STATEHOOD AS POLITICAL COMMUNITY

Alex Green argues that states arise under contemporary international law only when two abstract conditions are fulfilled. First, emerging states must constitute 'genuine political communities': collectives within which particular kinds of ethically valuable behaviour are possible. Second, such communities must emerge in a manner consistent with the ethical importance of individual political action. This uniquely 'Grotian' theory of state creation provides a clear legal framework comprising four factual 'antecedents' and five procedural principles, rendering the law of statehood both coherent and normatively attractive.

Alex Green is a senior lecturer at the University of York. His publications have appeared in periodicals such as the *Oxford Journal of Legal Studies*, the *Australian Year Book of International Law*, *Transnational Legal Theory*, and the *European Human Rights Law Review*. His research has been funded by the Modern Law Review Covid-19 Response Fellowship and the Hong Kong Research Grants Council Early Career Scheme award.

ASIL STUDIES IN INTERNATIONAL LEGAL THEORY

The purpose of the ASIL Studies in International Legal Theory series is to clarify and improve the theoretical foundations of international law. Too often the progressive development and implementation of international law has foundered on confusion about first principles. This series raises the level of public and scholarly discussion about the structure and purposes of the world legal order and how best to achieve global justice through law.

This series grows out of the International Legal Theory project of the American Society of International Law. The ASIL Studies in International Legal Theory series deepens this conversation by publishing scholarly monographs and edited volumes of essays considering subjects in international legal theory.

Books in the series

States, Firms, and Their Legal Fictions: Attributing Identity and Responsibility to Artificial Entities
Melissa J. Durkee

Rethinking the Relationship between International, EU and National Law
Lando Kirchmair

Consenting to International Law
Edited by Samantha Besson

The Death Penalty's Denial of Fundamental Human Rights
John Bessler

Theories of International Responsibility Law
Edited by Samantha Besson

Human Dignity in International Law
Ginevra Le Moli

Tipping Points in International Law: Commitment and Critique
Edited by Jean d'Aspremont and John D. Haskell

Ethical Leadership in International Organizations: Concepts, Narratives, Judgment, and Assessment
Edited by Maria Varaki and Guilherme Vasconcelos Vilaca

Whither the West?: Concepts on International Law in Europe and the United States
Edited by Chiara Giorgetti and Guglielmo Verdirame

International Law as Behavior
Edited by Harlan Grant Cohen and Timothy Meyer

Space and Fates of International Law: Between Leibniz and Hobbes
Ekaterina Yahyaoui Krivenko

Why Punish Perpetrators of Mass Atrocities?: Purposes of Punishment in International Criminal Law
Edited by Florian Jeßberger and Julia Geneuss

The Challenge of Inter-Legality
Edited by Jan Klabbers and Gianluigi Palombella

The Nature of International Law
Miodrag A. Jovanović

Reexamining Customary International Law
Edited by Brian D. Lepard

Theoretical Boundaries of Armed Conflict and Human Rights
Edited by Jens David Ohlin

Human Rights in Emergencies
Edited by Evan J. Criddle

The Theory of Self-Determination
Edited by Fernando R. Tesón

Negotiating State and Non-State Law: Global and Local Legal Pluralism
Edited by Michael A. Helfand

Jus Post Bellum and Transitional Justice
Edited by Larry May and Elizabeth Edenberg

Normative Pluralism and International Law: Exploring Global Governance
Edited by Jan Klabbers and Touko Piipaerinen

The Future of International Law: Global Government
Joel P. Trachtman

Morality, Jus Post Bellum, and International Law
Edited by Larry May and Andrew T. Forcehimes

Global Justice and International Economic Law: Opportunities and Prospects
Edited by Chios Carmody, Frank J. Garcia, and John Linarelli

Parochialism, Cosmopolitanism, and the Foundations of International Law
Edited by M. N. S. Sellers

The Role of Ethics in International Law
Edited by Donald Earl Childress III

The New Global Law
Rafael Domingo

Customary International Law: A New Theory with Practical Applications
Brian D. Lepard

International Criminal Law and Philosophy
Edited by Larry May and Zachary Hoskins

Statehood as Political Community

INTERNATIONAL LAW AND THE EMERGENCE OF NEW STATES

ALEX GREEN
University of York

CAMBRIDGE
UNIVERSITY PRESS

CAMBRIDGE
UNIVERSITY PRESS

Shaftesbury Road, Cambridge CB2 8EA, United Kingdom

One Liberty Plaza, 20th Floor, New York, NY 10006, USA

477 Williamstown Road, Port Melbourne, VIC 3207, Australia

314–321, 3rd Floor, Plot 3, Splendor Forum, Jasola District Centre, New Delhi – 110025, India

103 Penang Road, #05–06/07, Visioncrest Commercial, Singapore 238467

Cambridge University Press is part of Cambridge University Press & Assessment, a department of the University of Cambridge.

We share the University's mission to contribute to society through the pursuit of education, learning and research at the highest international levels of excellence.

www.cambridge.org
Information on this title: www.cambridge.org/9781009176323

DOI: 10.1017/9781009176309

First published 2024

A catalogue record for this publication is available from the British Library

Library of Congress Cataloging-in-Publication Data
NAMES: Green, Alex, 1988– author.
TITLE: Statehood as political community : international law and the emergence of new states / Alex Green, University of York.
DESCRIPTION: Cambridge, United Kingdom ; New York, NY : Cambridge University Press, 2024. | Includes bibliographical references and index.
IDENTIFIERS: LCCN 2023044233 | ISBN 9781009176323 (hardback) | ISBN 9781009176309 (ebook)
SUBJECTS: LCSH: State, The. | International law.
CLASSIFICATION: LCC KZ4002 .G74 2024 | DDC 341.26–dc23/eng/20231003
LC record available at https://lccn.loc.gov/2023044233

ISBN 978-1-009-17632-3 Hardback

To my Jendry

The new always happens against the overwhelming odds of statistical laws and their probability, which for all practical, everyday purposes amounts to certainty; the new therefore always appears in the guise of a miracle.

—Hannah Arendt, *The Human Condition*

Contents

Acknowledgements *page* xiii
List of International Instruments xv
List of International Judgements and Awards xix
List of Domestic Judgements and Legislation xxi

Introduction: Reconstructing the Law of State Creation 1
1 State Creation and the International Legal Order 2
2 Rational Reconstruction and International Law 8
3 The Law of State Creation 12
4 The Structure of This Book 15

PART I POLITICAL COMMUNITY 17

1 **Political Ethics and Community Membership** 19
1.1 Non-Voluntary Membership 21
1.2 Duties of Participation and Political Membership 22
1.3 Meaningfulness and Personal Narratives 29
1.4 Reasonableness 30
1.5 Two Objections 34
1.6 Authenticity and Self-Authorship 39
1.7 Two Requirements of Authenticity 40
1.8 The Ethical Value of Political Success 43
1.9 The Instrumental Ethical Value of Political Products 44
1.10 Conclusion 45

2 **Political Action and Valuable Institutions** 48
2.1 Archetypal Instances of Political Action 48
2.2 Politics and Violence 52
2.3 Violence as Politics? 54
2.4 Participation and Equality 56
2.5 Governance, Political Community, and Political Action 60
2.6 Conclusion 68

3 **The Antecedents of Statehood** 70
3.1 The Population Antecedent 72
3.2 The Territory Antecedent 75
3.3 The Effectiveness Antecedent 80
3.4 The Independence Antecedent 85
3.5 Conclusion 100

4 **Five Procedural Principles** 102
4.1 The Recognition Principle 103
4.2 The Referendum Principle 111
4.3 The Negative Self-Determination Principle 116
4.4 The International Peace Principle 122
4.5 The Territorial Integrity Principle 126
4.6 Conclusion 136

PART II STABILITY, LEGITIMACY, AND DEMOCRACY 139

5 **The Stability Thesis** 141
5.1 Characterising the Stability Thesis 142
5.2 Ambiguity over the Relevance of Recognition 145
5.3 Ambiguity within Declaratory View 147
5.4 Ambiguity within the Constitutive View 149
5.5 A Further Possibility and Some Conclusions 152
5.6 The Stability-Value of Consensus on the Emergence of States 154
5.7 The Stability-Value of Constitutive Recognition 156
5.8 The Stability-Value of the Declaratory Criteria 161
5.9 Conclusion 168

6 **The Legitimacy Thesis** 169
6.1 The Legitimacy Question 170
6.2 Investigating Legitimacy 172
6.3 Buchanan's Challenge 178

6.4 Hobbes' Thesis 181
6.5 Civil Incorporation 188
6.6 Popular Consent 192
6.7 Conclusion 197

7 **Democratic Legitimacy** 198
7.1 Rights-Based Legitimacy 199
7.2 Representative Government in International Practice 204
7.3 Equality, Majority Rule, and the Justification Gap 207
7.4 Accountability 218
7.5 Conclusion 222

Conclusion: The Nature and Resilience of Statehood 223
1 Resilient Statehood: Matters of Continuity and Extinction 225
2 The Idea of Statehood: Questions of 'Nature' or 'Essence' 229

Bibliography 237

Index 251

# Acknowledgements

It is hard to say precisely when this monograph began to take shape, for although state creation was the eventual subject of my doctoral thesis, my research topic changed considerably over the years. Initially, I was determined to produce a political theory of the entire international legal order; I must thank Stephen Guest for disabusing me of that notion. Although Stephen was my first supervisor, both timing and the job market determined that I would have three more, all of whom deserve independent thanks. I am grateful to Douglas Guilfoyle for his kindness and support, which continues to this day. I am grateful also to Martins Paparinskis, whose encyclopaedic knowledge of international law is as inspiring today as it was intimidating at first. Finally, I am indebted to Riz Mokal, whose rare mixture of warm solidarity, searing intellectual engagement, and personal integrity was without equal.

Thanks are also due to my doctoral and part-time colleagues at University College London. Early career academics stand or fall depending upon their professional networks, and I am fortunate that these friends provided me with such solid ground upon which to stand. In particular, I must thank Raquel Barradas de Freitas, Simon Palmer, Lea Raible, Rebecca Smith, Oisin Suttle, and Ilias Trispiotis, whose inexhaustible capacity for academic discussion outpaces even my own. Since gaining stable employment, to this list must be added Jason Beckett, James Greenwood-Reeves, Alexandra Hearne, Tamsin Paige, Alex Schwartz, Jo Shaw, Scott Veitch, and Emmanuel Voyiakis. I am also indebted for the many exchanges I've enjoyed at conferences, workshops, and seminars, including one particularly memorable occasion with the late James Crawford. Indeed, my luck has been such that would be impossible for me to list here every colleague properly deserving of thanks.

On the publication side of things, I want to thank Tom Randall and the others at Cambridge University Press (CUP) who supported me throughout the production of this book. It can be daunting for junior scholars to submit their first monograph proposal, and I could not have asked for better or more understanding recipients. Some elements of my argument borrow from material I have previously published, and I am particularly grateful to CUP for the opportunity to expand upon this here: 'Non-Positivist Legal Pluralism and Crises of Legitimacy in Settler-States' (2019) 14(2) JCL 267 (with Jennifer Hendry); 'Three Models of Political Membership: Delineating "The People in Question"' (2021) 41(2) OJLS 565; 'The Precarious Rationality of International Law: Critiquing the International Rule of Recognition' (2021) 22(8) GLJ 1613; '*The Creation of States* as a Cardinal Point: James Crawford's Contribution to International Legal Scholarship' (2023) 40(1) AYBIL 67; 'Successful Secession and the Value of International Recognition' in Jure Vidmar, Sarah McGibbon, and Lea Raible (eds) *Research Handbook on Secession* (Edward Elgar 2023); and 'A Political Theory of State Equality' (2023) 14(2) TLT 178.

Outwith the workplace, I must thank Joshua Ballantyne and Nathanael Mannone, without whose engagement this text would lack whatever political and social nuance it has come to possess. Thanks are also due to my brother, Edmund Green, whose determination and kindness remain a personal inspiration. Beyond these particular individuals, I am grateful to my many wonderful friends and the supportive members of my family, without whom life (and writing) would have been a lot less fun. Finally, particular gratitude is owed to three people. First, to my parents, Gillian and Timothy Green, who have loved and encouraged me my entire life. The value they place upon education, and the love of knowledge they have instilled in me, has carried me through. The existence of this book is due in no small part to them, and I hope that what follows does them some justice. Finally, my thanks, respect, adoration, and awe are given fully and completely to Jennifer Hendry. She is my companion, lover, and even my occasional co-author (this feat alone shows her patience to be superhuman). To say that she has been 'supportive' would be damning her with faint praise: she is the light that has guided my path. I hope that she will do so forever.

List of International Instruments

Agreement between the India Taipei Association in Taipei and The Taipei Economic and Cultural Center in New Delhi on The Promotion and Protection of Investments (adopted 17 October 2002, entered into force 28 November 2002), 153

Agreement between the Taipei Economic and Trade Office in Thailand and the Thailand Trade and Economic Office in Taipei for the Promotion and Protection of Investments (adopted and entered into force 30 April 1996), 153

Agreement respecting the Administration of Kelantan (Great Britain-Kelantan) (adopted 22 October 1910) 103 BFSP 518, 90

Agreement signed by the Chief of Bahrain (Great Britain-Bahrain) (adopted 22 December 1880), Charles Aitchison, Treaties, *Agreements and Sanads Relating to India and Neighbouring Countries* (1933), Vol. XI, 237, 96

American Convention on Human Rights (adopted 22 November 1969, entered into force 18 July 1978) 1144 UNTS 143, 205

Charter of Paris for a New Europe (1991) 30 ILM 193, 202

Charter of the United Nations (adopted 26 June 1945, entered into force 24 October 1945) 1 UNTS XVI, 2, 100, 116, 159

Council Directive 2013/36/EU of 26 June 2013 on access to the activity of credit institutions and the prudential supervision of credit institutions and investment firms, amending Directive 2002/87/EC and repealing Directives 2006/48/EC and 2006/49/EC Text with EEA relevance [2013] OJ L176/338, 42

Council Regulation (EU) 575/2013 Capital Requirements Regulation [2013] OJ L176/1, 42

Covenant of the League of Nations (adopted 28 June 1919, entered into force 10 January 1920), 100

European Community, 'Declaration on Yugoslavia and on the Guidelines on the Recognition of New States' (1992) 31 ILM 1485, 84

'Identification of Islands and Standardization of Their Names', submitted by Indonesia to the 11th United Nations Conference of the Standardization of Geographical Names (8–17 August 2017) (30 June 2017) E/CONF.105/115/CRP.115, 76

Inter-American Commission on Human Rights Resolution 01/09 (17 May 1990) OEA/Ser.L/V/11.77, doc. 7, rev.1, 206

International Covenant on Civil and Political Rights (adopted 16 December 1966, entered into force 23 March 1976) 999 UNTS 171, 205

International Law Commission (ILC) 'Unilateral Acts of States: Report of the Working Group – Conclusions of the International Law Commission on Unilateral Acts of States' (20 July 2006) UN Doc. A/CN.4/L./703, 9
ILC 'Draft Articles on Diplomatic Protection with Commentaries' 9 August 2006 UN Doc A/61/10, 2
ILC 'Report of the International Law Commission on the Work of its 58th Session' (1 May–9 June and 3 July–11 August 2006) UN Doc A/61/10, 9
ILC 'Report of the Study Group on Sea-Level Rise in Relation to International Law' (15 July 2022) UN Doc A/CN.4/L.972, 225
ILC 'Sea-Level Rise in Relation to International Law: Second Issues Paper' (19 April 2022) UN Doc A/CN.4/752, 72, 225
Montevideo Convention on the Rights and Duties of States (adopted 26 December 1933, entered into force 26 December 1934) 165 LNTS 19, 80
Organisation of American States, 'Texts Approved by the General Assembly at Its Sixteenth Special Session in Connection with the Amendments to the Charter of the Organization' OEA/Ser.P/ AG/doc. 11 (XVI-E/92) (14 December 1992), 206
Protocol to the European Convention for the Protection of Human Rights and Fundamental Freedoms (adopted 20 March 1952, entered into force 18 May 1954) 213 UNTS 262, 205
Sino-Japanese Dispute – Advisory Committee of the Special Assembly, Resolution of 24 February 1933 (1933) League of Nations Official Journal Spec Supp 101/I, 87, 92
State Treaty for the re-establishment of an independent and democratic Austria (adopted 15 May 1955, entered into force 1955) 58 UKTS 3, 79
The Comprehensive Peace Agreement between The Government of The Republic of The Sudan and The Sudan People's Liberation Movement/Sudan People's Liberation Army (adopted 9 January 2005), 113
Treaty Between Great Britain and the Chief of Bahrain (Great Britain-Bahrain) (adopted 22 March 1892) 176 CTS 467, 96
Treaty Concerning the Establishment of the Republic of Cyprus (adopted and entered into force 16 August 1960) 382 UNTS 8, 79
Treaty establishing the relations of France with the Principality of Monaco (with exchange of letters) (adopted 17 July 1918, entered into force 23 June 1919) 981 UNTS 363, 96
Treaty intended to adapt and strengthen friendship and cooperation relations between the Principality of Monaco and the French Republic (adopted 24 October 2002, entered into force 1 December 2005) 48 AFDI 792, 96
Treaty of Lisbon amending the Treaty on European Union and the Treaty establishing the European Community [2007] OJ C306/1, 95
Treaty of Peace with Italy (adopted 10 February 1947, entered into force 15 September 1947) 49 UNTS 3, 79
Treaty of St Germain-en-Laye (adopted 10 September 1919, entered into force 16 July 1920) 226 CTS 8, 79
United Nations General Assembly (UNGA) 'Question of East Timor: Report of the Secretary General' (5 May 1999) UN Doc A/53/951 'Annex I: The Agreement between the Republic of Indonesia and the Portuguese Republic on the Question of East Timor'; 'Annex II: The Agreement Regarding the Modalities for the Popular Consultation of the East Timorese through a Direct Ballot', 112
UNGA Resolution 273 (11 May 1949) UN Doc A/RES/273(III), 121
UNGA Resolution 377A (V) (3 November 1950) UN Doc A/RES/377(V)A, 124

UNGA Resolution 1498 (XV) (22 November 1960) UN Doc A/RES/1498(XV), 164
UNGA Resolution 1514 (VX) (14 December 1960) UN Doc A/RES/1514(XV), 2, 100, 111
UNGA Resolution 1541 (XV) (15 December 1960) UN Doc A/RES/1541(XV), 100, 163
UNGA Resolution 1599 (XV) (15 April 1961) UN Doc A/RES/1599(XV), 164
UNGA Resolution 2022 (XX) (5 November 1965) UN Doc A/RES/2022(XX), 117, 148
UNGA Resolution 2024 (XX) (11 November 1965) UN Doc A/RES/2024(XX), 117, 148
UNGA Resolution 2625 (XXV) (24 October 1970) UN Doc A/RES/25/2625(XXV), 100, 111, 116, 148, 231
UNGA Resolution 2758 (XXVI) (25 October 1971) UN Doc A/RES/2758(XXVI), 105
UNGA Resolution 2775E (XXVI) (29 November 1971) UN Doc A/RES/2775(XXVI) E, 118, 148
UNGA Resolution 2793 (XXVI) (7 December 1971) UN Doc A/RES/2793(XXVI), 136
UNGA Resolution 2923E (XXVII) (15 November 1972) UN Doc A/RES/2923(XXVII) E, 118
UNGA Resolution 2937 (XXVII) (29 November 1972) UN Doc A/RES/2937(XXVII), 134, 152
UNGA Resolution 3151G (XXVIII) (14 December 1973) UN Doc A/RES/3151(XXVIII) G, 118
UNGA Resolution 3171 (XXVIII) (17 December 1973) UN Doc A/RES/3171(XXVIII), 2
UNGA Resolution 3181 (XXVIII) (17 December 1973) UN Doc A/RES/3181(XXVIII), 135
UNGA Resolution 3203 (XXIX) (17 September 1974) UN Doc A/RES/3202(XXIX), 152
UNGA Resolution 3324E (XXIX) (16 December 1974) UN Doc A/RES/3324(XXIX)E, 118
UNGA Resolution 3411D (XXX) (28 November 1975) UN Doc A/RES/3411(XXX)D, 118, 148
UNGA Resolution 31/6A (26 October 1976) UN Doc A/RES/31/6A, 118
UNGA Resolution 67/19 (29 November 2012) UN Doc A/RES/67/19, 151
UNGA Resolution 68/262 (27 March 2014) UN Doc A/RES/68/262, 123
UNGA Resolution ES-11/1 (2 March 2022) UN Doc A/RES/ES-11/1, 124
United Nations Human Rights Committee 'General comment adopted by the Human Rights Committee under article 40, paragraph 4, of the International Covenant on Civil and Political Rights' (27 August 1996) UN Doc CCPR/C/21/Rev.l/Add.7, 205
United Nations Security Council (UNSC) 'Note by the President of the Security Council' (21 September 1979) UN Doc S/13549, 118
UNSC 'Report of the Secretary-General on the situation in Somalia' (19 December 2000) UN Doc S/2000/1211, 6, 131
UNSC 'Report of the Secretary-General on the Situation in Somalia' (11 October 2001) UN Doc S/2001/963, 131
UNSC 'Report of the Secretary-General on the Situation in Somalia' (21 February 2002) UN Doc S/2002/198, 131
UNSC 'Report of the Secretary-General on the Situation in Somalia' (25 October 2002) UN Doc S/2001/1202, 131
UNSC Resolution 1246 (11 June 1999) UN Doc S/RES/1246, 112
UNSC Resolution 143 (13 July 1960) UN Doc S/RES/143, 164
UNSC Resolution 145 (22 July 1960) UN Doc S/RES/145, 164
UNSC Resolution 146 (1 August 1960) UN Doc S/RES/146, 164
UNSC Resolution 217 (20 November 1965) UN Doc S/RES/217, 110
UNSC Resolution 242 (22 November 1967) UN Doc S/RES/242, 123

UNSC Resolution 253 (29 May 1968) UN Doc S/RES/253, 110
UNSC Resolution 264 (20 March 1969) UN Doc S/RES/264, 118
UNSC Resolution 277 (18 March 1970) UN Doc S/RES/277, 110
UNSC Resolution 351 (10 June 1974) Un Doc S/RES/351, 152
UNSC Resolution 402 (22 December 1976) UN Doc S/RES/402, 118
UNSC Resolution 407 (25 May 1977) UN Doc S/RES/407, 118
UNSC Resolution 417 (31 October 1977) UN Doc S/RES/417, 118
UNSC Resolution 478 (20 August 1980) UN Doc S/RES/478, 123
UNSC Resolution 541 (18 November 1983) UN Doc S/RES/541, 111
UNSC Resolution 550 (11 May 1984) UN Doc S/RES/550, 111
UNSC Resolution 556 (23 October 1984) UN Doc S/RES/556, 118
UNSC Resolution 581 (13 February 1986) UN Doc S/RES/581, 118
UNSC Resolution 662 (9 August 1990) UN Doc S/RES/662, 123
UNSC Resolution 1483 (22 May 2003) UN Doc S/RES/1483, 176
UNSC Resolution 1546 (8 June 2004) UN Doc S/RES/1546, 176
UNSC Resolution 1619 (11 August 2005) UN Doc S/RES/1619, 176
UNSC Resolution 1637 (8 November 2005) UN Doc S/RES/1637, 176
UNSC Resolution 1700 (10 August 2006) UN Doc S/RES/1700, 176
UNSC Resolution 1723 (28 November 2006) UN Doc S/RES/1723, 176
UNSC Resolution 2249 (20 November 2015) UN Doc S/RES/2249, 128
UNSC 'The Question of East Timor: Report of the Secretary-General' (1999) UN Doc A/53/951, 112
UNSC Verbatim Record (21 February 2022) UN Doc S/PV.8970, 124, 125

List of International Judgements and Awards

Accordance with International Law of the Unilateral Declaration of Independence in Respect of Kosovo (Advisory Opinion) [2010] ICJ Rep 403, 108

Allegations of Genocide under the Convention on the Prevention and Punishment of the Crime of Genocide (Ukraine v Russian Federation) (Application Instituting Proceedings) General List No. 182 [2022] ICJ 1, 125

Allegations of Genocide under the Convention on the Prevention and Punishment of the Crime of Genocide (Ukraine v Russian Federation) (Provisional Measures, Order of 16 March 2022) [2022] ICJ Rep 211, 136

Application of the Convention on the Prevention and Punishment of the Crime of Genocide (Bosnia and Herzegovina v Serbia and Montenegro) (Preliminary Objections: Judgement) [1996] ICJ Rep 595, 112, 157

Application of the Convention on the Prevention and Punishment of the Crime of Genocide (Bosnia and Herzegovina v Serbia and Montenegro) (Pleadings: Memorial, Bosnia and Herzegovina) [2007] ICJ Rep 43, 119

Armed Activities on the Territory of the Congo (New Application: 2002) (Democratic Republic of the Congo v Rwanda) (Jurisdiction and Admissibility: Judgment) [2006] ICJ Rep 6, 9, 158

Barcelona Traction, Light and Power Company Ltd (Belgium v Spain) (Merits) [1970] ICJ Rep 3, 157

Case C-6/90 *Andrea Francovich and Danila Bonifaci and Others v Italian Republic* [1991] ECR I-05357, 95

Case C-632/20 *Spain v Commission* (CJEU, 17 January 2023), 155

Case Concerning East Timor (Portugal v Australia) (Merits) [1995] ICJ Rep 90, 157

Case Concerning Military and Paramilitary Activities in and against Nicaragua (Nicaraagua v United States of America) (Merits) [1986] ICJ Rep 14, 127, 158, 205

Chiiko Bwalya v Zambia (27 July 1993) Communication No. 314/1988 CCPR/C/48/D/314/1988, 205

Conference on Yugoslavia, Arbitration Commission, Opinion 1 (1991) 92 ILR 162, 72, 81, 115, 150

Conference on Yugoslavia, Arbitration Commission, Opinion 5 (1992) 92 ILR 188, 112, 203

Conference on Yugoslavia, Arbitration Commission, Opinion 6 (1992) 92 ILR 182, 112, 203

Conference on Yugoslavia, Arbitration Commission, Opinion 7 (1992) 31(6) ILM 1512, 203

Conference on Yugoslavia, Arbitration Commission, Opinion 8 (1992) 31(6) ILM 1521, 80

Conference on Yugoslavia, Arbitration Commission, Opinion 9 (1992) 31(6) ILM 1523, 80

Conference on Yugoslavia, Arbitration Commission, Opinion 10 (1992) 92 ILR 206, 109
Corfu Channel (United Kingdom of Great Britain and Northern Ireland v Albania), (Merits) [1949] ICJ Rep 4, 159
Customs Regime between Germany and Austria (Germany v Austria) PCIJ Rep Series A/B No. 41, 86
Cyprus v Turkey (2002) 35 EHRR 30, 117
Deutsche Continental Gas-Gesellschaft v Polish State (1929) 9 Recueil TAM 336, 13, 72, 81
Greek Case (1969) 2 Yearbook of the European Convention on Human Rights 186 (Report of 5 November 1969), 205
Ilaşcu and Others and Romania (intervening) v Moldova and Russian Federation (2005) 40 EHRR 1030, 123
International Registration of Trade Mark (Germany) Case (1959) 28 ILR 82, 128
Island of Palmas Case (or Miangas) (United States v Netherlands) (Award) (1928) II RIAA 829, 75
Jurisdictional Immunities of the State (Germany v Italy: Greece intervening) (Merits) [2012] ICJ Rep 99, 116, 231
Legal Consequences for States of the Continued Presence of South Africa in Namibia (South West Africa) notwithstanding Security Council Resolution 276 (1970) (Advisory Opinion) [1971] ICJ Rep 6, 110
Legal Consequences of the Construction on a Wall in Occupied Palestinian Territory (Advisory Opinion) [2004] ICJ Rep 136, 123, 157
Loizidou and Cyprus (intervening) v Turkey (1997) 23 EHRR 513, 117
Matthews v United Kingdom (1999) 28 EHRR 361, 206
Monastery of Saint Naoum (Advisory Opinion) PCIJ Rep Series B No. 9, 75
North Sea Continental Shelf (Federal Republic of Germany v Denmark; Federal Republic of Germany v Netherlands) (Merits) [1969] ICJ Rep 3, 75
Nottebohm Case (second phase) (Liechtenstein v Guatemala) (Merits) [1955] ICJ Rep 4, 74
Nuclear Tests (Australia v France) (Merits) [1974] ICJ Rep 253, 9
Nuclear Tests (New Zealand v France) (Merits) [1974] ICJ Rep 457, 9
Reparation for injuries suffered in the service of the United Nations (Advisory Opinion) [1949] ICJ Rep 174, 3
Socialist Party and Others v Turkey (1999) 27 EHRR 51, 205–206
Socony Vacuum Oil Co. Claim (1954) 21 ILR 55, 92
Western Sahara (Advisory Opinion) [1975] ICJ Rep 12, 111, 164

List of Domestic Judgements and Legislation

Amending Act of 1786 (UK), 91
An Act relating to criminal offenses, 31 March 1976, Act A327; P.U. (B) 139/1976 (Malaysia), 49
An Act to consolidate the law relating to criminal offences 1871 (Singapore), 49
Bill of Rights 1689 (UK), 91
Case of Proclamations [1607] EWHC J23 (KB) (UK), 220
Constitution of the Federal Republic of Yugoslavia 1992 (Federal Republic of Yugoslavia), 113
Constitution of the Republic of Cyprus, 16 April 1960 (Republic of Cyprus), 113
Criminal Code (Cap. 195), 29 December 1838 (Mauritius), 49
Cyprus Act 1960 (UK), 97
Declaration of the Establishment of the State of Israel, 14 May 1948 (State of Israel), 121
Dissolution and Calling of Parliament Act 2022 (UK), 221
Dobbs v Jackson Women's Health Organization 597 US ___ (2022), 64
East India Company Act 1784 (UK), 91
Entick v Carrington & Others [1765] EWHC KB J98 (UK), 91
Executive Order 14065 – Blocking Property of Certain Persons and Prohibiting Certain Transactions with Respect to Continued Russian Efforts to Undermine the Sovereignty and Territorial Integrity of Ukraine, 21 February 2022 (United States), 124
Executive Order No. 71. On the Recognition of the Donetsk People's Republic, 21 February 2023 (Russian Federation), 124
Executive Order No. 72. On the Recognition of the Lugansk People's Republic, 21 February 2023 (Russian Federation), 124
Federal Constitution of the Swiss Confederation, 18 April 1999 (Swiss Confederation), 216
Financial Services and Markets Act 2012 (UK), 42
Fixed-term Parliaments Act 2011 (UK), 221
Government of India Act 1858 (UK), 91
Hagi-Salad v Ashcroft, 359 F 3d 1044, 1046 (8th Cir 2004, Loken CJ) (United States), 131
Judgment of 30 October 2003, 4 UE 4952/96.A (Hesse Administrative Court, Kassel) (Federal Republic of Germany), 131
Reference by the Lord Advocate of devolution issues under paragraph 34 of schedule 6 of the Scotland Act 1998 [2022] UKSC 31 (UK), 130
Reference re Secession of Quebec [1998] 2 SCR 217 (Canada), 109

Regulating Act 1773 (UK), 91
Roe v Wade 410 U.S. 113 (1973) (United States), 64
Status of Bophuthatswana Act, 1977 (No. 89 of 1977) (South Africa), 117
Status of Transkei Act, 1976 (No. 100 of 1976) (South Africa), 117
Status of Venda Act, 1979 (No. 107 of 1979) (South Africa), 117
Status of Ciskei Act, 1981 (No. 110 of 1981) (South Africa), 117
The Act on the Referendum on State-Legal Status of the Republic of Montenegro, Official Gazette of the Republic of Montenegro, No. 12/06 (2 March 2006) (Republic of Montenegro), 113
The Republic of Cyprus Order-in-Council, SI 1960, No. 1363, p. 1174 (UK), 97

Introduction

Reconstructing the Law of State Creation

This book is about the creation of states. It argues that international law permits state creation only when two abstract conditions are fulfilled. First, emerging states must constitute what I call 'genuine political communities': collectives within which particular kinds of ethically valuable behaviour are possible. Second, such communities must emerge in a manner consistent with the ethical importance of individual political action. These two conditions ground, justify, and nuance several more concrete and familiar legal propositions, such as the notion that new states must have 'effective' governments and that they cannot emerge via the unlawful use of force. Together, they enable the law governing the creation of new states to be reconstructed as a normatively coherent whole, with an intelligible and attractive set of philosophical foundations. Throughout what follows, I call this explanatory and justificatory framework 'statehood as political community'.

The legal claims presented in this book are highly unorthodox for two reasons. First, they require attention to ethical, moral, and philosophical concepts that have hitherto received very little attention from doctrinal scholars. Second, they utilise an approach to the identification of legal principles that many readers may consider alien. Rather than proceeding solely with recourse to the relevant social facts, such as treaty texts or patterns of behaviour among states, this text seeks to ascertain the content of international law through a 'rational reconstruction' of those facts, which places the normative attractiveness of putative laws on an equal footing with their factual provenance. This approach, and its relationship to the widely accepted sources of international law, is explained in greater detail in Section 2 of this Introduction. First, however, an overview of state creation within the international legal order, and of its political importance, shall be provided. These two tasks being complete, I then outline the legal framework I endorse and summarise the argumentative structure of this book as a whole.

1 STATE CREATION AND THE INTERNATIONAL LEGAL ORDER

We live in a world of states. With the exception of the high seas, outer space, and the continent of Antarctica, the entirety of our currently inhabitable environment falls within the jurisdiction of one state or another. States are some of the most powerful entities on our planet in terms of their social, environmental, and economic influence. For instance, almost without exception, it is states alone that possess full military capacity. Moreover, it is characteristically through independent statehood that political communities exercise collective self-determination,[1] gain a sense of shared identity,[2] and enjoy legal benefits such as diplomatic protection and rights of residence and return in relation to a particular territory.[3] When coupled with the fact that states are the primary creators and interpreters of international law,[4] any suggestion that a new community has joined this company of leviathans must be taken very seriously.

It is also no surprise that moments of state creation can be so politically controversial. Communities seceding from their 'parent' states characteristically take with them the people and natural resources within their new territories,[5] along with any rights to maritime territory and airspace associated with that land.[6] The political opposition faced by contemporary independence movements, such as those in Catalonia, Hong Kong, or Scotland, demonstrates the extent to which the governments of established states can be resistant to any alteration of their extant borders. Moreover, even if territorial distribution were not a zero-sum game, the creation of new states would nonetheless have sweeping legal implications. Emerging as a state for legal purposes establishes the new entity within a complex network of international 'jural relations', including rights, duties, liberties,

1 Charter of the United Nations (adopted 26 June 1945, entered into force 24 October 1945) 1 UNTS XVI: Article 1(2); United Nations General Assembly (UNGA) Resolution 1514 (VX) (14 December 1960) UN Doc A/RES/1514(XV).

2 Sari Nusseibeh, *What Is a Palestinian State Worth?* (Harvard University Press 2011) 61–70.

3 For example: International Law Commission (ILC) 'Draft Articles on Diplomatic Protection with Commentaries' 9 August 2006 UN Doc A/61/10: Article 1.

4 Rosalyn Higgins, *Problems and Processes: International Law and How We Use It* (Oxford University Press 1994) 17–38; Vaughan Lowe, *International Law* (Oxford University Press 2007) 90–97.

5 James Crawford, *The Creation of States in International Law* (Oxford University Press 2006) 52–53; UNGA Resolution 3171 (XXVIII) (17 December 1973) UN Doc A/RES/3171(XXVIII).

6 Suzanne Lalonde, 'The Role of the *uti possidetis* Principle in the Resolution of Maritime Boundary Disputes' in Christine Chinkin and Freya Baetens (eds.), *Sovereignty, Statehood and State Responsibility: Essays in Honour of James Crawford* (Cambridge University Press 2015).

and powers.[7] This juridical positioning brings not only formal equality with other states but also a range of entitlements that are substantively beneficial.[8] For example, it is by now well established that the Russian Federation's 2014 military occupation of the Crimea was contrary to international law. However, explaining *why* requires invoking the territorial integrity of Ukraine, which the latter holds by virtue of its statehood.[9] Indeed, if we understand the legal personality of a given community as its capacity to 'avail itself of obligations' at the international level,[10] statehood supplies the archetypal reason why that capacity exists. This reason-giving role is what it means for statehood to be an international legal status: states hold a unique place within the international community, and it is their statehood that establishes this fact.[11]

As a result, to borrow from James Crawford, 'the criteria for statehood are of a special character, in that their application conditions the application of most other international law rules'.[12] Given this point, it might seem natural that international legal practice would provide clear answers about when and how states emerge, as well as an evident justification for why those answers hold. However, nothing could be further from the truth. The law of state creation is notoriously contentious and complex, characterised more by scholarly disagreement and ambiguity in legal practice than by settled uniformity in either sphere. The extent of this actual and potential disagreement is a point I shall return to later on; however, a brief exemplification is necessary here

7 Wesley Newcomb Hohfeld, 'Fundamental Legal Conceptions as Applied in Judicial Reasoning' (1917) 26(8) *The Yale Law Journal* 710.

8 As Crawford notes, there is no automatic correspondence between statehood and the *complete* list of jural relations that hold in relation to a particular state (Crawford (n 5) 44). Not all communities will have the same treaty obligations, nor will customary law entail the same set of rights for every state. Different states will have signed and ratified different treaty texts and customs may apply to different communities in different ways. For example, a customary standard that requires all states to respect the territorial waters of coastal communities will entail *duties* for every seafaring state but *rights* only for those that possess a coastline.

9 Thomas Grant, 'Annexation of Crimea' (2015) 109(1) *American Journal of International Law* 68; Anne Peters, 'Crimea: Does "The West" Now Pay the Price for Kosovo?' *EJIL: Talk!*, 22 April 2018: www.ejiltalk.org/crimea-does-the-west-now-pay-the-price-for-kosovo/ (last accessed 2 October 2023).

10 *Reparation for injuries suffered in the service of the United Nations* (Advisory Opinion) [1949] ICJ Rep 174, 178.

11 Indeed, normative status in general can be understood in terms of the positionality it establishes within a given community, for which status within the international community is no exception, see: Thomas Nagel, 'Personal Rights and Public Space' (1995) 24(2) *Philosophy & Public Affairs* 83, 85.

12 Crawford (n 5) 45.

since much of what motivates this text comes from my desire to move forward within our otherwise deadlocked doctrinal debates.

Consider the debate that still exists over the legal effect of foreign recognition on the accrual of statehood. This so-called 'great debate' between the constitutive and declaratory views of recognition is something I return to in Chapters 4 and 5; however, for now, it suffices to remark upon the wide divergence that still pertains, even within anglophone scholarship. The constitutive view, in a nutshell, is that acts of foreign recognition by the governments of already established states themselves establish the statehood of nascent entities. This was the view, in essence, of Hersch Lauterpacht.[13] The declaratory view, by contrast, holds that recognition serves merely to acknowledge new states, which arise only once some set or other of independent legal criteria have been satisfied. This was, for instance, largely the position that Crawford endorsed.[14] It has been argued by some that the declaratory view predominates within anglophone scholarship;[15] however, this is no longer really the case, if indeed it ever was. By way of example, taking two recent and particularly influential texts, Rowan Nicholson and Jure Vidmar adopt two discrete and opposing views. Nicholson argues that statehood can in general arise whenever 'effectiveness' (in the sense of demonstrable factual control of both territory and population) is established.[16] However, although this puts him in agreement with those such as Crawford, who adopt a declaratory position, he in fact rejects that view, arguing instead that statehood can *also* accrue as a result of foreign recognition, even though effectiveness itself is absent.[17] Although he agrees with Nicholson on the possibility of foreign recognition acting as an independent basis for state creation, Vidmar takes yet another approach, arguing that the emergence of new states is always the result of a legally governed international political process, through which state creation via foreign recognition represents only one possible route.[18] Frustratingly, all three contemporary authors (Crawford, Nicholson, and Vidmar) each advance their respective and conflicting positions as the single correct interpretation

[13] Lauterpacht's analysis was in fact quite a bit more nuanced than this simple characterisation implies, due largely to his own non-positivist methodology, see: Hersch Lauterpacht, *Recognition of States in International Law* (Cambridge University Press 1947) 1–78.

[14] Crawford (n 5) 26–28.

[15] Ibid 25; Steven Ratner, *The Thin Justice of International Law: A Moral Reckoning of the Law of Nations* (Oxford University Press 2015) 184–187.

[16] Rowan Nicholson, *Statehood and the State-Like in International Law* (Oxford University Press 2019) 106–108.

[17] Ibid 127–142.

[18] Jure Vidmar, *Democratic Statehood: The Emergence of New States in Post-cold War Practice* (Hart Publishing 2013) 239–253.

of largely the same set of social facts: the same treaties, recognition practices, UN General Assembly Resolutions, and so on.

In light of such disagreement, some scholars are drawn to the view that there is no law at all governing state creation: how can there be any such law, they argue, when so many conflicting but otherwise plausible interpretations of the same social facts exist?[19] Such sceptics often consider state creation to be 'pre-legal',[20] following Lassa Oppenheim's famous contention that the 'formation of a new State is…a matter of fact, and not of law'.[21] For instance, Anthony Carty argues that '[l]aw governs neither the coming into existence nor the disappearance of states', whilst Duncan French suggests that '[w]ith no central organizing agency either to prescribe the specific conditions of or to determine the attainment or otherwise of the requirements of statehood, international law on this issue remains notionally mandatory, apparently persuasive, but ultimately contingent upon claim and response'.[22]

Unsurprisingly, I disagree with these conclusions. However, given the controversial nature of state creation and the scholarly disagreement that persists in relation to the relevant law, clarity over how precisely we should proceed when attempting to discover that law is particularly important. Indeed, I suspect that both the extent of our existing doctrinal disagreements, and the illusion of indeterminacy that such disagreements create, turns in large part on the method of identifying international law that currently dominates, both within the law of state creation and elsewhere.[23] This method, which is called either 'formalism' or 'positivism', depending upon one's legal tradition, focuses entirely upon establishing international laws by pointing to some set of social facts upon which they are taken to be grounded.[24] In the

[19] This claim often has roots in the postmodern critique that international law in general lacks determinacy, see: Martti Koskenniemi, *From Apology to Utopia: The Structure of International Legal Argument* (Cambridge University Press 2006) 586.

[20] Jean d'Aspremont, 'The International Law of Statehood: Craftsmanship for the Elucidation and Regulation of Births and Deaths in the International Society' (2014) 29 *Connecticut Journal of International Law* 201, 205.

[21] Lassa Oppenheim, *International Law: A Treatise, Volume 1* (Longmans, Green, and Company 1905) 264.

[22] Anthony Carty, *The Decay of International Law? A Reappraisal of the Limits of Legal Imagination in International Affairs* (Manchester University Press 1986) 43; Duncan French (ed.), *Statehood and Self-Determination: Reconciling Tradition and Modernity in International Law* (Cambridge University Press 2013) 2.

[23] For my views on this issue in general, see: Alex Green, 'The Precarious Rationality of International Law: Critiquing the International Rule of Recognition' (2021) 22(8) *German Law Journal* 1613.

[24] The clearest theoretical rendition of this approach can be found in: John Gardener, 'Legal Positivism: 5½ Myths' (2001) 46 *American Journal of Jurisprudence* 199.

case of state creation, this means paying exclusive attention to facts such as the foreign recognition of nascent entities, the text and legislative history of relevant treaty provisions, and any salient comments made by international courts and tribunals.

Social facts of this kind are descriptive, in that when we identify them, we do so via propositions about what has been done, said, or thought, rather than by making arguments about what *ought* to be entailed, either in belief or in deed, by virtue of these facts pertaining. The difficulty with this approach is that, for any given set of such facts, there is an indefinitely large number of putative legal standards that might be entailed.[25] This is demonstrated by the divergence of scholarly opinion already cited: working from largely the same set of international legal practices, various positivist authors advance starkly different and incompatible views of what it takes for new states to emerge. What is more, such common and exclusive reliance upon social fact means that there is no way to solve their disagreements. Discrete facts, such as the non-recognition of some particular entity, that function as paradigms under one approach appear as aberrant cases under another, with no means to determine which characterisation should be preferred. For example, Gérard Krejin argues that the circumstances of the Federal Republic of Somalia in the 1990s were 'a nail in the coffin of the declaratory theory'.[26] In 1991, during a protracted civil war that has continued on and off ever since, the territory of what is now the Republic of Somaliland purported to secede.[27] In the decades that followed, Somalia itself was frequently without effective government, while Somaliland swiftly gained relative 'calm' and maintains it to this day.[28] Nonetheless, Somalia continues to receive foreign recognition, whereas Somaliland has received none.[29] Jure Vidmar and Lea Raible effectively endorse Krejin's analysis, arguing that Somaliland cannot be a state because without foreign recognition or the consent of its parent state, the secession of Somaliland is forestalled by the principle of territorial integrity.[30] For these authors, and all others who reject the declaratory view, Somaliland thus constitutes a paradigmatic case: clear proof that statehood is not

[25] Mark Greenberg, 'How Facts Make Law' (2004) 10 *Legal Theory* 157, 181.

[26] Gérard Krejin, *State Failure, Sovereignty and Effectiveness: Legal Lessons from the Decolonization of Sub-Saharan Africa* (Nijhoff 2004) 355.

[27] Helen Metz, *Somalia: A Country Study*, 4th edition (Library of Congress 1993) 169–170.

[28] United Nations Security Council (UNSC) 'Report of the Secretary-General on the Situation in Somalia' (19 December 2000) UN Doc S/2000/1211, para 34.

[29] Crawford (n 5) 415.

[30] Jure Vidmar and Lea Raible, 'State Creation and the Concept of Statehood in International Law' in Jure Vidmar, Sarah McGibbon, and Lea Raible (eds.), *Research Handbook on Secession* (Edward Elgar 2022) 21.

something that arises in response to discrete legal criteria but instead a status constituted by international legal processes, including those of foreign recognition. Conversely, for scholars such as Crawford and Nicholson, Somaliland is an aberrant case, best understood as an exception to the rule that factual effectiveness is sufficient for state creation.[31] They stop short of arguing that it possesses statehood, yet advance no convincing reason for why this is not so. Indeed, Nicholson himself puts this methodological problem in a persuasive manner:

> …not every case of apparently divergent practice is necessarily evidence of anything…in an area of law as politicized as statehood, some divergent or potentially misleading practice might still emerge. The scholar of statehood cannot always assume that the practice of states is invariably consistent with international law, then form a conclusion from that practice about whether a particular entity is a state, and then work backwards to an explanation. An attempt to resolve every anomaly by that method might lengthen the list of exceptions and caveats until it really is doubtful whether any 'general' rules remain.[32]

This is undoubtedly true, in that no legal theory can possibly aim for total explanatory power, unless we are to abandon the obvious truth that sometimes laws are broken. However, Nicholson's sensible admission does nothing to address the more fundamental issue that we must have some means to discriminate between various plausible but nonetheless competing theories. Debate will persist, in other words, unless we can find some way to identify which principles of state creation we *should* endorse, amongst the complete set of those that *might* explain the preponderance of international practice. The problem here is that such an answer cannot be provided by social facts alone. Even a rejection of obviously absurd or deeply unjust legal standards must rely on something beyond the descriptive. We must, in other words, rely upon the sort of normative considerations that positivism excludes as the ultimate bases or 'grounds' of international law. In the following section, I outline my own approach, which proceeds in precisely this manner. My aim is to generate an account of the law that governs state creation that is not only doctrinally apt but also independently appealing, in that it makes normative sense for us to endorse *this* account of the law rather than any other. Naturally, I do not expect to convince every reader. Nonetheless, by shifting the terms of debate onto an explicitly normative footing, I hope that we can at least begin having disagreements of a more productive kind.

[31] Crawford (n 5) 417; Nicholson (n 16) 190–192.
[32] Nicholson (n 16) 191.

2 RATIONAL RECONSTRUCTION AND INTERNATIONAL LAW

I offer what Habermas calls a 'rational reconstruction' of state creation.[33] At its most basic, this is an interpretation of one or more texts, social practices, speech acts, or practical maxims.[34] Given my object of study, my own reconstruction focuses upon the complete set of international legal practice concerned with the creation of states. By 'international legal practice' I intend a deliberately inclusive set of descriptive facts. These encompass not only the text but also the social and historical context of international instruments, including but not limited to formally binding treaties, as well as that of international judgments and official statements about state creation made by the representatives of established states.[35] They also include, as one might expect within a book on state creation, international recognition practices. International laws themselves, whether thought of as genuine normative principles,[36] distinctly legal norms, or social rules,[37] are different in kind from these descriptive facts about what particular people, such as state representatives and international judges, did, said, or believed.[38] Nonetheless, some of these more basic facts have *prima facie* legal relevance. For instance, the text of treaty documents, the law-related statements of state representatives, and the judgements of international courts and tribunals are all presumptively relevant to the content of international law, as are the custom-forming behaviours undertaken by state representatives and other international actors, which lack any obvious semantic content.[39] The challenge is to explain how these more basic facts

[33] Jürgen Habermas, *Moral Consciousness and Communicative Action*, Christian Lenhardt and Shierry Nicholson (trans.) (Polity Press 1992) 29–32.

[34] Ibid 29.

[35] In adopting this broad understanding of legally relevant material, I follow: Greenberg (n 25) 157.

[36] By 'genuine normative principles' I mean abstract formulations that capture some set of other-regarding reasons that actually apply to us, as a matter of normative fact. I take 'facts' in this context to mean 'true propositions', see: Frank Ramsey, 'Facts and Propositions' in *Proceedings of the Aristotelian Society, Supplementary Volumes, Vol. 7, Mind, Objectivity and Fact* (1927) 153–206; Peter Strawson, 'Truth' (1949) 9(6) Analysis 83. Following this approach, a 'legal fact' is a 'true proposition of law', whilst a 'normative fact' is 'a proposition that is normatively true'. My previous references to 'descriptive facts' and 'social facts' have similar connotations, denoting true propositions about what is the case in our natural or social worlds. Normative facts pertain to the extent that they are supported by the normative reasons that actually apply to us, whether those reasons are all-things-considered or only *pro tanto*.

[37] The latter two possibilities are most famously forwarded by Hans Kelsen ('The Pure Theory of Law and Analytical Jurisprudence' (1941) 55(1) *Harvard Law Review* 44) and Herbert Hart (*The Concept of Law*, 2nd edition (Oxford University Press 1994) 79–99).

[38] Greenberg (n 25) 157–159.

[39] Jean d'Aspremont, *Formalism and the Sources of International Law* (Oxford University Press 2011) 161–174.

ground and explain the normative content of international law: why, in other words, they should be taken to produce one particular set of international legal standards, rather than any other.

Placing this material within the context of the traditional 'sources' of international law, as enumerated for example within Article 38(1) of the Statute of the International Court of Justice (ICJ),[40] 'international legal practice' includes at least all the relevant descriptive facts ordinarily used to establish the pedigree of putative legal standards under each of the three primary sources: international conventions, international custom, and general principles of law.[41] In addition, I sometimes reference the unilateral acts of states, which some lawyers invoke either as independent sources of legal obligation or as evidence of customary law.[42] Whatever the traditional classification of such material might be, what matters for the purposes of my argument is its descriptive nature and its putative legal relevance.

What distinguishes rational reconstruction from other interpretive approaches to such material is its relation to normative reasons.[43] Rather than 'merely' settling upon legal principles that more-or-less fit the relevant international practice, rational reconstruction assumes that any plausible conception of the law must also have an immanent rationality, which the interpreter therefore should explicate. Such reconstructions take seriously, in other words, the idea that the prescriptive content of international law

[40] 18 April 1946.

[41] The standard positivist view of international law insists that only the facts implicated by these 'formal' sources have a direct law-determining role: they are not only necessary for the existence and validity of international legal norms but also sufficient (Hugh Thirlway, *The Sources of International Law* (Oxford University Press 2014) 8–9). As such, positivists see the grounds of international law as exhausted by material such as the text of treaty documents, along with any relevant reservations; the behaviour and statements of state representatives that suggest the existence of customary norms; and any textual or behavioural evidence of generally recognised legal principles that are neither customary nor treaty based. Rational reconstruction rejects this exclusive reliance upon social fact, in the manner I outline below.

[42] ILC 'Unilateral Acts of States: Report of the Working Group – Conclusions of the International Law Commission on Unilateral Acts of States' (20 July 2006) UN Doc. A/CN.4/L./703; ILC 'Report of the International Law Commission on the Work of its 58th Session' (1 May–9 June and 3 July–11 August 2006) UN Doc A/61/10; *Nuclear Tests (Australia v France)* (Merits) [1974] ICJ Rep 253, paras. 43–46; *Nuclear Tests (New Zealand v France)* (Merits) [1974] ICJ Rep 457, paras. 46–49; *Armed Activities on the Territory of the Congo (New Application: 2002) (Democratic Republic of the Congo v Rwanda)* (Jurisdiction and Admissibility: Judgment) [2006] ICJ Rep 6, para. 50.

[43] Following Derek Parfit, I take 'reasons' to be 'considerations that count either in favour or against something' and 'normative reasons' to be 'considerations that count in favour of doing or not doing something', either simpliciter or in some specific manner (such as with particular intentions, attitudes, and so on), see: *On What Matters: Volume One* (Oxford University Press 2011) 31.

reflects some set of independently attractive normative reasons, such that part of what it means to discover the law on any given topic is to identify those reasons and articulate why they matter. This means that the interpreter must place as much emphasis upon the normative attractiveness of any putative laws as upon their descriptive or historical basis within a given text or practice. To borrow language from Ronald Dworkin, this means finding an appropriate balance between the interpretive dimensions of 'fit' and 'justification' when ascertaining the content of international law.[44] All of this follows because, to quote Habermas, international law, like any reason-giving practice, can only be properly understood in light of the reasons that animate it, and 'reasons can be *understood* only insofar as they are taken seriously as reasons and *evaluated*' [emphasis in original].[45] As mentioned above, this may strike more rigidly doctrinal international lawyers as somewhat alien, given that it requires explicit reliance upon moral, political, and other forms of normative argumentation when developing an account of the relevant law. Chapters 1 and 2 of this monograph, for example, are almost wholly exercises in normative political theory, within which international legal practice itself features only sparingly. They comprise, as it were, the 'justificatory' part of my argument. Conversely, Chapters 3 and 4 focus far more upon the 'fit'-based demonstration that my normative arguments – about the nature and value of politics, the function of governance institutions, and so on – have explanatory power in relation to our legal practices, such that they help to 'fix' which version of the law of state creation we *should* accept.

Although rational reconstruction of this sort is now uncommon within anglophone international legal scholarship, it is by no means unprecedented. Both Başak Cali and John Tasioulas have advocated for a similar 'interpretivist' approach within both international law as such and the identification of customary international law in particular.[46] Its true provenance, however, lies in the 'workable synthesis of natural law and State practice' that Lauterpacht famously described as 'Grotian'.[47] As Georg Schwarzenberger describes this approach, which was most prevalent in the first half of the last century, the Grotian must:

[44] Ronald Dworkin, *Law's Empire* (Hart Publishing 1986) 50–53.

[45] Habermas (n 33) 30.

[46] Başak Cali, 'On Interpretivism and International Law' (2009) 20(3) *European Journal of International Law* 805; John Tasioulas, 'In Defence of Relative Normativity: Communitarian Values and the Nicaragua Case' (1996) 16(1) *Oxford Journal of Legal Studies* 85.

[47] Hersch Lauterpacht, 'The Grotian Tradition in International Law' (1946) 23(1) *British Yearbook of International Law* 1, 5.

> examine customary law, treaties and the general principles of law as recognized by all civilized States and…search in the practice of States for traces of an infiltration of morality into the system of international law and, accordingly, would either exclude or apply conceptions of international morality.[48]

In the present century, we should have no patience for racially loaded talk of 'civilised' states; however, the Grotian approach can and should survive such anachronisms. As the point is powerfully put by J. L. Brierly:

> We are too often tempted to forget the link between law and morals is much more fundamental than the difference between them and that the ultimate basis of the obligation to obey the law can only be a moral one.[49]

In all essentials, this is the position I adopt here. Rational reconstruction is the contemporary inheritor of the Grotian tradition, understanding international legal practice primarily in terms of whatever genuine normative reasons – 'morals' in Brierly's text – present that practice in its best evaluative light. It is to this extent (but to this extent only) a variety of 'natural law',[50] which helps to explain the terms of Lauterpacht's own characterisation. Much of the legal controversy my arguments contain is therefore explicable in largely Grotian terms. Not only do I advance substantive positions at odds with many, if not all, of the positivist authors referenced above, but my approach to elucidating state creation departs from very different theoretical assumptions about the nature of international legal argument.

On my understanding, to borrow once more from Dworkin, international law constitutes a 'branch of political morality',[51] albeit a very narrow and discrete one. It is the morality that follows from our established history of international legal practices, when those practices are taken seriously by us as reason-giving and reconstructed in their best evaluative light. It does not exhaust the morality of international relations: I do not assume that the law of state creation is normatively binding 'all-things considered', even when it comes to questions of international recognition. Nonetheless, I do assume all international law to be at least moral in character, such that it makes sense to reconstruct state creation as a normatively coherent whole. As such, the

48 Georg Schwarzenberger, *Power Politics: An Introduction to the Study of International Relations and Post-war Planning* (Jonathan Cape 1941) 154.

49 James L. Brierly, 'The Shortcomings of International Law' (1924) 5 *British Yearbook of International Law* 4, 16.

50 Both Lauterpacht's 'Grotian' approach and my own 'rational reconstruction' differ quite markedly from the natural law of Grotius himself: Hugo Grotius, *De Jure Belli ac Pacis, Book I* (1652) 1.10.1.

51 Ronald Dworkin, *Justice for Hedgehogs* (Belknap Press 2011) 405.

argument in this book can therefore be understood not only as an attempt to move beyond the doctrinal deadlock that positivism has engendered, although that is my primary aim. It is also a characterisation of the 'inner morality' of state creation, which establishes this area of international law as presumptively binding upon every potential participant within the international legal order, including state representatives themselves. Moving beyond our doctrinal deadlock requires us to discriminate between the various competing legal theories that can be constructed on the basis of past practice. However, doing so is only possible by asking which theory (from now on, which 'reconstruction') we *should* adopt, on the basis that it provides the best available balance of fit and justification. Only a reconstruction such as this can disclose a law of state creation that can be viewed as *binding for us*. Statehood as political community, I contend, is that reconstruction.

3 THE LAW OF STATE CREATION

Given the unorthodox nature of what is to follow, this section aims to make my argument more digestible by summarising the legal positions I endorse. Doctrinal lawyers will find much here that is familiar and some that is more controversial. Non-lawyers, who might be reading this text through the lens of legal and political theory rather than international law, may find this roadmap particularly useful when reading Chapters 3, 4, and 5, which contain some rather dense analysis of international legal practice.

Statehood as political community, as noted at the outset of this Introduction, understands international law to impart statehood only upon the satisfaction of two abstract conditions. First, emerging states must themselves constitute genuine political communities. Second, they must emerge in a manner that respects the ethical value of individual political action. These two abstract conditions map onto two sets of more concrete principles, explicated in Chapters 3 and 4, respectively. The first set establishes what I call the 'antecedents' of statehood: those factual prerequisites necessary for plausible claims to emerge as a state. The second set is procedural in nature, providing both restrictions upon the manner in which new states can emerge and also things that can be accomplished or received by a nascent community to bolster the presumptive plausibility of its emergence.

Turning first to the antecedents of statehood, a presumptively plausible statehood claim requires four factual perquisites: a permanent population; a more or less defined territory; an effective government; and relative political independence. These will be familiar to international lawyers from sources such as Article 1 of the 1933 Montevideo Convention on the Rights and Duties of States,[52] as well as the famous arbitral award in *Deutsche Continental Gas-Gesellschaft v Polish State*.[53] Rather than understanding these antecedents as immutable and inflexible criteria, requiring fulfilment in the same manner and to the same degree in every case, statehood as political community understands them to be four discrete but interconnected indicators that the value of politics is sufficiently instantiated within a particular context for a nascent political community to exist there. Since each such factor is explicable in terms of a shared moral and ethical foundation, their collective application to any given set of facts requires holistic judgement, the fundamental question being whether or not an independent political community can be said to have emerged. Although such judgements must be made with an eye to contemporary social context and historical peculiarities, a brief overview of what each antecedent characteristically requires is instructive.

The population antecedent requires the territory upon which the relevant community exists to have a body of habitual residents. This population does not have to be of any particular size, but it must have the capacity to persist as a more or less identifiable group over time. The territory antecedent requires two things: first, a unit of geographical space within which valuable political activity can occur; and second, more or less determinate boundaries to that unit, such that the relevant community can be at least partially defined in territorial terms. The effectiveness antecedent requires governments to exercise territorial control so as to promote ethically valuable politics to some non-negligible degree. This requires not only sufficient law and order to maintain civil peace but also governance that facilitates individual political action. As such, although the social fact of actual governmental control is characteristically necessary, claims to effectiveness can be bolstered by credible commitments to protect relevant human rights, such as freedom of speech and association, or by the institution of suitably representative institutions.

Conversely, 'effective control' that demonstrably undermines ethically valuable politics will actually undermine the satisfaction of this antecedent: whatever may have been true in the past, contemporary international law cannot be rationally reconstructed so as to licence tyranny. Finally, the independence antecedent requires that effective governments also be relatively autonomous *vis-à-vis* other states. Practically speaking, independence is established wherever inter-governmental domination is absent: a matter which can be ascertained in both 'formal' and 'actual' terms. Formal independence holds to the extent that the ordinary linguistic meaning of particular treaty texts, constitutional

[52] Montevideo Convention on the Rights and Duties of States (adopted 26 December 1933, entered into force 26 December 1934) 165 LNTS 19.

[53] *Deutsche Continental Gas-Gesellschaft v Polish State* (1929) 9 Recueil TAM 336, 344.

documents, and so on, characterise the relevant government and institutions as collectively autonomous, whilst actual independence holds insofar as those same institutions exercise effective territorial control on their own part, rather than merely nominally, or as proxies for the effective control of some foreign entity. If the antecedents of statehood can be cumulatively satisfied to a sufficient degree, a nascent community gets, as it were, 'halfway home'.

Turning now to the relevant procedural principles, these can be split into two subsets. First, there are two principles that condition state creation by establishing processes through which political action can be either instantiated or enhanced. These are the 'recognition principle' and 'referendum principle', which concern, respectively, the effects of foreign recognition and the salience of independence referendums. Second, there are three principles that condition state creation by prohibiting, or rendering far more onerous, the emergence of new states through means that undermine political ethics. These are the 'negative self-determination principle', the 'international peace principle', and the 'territorial integrity principle'. All five share the same set of moral and ethical foundations. They each denote a way in which state creation can be accomplished consistently with the value of politics, such that the emergence of new entities is transactionally respectful *vis-à-vis* individual political action. Entities arising in violation of the first subset of principles characteristically cannot emerge as states. Conversely, although communities that emerge without widespread foreign recognition or an appropriate referendum will characteristically find it more challenging to demonstrate statehood, even a total absence of both is not necessarily fatal. A brief summary of these procedural principles will also be instructive.

The recognition principle holds that formal recognition by foreign governments, whilst not necessary for state creation, can strengthen an extant statehood claim unless such recognition would, in all the relevant circumstances, actually undermine or disrespect the ethical value of politics. Where tyrannical or wholly anarchic entities emerge, a collective duty not to recognise those entities supplants the default liberty that each state enjoys to grant recognition. The referendum principle holds that an independence referendum should accompany state creation unless requiring one would be unjustifiable, considering all the relevant circumstances. However, violation of this principle does not automatically disqualify nascent communities from emerging as states. Instead, where the lack of referendums is not appropriately justified, a rebuttable presumption against statehood arises. This presumption can be overcome by communities that have manifestly satisfied the antecedents of statehood and have otherwise emerged in a manner consistent with political ethics.

More categorical by far are the restrictions imposed by the international peace principle and the negative self-determination principle. Taking the former, an irrebuttable presumption against statehood arises where an entity is created via the unlawful threat or use of force. Taking the latter, where entities arise so as to cause the disenfranchisement or political subordination of a significant portion of an extant population, statehood is blocked until that situation is resolved. Disenfranchisement and subordination of this kind may present itself as an ongoing feature of the emerging entity's governance, such as the text and application of its basic legal instruments, or as something that was done so that the entity in question could arise in the form that it did, such as the mass expulsion of persons from its territory. Finally, the territorial integrity principle establishes a rebuttable presumption against statehood wherever state creation is attempted without either the consent or the dissolution of the parent state. (Where a parent state either consents or has dissolved, there is no contravening claim in relation to which the normative weight of territorial integrity attaches.) This presumption can be overcome where nascent entities have either or both widespread foreign recognition and a clear instantiation of political community through the antecedents of statehood, assuming that no other procedural principles have been breached. Moreover, the presumption can be removed altogether in circumstances where the nascent entity gains a right to remedial secession. In the latter case, such a right arises where the normative basis for territorial integrity itself is undermined *vis-à-vis* the seceding entity, by virtue of extreme violent oppression exacted upon the population of the territory in question.

As argued in what follows, these antecedents and procedural principles provide a framework for judgement on matters of state creation that is rationally intelligible as binding international law. It not only 'fits', and so explains, a sufficiently broad range of international legal practice, but also presents the law of state creation as a coherent and normatively appealing whole, which state representatives and other international legal actors can, without self-contradiction, comply with *as law*. This is not to say that statehood as political community is normatively perfect, such that the legal *status quo* it identifies could not conceivably be improved upon. However, it does entail that the law of state creation possesses a presumptively justifiable normative foundation, such that it makes sense for international legal actors to comply with it, at least until the practice upon which it is based alters sufficiently for its prescriptive content to change as well.

4 THE STRUCTURE OF THIS BOOK

My argument to that end is divided into two parts. Part I establishes my positive case, and Part II examines and rejects reconstructions of the relevant law that are at odds, in various ways, with my own. Chapters 1 and 2 explain what

I take political community to entail, whilst Chapters 3 and 4 demonstrate its explanatory and justificatory power in relation to international legal practice. Chapter 1 establishes what it takes for us to belong to particular political communities and how such membership brings distinct ethical value to our lives, enabling us to live both more meaningfully and more successfully. Chapter 2 further details the kinds of activity required to realise this value, as well as arguing for three important ways in which the governance institutions characteristic of contemporary states support its realisation. Chapter 3 uses these insights to identify and justify the antecedents of statehood, whilst Chapter 4 employs the same theoretical framework to identify the five procedural principles that condition the accrual of statehood to entities with presumptively plausible claims of the relevant kind.

Taken collectively, these first four chapters establish statehood as political community as a coherent and normatively appealing account of state creation. Part II bolsters this position by constructing and critiquing two alternative reconstructions, each of which is at odds with statehood as political community in some way. Chapter 5 considers what I call the 'stability thesis': the view that the law of state creation is primarily explicable, not in terms of political ethics but rather in relation to the value of maintaining international peace and friendly relations. Ultimately, although I accept the importance of this goal (statehood as political community also values it), I argue that no plausible reconstruction of contemporary practice could make peace its primary organising idea. Chapter 6 introduces another alternative, which I call the 'legitimacy thesis': the view that no state can emerge without a normatively legitimate government. I argue against this in general terms at first, before turning in Chapter 7 to a more specific iteration of that same argument: the view that gaining statehood is impossible for nascent communities without sufficiently democratic governance institutions. In both cases, I argue that any normatively plausible threshold for governmental legitimacy would be too demanding to function as a condition for the emergence of new states.

In addition to bolstering my argument for statehood as political community, the negative conclusions reached in Part II help extend my analysis into two adjacent questions. These concern, respectively, what we might call the 'nature' or 'essence' of legal statehood, on the one hand, and questions of state continuity and extinction, on the other. This text offers no conclusive view on either topic; however, my Conclusion presents some indicative thoughts on both, drawn from the arguments of both parts.

PART I

POLITICAL COMMUNITY

1

Political Ethics and Community Membership

International law permits the creation of new states only when they emerge as genuine political communities. Such communities are 'genuine' because they are capable of instantiating certain important ethical values and 'political' because those values relate to the importance of individual political activity. What is more, no new state can emerge unless the *manner* of its creation demonstrates appropriate respect for the value of politics as a distinct domain of ethical behaviour. Taken together, these claims provide the core thesis of this book: that the law of state creation is concerned with political community and that properly explicating this law requires paying political ethics due attention. In this chapter, I begin outlining the relevant ethical considerations. My focus shall be upon the normative foundations of political community, understood through the lens of membership. By understanding what it means to belong to a political community – and why this belonging forms such an important part of human life – we can better grasp why international law makes the observable emergence of such communities a necessary condition for state creation.

To begin, a brief word on the meaning of 'ethics' and 'politics'. By ethics, I mean issues pertaining to how we should live our lives: what makes for a successful life and one that is 'lived well'.[1] I presume that issues of this kind have a certain objectivity to them, in that there is more to living a good life than believing oneself to have done so, and that we are capable of being mistaken, both individually and on a societal level, about what 'living well' really means.[2] This is not to suggest that there is only one way of succeeding in these respects. Holding ethical truths to be independent of our beliefs about them is not to deny that there are many different ways of responding to the challenge of our existence. It does however commit us to believing that it is possible for

1 Ronald Dworkin, *Justice for Hedgehogs* (Belknap Press 2011) 13–15, 197–198.

2 Matthew Kramer, *Objectivity and the Rule of Law* (Cambridge University Press 2007) 4.

us to make ethical mistakes: that choosing to live one way rather than another might diminish the overall success of our lives, or lead to them being less meaningfully lived, when considered in the round. This ethical perspective, which will no doubt strike some as controversial, trades on the intuition, noted by Dworkin, that each human life truly matters, not just *to* those living them but *as such*, and that a life wasted provides a genuine and universal reason for regret.[3]

At bottom, my ethical claim in this chapter is as follows. Political communities matter because politics, understood as a characteristic kind of human activity, provides important opportunities for us to lead successful and meaningful lives. Unlike many accounts of politics and its connection to the related ideas of 'publicity' and 'society', my account does not demarcate either a logical or sociological category of human action.[4] Instead, it concerns politics as a distinct and important domain of morally salient behaviour. In what follows, I use 'morality' to denote the genuine normative reasons we each have for behaving in particular ways *vis-à-vis* other people. International law, I as alluded to in the Introduction, should be considered a domain of morality insofar as it provides a distinct set of genuine reasons for state representatives (and other international legal actors) to behave in particular ways towards others. Like ethics, morality possesses a certain objectivity: we can be mistaken about what we owe to others and we can, in a number of intelligible ways, act *wrongly* in relation to them. As such, politics – understood as its own moral domain – relates to the genuine reasons each of us have to behave in particular ways towards our compatriots: those individuals with whom we share a political community and who, along with ourselves, constitute that community in the way that this chapter describes. The law of state creation, as I argue in later chapters, both responds to and respects the ethical importance of these distinctly political obligations. It makes the existence of a physical and juridical space within which politics can take place a necessary condition for state creation and only bestows that status upon entities that emerge in a manner consistent with respect for the ethical value of politics.

As a result of how I conceptualise politics, some things that are commonly considered 'political' fall outside my characterisation in a manner that might feel counter-intuitive to some readers. For instance, Carl von Clausewitz's

3 Dworkin (n 1) 205–206.

4 Compare, for example: Hannah Arendt, *The Human Condition*, 2nd edition (University of Chicago Press 1998) 22–78; with Jürgen Habermas, *The Structural Transformation of the Public Sphere: An Inquiry into a Category of Bourgeois Society*, Thomas Burger (trans.) (Polity Press 1989) 57–88; and Max Weber, 'Politics as a Vocation' in H. H. Gerth and C. Wright Mills (eds.), *From Max Weber: Essays in Sociology* (Routledge 1991) 77–128. See also: Carl Schmitt, *The Concept of the Political*, George Schwab (trans.) (University of Chicago Press 1996).

famous claim that 'War is the continuation of politics with other means' is contrary to that characterisation, to which large-scale organised violence and domination are anathema.[5] Similarly, the use of 'political' as a pejorative to connote calculated or power-hungry behaviour is not engaged with. By excluding such usage, I do not seek to police the way in which the word 'politics' is used, nor do I pretend towards any kind of necessary truth about our shared concept(s) of politics, more broadly speaking. My aim is more discrete: to describe a unique and important domain of morally salient human behaviour and to demonstrate how the law of state creation, properly understood, both responds to and is informed by its ethical importance.

This chapter begins that argument by examining political membership as a source of moral obligation and investigating the ways in which obligations of this kind create distinct ethical opportunities. First, it argues for two moral duties that each of us have to participate in political activity. Second, it claims that these duties not only reflect important reasons we have for 'doing politics' but also demarcate the membership of our political communities. These arguments – constructed simultaneously – provide 'political community' with a moral core around which its ethical elements coalesce. Finally, this chapter sets out these ethical elements, which take the form of several distinct opportunities that become available when we belong to communities constituted by the two moral duties I advance. As noted above, it is these claims about the ethical importance of political communities that provide the ultimate basis for the account of international law forwarded by this book.

1.1 NON-VOLUNTARY MEMBERSHIP

I argue that the moral obligations providing the normative core of political community are: (i) our collective duty to avoid endemic conflict within our communities by supporting appropriate governance institutions and (ii) our remedial duties to promote autonomy and equality within those communities. They correspond to two conditions for political membership, which I shall call the 'residence' and 'beneficiary' conditions. Together, they yield the following proposition:

> *Non-Voluntary Membership*: any person (P) is a member of a given political community (C), where: (1) P habitually resides in the geographical area in relation to which C exits; and/or (2) P routinely benefits from the coercion of other people by the government of C.

5 Carl von Clausewitz, *On War*, Michael Howard and Peter Paret (eds.) (Princeton University Press 1984) 87.

The residence condition corresponds to our collective duty to avoid endemic conflict, whilst the beneficiary condition corresponds to our remedial duties to promote autonomy and equality. Both of these membership conditions, and the moral duties that explain their normative significance, are presented in Section 1.2 through discussion of what I call 'the hazards of living together' and 'the hazards of being governed'.[6]

Sections 1.3 and 1.4 explain the first ethical opportunity enabled by membership within the political communities that these two duties ground. This is the chance to behave 'reasonably' in relation to our moral obligations, which is presented as one dimension of living what I call a 'meaningful' life. Section 1.5 responds to two objections that these moral and ethical claims might face. Moving on, Sections 1.6 and 1.7 set out the second ethical opportunity that political membership enables: the chance to lead an 'authentic' life, which forms the second dimension of living meaningfully. Turning from ethical meaningfulness to ethical success, Section 1.8 contemplates the value of individual political achievements as part of an overall successful life, whilst Section 1.9 canvasses the instrumental value of political 'products' as logistical and cultural prerequisites for such lives. Taken together, these considerations support my larger claim that political communities are ethically beneficial and that international law both recognises and protects that benefit by making political community both a necessary condition for the emergence of legal statehood and the normative foundation for the procedural principles that the law of state creation imposes.

1.2 DUTIES OF PARTICIPATION AND POLITICAL MEMBERSHIP

This section argues that there are at least two distinctly political moral duties. These duties are 'special' in that they are owed only to compatriots,[7] and 'modest' in that, rather than existing only within perfectly just or wholly legitimate communities, they pertain in a world 'settled by historical chance and the actual course of events'.[8] The first is the collective duty that geographically proximate individuals share to uphold civil peace within the territorial boundaries established by the governance institutions to which they are subject.

[6] Elements of this argument, including the principle of *Non-Voluntary Membership*, appeared in: Alex Green, 'Three Models of Political Membership: Delineating "The People in Question"' (2021) 41(2) *Oxford Journal of Legal Studies* 565.

[7] Christopher Wellman, 'Friends, Compatriots, and Special Political Obligations' (2001) 29(2) *Political Theory* 217.

[8] Jürgen Habermas, *Inclusion of the Other: Studies in Political Theory* (Polity Press 1998) 116.

The second is the duty that each individual has to contribute their fair share towards advancing the autonomy and equality of their compatriots.

Both duties are essentially duties to participate in that they require individuals to engage in particular kinds of political activity. The arguments supporting them also entail that we belong to a distinct political community when: (i) we inhabit the land upon which it exists, so that we habitually live alongside the population of that place and/or (ii) we benefit from the coercive rule of its government, where that use of coercion violates the autonomy and equality of others. These membership conditions and their attendant political obligations arise from two characteristic moral hazards created by the current human condition: (i) the fact that we must live together and (ii) the fact that doing so peaceably usually requires the creation of coercive institutions.

1.2.1 *The Hazards of Living Together*

The 'residence condition' of political membership, which views habitual residence within a particular territory as sufficient for membership within the political community that territory demarcates, builds upon an argument in the liberal tradition. In brief, that argument holds geographically proximate individuals to possess a collective duty to avoid lapsing into endemic conflict by supporting institutions that are conducive to civil peace.

It begins with three, partly empirical, premises. The first is that failures of coordination and collaboration amongst people making incompatible claims to limited resources can create endemic conflict.[9] The second is that endemic conflict risks creating circumstances of extreme distributive injustice,[10] whereby resources are: (i) allocated solely on the basis of violence; (ii) wasted due to high transaction costs; and (iii) insufficiently secure for reliable personal and collective use. The third premise is that this unjust situation is most likely to emerge where individuals are geographically proximate: people in physical isolation face few (if any) coordinative or collaborative challenges.[11]

These premises support the following conclusions. First, because almost all individuals already live within geographically grouped social units, 'the frequency, density, and mutual entanglement' of potential conflict is particularly

[9] Martin Loughlin considers this potential for conflict the conceptual core or 'first order' of the political (*The Idea of Public Law* (Oxford University Press 2004) 33).

[10] Immanuel Kant, *The Metaphysics of Morals*, Lara Denis (ed.), Mary Gregor (trans.) (Cambridge University Press 1996) 89–90; Jeremy Waldron, 'Special Ties and Natural Duties' (1993) 22(1) *Philosophy & Public Affairs* 3, 14.

[11] Waldron (n 10) 15.

pronounced within those units.[12] Therefore, second, habitually living upon the territory of a particular community enhances the risk that an individual will contribute to conflict there. (That they may not have chosen to live within that community is irrelevant: the risk exists whether they chose to run it or not.) Third, on the plausible additional premise that we should avoid contributing to unjust states of affairs,[13] it is thereby instrumentally important for geographically proximate collectives to prioritise relatively harmonious relations amongst themselves before turning their eyes further afield. On this account, it is the relative proximity of people that matters: living alongside each other creates the problem, so social organisation must provide the solution.

Averting endemic conflict within a particular territory characteristically requires some kind of legal order and a government capable of employing coercive power.[14] Enlightenment liberal theorists, such as Kant, famously used this fact to justify moving from a 'state of nature' into a legally constituted polity.[15] However, the same considerations also provide a reason to prevent the collapse of extant governmental arrangements that avoid endemic conflict,[16] assuming that those arrangements are at least somewhat more just than the anarchic circumstances they forestall. This is entailed because any obligation to eliminate unjust circumstances implies (all other things being equal) an obligation to prevent their re-emergence. Governments can uphold civil peace in several ways and, in the ordinary course of events, possess the primary obligation to do so. However, individuals can also help to forestall endemic conflict by acting alone and in concert with others, typically by promoting, supporting, or at least tolerating, governance practices that prevent anarchy.[17]

Individuals with this capacity, and who are habitually resident within a particular territory, have a special, collective obligation to secure and uphold civil peace that runs parallel to the obligation of their government to do the same. This duty is collective in the sense that, whilst the complete set of individuals concerned are obligated to secure civil peace as a group, no one individual amongst them is bound to forestall endemic conflict alone. It is special in the sense that it pertains only amongst the habitually resident *qua*

[12] Jeremy Waldron, 'Two Concepts of Self-Determination' in Samantha Besson and John Tasioulas (eds.), *The Philosophy of International Law* (Oxford University Press 2010) 411.

[13] John Rawls, *A Theory of Justice* (Belknap Press 1999) 115.

[14] Waldron (n 12) 411.

[15] Kant (n 10) 86.

[16] Waldron (n 10) 15–17; Waldron (n 12) 411.

[17] What this requires in terms of specific acts will depend on the circumstances. However, once our compatriots have begun this undertaking, our duty may take on an element of reciprocity. This makes fairness relevant, see: Margaret Moore, 'Is Patriotism an Associative Duty?' (2009) 13(4) *The Journal of Ethics* 383, 388–390.

community members and not also amongst 'outsiders'. For example, the government and laws of the French Republic are primarily constituted to address the distribution of rights and duties within France and, as a result, speak directly to the maintenance of civil peace amongst those who live there. This relationship is not contingent because 'it depends on the difference between being one of the parties in respect of whose interests…[an] institution is [sufficiently] just, and being a person who is merely capable of interfering with a [sufficiently] just institution in some way'.[18] The special nature of this duty serves to pick out habitual residents as members of a territorially grounded political community on the basis of their ongoing contribution to the potential for endemic conflict within that community ('the residence condition' of membership).[19]

1.2.2 *The Hazards of Being Governed*

By throwing us together with other people, history creates moral hazards. Geographically proximate individuals share a collective duty to uphold civil peace within the territorial boundaries established by the institutions to which they are subject. When they succeed in securing the conditions that this special duty requires, that territorial unit yields a nascent political community. However, as Weber teaches us, this is typically achieved through state monopoly on coercive power,[20] which makes the normative profile of such communities somewhat complex.

Coercive rule is presumptively problematic because coercion presumptively violates both autonomy and equality. This is so for two reasons. First, coercion as such consists in manipulating people into pursuing ends that they would not otherwise have chosen, and so violates autonomy.[21] Second, it also presumptively violates equality because manipulation of this kind aims at one person becoming subject to the will of another, creating a relationship of subordination. For these reasons, political communities appear morally paradoxical: characteristically, they emerge in fulfilment of one collective duty by violating other moral precepts. For such communities to be both legitimate

18 Waldron (n 10) 19.

19 Such residence need not be uninterrupted. It turns on the empirical question of where a given person lives large portions of their life. It will include those who have a habit of residing in the territory of more than one political community but not those who are merely visiting or otherwise travelling through the territory in question. This ground yields a conception of membership quite distinct from membership in a national group: our relationship with the other members of our community is one of compatriotism, not shared identity.

20 Weber (n 4).

21 Robert Nozick, *Socratic Puzzles* (Harvard University Press 1997) 15–44.

and just, this circle must somehow be squared, presenting what I shall call the 'autonomy and equality problems'.

Rendering coercive rule compliant with autonomy and equality is a demanding task.[22] Not only must civil peace be maintained within the relevant territory but there must also be general compliance with fundamental human rights.[23] Moreover, no community could truly guarantee autonomy and equality in the face of coercive rule without governance by law and genuine democracy.[24] Finally, and this is perhaps the most exacting hurdle, it is difficult to see how any community could be meaningfully egalitarian or respectful of individual autonomy unless the overwhelming majority of its laws were substantively conducive to implementing those values.[25] Considering this, it seems likely that most political communities will fail to resolve the autonomy and equality problem conclusively, such that at least some coercive rule within them will be morally unjustified.

What is the moral position of individuals subject to coercive rule of this kind? Certainly, their governments owe them better guarantees of autonomy and equality, but what, if anything, do they owe each other? In this subsection, I suggest that such individuals have an obligation to advance both autonomy and equality within their communities and that this obligation further underwrites their community membership, forming what I shall call the 'beneficiary condition' (for reasons that shall become apparent).

When our governments fail to secure autonomy and equality, we should act in pursuit of these values ourselves. We have, I contend, a presumptive duty to do our fair share towards promoting autonomy and equality within our communities. There are at least two reasons for this. The first turns on the causal relationship between governments and their subjects. Not only is the need to avoid endemic conflict a possible motivation for the creation of governments but the habitual residents of a particular territory form an important resource with which governments support themselves. In this way, habitual residents as a set are often doubly causally responsible for coercive rule, in addition to being subject to it. This point should not be overstated: that I caused X, in the sense of forming part of the collectively sufficient conditions that gave rise to it, is not sufficient to say that I am morally liable for ameliorating X. Unlike the potential for injustice that we create by living in relative proximity,

[22] See Chapters 6 and 7 for more detailed discussion of this issue.

[23] Allen Buchanan, *Justice, Legitimacy, and Self-Determination: Moral Foundations for International Law* (Oxford University Press 2004) 266–267.

[24] That is, not just the presence of nominally democratic or representative institutions. On this point, see: Ronald Dworkin, *Freedom's Law* (Harvard University Press 1996) 15–24.

[25] Charles Beitz, *Political Equality* (Princeton University Press 1989) 64.

coercive rule characteristically arises from the actions of a minority who are asymmetrically placed *vis-à-vis* the general population. In some cases, one or more individuals within the relevant government may be individually culpable for particular violations of autonomy or equality, and even where this is not so, the government itself may be culpable as a collective agent.[26] However, as Miller points out, the 'causal relationship suffices to pick [us] out from the universe of others' potentially obligated to attempt a remedy.[27] This is particularly important when no individual is morally culpable in their own right or the relevant government seems unwilling to take the appropriate steps. Causality picks out habitual residents as special in a relevant way.

The second reason why being governed often generates the special duty I am contemplating may seem more controversial. I argue that we have remedial reasons to promote autonomy and equality because we typically gain special benefits from the governmental coercion of those we live alongside.[28] These benefits extend beyond the forestalling of conflict between geographically proximate individuals: contemporary governments are more invasively coercive than simple peace-keepers. Consider the provision of public transportation, either through nationalisation or public procurement, or the provision of other utilities, such as public libraries and recreational space. Although these benefits are not primarily directed towards avoiding endemic conflict, they are funded by taxes that, at least ultimately, are collected via coercion.

Whether an individual experiences a net benefit from being governed will depend upon their circumstances. However, it seems plausible that many of us are better off under functioning governments than we would be otherwise.[29] This probably cannot justify very exacting political duties, such as a

26 Christian List and Philip Pettit, *Group Agency: The Possibility, Design, and Status of Corporate Agents* (Oxford University Press 2013) 153–169.

27 David Miller, *National Responsibility and Global Justice* (Oxford University Press 2007) 101–102.

28 This claim has some similarities to Rawls' argument for a duty to support just institutions on the basis of fair play because of the emphasis both place upon social benefits and burdens (John Rawls, 'Legal Obligation and the Duty of Fair Play' in Sidney Hook (ed.), *Law and Philosophy* (New York University Press 1964) 3–18). However, it differs markedly in two respects. First, it is not primarily concerned with the *distribution* of benefits and burdens so much as with the fact that various individuals benefit from the *prima facie* wrongful burdening of others *no matter how the distribution falls*. Second, at least in the first instance, it does not provide us with duties to support (just) institutions so much as duties to promote the reform of morally problematic ones.

29 Strictly speaking, the duty I outline here applies even to those who are not net beneficiaries. Since compliance with autonomy and equality can be assessed one act at a time, we can arguably gain special remedial duties from the governmental perpetration of individual coercive acts.

duty to obey the law.[30] It is also insufficient, taken in isolation, to resolve the autonomy and equality problems. However, precisely because of this point, it is a plausible basis for individual duties to contribute our fair share towards increasing overall compliance with autonomy and equality within our respective political communities.

To recap, coercion is presumptively wrong because it manipulates us into pursuing ends that we would not have otherwise chosen and subordinates us to those who should treat us as equals. Many people benefit from such presumptive violations of autonomy and equality within contemporary political communities. The benefits of civil peace cannot justify coercive acts that are unnecessary for the maintenance of that peace, so governance beyond that point is presumptively problematic. A solution to the autonomy and equality problem is required for the wrongfulness of coercion to be addressed. This has at least two important implications. First, governments that provide their subjects with benefits whilst *failing* in this respect are morally enjoined to remedy their failure. Second, and crucially for present purposes, if governments are either unwilling or unable to secure autonomy and equality within their communities, it falls upon those receiving the benefits of governance to do their fair share towards promoting those values. In many contemporary communities, where the benefits of governance are various and the coercive acts securing them pose the autonomy and equality problems, this will likely encompass most people who find themselves being governed.[31]

An analogy is useful to establish the plausibility of this position. The law of unjust enrichment, as developed in Anglo-American jurisprudence, supposes that we can be morally liable for gaining at the expense of another without being morally *culpable* for doing so.[32] In a paradigmatic case, you are unjustly enriched at my expense when I transfer title over a sum of money to you, mistakenly believing myself to be paying off a debt.[33] There is no debt, so I am, as it were, unintentionally gifting you the money. You are clearly blameless, as the mistake was mine. However, you are nonetheless liable to pay me back an equal sum. Your duty to correct the unjust circumstances exists

30 Ronald Dworkin, *Law's Empire* (Hart Publishing 1986) 194.

31 It also holds, albeit to a lesser degree, where governments *characteristically* uphold autonomy and equality but nonetheless violate it on occasion. This follows from our ability to assess the wrongfulness of individual actions. For more on the latter point, see Chapter 6.

32 Kit Barker, 'The Nature of Responsibility for Gain: Gain, Harm, and Keeping the Lid on Pandora's Box' in Robert Chambers, Charles Mitchell, and James Penner (eds.), *Philosophical Foundations of the Law of Unjust Enrichment* (Oxford University Press 2009) 152.

33 Peter Birks, *Unjust Enrichment*, 2nd edition (Clarendon Press 2005) 3–19.

notwithstanding your lack of fault.[34] I suggest that those routinely benefiting from morally problematic coercive rule stand in a similar position: through no immediate fault of their own, they have gained at the expense of moral wrongs done to others. In circumstances where the guilty party – that is, the relevant government – is either unwilling or unable to address this, it is incumbent upon such 'political beneficiaries' to do what they can.[35] Characteristically, this will require them to put pressure on their governments via political action.

This kind of remedial duty is special, in the sense that it pertains only amongst people connected by the bonds of political community and so helps to define those bonds. It ties us to our burdened compatriots in a way that non-beneficiaries are not tied and, importantly, pertains whether or not the community-wide allocation of benefits and burdens is fair. Indeed, it bites particularly hard when that allocation is *not* fair. Finally, and most importantly for present purposes, this duty provides the second ground for political membership: we belong to a given community to the extent that we routinely benefit from the coercive activity of its government (the 'beneficiary condition').[36]

1.3 MEANINGFULNESS AND PERSONAL NARRATIVES

I have argued that we owe our compatriots two special obligations. First, we have a collective duty to uphold civil peace by supporting appropriate governance institutions, so that endemic conflict does not subject us all to circumstances of extreme injustice. Second, each of us has remedial obligations to contribute towards the autonomy and equality of our compatriots wherever and whenever our governance institutions fail properly to respect those two values. These duties are first and foremost duties of participation, which require us to act politically in furtherance of their mandated ends.

This section, together with Sections 1.4, 1.6, and 1.7, argues that performing these duties via action of this kind enables us to live 'meaningful' lives. There are two dimensions to this. First, it allows us to act 'reasonably'. Second, engaging in the kind of behaviour that these special duties require can constitute an 'authentic' means for 'self-authorship'. Both elements relate to the ethical

34 Ibid 148–150.

35 Miller (n 27) 102–103, suggests this as a potential basis for 'remedial' obligations, although he does not make an argument for political duties along those lines.

36 'Routine benefit' should not be confused with 'net benefit'. The former refers to the regularity and frequency with which the benefits of coercion accrue, not to the relative value of those benefits. The requirement of *routine* benefit captures the intuition that we cannot become members of a community simply by *visiting* the territory upon which it supervenes, even though we may very well benefit from the coercion of its population during our visit.

value of attempts: that I attempted to achieve something I believed to be good, or that I attempted to do what I considered to be right, carries a type of value that is not captured by my eventual success or failure. I discuss the value of such attempts in general terms here, set out the requirements of reasonableness in Section 1.4, and those of authentic self-authorship in Sections 1.6 and 1.7.

Ethically valuable attempts help to create something – a history or 'personal narrative' of our doings – in relation to which the overall meaningfulness of our lives can be judged.[37] When we act, politically or otherwise, our actions imply particular attitudes. Whether we play games, till fields, or write poetry, our actions express an endorsement of the permissibility, importance, or necessity of what we undertake. This endorsement is not always conscious or intentional. We often give such things no thought at all. However, it is always latent. While we have the capacity for moral and ethical judgement, we cannot avoid this implicit endorsement. It is part of being a self-aware moral agent.[38] As time passes, we accrue a history of action and inaction, each item of which may instantiate or abrogate meaningfulness and success. Our characters may be transient, changing throughout our lives. Our history is transitive and attaches to us no matter how we have changed. This is captured most evocatively by Arendt:

> In acting and speaking, men show who they are…This disclosure of "who" in contradistinction to "what" somebody is – his qualities, gifts, talents, and shortcomings, which he may display or hide – is implicit in everything somebody says and does. It can be hidden only in complete silence and perfect passivity…[39]

As my discussion of reasonableness and authentic self-authorship will exemplify, each of us is uniquely placed to determine the meaningfulness catalogued by our own personal narratives. Just as I cannot make your actions authentic or reasonable, neither can you render mine so. Therefore, insofar as our personal narratives matter objectively, each of us has *ethical* reasons to instantiate as much meaningfulness within them as we can.

1.4 REASONABLENESS

Living meaningfully requires that we avoid behaving selfishly or myopically, such that we lack reasonableness. For instance, if I ignore my obligations to my family because they hamper my success as an academic lawyer, I may succeed

37 Dworkin calls this the 'performance value' of our lives: (n 1) 197–198.
38 Ibid 241–247.
39 Hannah Arendt, *The Human Condition*, 2nd edition (University of Chicago Press 1998) 179.

in authentic self-authorship (see below), but I will nonetheless have exhibited unreasonable ambivalence towards those obligations. Ethically speaking, this diminishes the value of my attempts because they necessarily partake of my failure to address the *moral* challenge set by the circumstances of my existence. This is not to say that reasonableness (and thereby meaningfulness) requires us to pursue only that which is actually right or good. A failure to behave reasonably in relation to one's family is not a failure to identify an appropriate personal goal. Instead, that failure consists in not recognising that there are elements of living meaningfully that one has no choice but to accept. I owe my family a number of moral obligations, and I live a less meaningful life to the extent that I do not recognise this and respond appropriately. This does not mean that I must pursue my goals in a perfectly moral fashion. However, it does require that I attempt to meet the moral obligations that I actually possess.

As mentioned above, the existence of a moral duty is an objective matter: whether or not I believe myself to have familial obligations is distinct from whether or not I actually have them. Reasonableness is sensitive to this objectivity. It requires that, whilst we may have an imperfect understanding of the *content* of our moral obligations, we nonetheless acknowledge and respond to their *existence* by attempting to comply with them to the best of our ability.[40] I do not always behave unreasonably by failing to discharge my duty, say, to my family, even though I will behave wrongly by doing so. However, I will lack reasonableness to the extent that I fail to understand or acknowledge that I have obligations of this kind or if, having acknowledged them, I am indifferent to what they require.

Reasonableness is a scalar property. For instance, an inchoate belief that we should behave 'appropriately' towards strangers falls within the bounds of reasonableness, even if it is *less* reasonable – by virtue of being less accurate – than believing in a duty to prevent strangers from coming to harm when the cost to ourselves is low.[41] This connection between reasonableness and moral accuracy shows why being reasonable always requires more than honest belief. I may genuinely believe that I have no obligations to those with whom I lack a personal relationship. However, this belief would be unreasonable insofar as it is unresponsive to the existence of the obligations that I in fact

40 Whilst similar to the conception of reasonableness advanced by Thomas Scanlon (in particular, see: *What We Owe Each Other* (Belknap Press 1998) 33), mine is normatively thinner. Scanlon believes that judgements of reasonableness not only 'presupposes a certain body of information and a certain range of reasons which are taken to be relevant' but also include 'what these reasons, properly understood, in fact support' (ibid 192).

41 I assume such a duty, see: Peter Singer, 'Famine, Affluence, and Morality' (1972) 1(1) *Philosophy & Public Affairs* 229.

possess. Summarising these observations, we can say that reasonableness turns on: (i) the degree of correspondence between what I should do and how I in fact behave and (ii) the conscientiousness with which I attempt to render my pursuit of personal projects consistent with what I believe my obligations to be. My life as a whole has been lived reasonably to the extent that my personal narrative has instantiated these two elements.

For reasonableness to pertain in relation to any single action, both elements must be present to some extent. Consider someone who incorrectly denies the existence of an entire 'domain' of morally important activity, not out of ignorance or indifference, but after diligent reflection.[42] The two moral duties that I argued we owe to our compatriots are distinct from those that we owe within our inter-personal relationships[43] and those that we owe to all other moral subjects. If I am right about the existence and content of those duties, then whether or not we have lived reasonably is partly dependent upon how we have engaged in politics. However, we can imagine an attenuated sort of egoist who, after philosophically informed, sustained, and conscientious reflection, comes to believe that no political obligations exist. Instead, they hold that we only owe obligations to those we care about on a personal level.[44] Assuming that this sort of person lives in accordance with these beliefs, can we really describe them as unreasonable? Notwithstanding the fact that they may have agonised over the notion of political obligation, I believe that we can. Lives that deny the importance of politics can be authentic (see below) and praiseworthy to that extent. But denying the existence of all political obligations is ethically hazardous. By acting on the assumption that we owe *something* to those within our political communities, the most we risk is trying and failing to live justly. However, by acting on the denial that there is anything to owe, we risk failing to try at all. Our attenuated egoist therefore faces an ethical tragedy: authenticity requires them to risk behaving unreasonably, whilst hedging their bets would result in an inauthentic life.

This assumes the truth of my previous claims: if we owe nothing to our compatriots, then it is impossible to act unreasonably in relation to them, and the meaningfulness of the egoist's personal narrative will not suffer. As will become

42 A 'domain', in this sense, is an area of activity that can be provisionally demarcated in terms of the kinds of moral reason that characteristically apply to us when we engage in it. Politics is one such domain, promising is another.

43 Such relationships include associations of friendship, family, and romantic attachment but also promissory commitments, other voluntary associations, and assumptions of responsibility.

44 This is a particularly extreme articulation of what Thomas Nagel calls the 'personal standpoint', by virtue of which something matters (only) because it matters *to someone* (*Equality and Partiality* (Oxford University Press 1995) 11–18).

apparent, because it is partially hostage to moral truth, reasonableness is more demanding than authenticity. But this is appropriate. Within the relatively minimal constraints described in Section 1.7, we should be free to make judgements about what is worth pursuing in life. Being ethically free in this way is entailed by the importance of us authoring our own personal narratives.[45] However, part of the challenge of living meaningfully is doing so alongside others who are ethically enjoined to do the same. What we owe *them* should not depend solely on what we believe to be important, whether we believe it authentically or otherwise.[46] Our duty to make our personal narratives authentic, which comes from our unique capacity to determine the authenticity of our own actions, is insufficient to determine the relation in which we stand to the lives of others. Morality requires that we do what is right, not simply what seems right to us. However, if living meaningfully required perfectly moral action, we would all be doomed to ethical failure. Our ethical obligation to act reasonably bridges this gap between morality and ethics. It allows us to succeed ethically whilst failing morally, yet nonetheless remains sensitive to the fact that the morality of our actions is not exhausted by the authenticity of our attempts.

Assuming that I am correct about the duties we owe to our compatriots, we can exhibit reasonableness when we act politically. For instance, whether or not a particular tax or disability welfare regime is appropriate concerns distributive justice. Questions of distributive justice are paradigmatic of political morality, addressing whether governance is sufficiently egalitarian. If you support a libertarian scheme, whilst I prefer something based on the Rawlsian difference principle,[47] we are disagreeing over a moral issue of political scope. This means that if we pursue our convictions through individual or collective participation, we are making attempts towards meeting our moral obligations and, because such attempts exhibit reasonableness, we will both have succeeded ethically to at least some extent.[48]

45 Dworkin (n 1) 210–213.

46 Nagel (n 44) 15–16.

47 John Rawls, *Political Liberalism* (Columbia University Press 1993) 5–6.

48 Consider the Jordanian uprisings beginning in January 2011, which targeted, amongst other things, a perceived democratic deficit in Jordan's constitutional monarchy. Those protesting pushed for greater legitimacy within their political community, exhibiting reasonableness in so doing. This sort of effort is the most visible way to meet our ethical duties through political action: placing popular pressure on government through collective demonstration. Voting (where it is available to us) is another means of doing so, as is individual action taken outside electoral contexts, such as writing to, or otherwise petitioning, government on matters of public interest. For an interesting report on this, see: Andrew Spath, 'Change Without Revolution: Jordan's Missed Opportunity?' *New Middle East*, 2011: http://new-middle-east.blogspot.co.uk/2011/04/change-without-revolution-jordans.html (last accessed 2 October 2023).

Conversely, the capacity to act reasonably in politics brings with it an ethical hazard. If we owe political obligations, then, under normal circumstances, our lives will lack a degree of meaningfulness unless we engage in at least *some* reasonable political action. This is not an 'all or nothing' issue: because the meaningfulness of a life turns on how much meaningful action it contains, the overall meaningfulness of a personal narrative is a scalar property. However, all other things being equal, our ethical duties to engage in political action cannot be avoided without some degree of failure on our part. This matters because a failure to behave reasonably in relation to a morally important domain of activity is always significant; an individual's personal narrative must be judged holistically.

1.5 TWO OBJECTIONS

Some might find my suggestions problematic. In particular, they may take issue with my second justification for our individual, remedial duties to promote the autonomy and equality of our compatriots. The benefits bestowed upon us by governments are often unsolicited and might have been rejected by some people if opt-outs had been offered.[49] Given this possibility, why should private individuals gain *any* obligations from receiving the benefits of governmental coercion? Whilst it might seem appealing, this objection risks begging the question: it implicitly assumes that all political obligations are basically voluntary, which my argument explicitly denies.[50] However, what if we modify the objection? Our governments owe us special duties because they coerce us. These include duties to secure civil peace, as well as to render any further uses of coercion compatible with the autonomy and equality of all. Given this, is it not unnecessary and, in any event, overly burdensome for private individuals to have special moral duties to their compatriots? Framed in this manner, the objection can be levelled at both the duties that I claim we owe to our compatriots, as well as at the ethical requirements of reasonableness I argue to follow from them.

The high degree of responsibility that attaches to governments, and even the relatively greater logistical potency they possess, does not entail that supplementing their activity will never be morally required. Government officials, like any other human agent, can be unwilling or unable to comply with

[49] Robert Nozick, *Anarchy, State and Utopia* (Basic Books 1974) 90–95; John Simmons, *Moral Principles and Political Obligations* (Princeton University Press 1979) 129.

[50] Samuel Scheffler, *Boundaries and Allegiances, Problems of Justice and Responsibility in Liberal Thought* (Oxford University Press 2001) 71–72.

their obligations. Given the importance of promoting civil peace, autonomy, and equality, it seems unacceptable to let this lie: there should be some person or group with 'secondary responsibility' for promoting these ends, should governments fail.[51] In this connection, the scope of the duties I have proposed is crucial. Morally, they are quite modest: we are enjoined only to do our *fair share* towards promoting and/or supporting civil peace, autonomy, and equality. Their ethical corollaries are more modest still: we need only make reasonable attempts towards fulfilling these moral obligations. What is more, the application of such principles will depend upon the circumstances in particular political communities, such as the distribution of resources amongst their members, the structure of their governance institutions, and the uses to which governmental coercion is typically put. The more impotent an individual finds themselves through circumstances beyond their control, the less these duties will demand from them. Seen in this light, they are far less demanding than many other moral and ethical obligations we might be thought to hold.

Given the relatively modest nature of these duties and the importance of civil peace, autonomy, and equality, in what sense might the former be too burdensome? I anticipate two concerns. First, none of the arguments advanced above demonstrate that 'ordinary' members of political communities are individually culpable for the harm caused by endemic conflict or coercion: are special duties like those contemplated too burdensome without culpability of this kind? Second, do the moral duties I have identified place too much strain upon individual resources, even though we are only enjoined to do our fair share?

1.5.1 *Remedial Duties without Personal Culpability*

Taking the first concern, our contribution to the potential for endemic violence in a particular place does not entail that we will each be individually culpable, not to mention culpable to the same degree, should it actually emerge. Some of us may be individually culpable and some not, or else the nature of our collective failure might be so complex that no individual can be deemed personally culpable. What is more, a purely causal contribution to the existence of morally problematic coercion is typically insufficient to make us morally culpable for it. Similarly, insofar as I am an innocent beneficiary of governmental coercion, I am not distinctively to blame for any consequent

[51] I take the language of primary and secondary responsibility from: Leif Wenar, 'Responsibility and Severe Poverty' in Thomas Pogge(ed.), *Freedom from Poverty as a Human Right* (Oxford University Press 2007) 264.

violations of autonomy and equality. We may feel uncomfortable conceding the existence of moral duties to engage politically in the face of this.

Nonetheless, it is generally accepted in both political theory and legal practice that we can have special obligations without having committed a wrong. This is so even when, to reference the earlier version of this objection, we have not consented to those obligations falling upon us. Most of us believe that we have obligations to friends and family that are non-voluntary and do not arise in response to individual wrongdoing. If these intuitions are not enough, consider once again the analogy drawn above between our remedial duties to engage in political action on the one hand and the law of unjust enrichment on the other. Briefly considering what justifies this analogous area of law will help establish the presumptive plausibility of non-voluntary duties that can arise without fault: if we can do so, then the above-noted 'culpability objection' will seem less serious.

There are a number of potential explanations for why restitution is morally required once an unjust enrichment occurs. It does not matter for present purposes which provides the best available reconstruction of Anglo-American legal practice. Our present task, which is to consider whether remedial obligations to act politically can be justified by a non-consensual, non-fault-based principle, can be served by examining the plausibility of a 'corrective justice' approach. Consider once more the paradigmatic case of unjust enrichment: the mistaken payment of a non-existent debt. According to Barker and Weinrib, we must give any mistakenly transferred money back out of respect for the pre-existing property right of the original owner.[52] For ease of analysis, assume that this prior right was morally justified, *inter alia*, by the importance of that owner's capacity to use the object of their right (the money) to further whatever morally permissible ends they chose. The original owner mistakenly used their money in pursuit of a non-existent end (discharge of the imagined debt), and so their action did not match their intentions. Although their mistaken payment legally transfers ownership to the enrichee, this is so for instrumental reasons, such as certainty and speed of commerce at the societal level. The duty of restitution exists 'precisely to recognize and reverse the moral problems which this necessary instrumentalism creates'.[53] The law as a whole thereby protects the original owner's prior legal right whilst facilitating other goods. The enrichee's duty of restitution exists because they are the person with whom the legal entitlement to the

[52] Barker (n 32) 169; Ernest Weinrib, *The Idea of Private Law* (Oxford University Press 2012) 140–141; Ernest Weinrib, 'Restoring Restitution' (2005) 91(3) *Virginia Law Review* 861, 868–870.

[53] Barker (n 32) 169.

object of the original owner's *moral* right now rests. No moral wrongdoing or voluntary action on the enrichee's part was necessary to put them in that position. Nonetheless, it would be impossible for them to respect the original owner's prior legal (and present moral) entitlement to the money without performing restitution. Replacing it with as much as and good from another source – say, a state fund – would not reflect the enrichee's status as the beneficiary of the original owner's loss. This cogent and, I suggest, normatively attractive account of unjust enrichment demonstrates the moral sense in our possessing certain remedial duties even without personal culpability. That is enough to render the remedial duties that motivate the beneficiary condition of political membership plausible and provide an intuitive reason to reject the culpability objection raised above.

1.5.2 *Modest Political Burdens*

This sketched explanation of unjust enrichment not only demonstrates the plausibility of duties other than those acquired by wrongdoing or volition. It also serves as a useful comparison when asking whether we would be overburdened by a duty to do our fair share of political action. This addresses the second objection contemplated above: does political action require so much from us that we will be unjustifiably restricted from engaging in other ethically valuable activity? The quick answer would be that 'our *fair* share' necessarily implies not. However, this misconstrues the concern, which is that any such duty – even the relatively minimal one contemplated above – would be too burdensome to place upon private individuals.

The duty of restitution we acquire when in receipt of an unjust enrichment is both a primary moral duty and a legal liability. By contrast, our duties to engage in political action are secondary duties, characteristically without legal liability.[54] Both points of difference are significant. All other things being equal, it is more burdensome to have a primary duty than a secondary one. Whether they are individuals or groups, the holders of primary duties are uniquely responsible for ensuring that performance of their duty is achieved. Only if they fail or refuse to act do the secondary duties of others become engaged. When benefiting from an unjust enrichment, your private law duty of restitution is one that you alone owe. The judicial organs that guarantee your restitution only become obligated in the event of your failure to act.

54 In some jurisdictions, this is not always so. In Australia, for example, voting (which is one archetypal mode of political action) is compulsory and to that extent more burdensome. For more on the various modes of political action available in contemporary states, see Chapter 2.

In the case of secondary duties, however, the individual or group with the primary duty does not lose their obligations just because their failure to act has obligated someone else. Indeed, secondarily obligated individuals may gain rights against the primary duty-holder. In the political context, a government employing coercion should *always* safeguard the autonomy and equality of those it governs, including those who have remedial duties to contribute fairly towards the correction of its wrongful behaviour. However, when that government fails to secure these values, it comes under additional duties to the remedially responsible: to the extent that the duty to correct any unjustified coercion is a burden to such people, governments have an additional reason to amend their ways. Returning to the comparison, if a primary duty to reverse an unjust enrichment can be a justifiable burden, then a secondary duty to address violations of autonomy and equality would also seem justifiable.

The distinction between moral and legal liability is even more important. Section 1.5.1 contemplated the *moral* liability of an unjustly enriched individual, which in the private law context required restitution. However, private law also establishes the judicial enforceability of that duty. Since this form of liability is coercively enforceable, it is far more burdensome than 'mere' moral liability. Moral duties to act politically are characteristically not legally enforceable. To the extent that enforceable private law duties are not unjustifiably burdensome, we are provided with an additional reason to believe that non-enforceable political duties are not overly burdensome either.

Perhaps neither the form nor magnitude of the duty matters so much as its pervasiveness. The private law duty to reverse unjustified gains only applies when we are in receipt of such gains. Conversely, a duty to engage politically is, *ex hypothesi*, a demand that we almost always face. For instance, if: (i) most modern governments routinely violate autonomy and equality and (ii) most of us routinely benefit from their use of coercion, then most of us will have a standing duty to act politically. Whilst the resource drain of an individual instance of political action is not too great, an ongoing duty might be, cumulatively speaking. To answer this concern, we should remember that our proposed moral duties are to do our fair share towards promoting and/or supporting civil peace, autonomy, and equality through political action, whilst our supervening ethical duties require only reasonable attempts towards securing those ends.

The burden established by the moral element of this standard is minimal. Duties to *promote* and *support* civil peace, autonomy, and equality do not entail a duty to *secure* those ends. Governments have the latter duty, but individuals characteristically do not. This mirrors the different reasons at play. Governments have extensive duties by virtue of undertaking systematic coercion. Individuals do not. Their obligations are, as I have argued, based on their collective creation of the risks of endemic conflict, their causal relation to coercive governance, and their status as routine beneficiaries of coercion. Taken individually, these are weaker grounds for moral liability than attempting to coerce others. Concordantly, the duties that arise as a result of these grounds are less invasive. Private individuals do not fail morally when they are unable to bring about the required changes in their communities. Instead, failure occurs when they do not take the actions that should be expected of them, given their particular circumstances. For instance, a people suddenly facing violent oppression from a military coup will likely have a duty to offer some resistance.[55] However, they are not required to take *whatever* steps would be necessary to remove their oppressors.

The exact moral requirements that political membership places upon each individual are not as important for present purposes as the resultant ethical ones: individuals will succeed ethically when they respond reasonably to the fact that *some* manner of political action is required. That requirement may be burdensome to some extent, but it is hardly excessive, given the characteristic importance of the goals to be served. Furthermore, since the moral duty to be political requires only an appropriate *contribution*, no private individual needs to take up their burdens alone. Given the size of contemporary communities, most will share their duties to act with sizeable multitudes. The benefits of collective activity often outweigh the cost borne by each participant. Consider the January 2017 'Women's March', which responded to the perceived chauvinism of the newly inaugurated President of the United States. Such mass demonstrations can have immense expressive power, whereas the cost for each participant is typically low: usually, the only thing lost is the time and expense of attending. In light of the above, the case for the overwhelming burdensomeness of a duty to act politically is rather weak.

1.6 AUTHENTICITY AND SELF-AUTHORSHIP

The second dimension of living a meaningful life that political membership enables concerns the 'authenticity' expressed by our attempts to live according to personal judgements of value. To use Dworkin's example, an artist who could have been admired for producing conventional work but nonetheless risks an innovative project may eventually fail. Nonetheless, they have arguably made the more meaningful choice by taking the risk: it speaks to the

55 Candice Delmas, *A Duty to Resist: When Disobedience Should Be Uncivil* (Oxford University Press 2018).

seriousness with which they take their art and the value to be found there.[56] The same value can be found in attempts to meet the two moral duties detailed above. My efforts to create support for constitutional reform may fall on deaf ears or be successfully undermined by those with conflicting agendas. Nonetheless, the fact that I pursued what I believed to be just and fair evidences the honesty (and perhaps courage) with which I approached the issues in question. This cannot be diminished by a lack of success. To the extent that I have engaged in such attempts, I have authentically approached the challenge of my existence.

Subject to certain qualifications, authenticity cannot be negated by my being mistaken about the objective value or rightness of the goal or act I pursued. Questions of value are sometimes controversial, and living authentically requires us to pursue what we honestly believe to be worthwhile, even (or perhaps particularly) when others disagree with us. More to the point, although the value of such attempts assumes the possibility of achieving valuable ends, it is not contingent upon the objective potential for success in any particular case. Just as I might be destined to fail due to events beyond my control, so too might I be destined to fail because what I honestly believed to be worthwhile is in fact not so. It nonetheless remains that I took steps towards authoring an authentic personal narrative.

Note the distinction between authenticity and autonomy. Autonomy is best understood in terms of what might be called 'non-domination': it requires that we are not manipulated into pursuing ends that we would not have otherwise chosen to prioritise. This is a necessary but insufficient condition for authentic action.[57] When our autonomy is respected, we have the capacity to behave authentically, but we may still fail to do so. For instance, a young person's parents may refrain from putting pressure upon her to choose a particular career, but that does not entail that her eventual choice will be one that conforms to her beliefs about what matters. Her choice may be made capriciously or otherwise be inconsistent with her ethical reasons to self-author.[58]

1.7 TWO REQUIREMENTS OF AUTHENTICITY

There are at least two normative restrictions upon our ability to be authentic. The first is moral: we must pursue only those goals or actions that are consistent with the value of *all* individuals developing more or less authentic personal

56 Dworkin (n 1) 199.
57 Ibid 212.
58 Simone de Beauvior, *The Ethics of Ambiguity*, Bernard Frechtman (trans.) (Citadel Press 1948) 25.

narratives. Under normal circumstances, someone who seeks to destroy, dominate, or wholly exclude others from political and social life implicitly denies the value of those individuals' self-authorship. Unless there is a reason why some person or class of people do not merit self-authorship, such acts of destruction, domination, and exclusion imply a denial of self-authorship's *general* value. It is hard to imagine what such a reason could be. For instance, why should my being an agnostic, heterosexual, white, English, human male make me any more deserving of the opportunity to act authentically than other beings capable of making judgements about value?[59]

Such implicit denials have an ethical impact because they necessarily qualify the authenticity of our attempts, even though they cannot completely remove that value. We can self-author as vicious or callous, and, though this may seem puzzling, there is at least some value in our doing so. Acting authentically does not mean pursuing only what is objectively good. I may honestly believe that an egotistical or malicious life is well-lived. For example, a plausible interpretation of some of Nietzsche's work suggests that he considered extreme cruelty to be consistent with greatness of character and that greatness of character was objectively worth having.[60] If I honestly act on similar beliefs, those parts of my personal narrative will track my understanding of what matters. However, imagine that this includes acts of murder. By killing others, I deny them the chance to behave authentically. By doing so without justification, I implicitly deny the value of authenticity *tout court*. By generally denying this value, I implicitly deny that my own self-authorship partakes of it: if there is no such value, it cannot be instantiated in my actions. This denial does not change the fact that the meaningfulness of my actions *does* matter: that is an objective issue. However, it does prevent my actions from fully instantiating the value of authenticity. Since I can only be fully authentic by acting consistently with the importance of my own self-authorship, any behaviour that implicitly denies the authenticity-value of my actions cannot be fully authentic.[61] I may not realise that I am engaged in such a denial, but that does not matter. The confused nature of my actions itself inflicts the ethical damage: whilst still an instance of self-authorship, my behaviour is imperfectly authentic.

Like reasonableness, authenticity is, to this extent, a scalar property. Some actions can be *more* authentic than others by virtue of their content and one's

[59] Dworkin (n 1) 256–257; Nagel (n 44) 11.

[60] Friedrich Nietzsche, *Beyond Good and Evil*, R. J. Hollingdale (trans.) (Penguin Books 2003), 149, 159, 195–196, 204; Friedrich Nietzsche, *Thus Spoke Zarathustra*, Graham Parks (trans.) (Oxford University Press 2005) 10–17.

[61] Dworkin (n 1) 212.

mental state whilst engaging in them. Consciously accepting the importance of self-authorship will no doubt enhance the authenticity of what I do, but it is neither necessary nor sufficient. I can behave with authenticity even if I have never thought about my actions in those terms. I may have an intuition that certain of my decisions 'really matter', or I may simply behave as though they do without really thinking about it at all.

The second restriction upon our ability to act authentically is that we must honestly (in the absence of psychosis) believe that our attempts are feasible. Because the notion of valuable attempts necessarily assumes the possibility of valuable ends, I cannot make a meaningful attempt where it seems to me that there is virtually no chance of success. A life dedicated to creating a school of magic in Scotland would be wasted, due (in part) to the mundane nature of our universe. For slightly different reasons, it would waste my time to run for President of the United States of America, given that I was born on a small island off the South coast of England. Admittedly, one can self-author as a fool or failure. There may even be some value in it, albeit of a different kind. If they are not caused by delusions, the actions of a committed Don Quixote – charging at imaginary giants – may instantiate *autonomous* living. Such a life may even be fun. Nonetheless, the knowing pursuit of a pointless enterprise cannot count as an authentic attempt towards something of value.[62] It makes a mockery of the ethical reasons we each have for constructing our personal narratives.

These are unusual cases. We should neither overestimate nor misconstrue feasibility. Even seemingly hopeless attempts can have authenticity. When Rosa Parks and those who emulated her refused to yield to racist domination, even the slimmest chance of making a difference was sufficient to render their attempts authentic. What is more, we can deliberately attempt something in the hopes that our anticipated failure will have an expressive impact, or else that we will achieve something other than our stated goals. Many of those involved in the Occupy Movement must have known or suspected that fundamentally altering global financialism was a hopeless aim. Nonetheless, by publicly railing against it, they contributed to a transnational political ethos that may well have informed the more stringent financial regulation that we now enjoy.[63] The strategy of asking for more than we expect is a well-known

[62] de Beauvior (n 58) 28.

[63] See, for example: Financial Services and Markets Act 2012 (UK); Council Regulation (EU) 575/2013 Capital Requirements Regulation [2013] OJ L176/1; Council Directive 2013/36/EU of 26 June 2013 on access to the activity of credit institutions and the prudential supervision of credit institutions and investment firms, amending Directive 2002/87/EC and repealing Directives 2006/48/EC and 2006/49/EC Text with EEA relevance [2013] OJ L176/338.

negotiation tactic, and we should not read a lack of feasibility into such political manoeuvring too readily.

1.8 THE ETHICAL VALUE OF POLITICAL SUCCESS

Both dimensions of ethical value discussed so far relate to the meaningfulness of our lives, which concerns the manner in which we choose to respond to the (moral and ethical) challenges we face. Sections 1.9 and 1.10 argue that responding to the two moral duties described in Section 1.2 can also facilitate our leading *successful* lives. Rather the focusing on the value of our attempts, this turns on the extent to which we manage to behave rightly and achieve ends that are actually good. To this extent, success should be understood in objective terms: did we really do something of value, rather than just believing that we did so?[64]

My claim in this section is that our political actions can make our lives more successful by counting as personal achievements. Relatively few of us will ever filibuster a senate or spearhead a civil society campaign, but it would be myopic to assume that personal political achievement is the exclusive province of statesmen.[65] Contributing to the creation or realisation of valuable movements and institutions can give meaning to human existence, even if the role that we each play is as one amongst many. For every Martin Luther King Jr., there are multitudes who contribute in less visible ways, without which power and influence would be impossible. Hume's emphasis on the passive power held by the governed is apposite here, as is Lenin's observation that politics 'begins where masses are'.[66] The vast majority of us provide small, commonplace contributions to the creation and augmentation of our political communities, whether through the opinions we express in political discussion or by the claims we make upon governance institutions. The engaged citizen who takes part in public debate (whether through writing, speech, or physical demonstration), who votes wherever she is able, and who makes good use of her legal rights is the paradigm example of this in the Western world, but even she represents just a few modes of action amongst many.

The degree to which we dedicate ourselves to political projects will vary from person to person. However, when we contribute to a political success, we can consider ourselves to have accomplished something valuable, even

64 Dworkin (n 1) 197–198.

65 Richard Evans, *In Defence of History* (Granta Books 1997) 161–190; E. H. Carr, *What Is History?* (Penguin Books 1987) 31–55.

66 Hume, *Essays, Moral, Political, and Literary*, I.IV.1; Vladimir Ilich Lenin, *Lenin, Selected Works: Volume 7* (Progress Publishers 1961) 295.

if the exact nature of that value will depend upon the nature of the success. For instance, the negotiations that led to the fall of apartheid in South Africa between 1990 and 1993 were an important episode in that state's political development. However, they took place only because of a more diffuse political background in which numerous individuals played a part. Early strikes, boycotts, and organised acts of civil disobedience were conducted by South Africans under the leadership of the African National Congress and its 1952 Defiance Campaign. Around 8,000 people were arrested during this movement for their attempts to resist the enforcement of racial segregation.[67] Each of those individuals can count the fall of apartheid as a success in which they played an active role, notwithstanding the fact that their individual causal contribution might be difficult to discern. The point is not that each individual was a necessary actor without which the world would not have changed. It is enough that each person contributed to a collection of actions that were cumulatively sufficient for that outcome to have taken place.

1.9 THE INSTRUMENTAL ETHICAL VALUE OF POLITICAL PRODUCTS

There are many ways we can strive for personal success, lots of which have little to do with politics. Some of us endeavour to understand the nature of our universe, whilst others focus on the value to be found in inter-personal relationships. Others still turn their attention to music, whilst many make raising children their focus. However, political endeavours differ from these examples in that without at least some people succeeding in them, other avenues of human activity become much harder to pursue. This is the final way in which political membership creates ethical opportunities: our political successes can facilitate further personal success by providing independently valuable things in which we can partake. To take just one example, cultural and social institutions that enrich our lives, such as public displays of sporting prowess or musical skill, are generated as much by political activity as by the individual skill of the performers. Any concert, public competition, or play relies upon a complex background of logistical collaboration, social toleration, and economic facilitation to provide the physical and social space within which it takes place. It is through political activity that these are provided: activity that extends beyond the efforts of particularly involved individuals, into that undertaken by society at large.

[67] 'The Defiance Campaign', *South Africa: Overcoming Apartheid Building Democracy*: http://overcomingapartheid.msu.edu/multimedia.php?id=65-259-9 (last accessed 2 October 2023).

This instrumental value of politics is complex and often difficult to trace causally. Individual political acts that seem insignificant on their own can combine with others to have far-reaching effects. The clearest example is voting. Individual votes have an extremely limited causal impact but, in aggregate, can change the social landscape of entire continents. Consider the 2016 referendum in the United Kingdom, in which a majority voted to leave the European Union, thereby altering the dynamic of international relations within Europe. Chapter 2 outlines a number of ways in which politics outside the ballot box can have this aggregate effect, most of which are more causally complex still. But, however they emerge, the consequences of politics can provide us with ethical opportunities that we would otherwise lack. So many individual undertakings rely upon a background of cooperation and mutual tolerance that most personal projects are only possible by virtue of collective action somewhere along the line.[68] I may consider the life of an artist or priest to be particularly worthwhile, but unless my political community provides logistical, social, and economic support for art and religion, my desire to engage in those things will be frustrated.[69] This is not to say that a successful life would be impossible without the support of political activity. But without it, the modes of potential success open to us would be greatly diminished.

1.10 CONCLUSION

It may seem odd for a book concerned with state creation to begin with such an in-depth discussion of individual flourishing. Ethics – even political ethics – can seem very far removed from the substantive principles of international law. This book, however, is motivated by the conviction that this is not so: despite its somewhat unsalutary history, international law – and particularly those aspects that deal with state creation – is deeply intertwined with the value of individual human lives. My ultimate claim, that state creation, as regulated by international law, is grounded upon an appreciation for the value of politics, possesses much of its explanatory power only because of the links that exist between law and ethics.

With that connection in mind, this chapter argued for a particular understanding of what it means to belong to a political community, based upon

[68] Plato, 'Crito' in Harold Tarrant (ed., trans.) and Hugh Tredennick (trans.), *The Last Days of Socrates* (Penguin Classics 2003) 90–91, 50d.

[69] Support can come by way of permission to engage in the relevant activity, even though this liberty is otherwise unsupported. The mere interaction of different lifestyles and modes of existence necessarily has an economic and social effect upon a political community, such that tolerance of any activity will come with some cost, even if that cost seems negligible.

two special kinds of moral duty that we owe to our compatriots. These are: (i) our collective duty to avoid endemic conflict within our communities by supporting appropriate governance institutions and (ii) our remedial duties to promote autonomy and equality within those communities. My arguments in support of these two political obligations also established the following principle of community membership:

> *Non-Voluntary Membership*: any person (P) is a member of a given political community (C), where: (1) P habitually resides in the geographical area in relation to which C exits; and/or (2) P routinely benefits from the coercion of other people by the government of C.

Political communities constituted on this basis characteristically create four kinds of ethical opportunity. The first two relate to the meaningfulness of our lives, concerning the extent to which we live reasonably and authentically self-author. The second two concern whether our lives have been successful in an objective sense: performing our duties can lead to personal successes and also create opportunities for further ethically valuable activity that would otherwise not be available to us. This, I suggest, already tells us a great deal about the ethical value of contemporary states.

These four kinds of ethical opportunity can sometimes be realised through single actions. Most obviously, many authentic political acts will also be reasonable. For instance, when someone lends their support to a national labour movement, they authentically pursue their own conception of what matters and act reasonably in relation to their political obligations. However, both authenticity and reasonableness assume the value of ethical successes, as set out in Sections 1.9 and 1.10: valuable attempts are possible only where valuable ends are feasible. Similarly, many personal political successes will be such as to provide further opportunities for ethically valuable activity, both for the successful individual and for others. This being so, it is possible for a single political action to be doubly meaningful, a personal success and a condition for further ethical successes.

Nonetheless, the distinctions drawn in this chapter matter. The moral duties we owe to our compatriots define the ethical core of political community, presenting us with challenges that we cannot avoid without diminishing the overall meaningfulness of our lives. However, we can authentically supererogate these duties. This happens when we contribute *more* than our fair share to the promotion of civil peace, autonomy, and equality, or when we push for public goods beyond these three things. Such actions meet the standard of reasonableness, but – particularly where supererogation is intentional – they must be understood as authentic attempts at going *beyond* the call of duty. Examples include acts by which people risk (or voluntarily end) their own lives, such as the individuals involved in the 1981 Irish hunger strike or the unidentified rebel who stood before a column of tanks in Beijing, following the violent suppression of the 1989 Tiananmen Square protests.[70] Supererogation is significant because it exemplifies the distinctiveness of authentic acts as engagements with a particular community.

Taken together, the arguments of this chapter present the core of 'political community' as a moral and ethical concept, forming the foundation upon which my account of state creation shall be built. Chapter 2 elaborates further upon politics as a distinct domain of human activity and discusses the role that state institutions play in its realisation.

[70] An interesting collection of journalistic perspectives on this 'Tank Man' can be found in: Patrick Witty, 'Behind the Scenes: Tank Man of Tiananmen', *The New York Times*, 3 June 2009: http://lens.blogs.nytimes.com/2009/06/03/behind-the-scenes-tank-man-of-tiananmen/ (last accessed 2 October 2023).

2

Political Action and Valuable Institutions

The account of international law presented in this book contends that the principles of state creation are best elucidated with reference to political ethics. Chapter 1 advanced an understanding of those ethics. This chapter bridges the gap between that discussion and the rational reconstruction of international law presented in Chapters 3 and 4. It does so by shifting focus from individual ethics to the facilitative role played by state institutions in respect of ethically valuable political action. This shift has three stages. First, I provide an illustrative discussion of political action designed to further characterise this domain of human activity. This comprises a non-exhaustive list of behaviours that constitute political action and a conceptual account of the relationship between violence and politics. Second, I examine further how political action relates to equality, with particular attention to the permissibility of prioritising the participation of our compatriots. Third, I establish some normative connections between political action and state institutions, arguing that the latter are highly advantageous – and perhaps essential – to realise the ethical value of politics. Specifically, I claim that such institutions are characteristically: (a) 'artefacts' created by intrinsically valuable political action, (b) 'focuses' at which much of our political action is aimed, and (c) both conditions for, and examples of, 'forums' within which such action can be conducted.

2.1 ARCHETYPAL INSTANCES OF POLITICAL ACTION

The next three sections elaborate upon the conception political action constructed in this book. In this section, I outline some paradigmatic instances of politics, which I divide into two categories: 'direct' and 'diffuse' action. On the conception of political ethics advanced here, behaviour counts as 'political' to the extent that it responds to the two moral duties that, as argued in Chapter 1, pertain amongst compatriots. This has two consequences. First, the activities listed in this section are non-exhaustive: the form that political action takes in a particular community will depend to some extent upon that community's governance institutions, cultural traditions, and other social practices. What I have to say in the following two subsections is designed only to characterise politics rather than to dispose of it in any kind of exhaustive or definitional manner.

Second, the political and non-political, on my conception, differ from the more familiar distinction between the public and private. I treat many issues falling within what is commonly accepted to be the 'private sphere' as political in character. One example is sexuality: governmental support (or toleration) of the sexual subordination of women and the victimisation of transgender and homosexual persons are serious violations of equality – and so are political in nature – notwithstanding the 'private' social spheres within which such issues often arise. It is well known that governments often abandon women to the risk of sexual violence in their home environments[1] and that many legal systems still do not permit sexual intercourse between consenting adults of the same gender.[2] The 'public' or 'private' nature of such issues is less important for my purposes than their relation to the moral duties that we owe to our compatriots. Each of us have (secondary) obligations to oppose this kind of oppression within our political communities, making questions of sexuality political, at least to that extent. What I have to say within the next two subsections should be read with this in mind.

2.1.1 *Direct Action*

This occurs when individuals have unmediated interaction with either the government or the governance institutions of a particular political community. The analytical importance of parsing between these two things is outlined in Chapter 6. For present purposes, it suffices to say that governments are the people who exercise political power within a given community, whereas governance institutions are the legal and other frameworks through which they do so. Interaction with the latter is usually easier for those professionally engaged in politics, such as elected officials or civil servants. Not every aspect

[1] See generally: Mary P. Koss, Lisa Goodman, Louise Fitzgerald, Nancy Felipe Russo, Gwendolyn Puryear Keita and Angela Browne, *No Safe Haven: Male Violence against Women at Home, at Work and in the Community* (American Psychological Association 1994).

[2] For example: An Act to consolidate the law relating to criminal offences 1871 (Singapore), Section 377A; Criminal Code (Cap. 195), 29 December 1838 (Mauritius), Section 250; An Act relating to criminal offenses, 31 March 1976, Act A327; P.U. (B) 139/1976 (Malaysia), Section 377.

of their work will be 'political', although formulating and implementing policy certainly offers the possibility for ethically valuable action. Outside that context, the most obvious example of direct action is voting, either in elections or referendums. However, most communities rely upon voting relatively infrequently, such that it cannot be considered the most commonplace means of direct participation. In some states, voting in local government elections is supplemented by opportunities to participate in consultations on regional policy. Since politics also relates to local issues, such activity counts as direct participation. To take one more example, legal actions taken in relation to particular governance activities, such as judicial review or private lawsuits, enable individuals and groups to act directly via governance institutions (in this case, courts).

There is also direct action where private individuals communicate or consult with governments, unmediated by governance institutions. Writing to a political representative or attending 'discussion workshops' with them are paradigmatic examples of this. Lobbying government departments is also paradigmatically political. Given this, individuals working (either professionally or voluntarily) for civil society organisations, as well as the participants in some kinds of public service-related trade union activity, can be considered to take political action routinely. Whilst fire fighters and doctors (for example) are not professional political actors, their participation in strikes and protests is an important means of directly engaging with governments, given their connection with public safety and wellbeing. Furthermore, where communities have political parties with which private individuals can associate, taking part in their activities is an important means through which individuals can engage in direct forms of collective action. Finally, public protest can count as direct action, at least when clearly aimed at governments. The 2019 Hong Kong protests and the 2022 Russian protests opposing the invasion of Ukraine were instances of this kind.

2.1.2 *Diffuse Action*

Unlike direct action, 'diffuse' participation contributes exclusively to the political 'ethos' or 'culture' of a particular community.[3] It forms, as it were, part of the political background against which direct action takes place. Since

[3] For an interesting case study, see: Maarten Hajer, 'Discourse Coalitions and the Institutionalization of Practice: The Case of Acid Rain in Britain' in Frank Fischer and John Forester (eds.), *The Argumentative Turn in Policy Analysis and Planning* (Duke University Press 1993) 43–76.

governmental power is always at least to some extent hostage to the tolerance of the governed (see the following section), governments attempting to rule through largely non-violent means must remain relatively receptive to the political ethos of their community. This will often not be as straightforward as 'giving the people what they want': political communities are usually too diverse for uniform popular sentiment.[4] However, maintaining an appearance of acceptability is crucial to ensure stable rule.[5] The result is that, where individuals contribute to political discourse in a particular community, their actions form part of the behaviour that collectively determines the ethos to which their government responds.[6] This complex and remote causal impact is insufficient to provide governments with genuine legitimacy (see Chapters 6 and 7). However, it is enough to instantiate the ethical values outlined in Chapter 1. For instance, authentic and reasonable activity is perfectly consistent with being one of an immense and relatively disorganised multitude, individually contributing, and collectively constituting, a political ethos.

Some of the most visible individual contributions to political ethos come from those who write, either in print or digitally, on issues concerning governance. However, political speech can have similar impact. Journalists, pundits, and public intellectuals are particularly clear instances of this. Political communication of this kind will typically be more impactful the more people it reaches. However, even relatively private discussions can help to shape the individual attitudes that cumulatively determine the ethos of a political community.[7] To this we might add non-verbal or otherwise allegorical political expression, through art, film, poetry, literature, or humour. To some extent, even the consumption of this material, when it is widespread enough to have a noticeable impact, has a political dimension. Boycotts and 'cancelling' are apposite here. Acts of association can have a similar effect. The mere joining of particular groups, such as trade unions or political parties, and the eschewing of others, whether by withholding membership, attention, or, in commercial contexts, custom and investment, can have an expressive impact when

4 Furthermore, it is unusual for this kind of political ethos to develop through community-wide interaction. Far more usual is the development of informal 'deliberative enclaves' within which discussion takes place, see: Cass Sunstein, 'The Law of Group Polarization' (2002) 10(2) *Journal of Political Philosophy* 175, 176.

5 Niccolò Machiavelli, *The Discourses*, Leslie J. Walker (trans.), Bernard Crick (ed.) (Penguin 1983) i.4.

6 To use Loughlin's language (*The Idea of Public Law* (Oxford University Press 2004) 99–113), a great deal of 'constitutive power' is bound up in the political discourse of communities which are not ruled solely through violent means.

7 John Parkinson, *Democracy and Public Space: The Physical Sites of Democratic Performance* (Oxford University Press 2012) 39.

undertaken by sufficient numbers. Action of this diffuse sort will characteristically comprise the vast majority of the behaviour that populates the political domain of our personal narratives.

2.2 POLITICS AND VIOLENCE

The line of argument I adopt in this book denies war the status of 'political action'. This, some may well think, runs contrary to the common-sense thought that force is a frequently used political tool in international relations. There is indeed a sense in which war is 'political' when used to advance governmental agendas and to secure or undermine intergovernmental relationships. But this is 'politics' only in the broader sense of ordinary English. Widespread violence must be considered inimical to ethically valuable politics in the sense with which I am concerned. Where truly endemic violence persists, most private individuals will not be free to act politically, being limited by necessity to securing their personal safety. At the very most, private individuals might be able to respond to circumstances of war or violent anarchy by attempting, on a collective basis, to bring about an end to that unjust state of affairs. However, in contemporary armed conflict, the potency of individual non-combatants is typically quite limited in this regard. In this respect, our duty to restore a civil condition, when faced with endemic violence, is more akin to a duty to *enter into* politics than a political duty as such.

At a conceptual level, the opposition of politics and violence is best accessed via Hannah Arendt's distinction between violence and power, which tracks an important moral distinction between violence as a governmental tool and politics as a process of collective self-determination. Arendt defined power (in its political sense) as the potential that attaches to multitudes by virtue of their collective capacities, whilst describing violence as the capacity of select groups or individuals to threaten physically or overwhelm (and thereby dominate) larger groups.[8] For her, power 'is never the property of an individual; it belongs to a group and remains in existence only so long as the group keeps together'.[9] Power need not be bound up with collective actions. It can be potential or passive, such that when 'we say of somebody that he is "in power" we actually refer to his being empowered by a certain number of people'.[10] Violence, by contrast, is the means through which an individual or sub-group can overcome the superior potency of the many: 'the implements of violence… are

[8] Hannah Arendt, *On Violence* (Harcourt 1970) 42.
[9] Ibid 44.
[10] Ibid.

designed and used for the purpose of multiplying natural strength until, in the last stage of their development, they can substitute for it'.[11] Arendt understood that violence often coincides with power.[12] To rehearse Hume's observation, governments that rule coercively can typically do so only with the tolerance of their populations, for the power of the many far outweighs the potency of the few.[13] This distinction between power and violence is nonetheless useful, as it helps to explicate both the role of politics within contemporary governance and the ways in which endemic violence can suppress political action. I shall take these points in order.

In the same way that Arendtian power is bound up with collective potential, ethically valuable politics prises our ability to contribute to the cooperative or cumulative augmentation of our political communities. Public goods that provide us with distinct ethical opportunities may be supported by governments, but they also depend upon the popular support that those governments receive. True, some individuals will only contribute to these goods (for example, by paying tax) because they are coerced into doing so. However, it seems likely that many others will feel an obligation to contribute.[14] Such an impulse may not be theoretically worked out, particularly as regards the ethical framework developed in Chapter 1. Some people may react purely instinctively to their obligations or believe that convention requires them to toe the line. Whatever the case, it is difficult to imagine how governments could provide any form of public good without people to support them, either passively or actively. Violence – in this context the use of governmental coercion to promote compliance – can only secure the state against a minority of potential dissenters. It is the 'last resort' of a regulatory process that assumes compliance to be the norm.[15] As Arendt tells us, in 'a contest of violence against violence the superiority of the government has always been absolute; but this superiority lasts only as long as the power structure of the government is intact'.[16] Politics, to that extent, precedes governmental violence and must be considered conceptually distinct for that reason.

Moving on to the second point, where violence is endemic, valuable political activity is often difficult if not altogether impossible. In this regard, both

[11] Ibid 46.
[12] Ibid 47.
[13] Hume, *Essays, Moral, Political, and Literary*, I.IV.1. See also: Loughlin (n 6) 81–83.
[14] H. L. A. Hart, *The Concept of Law*, 3rd edition (Oxford University Press 2012) 80.
[15] Arendt (n 8) 51; A similar point is raised by Leslie Green in his Introduction to Hart's *The Concept of Law* (page xxx). Sanctions, Green tells us, are 'the law's Plan B. Plan A is that its subjects should conform to it without further supervision'.
[16] Arendt (n 8) 48.

Kant and Hobbes were correct in their assessment of 'the state of nature'. If we imagine a hypothetical state of endemic violence, it is easy to see why, as Kant argued, undertaking valuable projects would be cripplingly difficult,[17] in no small part because, as Hobbes feared, every individual would be entirely preoccupied with their own immediate safety.[18] Consider the case of the Syrian Arab Republic, where the impact of governmental, paramilitary, and foreign violence has caused the destruction and forced relocation of much of that state's population.[19] The policies of foreign governments no doubt affect Syria, such that the politics of those other states may affect its future. But *Syrian* politics, understood as the more or less stable political interaction amongst and between its populace and government, has been crippled by civil war. At various points over the previous decade, Syria's government itself was reduced to fighting for its own survival. However, whilst we may justly condemn Bashar al-Assad, it remains true that under such violent conditions, the provision of public goods is crippled, and the necessity of individual and collective self-defence eliminates most other opportunities for authentic and reasonable self-authorship. In a state of perpetual war, collective action might persist through the organisation of competing military or, more likely, paramilitary organisations.[20] However, this is collective action of a severely limited sort. It contemplates only the use of violence to bring about more peaceful circumstances. The ethical richness and complexity of ordinary political life is absent. This provides us with a reason to treat violence and politics as inimical (and so distinct), at least insofar as violence may become endemic. This opposition, as we shall see in Chapter 4, is of particular consequence *vis-à-vis* the procedural principles that international law imposes upon state creation.

2.3 VIOLENCE AS POLITICS?

The previous section argued that governmental violence characteristically requires a degree of popular empowerment. Furthermore, Chapter 1 argued that governmental coercion can be used to secure the circumstances of politics

17 Immanuel Kant, *The Metaphysics of Morals*, Lara Denis (ed.), Mary Gregor (trans.) (Cambridge University Press 1996) 38–39, 44–45, 89–90.

18 Thomas Hobbes, *Leviathan* (Penguin Classics 1997) 84.

19 At the time of writing, around 5.2 million people have fled Syria, see: 'Syrian Regional Refugee Response', The Office of the United Nations High Commissioner for Refugees, last updated 24 August 2023: https://data.unhcr.org/en/situations/syria (last accessed 2 October 2023).

20 Traditional military groups have far too strict a command structure to admit much in the way of meaningful political action.

against violent disruption. These relationships between governance and stable political communities are particularly important to the rational reconstruction undertaken in this book, as will be expanded upon below. They show that, notwithstanding the tension between politics and violence, there can also be interdependence between them. But can violence, at least when it falls short of making war, ever *constitute* political action?

Isolated acts or even limited campaigns of violence can be used to make political statements: my conception of politics would be problematically counterintuitive to the extent that it completely denied this. The suffragette movement in the United Kingdom, and the Women's Social and Political Union in particular, are famous for having used militant tactics in an attempt to promote equal voting rights across the genders.[21] We might also cite the violent actions of Umkhonto we Sizwe in undermining apartheid in South Africa, or the 2005 French riots, driven as they were by the rioters' perceptions of their own social marginalisation. More recently, the violence associated with the Black Lives Matter movement seems almost paradigmatically political. The question is: did the violent behaviour of such movements, which clearly engaged with issues of social justice and governmental legitimacy, count as valuable political action in the sense with which I am concerned?

Exactly when violence counts as an all-things-considered morally appropriate mode of political action is not at issue. The objective permissibility or necessity of political violence will depend upon the circumstances.[22] More pressing is whether violence can instantiate the value of politics, as discussed in Chapter 1. Can acts of violent protest be reasonable and authentic responses to the moral duties that we owe our compatriots? Despite the conceptual distinction and tensions between politics and violence, there is no reason to deny this *a priori*, assuming that the person perpetrating these violent acts has: (a) an honest belief that they are relatively likely to succeed, (b) a simultaneous belief in their moral necessity, both in terms of means and ends, and (c) both of these beliefs (at least inchoately) track some set of moral obligations that actually exist, even if they are imperfectly understood by the individual in question. These requirements are, to be clear, no more nor less than the requirements of authenticity and reasonableness – articulated in Chapter 1 – as they apply to violent acts. That at least some acts of violence might satisfy these desiderata seems plausible.

[21] Martin Pugh, *State and Society: A Social and Political History of Britain since 1870*, 4th edition (Bloomsbury 2012) 152; Bob Whitfield, *The Extension of the Franchise, 1832–1931* (Heinemann 2001) 152–160.

[22] For example: Avia Pasternak, 'Political Rioting: A Moral Assessment' (2019) 46(4) *Philosophy & Public Affairs* 384.

I will say no more about this here, save to mention one further restriction that appears essential. One moral limitation upon the ethical value of our violent actions is that, as putative acts of self-authorship, they must be consistent with the value of self-authorship in general. As argued in Chapter 1, this value cannot be coherently instantiated in acts that implicitly deny it: violent politics will have limited authenticity-value if it is a sufficiently proximate cause of the destruction, domination, or political exclusion of sentient beings under circumstances where we know or ought to know that such a risk was material.[23]

2.4 PARTICIPATION AND EQUALITY

The existence of genuine political community is not contingent upon the realisation of a fully egalitarian society. This does not mean, however, that equality is otiose as far as political ethics is concerned. As argued in Chapter 1, it is partly through our responses to inequality that political action allows us to lead meaningful lives. Moreover, even though political community itself does not require perfectly egalitarian policies, it does require circumstances conducive to two normative baselines that can be characterised in broadly egalitarian terms. First, all other things being equal, each member of the relevant community should be permitted to exercise their capacity to undertake at least some form of political action, such that they can be considered potential participants. Second, each individual must be permitted to act politically in relation to their own communities (and not, that is, simply in relation to any community that may permit their participation). These two normative baselines have egalitarian implications, notwithstanding their minimalism. To the extent that any society fails to meet these standards – for example, by excluding a significant minority of its population from public life – it will, to that extent, undermine its credentials *as* a political community. This holds for reasons similar to those discussed in Chapter 1: insofar as a community unjustifiably denies the value of some minority acting politically, it thereby implicitly denies the value of political action *tout court*. This point, as Chapter 4 demonstrates, has particular importance when elucidating some of the procedural limitations international law places upon state creation.

[23] I assume that, to count as political in the ethical sense, violent actions cannot *aim* at the death of sentient beings either. If it is wrong to risk a particular state of affairs, it is wrong to knowingly pursue it as well. The only circumstances in which either the destruction of (or the unilateral superimposition of one's own will upon) another sentient being seems consistent with the value of self-authorship are circumstances of self-defence and, under perhaps more stringent conditions, the defence of others. This matters because some political violence can be understood in terms of collective self-defence (Pasternak (n 22)).

These modest egalitarian constraints might concern readers with particularly cosmopolitan or democratic intuitions. First, in cosmopolitan terms, why should it matter which communities we get to participate within, as long as we can do politics somewhere? Second, if everyone is entitled to act politically in relation to their own communities, why are we not also entitled to political participation on a genuinely egalitarian basis: why does the ethical importance of politics not mandate full-blown constitutional democracy and egalitarian resource distribution?

2.4.1 *Prioritising the Participation of Compatriots*

To understand the importance of political participation within one's own community, we must return to the two conditions for political membership, outlined in Chapter 1:

> *Non-Voluntary Membership*: any person (P) is a member of a given political community (C), where: (1) P habitually resides in the geographical area in relation to which C exits; and/or (2) P routinely benefits from the coercion of other people by the government of C.

Both conditions turn upon the existence of special moral duties: to collectively forestall endemic conflict within our communities and, on an individual basis, to contribute our fair share towards countering any violations of autonomy and equality resulting from governmental coercion of which we are beneficiaries. This means that, ethically speaking, *Non-Voluntary Membership* is demarcated in terms of reasonableness rather than authenticity. Reasonableness, it should be remembered, turns upon the conscientiousness with which we respond to the existence of our moral duties, as well as the degree of correspondence between our actions and what we are, in fact, morally required to do, whilst authenticity turns instead upon the correspondence between our actions and our honestly held beliefs about what matters. Whilst these two dimensions of meaningfulness may hold equal ethical importance, they differ considerably in substance. Although we do not necessarily fail more profoundly by being unreasonable than by being inauthentic, authenticity can be instantiated in many kinds of action, political or otherwise, and need not be displayed in relation to any particular community. By contrast, our ethical duty to be politically reasonable exists *only* in relation to moral duties that bind us *vis-à-vis* particular communities. Our capacity to be politically reasonable therefore turns upon our ability to act in relation to the communities in question: we typically cannot act in a reasonable manner towards our own communities by participating elsewhere.

Imagine an individual who satisfies *Non-Voluntary Membership* but is prevented from participating within their own community. Perhaps they are imprisoned and shut off from all relevant means of action or are the victim of such an unjust distribution of resources that they are unable to do anything but struggle for survival. Bringing about these kinds of circumstances is presumptively wrongful for many reasons. However, one reason is the disrespect that it evidences for the political capacity of the person in question. Such individuals will not fail morally or ethically by being prevented from engaging with their obligations: the fact that performance was rendered impossible by the wrongful interference of others arguably removes such obligations from them.[24] But it is precisely because of this fact that undermining their political capacity is disrespectful. Intentionally or recklessly preventing others from taking political action risks implying that something about those people makes them unequal to the task or undeserving of the privilege. For instance, we may well think that when incarcerated individuals are denied political participation, they are treated as misbehaving children who are not capable (or not deserving) of participating in their communities. This devalues their capacity to be reasonable in relation to their political obligations and so denies them this dimension of meaningful activity.

If such disrespect is to be avoided, we must not be either internationally or recklessly prevented from engaging politically within our own communities. Those who are neither routinely resident within a particular community, nor routine beneficiaries of governmental coercion there, characteristically have no special moral duties towards the community in question. Preventing such people from participating does not risk the same disrespect instantiated by attempts to undermine the participation of community members, since there can be no implicit denial of the capacity to act reasonably in relation to moral duties that do not exist. Indeed, assuming that the political capacities of 'outsiders' are sufficiently recognised within their own communities, such people can always engage in reasonable political behaviour somewhere.[25]

What is more, wherever the opportunity for reasonable politics exists, the opportunity for authentic self-authorship exists as well. As long as outsiders

[24] On one account, the loss of these duties leaves intact the moral reason(s) the relevant individuals have to act politically (John Gardener, 'Reasons and Abilities: Some Preliminaries' (2013) 58(1) *American Journal of Jurisprudence* 63). Those reason(s) were sufficient to ground their duties, but only in the absence of wrongful prevention. According to this view, wrongful interference with political capacity operates as an *excuse* for non-compliance, even though non-compliance remains something to regret.

[25] This particular need for the recognition of *Non-Voluntary Membership* provides one reason amongst many for why being rendered stateless is so dangerous.

are afforded participation within at least one community, they also have some opportunity for authentic political action. Excluding them from participation in another community does not shut them off from a *necessary* avenue of authentic behaviour. As Dworkin argues:

> A person's authenticity is not compromised by limitations of nature or circumstance: not because he lacks athletic ability, or because taxation makes it impossible for him to live as he would most like, or because he lives in a technologically backward community. He does not then have as many colors on his palette, but the life he designs…may be just…as firmly the life that he rather than anyone else has designed.[26]

To summarise, *Non-Voluntary Membership*, based as it is upon the moral duties to our compatriots, presents a more fragile ethical challenge than our more abstract duty to act authentically. Preventing people from acting politically in relation to their own communities renders them unable to engage in a distinct kind of reasonable activity. Assuming that such 'insiders' would otherwise be able to face this challenge, intentionally or recklessly frustrating their engagement is disrespectful. Conversely, preventing 'outsiders' from political participation within other communities does not shut them off from either reasonable or authentic action *per se*. This is not to say that purely authentic political acts are unimportant, simply that their value does not require the same provision of opportunity that the capacity to act reasonably does.[27]

2.4.2 *Degrees of Participation*

Some modes of governance facilitate political participation more than others. Given this, why does the ethical importance of politics not require complete

[26] Ronald Dworkin, *Justice for Hedgehogs* (Harvard University Press 2011) 212.

[27] It is plausible that an analogous argument might apply in relation to 'duties of common humanity': one might claim that insofar as a person (P) is prevented from acting reasonably in relation to what they owe to non-compatriots for reasons of common humanity, P is treated disrespectfully *in the same way that they would be if they were prevented from acting reasonably in relation to their compatriots*. Whilst I take no definitive stance on this, one dissimilarity between political duties and duties of common humanity merits comment. P's *political* duties are owed to a discrete set of people (P's compatriots) by virtue of *Non-Voluntary Membership*. Conversely, P is less restricted when it comes to performing duties of common humanity. Preventing P from acting in relation to one group of non-compatriots (say, those in foreign state S1) but not another (those in S2) does not prevent P from responding reasonably to *all* of their duties of common humanity, taken as a set. Characteristically speaking, the same is not true of political duties: when P is prevented from acting reasonably in relation to their compatriots, there is no alternative set of individuals in respect of which P can undertake the ethical challenge of political action.

participatory equality, for instance, via radically egalitarian social democracy or some other appropriate institutional structure? The answer is that, as argued more fully in what follows, the instantiation of political community is scalar in relation to actual societies. Real communities differ in terms of the frequency, regularity, and profundity of their population's political activity. Similarly, actual governance institutions typically fall somewhere in between licencing absolute tyranny and instantiating the popular power of utopian democracy, such that their political value is always a matter of degree. A community in which all members have identical legal rights to political participation will instantiate the value of politics more than one in which they do not. Likewise, it is preferable *vis-à-vis* political community that each individual has an equal pool of material resources (such as time and wealth) with which to act politically.

However, a failure to guarantee either or both of these ideal conditions does not imply an absence of the relevant values. The value of politics can be instantiated to a non-negligible extent where the population of the relevant community is typically afforded the *de facto* ability to participate, even though their legal rights and material resources are unequal. As long as such people have minimally sufficient resources and protections to engage in reasonable and authentic activity, the community they belong to has non-negligible political value. As I argue in Chapter 3, international law characteristically permits state creation only where this minimal standard is met.

2.5 GOVERNANCE, POLITICAL COMMUNITY, AND POLITICAL ACTION

As argued earlier in this chapter, both governments and governance institutions can be the direct addressees of our political activity: they can, for example, be petitioned, protested, and, under some circumstances, sued. We can also convey our attitudes or intentions towards them in a more diffuse manner, using means as varied as journalism or jokes. Where the value of politics is instantiated sufficiently, institutions such as legislatures, councils, courts, and police almost always owe their initial and continued existence, at least in part, to the ongoing, often passive, tolerance and support of their subjects, as well as to the individual and collective political actions of those people. As argued in Chapter 1, such actions provide a range of ethically important benefits to us, some of which enable further valuable political action. Indeed, our very membership within discrete political communities turns upon distinct moral duties, which themselves have important ethical implications.

In this section, I add to these earlier claims, arguing that governments and governance institutions of various kinds characteristically bear three sorts of 'quasi-independent' moral value, each of which is downstream from the ethical importance of individual political action. I do not set out what kind of institutional arrangements maximise the values I describe; to that extent, my approach is pluralistic. I limit myself to claiming that, within genuine political communities, governments and the institutions within which they reside have value of their own: as 'artefacts' of political activity, 'focuses' for that activity, and 'forums' within which it can take place. The first of these three values is intrinsic, making governments and institutions valuable in a manner analogous to works of art. The second two are instrumental, relating more directly to the value of ongoing and potential political activity in the relevant community.

2.5.1 *Political Artefacts*

Although intrinsically valuable, the political acts that help constitute our personal narratives are ephemeral. Once complete, the value these actions instantiated becomes a matter of history. In this sense, politics constitutes a performance. However, any institutions produced by our aggregate or collective activity have a degree of permanence. Although governance institutions are created and sustained by political activity, their existence is typically independent of any particular political action or individual actor. Councils, commissions, parliaments, and adjudicative mechanisms endure as long as our collective practices sustain them. As such, so long as those practices continue, the institutions they support stand as intrinsically valuable monuments to whatever individual political activity helped 'fix' their existence: to use Martin Loughlin's words, governance institutions are 'an expression of the realm of the political'.[28] I argue that to the extent that we have a reason to respect political activity we also have a reason to respect the institutional products of that ethically valuable behaviour.

A comparison with art is revealing. It is intrinsically valuable that Salvador Dalí painted *Christ of Saint John of the Cross*. The fact that someone strove to make such a beautiful thing has its own significance, never mind that he succeeded. Political acts are similar: the mere act of supporting a democratic movement can have value that is not reducible to the eventual success or failure of that movement. However, the value of such attempts is only intelligible where valuable goals or ends are conceivable. Whether in the case of

[28] Martin Loughlin, *The Foundations of Public Law* (Oxford University Press 2010) 194 (citing Georg Jellinek, *Allgemeine Staatslehre*, 3rd edition (Springer 1922) 180). Unlike Loughlin I do not believe that political communities are 'a collective act of imagination' (ibid 197). As I hope to be clear from my argument so far, they possess objective moral and social existence.

Dalí painting *Christ of Saint John of the Cross* or your support for a political movement, the value of the attempt may not be hostage to the reality of the result but it is necessarily related to the *possibility* of success. This explains why success intuitively possesses an augmented ethical value when compared with meaningful failure. Due to the necessary connection between the value of an attempt and the value of what is attempted, a successful attempt partakes of that second value in the way that an unsuccessful one does not.

Both art and politics have products. These 'artefacts' can have an independent value from that of the acts that create them. Dalí's work is beautiful, which gives it value. It also brings people pleasure, which gives it value of another kind. An institution created or augmented through political action can enhance legitimacy or justice within the relevant community, as well as providing a number of other public and private goods to those within its jurisdiction. People can also rally around their institutions, taking a sense of pride or belonging in them, which, like Dalí's painting, gives them value of another sort. However, in both cases, the close ethical relationship between the act(s) of creation and their product cuts back the other way. A perfect replica of *Christ of Saint John of the Cross* would be as beautiful as the original and may bring as much pleasure. However, it would lack the value of having been produced by a meaningful act.[29] Similarly, state institutions imposed wholly by some foreign colonial power might produce justice or increase legitimacy (although this has rarely, if ever, been the case) but would lack, or at least have greatly reduced, artefactual value *vis-à-vis* the political communities they govern. By contrast, governance institutions produced by domestic political action will have value *as products* because they were produced by the aggregate or collective political acts of the relevant community. True, not all of the actions that collectively contributed to the nature and existence of an institution at a particular point in time will count, in the round, as ethical successes (although some of them almost certainly will). Nonetheless, many governance institutions with some degree of independent value will also be valuable as the artefacts of many directly and diffusely implicated, successful and unsuccessful, political attempts.[30] Due to the relative permanence of such institutions, they concretise the value of these attempts in such a way as to render the latter less fleeting than they would otherwise be. As Arendt puts it:

[29] This and other points about the value of art are taken from Dworkin (n 26) 197).

[30] It is particularly important not to discount the meaningfulness of authentic failures because the 'final result of political action often, no, even regularly, stands in completely inadequate and often even paradoxical relation to its original meaning' (Max Weber, 'Politics as a Vocation' in H. H. Gerth and C. Wright Mills (eds.), *From Max Weber: Essays in Sociology* (Routledge 1991) 117).

> The organization of the *polis*...assures the mortal actor that his passing existence and fleeting greatness will never lack the reality that comes from being seen, being heard, and, generally, appearing before an audience of fellow men, who outside the *polis* could attend only the short duration of the performance and therefore needed Homer and "others of his craft" in order to be presented to those who were not there.[31]

Imagine that I take a hatchet to Dalí's *Christ of Saint John of the Cross.* I would not only be destroying an object of beauty but a product of artistic genius. I do something bad when destroying a beautiful thing, but I also act wrongfully, by showing disrespect, when that thing has additional value as a *product.* My vandalism is harmful because it leaves the world worse off but disrespectful because it insults the achievement that Dalí's work represents. Something similar is true with respect to political institutions, although the analogy is not exact. For one thing, no political institution is an isolated work of genius. What is more, some attempts to reform or abolish governance institutions may show greater respect to them (and to the political activity which created them) than continuing to support their existence. In this respect at least, governance institutions are more like jokes insofar as each teller of a joke has the liberty to improve upon the telling. Private individuals that satisfy the beneficiary condition of *Non-Voluntary Membership* (see Chapter 1) have a moral duty to improve their governance institutions in an analogous manner. But this does not undermine the artefactual value of those institutions. Indeed, one way in which we can show respect for the past political activity of our compatriots is to interpret their activity as reasonable in the sense of having been aimed towards compliance with the political duties that they held. Where those duties included a remedial duty to enhance autonomy and equality, it would be no less reasonable and in no way disrespectful for us to attempt even radical changes to the status quo. Such changes, if both authentic and reasonable in themselves, must be understood as pursuing a collective project that we share with those who came before us. What the artefactual value of governance institutions does imply, and what the analogy with the destruction of Dalí's masterpiece brings out, is the wrongfulness of insufficient sensitivity to the value of what has gone before.

2.5.2 *Political Focuses*

As argued in Section 2.1, political activity can be either directly or diffusely related to governance. However, whether intentionally directed towards it or not, all political activity in contemporary societies is facilitated by

[31] Hannah Arendt, *The Human Condition*, 2nd edition (Chicago University Press 1998) 198.

governments exercising power, coercion, and physical violence in an observable manner. Contemporary political communities tend to be very large. At the time of writing, the People's Republic of China has a population well in excess of one billion, and even states that are many times smaller have populations in the tens of thousands.[32] Such large groups cannot organise themselves on a purely interpersonal, non-hierarchical basis.[33] This is not only a matter of communication. Even allowing for internet-based technologies, we are not capable of sustaining that volume of interpersonal interaction.[34] Print, digital, and social media allow information to be disseminated simultaneously to large groups. However, politics requires more than this: there must be something to talk *about* and act *in relation to*. Actual and conceivable governance provides the substance of political discussion. Without it political speech would flounder in the complexity created by our numbers and diversity.

Where governments act within publicly identifiable institutions in a sufficiently visible manner, their subjects have a focus for political activity that they would otherwise lack. Communities with functioning governments and visible institutions are more likely to converge productively in agreement and disagreement than they would otherwise. They can discuss and take positions on what the members of a particular institution should do, given the kind of entity that it is and the context in which it operates. (Should our leaders employ our military in a particular conflict? How should our local government tax us? Should the death penalty be available in our courts?) Past institutional practice can be a target for criticism and a rallying point for support: consider the famous example of *Roe v Wade* in the United States,[35] which at the time of writing has recently been overturned.[36] Even the structure and interrelation of institutions themselves can provide focus for action and debate. (Should voting in national elections be mandatory? Should we have a state religion? Should our courts ever strike down statutory texts?) Although reasoning in the abstract can help answer such questions, arguing and acting within a governmental and institutional context concretises and focuses our efforts.

[32] Discounting the somewhat atypical case of the Vatican City, the two smallest Member States of the United Nations, the Republic of Nauru and Tuvalu, both have a population of around 11,200, see: Nauru Bureau of Statistics website: http://nauru.prism.spc.int/ (last accessed 2 October 2023); 'Country Facts', Permanent Mission of Tuvalu to the United Nations website: www.un.int/tuvalu/tuvalu/country-facts (last accessed 2 October 2023)

[33] Loughlin (n 6) 5.

[34] Anthony Lincoln, 'FYI: TMI: Toward a Holistic Social Theory of Information Overload' (2011) 16(3) *First Monday*: http://firstmonday.org/ojs/index.php/fm/article/view/3051/2835 (last accessed 2 October 2023).

[35] 410 U.S. 113 (1973).

[36] *Dobbs v Jackson Women's Health Organization* 597 US ___ (2022).

This coordinating function holds even in circumstances of relative autocracy. A dictator or dominant class provide a very visible political target for protestors, reformers and revolutionaries: consider the internal political opposition to apartheid in South Africa or the government of Zine El Abidine Ben Ali in the Republic of Tunisia. The visibility of such regimes cannot make them just or legitimate, but it would be wrong to dismiss their value completely whilst they operate as effective political focuses. Admittedly, this value will be minimal where oppression is extreme or the resources available to private individuals are severely limited. However, relative civil peace and some degree of liberty will usually permit *some* ethically valuable politics, even on the part of the oppressed and destitute. To dismiss this possibility – and thereby reject the political nature of autocracy altogether – would be to risk dismissing the political action within those communities as well. We should distinguish autocracy, to this extent, from tyranny, which we might define as rule so oppressive, neglectful, or incompetent that valuable politics becomes characteristically impossible. None of this is to say that we must endorse autocratic regimes as either legitimate or just. We should not. However, there is more complexity – and more of value – within political ethics than that which can be exhausted by those two concepts alone.

2.5.3 *Political Forums*

As John Parkinson argues, politics is 'not merely the interplay of arguments and reasons in some abstract public sphere but is performed by people, with aims, on stages' and so needs a space within which to be undertaken.[37] While this space need not always be physical (it could be digital or print-based) at some point a physical space *will* be required, if for no other reason than to supply infrastructure. Characteristically, at least for politics to flourish, there will also need to be a juridical space, where the freedom to act politically is guaranteed by law. What I call a 'forum' for political activity can be one or a combination of these things: some space in which private individuals have a *de facto* and/or *de jure* capacity to engage in political action. In this subsection, I argue that governance institutions can be forums for political activity themselves, whilst governments can facilitate the creation of additional forums that do not fall within the constitutive practices of such institutions.

[37] Parkinson (n 7) 23 (Although Parkinson was discussing democracy, his claim holds for non-democratic politics as well).

Institutions themselves are forums to the extent that the practices, conventions, and principles constituting them allow for political participation.[38] Common examples are those institutions whose members are selected via popular participation. This includes legislative, judicial, and executive bodies subject to election, whether at the local or national level. Also relevant are institutions that, whilst not constituted on a participatory basis, have a function that allows for participation. For instance, the provision of adjudicative institutions necessarily involves the participation of private individuals, particularly (but not only) when the cases brought before those institutions directly implicate governments.

The characteristically rule-governed nature of governance institutions can be an advantage, whether those rules are parliamentary, adjudicative, or otherwise. As Parkinson explains, 'when we expect conflict to arise, we tend [towards]...settings where conflict can be encouraged yet contained, to place it in a more formal setting, with formal rules of engagement to civilize conflict'.[39] Governmental forums also tend to be rather visible: as I have argued, they can also operate as focuses for political activity. This matters because, to quote Parkinson once again, 'getting noticed and taken seriously is what matters, which means that claims need to be made in publicly visible and accessible places'.[40] This is not to say that less visible political activity is not important, either intrinsically or instrumentally. As I have argued, even wholly private political action can have value of both kinds insofar as it provides a diffuse contribution. However, institutional forums that are also focuses for activity typically create the possibility for political action with significant impact.

Even where popular participation is not afforded by the constitutive practices of institutions, governments can support other political forums by facilitating a social environment within which political activity can take place. The most obvious way they can do this is by generating practices that enable individuals to act collectively. Such practices can aim towards *de jure* protections, such as the formal freedom to associate and the right to promulgate particular forms of speech. They can also perform a *de facto* enabling role, for

[38] This is logistical and a matter of degree: to what extent do individuals have the opportunity to engage in authentic and reasonable political action within their governance institutions? Autocratic institutions will provide very little value of this kind, as will most traditions that do not have at least some commitment to the rule of law. However, as above, we should not dismiss any tradition of governance purely because it lacks perfect justice or legitimacy. The bar is much lower. Political participation within an institution need not be easy, pleasant, or even commonplace to have *some* ethical value of the kinds discussed.

[39] Parkinson (n 7) 40.

[40] Ibid 42.

instance, by helping to establish resource distributions that are conducive to individual political activity. Constitutional and legislative texts, adjudicative decisions, and executive orders all have the potential to perform both functions. However, the extent to which either is undertaken is contingent upon what is actually done or refrained from. This means – amongst other things – that the existence of ethically valuable politics can become contingent upon the effective protection of particular human rights. As noted in Chapter 3, this makes a putative state's potential compliance with international human rights law relevant to whether or not we should consider its government 'effective'.

The physical manifestations of governance institutions that serve as focuses for politics can create forums themselves. As Parkinson explains: 'groups can organize demonstrations at sites of power or sites of symbolic importance, perhaps adding a march from one site to another … [this] could involve stunts designed to attract the television cameras – remembering that news is about the unusual, the extraordinary, not the commonplace'.[41] This holds even in the absence of a guaranteed juridical space for political action, for instance, where the activity in question is illegal. Take the case of Greenpeace, which placed a number of protesters on the roof of Westminster Hall on the first day of the new parliament in 2009.[42] In that case, an institutional forum (or at least the building commonly associated with it) was used to engage with political issues in a manner *otherwise* than provided for by its constitutive practices. This not only links back to the importance of having *physical* spaces for politics but also shows that institutions can facilitate acts with symbolic meaning that would not be available otherwise: a protest outside the Kremlin only has the meaning it does because of the formal function that building serves.

However, the most pervasive influence governments and institutions can have on the creation of political forums is not contingent upon them being focuses for action. Politics, as I have argued, cannot thrive in conditions of endemic violence. Even violent political movements, be they protests or revolutions, require relative civil peace within which to organise themselves, and they must quickly secure (or at least lapse into) peace if they are not to produce anarchy. By securing relative domestic peace through the coordination of power and violence, governments can make politics possible. True, politics does not automatically thrive in the absence of civil war. Under extremely oppressive rulers authentic and reasonable action may be impossible.

41 Ibid.

42 'Greenpeace Protesters Spend Night on Parliament Roof' *The Guardian*, 12 October 2009: www.theguardian.com/environment/2009/oct/12/greenpeace-westminster-roof-protest (last accessed 2 October 2023).

But however insufficient stability may be for valuable politics, it is necessary. Indeed, with the exception of territories subject to particularly invasive tyrants or an endemic lack of necessary resources, any peaceful physical space provides the potential for valuable political acts. Even where it is less organised, stable territory can function like the Ancient Athenian *agora*, providing a stage upon which politics can be performed. As argued above, these acts need not even be particularly public. Private conversations, the telling of jokes and of stories can, in a diffuse manner, all contribute to the political ethos of a community. Legally secured freedoms help enable action of this kind. However, valuable politics can take place without them.

2.6 CONCLUSION

This chapter expanded upon the claims of Chapter 1 in a number of ways. First, it provided some paradigmatic examples of valuable politics. Rather than providing an exhaustive list, these were designed to supplement my earlier discussion of morality, ethics, and community membership, so that further instances of political activity can be identified by analogy as well as principle. This exercise also helped to establish the link between individual behaviour on the one hand and governments and governance institutions on the other.

Second, it discussed the relationship between power and violence, arguing that valuable politics is necessarily connected to the exercise of collective power whilst existing in a paradoxical relationship with both individual and governmental violence. Although acts of violence can count as political, endemic violence either destroys or severely limits our capacity for political action wherever it takes hold. This lays groundwork for several elements of the rational reconstruction that follows.

Third, this chapter explored the relationship between political action and equality. I argued for a distinction between full-blown egalitarianism and the more minimal requirements of inclusion and non-frustration that political ethics require. As Chapters 3 and 4 demonstrate, this allows us to rationally reconstruct the law of state creation in such a way as to explain the value that international law apparently locates in illegitimate regimes, whilst nonetheless conceptualising the idea of 'effective' and appropriately emerging statehood as coherent with particular human rights.

Fourth, this chapter described more fully the values that governments and governance institutions instantiate within genuine political communities. Specifically, I argued that they can be: (a) 'artefacts' created by political action, (b) 'focuses' at which much of our action is aimed, and (c) both conditions for, and examples of, 'forums' within which politics can be conducted.

This characterised genuine political communities as bound up with the 'quasi-independent' moral value of stable governance traditions. These modes of 'quasi-independent' value feature in my rational reconstruction of international law in several ways, not least of which is providing more than one normative foundation for what I call the 'antecedents' of statehood.

The discussion up to this point has been somewhat eclectic, but that is appropriate. The moral and ethical considerations captured by my conception of politics are not straightforward. They are not instantiated simply by the absence of conflict, and they do not only concern the relationship between the rulers and the ruled. Instead, they define the membership of political communities, establish the duties that pertain amongst compatriots, and characterise the relationships between such individuals, their governments, and the institutions through which those governments act. As the next two chapters argue, these complex elements are essential for properly comprehending how international law governs the creation of new states.

3

The Antecedents of Statehood

My argument began with an account of political membership built upon two duties that we owe to our compatriots. I used these normative resources to argue for the ethical importance of political action as a discrete form of human activity. Detailing the relationship between politics, on the one hand, and both violence and equality, on the other, I then bridged the gap between individual action and state institutions by demonstrating the quasi-independent value the latter possess as political artefacts, focuses, and forums. Taken collectively, this argument discloses a discrete conception of 'political community' and explains why living within such communities has such an impact upon the overall meaningfulness and success of our individual lives.

In this chapter, I argue that statehood characteristically arises only when these ethical elements become instantiated, such that state creation turns upon the extent to which putative states can be characterised *as* political communities of the relevant kind. This reconstruction explicates the legal elements without which, in the ordinary course of events, no plausible statehood claim can arise. These 'antecedents of statehood' are: (1) a permanent population, (2) a relatively determinate territory, (3) an 'effective' government, and (4) some degree of governmental independence.

In what follows, I examine each in turn, arguing that they are united by the same set of normative foundations: first, the ethical value of potential and actual political acts, second, the moral duties that exist between compatriots, which I identified in Chapter 1, and third, the 'quasi-independent value' of governments and the institutions within which they reside, as discussed in Chapter 2. These shared foundations provide the antecedents of statehood with normative weight, making them comprehensible as legal principles capable of guiding behaviour (that is, by providing justifiable conditions for plausible statehood claims). They also render the antecedents of statehood a coherent set, presenting them as a unified body of law. Finally, the normative resources of political community provide an additional constraint upon the content and application of statehood's antecedents – that is, over and above international legal practice – such that this content and application can be both more determinate and more precisely ascertained.

When it comes to the creation of individual states, evincing the satisfaction of some antecedents will be more important than demonstrating compliance with others, depending upon the circumstances. However, on the account of international law this chapter presents, none constitute immutable or exhaustive requirements for state creation. Instead, I argue that whether political community is sufficiently instantiated in any particular case must be investigated holistically, with an appreciation for historical peculiarities. In this respect, the antecedents of statehood are variables to be included in an overall exercise of judgement. Since no two states have the same political history, no two of them will instantiate political community by satisfying the antecedents of statehood in precisely the same manner.[1] For this reason, I do not detail the complete range of circumstances under which these antecedents can be sufficiently satisfied for statehood to arise. Instead, I provide a principled overview of each antecedent, with indicative examples where appropriate.

This principle-based approach both reflects, and is assisted by, the necessity of analogical reasoning when undertaking the kind of holistic judgement just mentioned. Since historical peculiarities differ, putative states inevitably instantiate political community to greater or lesser extents, making its overall instantiation scalar. Attempting to establish determinate thresholds along this scale would be problematic without something to justify such categorical distinctions. How and where should we draw the line between 'plausible statehood claim' and 'implausible statehood claim' if the instantiation of political community is a matter of degree? Philosophically speaking, it might be enough to admit indeterminacy in borderline cases. Nonetheless, international law *needs* thresholds against which claims of emerging statehood can be assessed. At one level, it will always fall to individual state representatives (and sometimes international adjudicators) to exercise judgement about when sufficient instantiation of political community pertains. But this would likely yield significant discoordination were it not for the ability to reason analogically, using paradigmatic instances of established statehood as interpretive guides, and by appealing also to past

[1] This explains the co-dependency that Janis Grzybowski identifies amongst the antecedents of statehood ('To Be or Not to Be: The Ontological Predicament of State Creation in International Law' (2017) 28(2) *European Journal of International Law* 409).

instances where emerging statehood has been in dispute, treating, in both instances, like cases alike. As observers of this process, we must place a certain degree of faith in the ability of state representatives to reason in this way. Rational reconstructions of state creation can establish what is salient for the accrual of that status, but they will always require application to particular facts.[2] Nonetheless, in what follows, I provide as extensive a characterization of the relevant antecedents as possible, so that determinate answers can more readily be ascertained.

3.1 THE POPULATION ANTECEDENT

The existence of this antecedent is well established within international legal practice. Most obviously, it is recognised in Article 1(a) of the Montevideo Convention on the Rights and Duties of States 1933.[3] Indeed, despite the fact that it focuses primarily upon *defining* states, rather than upon establishing conditions for their creation, Article 1 of that Convention helps to establish each of the first three antecedents discussed within this chapter. It reflects, for example, the approach taken in *Deutsche Continental Gas-Gesellschaft v Polish State*,[4] that adopted by the Badinter Commission, which was established by the European Community to advise on the collapse of the former Socialist Federal Republic of Yugoslavia,[5] and a considerable amount of state practice.[6] In terms of rational reconstruction, the point of this antecedent can be put quite simply: political community implies a *polity* amongst whom politics can take place. In this respect, the need for emerging states to have permanent populations reflects the 'residence condition' of *Non-Voluntary Membership*, discussed in Chapters 1 and 2. Those who live in relative proximity are normatively enjoined to support domestic governance institutions that forestall endemic conflict amongst them. Political communities exist in nascent form where geographically proximate individuals respond to the dangers of their

2 This point is revisited in Chapter 4, where (amongst other things) I discuss the importance of foreign recognition for determining whether attempts at state creation have been successful.

3 See also: Ian Brownlie, 'Relations of Nationality in Public International Law' (1963) 39 *British Yearbook of International Law* 284–320; James Crawford, *The Creation of States in International Law*, 2nd edition (Oxford University Press 2007) 52; Colin Warbrick, 'States and Recognition in International Law' in Malcolm Evans (ed.), *International Law*, 2nd edition (Oxford University Press 2006) 232.

4 *Deutsche Continental Gas-Gesellschaft v Polish State* (1929) 9 Recueil TAM 336, 344.

5 *Conference on Yugoslavia, Arbitration Commission, Opinion 1* (1991) 92 ILR 162, 164–165.

6 A great deal of this practice has recently been collated and endorsed by the International Law Commission, see: International Law Commission (ILC) 'Sea-Level Rise in Relation to International Law: Second Issues Paper' (19 April 2022) UN Doc A/CN.4/752.

mutual proximity, either by supporting extant governance institutions or by creating them anew.[7] Communities constituted on this basis enable their members to satisfy the ethical challenge that this duty poses, which imbues those members' lives with greater meaningfulness and the chance for at least one mode of political success.

The residence condition, like the duty to forestall endemic conflict which grounds it, is 'special' insofar as it applies only in relation to geographically proximate individuals. The ethical value these elements represent is therefore special in the same way: a challenge that exists only for geographically determined populations.[8] This normative distinctiveness allows us to better comprehend what manner of population might satisfy this antecedent. For instance, the value of a political community is not at all contingent upon the size of its membership. Individual political activity has much of the ethical value it does because of the moral challenge posed by our obligations to act within and in relation to existing collectives of people, however large they happen to be.[9] This explains why international practice supports no criteria for minimum or maximum population size when it comes to state creation: Tuvalu and the Republic of Nauru are no less states than the Republics of India or China.[10]

To take another example, it is well established in practice that an entity's population must have relative permanence.[11] This is at least consistent with the value of international stability (see Chapter 5). Populations are easier to define if they habitually reside within a particular territory. All other things being equal, the existence of states partly constituted on the basis of such populations should invite less controversy than those with membership conditions that admit greater fluctuation. However, stability does not exhaust the value of a polity that persists through time. Governments and governance institutions can only act as focuses and forums for politics where there are relatively stable groups of individuals to interact with them. Moreover, even where it takes place outside such institutions, politics requires an identifiable polity amongst

7 This accords with Wheaton's conception of statehood, which was drawn, in turn, from Cicero, see: Henry Wheaton, *Elements of International Law* (Clarendon Press 1936) 29.

8 This fits Baty's characterisation of the state as disclosing 'the existence among the people, or the bulk of the people, of a certain mutual reliance, not participated in by the outside world', see: Thomas Baty, *The Canons of International Law* (J. Murray 1930) 13.

9 By contrast, and also by way of counterexample, the egalitarian credentials of representative government are, due to the fact of human plurality, considerably diluted by large population size (see Chapter 7). This fact makes statehood as political community better placed to elucidate the population antecedent than the legitimacy thesis.

10 Crawford (n 3) 52.

11 Ibid.

and in respect of whom it can take place. True, some politics takes place online, where participants form distinct but more fluid 'populations', which are not tied to particular territories. Moreover, even some offline politics may concern transnational issues that transcend the concerns of any particular community. However, both kinds of activity would be impossible without the localised infrastructures that can be supported only by relatively organised, extant communities of geographically proximate people. Permanence facilitates such organisation and is therefore conducive to the formation of political community.

One more explanatory point bears remark, which sets statehood as political community apart from, for example, rational reconstructions premised upon the value of democracy, such as those discussed in Chapter 7. As Crawford notes, drawing from the decision of the International Court of Justice in the *Nottebohm Case*,[12] the population antecedent 'is not a rule relating to the nationality of [the] population [in question]…the grant of nationality is a matter that only States by their municipal law (or by way of treaty) can perform'.[13] From this, Crawford concludes that nationality 'is dependent upon statehood, not vice versa'.[14] Statehood as political community can explain why this is so, thereby underwriting *Nottebohm* with its own normative resources. Under *Non-Voluntary Membership*, we belong to a political community to the extent that we meet either the residence or beneficiary conditions. However, although these conditions track something of normative importance, neither is contingent upon a formal grant of citizenship. Indeed, as I have argued elsewhere, grants of citizenship are better viewed as means through which governments may respond to the normative demands placed upon them by their attempts to coerce us.[15] The granting of nationality enhances the autonomy and equality of a particular population by providing those individuals with an elevated status *vis-à-vis* domestic and international law. However, governments that coerce the populations of the territory they control *already* possess a normatively salient relationship with those people. Statehood as political community explains the nature of this relationship with the very same resources it uses to explain the distinction between 'populations' and 'nationals' as a matter of international law. The former already satisfy *Non-Voluntary Membership* and count towards evincing the statehood of putative entities under the relevant antecedent.

[12] *Nottebohm Case (second phase) (Liechtenstein v Guatemala)* (Merits) [1955] ICJ Rep 4, 23.

[13] Crawford (n 3) 52.

[14] Ibid.

[15] Alex Green, 'Three Models of Political Membership: Delineating "The People in Question"' (2021) 41(2) *Oxford Journal of Legal Studies* 565.

3.2 THE TERRITORY ANTECEDENT

Article 1(b) of the Montevideo Convention requires 'a defined territory'.[16] Although international lawyers do not always do so, care must be taken to separate territory as an antecedent of statehood from the connected but distinct concept of territorial title.[17] The former relates to the more or less identifiable geographical area over which the government of a putative state is able to exert the kind of control described in Section 3.3.[18] By contrast, territorial title concerns the *right* that states possess to have a particular area of the globe administered by *their* governments and institutions. Given my focus upon state creation, full consideration of territory as a right, rather than as an antecedent, is beyond the scope of this book. I give the former some attention in Chapter 4, but only to the extent that the territorial integrity of existing states is implicated in the procedural principles of state creation. In this section, I focus upon how political community explains the legal salience of territorial control as a matter of social fact.

Political community explains the importance of the territory antecedent in two ways. First, the physical elements of territory are conductive to the creation of focuses and forums for political activity. Second, the conditions for *Non-Voluntary Membership* are primarily met in relation to identifiable territorial units. Taking the first, politics must take place within, and in relation to, physical space. Territorial governance provides this in at least two ways. First, the physical area that it demarcates becomes a space within which politics can be performed. Political marches and rallies require roads, squares, and parks, whilst smaller scale interactions also require physical venues, be they coffee shops for private discussions or local halls for union and party meetings. In addition, such things require the logistical, economic, and cultural support that territorial governance characteristically provides.

[16] 'Defined' is potentially misleading: an indeterminate but broadly identifiable geographical area is sufficient. Disputes relating to some or all of a state's territory do not prevent that state from emerging or continuing. For instance, Albania joined the League of Nations well before its boundaries were settled (*Monastery of Saint Naoum* (Advisory Opinion) PCIJ Rep Series B No. 9, p. 10). This supported the ICJ's observation in the *North Sea Continental Shelf* judgement that there was 'no rule that the land frontiers of a State must be fully delimited and defined, and often in various places and for long periods they are not' (*North Sea Continental Shelf (Federal Republic of Germany v Denmark; Federal Republic of Germany v Netherlands)* (Merits) [1969] ICJ Rep 3, para 46).

[17] Cf. Hans Kelsen, *General Theory of Law and State* (Transaction Publishers 2005) 210–218.

[18] *Island of Palmas Case (or Miangas) (United States v Netherlands)* (Award) (1928) II RIAA 829, p. 840.

Perhaps even more importantly, *stable* territorial units are conducive to civil peace, and, as argued in Chapter 2, politics cannot take place amidst conditions of endemic violence. Where a government is in control of territory – assuming that it is not unusually tyrannical and that its people are not peculiarly bereft of resources – that territory provides a space within which the immediate demands of self-preservation do not dominate everyday life. Politics is characteristically possible only under such conditions. Institutions that act as focuses and forums for political activity require relatively stable territory upon which to exist and from which to draw resources, whilst individuals need relative security to undertake political projects that can count towards the overall meaningfulness and success of their lives.

This argument for the normative salience of territory has explanatory advantages. Establishing governance that enhances domestic stability does not always require a large contiguous territory, which explains why international practice prescribes no minimum territorial area,[19] as well as why there need be no contiguity in the territory of a state.[20] The Republic of Indonesia, which is comprised of some 17,504 separate islands,[21] is no less a state than the Republic of Kenya or the Republic of Bulgaria. As long as the governance of small, archipelagic, or otherwise fragmented territories reliably avoids endemic conflict, it can further the fulfilment of the duties we owe to our compatriots. As examples like San Marino and the Federated States of Micronesia show, neither small size nor fragmented territory necessarily leads to domestic instability, although the provision of some inhabitable *land* upon which politics can take place will almost always be necessary for political community to emerge.[22]

The second way in which political community normatively grounds the territory antecedent turns on the fact that the residence and beneficiary conditions of *Non-Voluntary Membership* are characteristically fulfilled in relation to identifiable territorial units. Take the residence condition first. As argued in

19 Thomas Franck and Paul Hoffman, 'The Right of Self-Determination in Very Small Places' (1976) 8(3) *New York University Journal of International Law* 331, 383–384.

20 Crawford (n 3) 47.

21 'Identification of Islands and Standardization of Their Names', submitted by Indonesia to the 11th United Nations Conference of the Standardization of Geographical Names (8–17 August 2017) (30 June 2017) E/CONF.105/115/CRP.115, p. 1.

22 This point holds only in relation to state creation – that is, to the *initial* independent instantiation of political community – and not to the separate issue of state continuity. As I have argued elsewhere, political communities should be held to survive even a total loss of inhabitable land, once established, at least under certain conditions, see: Alex Green, '*The Creation of States* as a Cardinal Point: James Crawford's Contribution to International Legal Scholarship' (2022) 40 *Australian Year Book of International Law* 67. See also my discussion of continuity in the Conclusion to this text.

Chapter 1, this corresponds to the proposition that physical proximity generates special duties amongst geographically defined polities to create and support institutions that avoid endemic conflict. These duties: (a) set conditions for living fully meaningful lives and (b) partly demarcate the membership of our political communities. Being geographically limited, they naturally cohere with the idea of territorially delimited states.

When arguing for the existence of these duties, I proceeded on the basis that the geographical units within which they pertain can be readily identified. In reality, no territory can be accurately identified without reference to international legal practices of territorial delineation and delimitation.[23] Without such practices to establish guidelines for the identification of particular territories, any reference to 'geographical area' or 'territorial unit' will be insufficiently determinate to attribute precise physical spaces to particular states. In a similar vein, the descriptive elements of territory as an antecedent of statehood do not so much *correspond* to the relevant geographical units as *establish* them for the purpose of grounding the residence condition of *Non-Voluntary Membership*.[24] As noted at the beginning of this section, this requires an area of the world over which the government of a nascent community maintains 'effective control'. The social fact of this control is what enables us to delineate discrete territorial units.

Statehood as political community provides a normative explanation for why the social fact of governmental control is a justifiable means for conducting such delineation. Without the ability to identify groups of individuals who live in relative geographical proximity, any attempt by those people to act upon the duties that exist between them would face unworkable indeterminacy. The factual requirement of territorial control sets boundaries for these duties, rendering political membership more determinate and allowing nascent communities to emerge. In so doing, it facilitates compliance with the duties that compatriots owe each other, increasing the likelihood of those people acting meaningfully in relation to them. This reflexive relationship between normative foundation and social fact is not only a hallmark of statehood as political community but also of rational reconstruction itself as a method for identifying *de lege lata*. It supports the rationality of the law on state creation as a set of reason-giving principles, as well as evincing the explanatory power of political ethics.

Turning to the connection between the fact of territorial control and the beneficiary condition of *Non-Voluntary Membership*, the benefits that

[23] This point helps to capture the 'complex function' that Baty attributes to the existence of states, see: Baty (n 8) 11.

[24] Steven Ratner, 'Land Feuds and Their Solutions: Finding International Law beyond the Tribunal Chamber' (2006) 100(4) *American Journal of International Law* 808, 809.

coercive government characteristically yields almost all require the management of physical space, either directly by governments themselves or by private individuals and other actors relying upon the stability and other opportunities that territorial governance provides. For example, the maintenance of public highways, the running of hospitals, and the propagation of cultural and artistic practices, all require the more or less effective management of land. Even activities such as online interaction, which lack any direct connection to land, rely upon a physical – and therefore territorial – infrastructure at some level. Considerations such as these suggest that, where governments exercise control over territory, the people living there are likely to be in routine receipt of the kinds of benefits contemplated by the beneficiary condition. In this respect, the territorial nature of states operates as a practical precondition for our remedial duties to promote autonomy and equality, such that the territory antecedent can be partly explained in terms of the ethical challenge that those duties represent. To put the same point another way, territory operates as a precondition for statehood because it is partly in response to what territorial governance enables that our ethically salient political membership is realised.

Naturally, there will be instances where the benefits of governance accrue to those outside the relevant territory. The most obvious example is that of migrant nationals living abroad, who nonetheless enjoy the benefits of, amongst other things, the diplomatic protection of their home states and the right to return there. However, even in such cases, territory is important. The power to offer protection, not to mention somewhere to return, is almost always contingent on the resources that territory provides.[25] Regardless, the *paradigmatic* connection between territory and the benefits of governmental coercion once more suggests that the territory antecedent is properly explicated by statehood as political community.

Governmental control of land is sometimes cited as only one of two allegedly independent means through which the territory antecedent can be satisfied. The other is receiving a grant of territory 'lawfully…from a prior sovereign, whether from another state through a treaty of cession or by way of state succession, including decolonisation'.[26] Despite the prevalence of

[25] It arguably counts in favour of the beneficiary condition, *qua* rational reconstruction, that it can explain the political membership of non-resident expatriates in addition to that of current residents.

[26] Ratner (n 24) 811. According to Crawford '[s]ince 1945, most new States have been created by explicit grant of independence from the previous sovereign…[and] [i]mmediate or relatively immediate grant of independence is by far the most common modern method of transfer of governmental authority' (Crawford (n 3) 330).

this view, caution must be exercised. Territory in the titular sense is always granted *to* some entity or another, even if the status of that entity is ambiguous at the relevant time.[27] In this respect, grants of territory most commonly take the form of relinquishments of land in the direction of another putative state,[28] which then has the opportunity to fulfil the territory antecedent in the usual manner.[29]

If territorial grants did not depend upon the prior existence of 'emerging' or 'putative' states in this way, the relatively common practice of new states being party to their 'constitutive' treaties would, at least in some circumstances, create a logical paradox.[30] States constituted *entirely* by treaties cannot without contradiction be party to those treaties: acts of creation cannot be undertaken by the things that they create.[31] There must be at least a putative state (or some other appropriate entity) capable of holding legal rights and obligations.[32] Such legal personality is never a brute fact: a normative status of some kind must attach to the relevant entity if its capacity to enter into legally binding relations is to be explained. Furthermore, the *extent* of that personality – that is, what kinds of legal relations it enables – is contingent upon the nature of the status in question. Statehood is the most commonplace international status that grounds the power to make treaties, suggesting that, in the usual course of events, state creation must turn upon something more than a treaty to which the nascent entity is party. The nascent entity, in other words, must

27 Ambiguity arises in particular where grants of *independence* are incremental, as the other antecedents of statehood will sometimes seemingly conflict with the absence of a full grant. See Section 3.4 and also: Crawford (n 3) 350.

28 Technically, international practice recognises: (a) abandonment (the simple withdrawal of territorial claims in favour of creating '*res nullius*'), (b) cession (the grant of territory to a state without independent title), and (c) relinquishment (the withdrawal of territorial claims in recognition of competing title). However, the practical distinction between abandonment and relinquishment is usually minimal (James Crawford, *Brownlie's Principles of Public International Law*, 8th edition (Oxford University Press 2012) 230).

29 Although territory is not a form of property, this mechanism is analogous to the directional abandonment of property, see: James Penner, *The Idea of Property in Law* (Oxford University Press 2000) 84–85. For examples of territorial relinquishment as a transfer of right, see: Treaty of St Germain-en-Laye (adopted 10 September 1919, entered into force 16 July 1920) 226 CTS 8, Arts 36, 38, 46–47, 53–54, 59, 89–91; Treaty of Peace with Italy (adopted 10 February 1947, entered into force 15 September 1947) 49 UNTS 3, Art. 23.

30 See, for example, the Treaty Concerning the Establishment of the Republic of Cyprus (adopted and entered into force 16 August 1960) 382 UNTS 8, to which Cyprus was party. See also the 're-establishment' of Austria via the State Treaty for the re-establishment of an independent and democratic Austria (adopted 15 May 1955, entered into force 1955) 58 UKTS 3, to which that entity was also party. (Cf. Crawford (n 3) 106.)

31 Plato, 'Euthyphro' in Harold Tarrant (ed., trans.) and Hugh Tredennick (trans.), *The Last Days of Socrates* (Penguin Classics 2003) 20–22.

32 Ibid 28–31.

be at least 'state-like' for the treaty to take effect.[33] Governmental control of territory is the usual basis upon which such 'state-like' personality can be exercised, and statehood as political community offers clear normative grounds for the legal salience of that factual antecedent.

Nonetheless, to rehearse a point made earlier on, the antecedents of statehood form part of a contextually sensitive and holistic framework for identifying successful state creation. That framework ultimately turns upon the adequate instantiation of political community: its component parts, including the antecedents of statehood, are not inflexible criteria, each of which must always be met. Under some circumstances, a grant of territorial title without extensive governmental control, or the simple absence of an alternative claimant in respect of a particular area of land, *may* be sufficient. Boznia-Herzegovina in 1992 was in the latter position, given that the former Yugoslavia had at that point ceased to exist,[34] whilst the Democratic Republic of the Congo was in the former position, due to its rather hasty grant of independence by Belgium.[35] Such cases are nonetheless atypical. At least in the case of the DRC, the majority of the explanatory work can arguably be attributed, not to Belgium's grant of title, but to the *uti possidetis iuris* principle, as that operated within the process of decolonisation (see below).

3.3 THE EFFECTIVENESS ANTECEDENT

As with the two antecedents already discussed, an 'effective government' is listed in Article 1 of the Montevideo Convention.[36] The notion that governmental effectiveness is central to plausible claims of emerging statehood is also supported by a number of leading scholars,[37] as well the Badinter

[33] Rowan Nicholson, *Statehood and the State-Like in International Law* (Oxford University Press 2019) 193–211.

[34] The Badinter Commission held that all resulting states were 'successor states', see: *Conference on Yugoslavia, Arbitration Commission, Opinion* 8 (1992) 31(6) ILM 1521, 1523 and *Conference on Yugoslavia, Arbitration Commission, Opinion* 9 (1992) 31(6) ILM 1523, 1524.

[35] Emizet François Kisangani, *The Context of Congo's Internal Wars, 1960–2010* (Lynne Rienner Publishers 2012) 11–16; Crawford (n 3) 56. Originally named the Republic of Congo in 1960, that entity was renamed the Democratic Republic of Congo in 1964, then the Republic of Zaire in 1971. It was renamed the Democratic Republic of Congo in 1997.

[36] Montevideo Convention on the Rights and Duties of States (adopted 26 December 1933, entered into force 26 December 1934) 165 LNTS 19, Article 1(c).

[37] Crawford (n 3) 55; Ratner (n 24) 186; James Lorimer, *The Institutes of the Law of Nations: A Treatise of the Jural Relations of Separate Political Communities* (William Blackwood and Sons 1883) 109; William Hall, *A Treaties on International Law* (Clarendon Press 1924) 18–19.

Commission, and the award in *Deutsche Continental Gas-Gesellschaft v Polish State*.[38] This position is also reflected in various items of state practice, whether they mention the Montevideo Convention or not.[39] The importance of effectiveness, however, is complicated by its apparently nebulous character: what does it mean for governments to be 'effective'? In non-legal contexts, effectiveness is usually measured in relation to some desired or mandated outcome. As such, it would appear that one must ask *what governments are for* before an answer can be gleaned. However, not only is that question complex and controversial, but there is no consensus on the matter to be found within legal practice. True, international law dictates various things that governments must do: protect human rights, refrain from the unlawful threat or use of force, and so on. Nonetheless, these obligations cannot themselves disclose a complete account of effective government. They are better viewed either as more-or-less articulated aspects of an unarticulated whole or as 'side constraints' upon what governments may do when pursuing their own conception(s) of effectiveness.[40]

Crawford, like most contemporary scholars, explains effectiveness in terms of territorial control, averring that 'international law lays down no specific requirements as to the nature and extent of this control, except that it include some degree of maintenance of law and order and the establishment of basic institutions'.[41] In practical terms, there is merit to relying upon social fact in this way. For instance, absent an explicit grant of territory, it is difficult to discern whether the territorial antecedent has been satisfied other than by identifying the presence of a distinct government in control of habitable land. Unfortunately, this eschewing of teleology for social facticity does little to address the problem noted above: antecedents like 'basic institutions' and 'some degree of…law and order' might be satisfied everywhere or nowhere, depending upon how they are understood and applied. In the same manner, the tribunal's discussion in *Deutsche Continental Gas-Gesellschaft*, which proceeded in terms of 'public power exercised over… territory' leaves many

38 *Conference on Yugoslavia, Arbitration Commission, Opinion 1* (1991) 92 ILR 162, 164–165; (n 4) 344.

39 For example, see: 'United States Department of State Press Relations Office Notice', 1 November 1976, as quoted in Eleanor McDowell, 'Contemporary Practice of the United States Relating to International Law' (1977) 71 *American Journal of International Law* 337.

40 A 'side constraint' is a deontological prohibition upon particular kinds of action, such that someone so bound may not procure any desired end via those means, even if the balance of other reasons suggests that doing so might be either permissible or required, see: Robert Nozick, *Anarchy, State, and Utopia* (Blackwell 1974) 28–33.

41 Crawford (n 3) 59.

conceptual questions unanswered.[42] Reliance upon social fact might aid determinacy, but we still require clarity of principle if we are to know which social facts we are to look for and when they pertain.

True, one can always reason by analogy with established cases. If one accepts, for example, that the Argentine Republic exhibits public power, exercised so as to effect sufficient territorial control, then one might use that instance of established statehood, along with others one is confident about, to guide one's judgement in more nebulous cases of state creation. Sometimes, the need to apply close scrutiny will also be ameliorated by the absence of any contrary claims to the territory in question. As with the emerging DRC, where the Kingdom of Belgium was estopped from asserting a contrary claim by its formal grant of Congolese independence,[43] or the emerging Bosnia-Herzegovina (then the Socialist Republic of Bosnia-Herzegovina), where the SFRY had dissolved and so could claim nothing, the absence of contrary claims makes it less important for the precise quality of government to be discerned, on the assumption that both the population and territory antecedents are demonstrably satisfied.[44]

Nonetheless, when difficult cases arise, and both the quality of territorial control and whatever title might follow from it are reasonably disputed, the effectiveness antecedent must be articulated in more than a purely nominal manner. Statehood as political community adopts a somewhat unorthodox answer to what constitutes 'effectiveness' in these circumstances, although it also accepts the social fact of territorial control to be salient, both legally and morally speaking. Effective government, to repurpose Mark Lindley's phrase, pertains wherever the governmental infrastructure is such that a population can be expected to become 'united permanently for political action' under its auspices.[45] Putative states must, in other words, be constituted so as to promote ethically valuable politics to some non-negligible degree. This entails, amongst other things, the forestalling of endemic violence, but also the creation of political focuses and forums, and at least some capacity for populations to contribute towards the creation of institutional artefacts, which might

[42] (n 4) 344. For example, what makes power 'public' as opposed to 'private'? Does the government of the Kingdom of Saudi Arabia wield public power, even though it is possessed almost entirely by the House of Saud? If we are to admit Saudi Arabia as an instance of public power, then what criteria of 'publicness' is international law deploying?

[43] The position of the DRC was thus doubly secured: first, by the principle of *uti possidetis iuris*, which guarded it against incursion by neighbouring entities; second, by the consent of Belgium, which prevented the reassertion of colonial power.

[44] Crawford (n 3) 59.

[45] M. F. Lindley, *The Acquisition and Government of Backwards Territory in International Law* (Longmans, Green, & Co 1926) 20–24.

come, through time, to signify the value of past political action within the community in question.

Discussion of these elements can be found in Chapter 2, alongside my characterisation of direct and diffuse political action. To recap briefly, political focuses can be either governments wielding coercive power or the institutions that they sit within, both of which serve as visible reference points for the targeting and coordination of political action. Without such focuses, contemporary political communities would be too large for the productive convergence of individual activity. Moreover, governance institutions can be forums for political activity themselves where they possess a participatory structure, and, insofar as the governments that sit within them maintain domestic peace, they can support the existence of further forums within the broader community. A forum in this sense is any space, including 'digital space', within which individuals enjoy a *de facto* capacity to engage in political action. Finally, governance institutions that are at least partly constituted by political activity have a kind of artefactual value, like artwork or jokes. They matter in part because they have been created by intrinsically valuable behaviour, albeit often in complex and causally obtuse ways. The vast majority of governance institutions in contemporary states instantiate all of these values to some non-negligible degree. There are of course outliers, where complete tyranny pertains or economic deprivation is effectively total; however, most paradigmatic instances of established statehood fit the former mould.

In addition to providing focuses, forums, and the potential for institutional artefacts, governance enables *Non-Voluntary Membership* because it is not only territorially delimited but also territorially *delimiting*. As outlined in relation to the territory antecedent, there is strong coherence between this fact and the residence condition of political membership. Collectively, extant populations have duties to forestall endemic conflict amongst their own number. However, the identification of such populations requires the delimitation of borders: rough notions of geographical proximity are insufficient to that end. The social fact of governmental control can, as I have argued, delimit a territory. When read together, the residence condition and the social fact of governmental control are mutually supporting: the former provides normative reasons that determine the salience of the latter, whilst the latter renders the geographical application of the former more determinate. Governance as such is also essential for *Non-Voluntary Membership*'s beneficiary condition. Wherever governments rule via coercion, the fact that their subjects benefit from their presumptively wrongful activity places a special duty upon those individuals to ameliorate this ongoing state of affairs by doing their fair share towards promoting autonomy and equality. Whenever we make reasonable attempts to pursue the moral duties that map onto the residence and beneficiary conditions, we have acted in an ethically meaningful way. Governance is 'effective', in one important sense, when it enables such ethically valuable action.

Since it requires this manifestation of potential, statehood as political community is more normatively demanding than most contemporary doctrinal accounts of the effectiveness antecedent. Governments that exercise territorial control but nonetheless, through their tyranny or incompetence, render all non-negligible individual engagement in politics impossible cannot be considered 'effective' in the relevant sense. However, given the broad range of governance styles and institutional arrangements that might facilitate political action to an adequate degree (again, see Chapters 1 and 2), this interpretation of effectiveness remains consistent with very many past instances of state creation. It is extreme cases that are excluded, which, or so I contend, actually enhances both the doctrinal plausibility of this approach and its explanatory power. For instance, the emergence of 'Islamic State' (or 'Daesh') had negligible value in terms of political community, even though its control of some regions was, in 2015–2019 at least, *factually* effective to some degree.[46]

This account of what it takes for governments to be effective – that is, effective catalysts for political action – also implies two ways in which effectiveness can be signified by emerging states during the process of state creation, beyond the demonstration of factual control. First, it suggests that governments can enhance their apparent effectiveness by making credible commitments to protect fundamental human rights, the enjoyment of which is conducive to political capacity. Authentic and reasonable political action is made easier, for instance, where freedom of association, expression, and movement are subject to effective legal guarantees. Second, where an emerging state makes plausible commitments to institute popular participation, through the provision of reasonably frequent and regular elections, for example, then its instantiation of political community will be more overt. In terms of international legal practice, these implications may help to explain the European Community Guidelines on the Recognition of New States in Eastern Europe and the Soviet Union (1991), which required EC Member States to recognise only those successor states to the SFRY that demonstrated 'respect for the provisions … in the Charter of Paris, especially with regard to…human rights'.[47]

[46] Excluding cases such as this also coheres with the 'negative self-determination principle' (see Chapter 4).

[47] European Community, 'Declaration on Yugoslavia and on the Guidelines on the Recognition of New States' (1992) 31 ILM 1485–1487.

Nonetheless, some caution is required here. Unlike some versions of the legitimacy thesis (see Chapters 6 and 7), statehood as political community does not *require* emerging states to make commitments of this kind in order to demonstrate effectiveness. Although liberal democracy might enhance political community, at least in some circumstances, it is not necessary for its instantiation or development. As such, plausible commitments to protect human rights or institute participatory governance may render satisfaction of the effectiveness antecedent more likely, all other things being equal; however, their absence cannot forestall such satisfaction. Not only does this reflect international legal practice, which does not support mandatory commitments of either kind (see Chapter 7), but it also coheres with the pluralistic nature of political community. There are many routes to providing domestic stability and even more to providing the focuses and forums that politics requires to thrive. Statehood as political community, expressed through the effectiveness antecedent, requires only that the potential for politics is evinced *somehow* and *to a non-negligible degree*.

3.4 THE INDEPENDENCE ANTECEDENT

Although not separately listed in the Montevideo Convention, the notion that governance must be independent has also been described as central to emerging statehood.[48] Like 'territory', 'independence' alludes to different legal ideas in different contexts. Most importantly, governmental independence as a *right* of states must be distinguished from independence as an *antecedent* of statehood.[49] Only the latter concerns me here. The Permanent Court of Arbitration in the *Island of Palmas* case characterised independence as the 'exercise [in relation to a proportion of the globe], to the exclusion of

[48] Crawford (n 3) 62; see also Hersch Lauterpacht, *Recognition in International Law* (Cambridge University Press 2012) 26.

[49] Nicholson (n 33) 94–96. For independence as a right of states, see: United Nations General Assembly (UNGA) Resolution 2625 (XXV) (24 October 1970) UN Doc A/RES/25/2625, 124; Alex Green, 'A Political Theory of State Equality' (2023) 14(2) *Transnational Legal Theory* 178. In the cited passage, Nicholson goes beyond the separation of antecedents from entitlements, arguing that 'the effectiveness criteria can explain which entities are states only if, in the last analysis, the criteria do not include prior possession of a right to exclusive jurisdiction'. Although the thrust of his argument is correct, this last point is mistaken. It is indeed possible for entities to emerge as states in part because they have a right to the benefits of statehood, as an international legal status. Insofar as they constituted self-determination units prior to their formal independence, erstwhile colonies had rights of precisely this kind (Crawford (n 3) 112–128). We might resolve this disagreement by holding such non-self-governing territories to possess the right *to a right* of exclusive jurisdiction; however, it is by no means clear what practical difference such an analytical step would make.

any other State, the functions of a State'.[50] As with effectiveness, political community provides this idea not only with normative foundations but also with more detailed and determinate legal content. Why this matters can be swiftly grasped, notwithstanding the availability of analogical reasoning, from the unhelpful tautology upon which the Permanent Court's definition rests. It is circular to assert that a nascent state becomes factually independent when it begins behaving like an independent state. Even if this problem could be overcome practically through comparison to the factual reality of already established states, the high level of abstraction at which such statements operate does little to parse between the very many social facts that either may, or may not, indicate independent government in such cases. In what remains of this chapter, I address this problem.

According to statehood as political community, substantially autonomous governance is legally salient for state creation because it is characteristically conducive to the existence of valuable politics. However, this general claim must be subject to an important proviso: independent governments that suppress all political activity *weaken*, rather than strengthen, their respective entities' claims to statehood. Moreover, as I argue below, although external limitations upon state behaviour resulting from the foreign domination of domestic governance are inconsistent with independence, other limitations are not. This distinguishes the independence antecedent from what we might call 'plenary sovereignty': the idea that paradigmatic states either do or should possess unrestricted legal and moral liberty, both internally and externally, such that any derogation from that liberty requires special justification no matter what its cause might be.[51] Whether any states have ever been 'sovereign' in this extraordinary sense is, to a certain extent, moot: plenary sovereignty fits poorly with the preponderance of international practice with which I am now concerned and, more importantly, it misconstrues the normative foundations of state creation. Unrestricted governmental liberty trades upon the alleged value of freedom in its 'bare' metaphysical sense,[52] which correlates to the absence of limitations upon action.[53] By contrast, as I argue

[50] (1928)2 RIAA 829, 893; see also 'the classic statement' (Crawford (n 3) 65) of Judge Anzilotti in the *Customs Regime between Germany and Austria (Germany v Austria)* PCIJ Rep Series A/B No. 41, 57–58.

[51] Louis Henkin, *International Law: Politics and Values* (Springer 1995) 8.

[52] Timothy Endicott, 'The Logic of Freedom and Power' in Samantha Besson and John Tasioulas (eds.), *The Philosophy of International Law* (Oxford University Press 2010) 247–249.

[53] I simplify here: metaphysical freedom can be limited in two ways. An entity can either be 'unfree' to do something (because they lack the capacity due to some fact about themselves) or 'not free' (because some other entity prevents them from doing what it would be otherwise capable of doing). Sovereignty in the plenary sense implicates only the second form of

below, the independence antecedent is concerned with non-domination. This pertains where foreign governments exhibit proper respect for the political capacities of a nascent state's population when the former act in relation to the government and governance institutions of the community in question. Inter-governmental domination, on the other hand, is exemplified by the position of colonies and puppet states, where independence is lacking (see below).

In paradigmatic independent states, the kind of governmental control described in Sections 3.2 and 3.3 is exercised wholly by the governments and institutions that *nominally* govern there.[54] For example, the institutions established by Republic of Peru's 1993 Constitution collectively exercise a meaningful degree of autonomous control over Peruvian territory. Any analysis of whether nominal governmental control accords with social reality is best pursued, at least for present purposes, through Crawford's distinction between the 'formal' and 'actual' indicators of independence.[55] As Nicholson notes, both sets of indicators are best viewed as social facts, albeit ones of slightly different kinds.[56] Formal indicators of independence include the semantic content of treaty texts, constitutional documents, and so on, which characterise a putative state's government and governance institutions as collectively autonomous, indicating that, according to the ordinary linguistic meaning of those texts at least, the community in question should be considered independent.[57] By contrast, actual independence holds to the extent that the relevant government or set of institutions function in a collectively autonomous manner.

Both sets of indicators merit observation, even though, as I explain below, statehood as political community places heavy emphasis upon social reality, to the extent that where governmental autonomy is formally indicated but actually absent, the independence antecedent is unlikely to be satisfied. Due to their publicly promulgated and largely textual nature, formal indicators of independence are typically easier to identify, at least outwith circumstances where the presence or absence of actual governmental autonomy is obvious. Whilst

abrogation and is best construed as: (a) an *erga omnes* right to be free from any limitation and/or (b) those capacities that enable the exercise of this right within a contemporaneous international community.

54 Krystina Marek, *Identity and Continuity of States in International Law* (Librairie E. Droz 1954) 180.

55 Crawford (n 3) 67, 72.

56 Nicholson (n 33) 96–97.

57 Crawford defines formal independence differently – in terms of the legal authority a given institution possesses (Crawford (n 3) 67) – whereas Nicholson provides no definition of his own beyond describing them as 'legally constructed facts' (Nicholson (n 33) 96). This definition, as such, is one of my own devising, albeit constructed to accord with the thrust of the positions that both authors adopt.

the existence of independence is, strictly speaking, separate from whether or not its presence is ascertainable, avoiding unnecessary controversy is always to be preferred, even if the value of international stability itself provides an insufficient basis upon which to rationally reconstruct the law of state creation (see Chapter 5). For this reason, statehood as political community accommodates the two epistemic presumptions suggested by Crawford when parsing between formal and actual independence.[58] First, where independence is formally indicated, the satisfaction of this antecedent should be presumed. Second, where formal dependence is signified instead, it should be assumed that the independence antecedent is absent. As noted above, however, either presumption can be overturned in the event that actual (in)dependence is clearly indicated. This approach has the twin virtues of avoiding logistically complex investigations into the social reality of emerging regimes while permitting dates of commencement to be more precisely delineated in circumstances where actual independence develops incrementally over time.[59]

3.4.1 *Inter-Governmental Domination and Actual Independence*

Notwithstanding the epistemic primacy of formal independence, the ultimate importance of actual independence warrants attention to that set of indicators first. Moreover, it is in relation to actual independence and its conceptual opposite, inter-governmental domination, that the normative foundations of the independence antecedent in general can be most clearly appreciated. Indeed, according to statehood as political community, actual independence is indicated wherever inter-governmental domination is *absent*, such that independence as an antecedent of statehood is best characterised in terms of *non-domination*. My aim in this subsection is to characterise inter-governmental domination, so that the inverse (independence) can be judged by contradistinction. To that end, briefly examining colonialism will best illustrate how domination of this sort both prevents and destroys the proper development of political community. There are two aspects to this: the first concerns the characteristic consequences of colonial domination; the second pertains to the *relational wrong* that all inter-governmental domination constitutes, whatever its consequences might be.

First, consider a consequentialist argument. Even leaving aside cases of colonial expansion where entire Indigenous communities were murdered, there have been several instances where, through a combination of genocide,

[58] Crawford (n 3) 88–89.
[59] For more on the issue of commencement, see: ibid 651–666.

non-recognition, and the dismantling of Indigenous governance institutions, colonialism has eliminated political communities that would otherwise most likely still exist.[60] There have also been many instances where surviving populations have been enslaved, subject to forced migration, and substantially deprived of access to necessary resources.[61] At its worst, in other words, colonial rule exhibits the very same tyranny that, in the previous section, I argued to render government 'ineffective'. Admittedly, the relationship between such brutality and inter-governmental domination is contingent. There is nothing about the domination of one government by another that *necessitates* such flagrant disregard for the value of human life. But this 'historical contingency' has manifested so frequently that it should be treated as practically inevitable. Whether we consider the material conditions of life within the Belgian Congo between 1908 and 1960,[62] or the oppressive rule of the British East India Company from 1757 to 1858,[63] the evidence for supposing that colonial rule is characteristically deleterious to individual political activity is strong.

Importantly, my point is not that 'precolonial' communities lacked either statehood or international legal personality, which colonial brutality thereafter prevented from developing. Indeed, the case for supposing otherwise in relation to precolonial communities is robust, even on a very restrictive reading of international law at the material times.[64] Instead, the consequentialist point above is simply that colonial rule, itself being paradigmatic of inter-governmental domination, has almost without exception coincided with activity that undermines the political capacity of affected individuals. To this, we must add another consequentialist concern. Insofar as colonial rule either subjugates or wholly replaces the exercise of power by precolonial governments, it becomes an exercise in 'foreign control overbearing the decision-making of the entity concerned on a wide range of matters…systematically and on a permanent basis'.[65]

[60] For example, see the visceral account of these trends within the Australian Aboriginal context by Irene Watson: *Aboriginal Peoples, Colonialism and International Law: Raw Law* (Routledge 2014) 67–144; 'Buried Alive' (2002) 13 *Law and Critique* 253.

[61] For instance, the physical, biological, and cultural genocide found in: The Truth and Reconciliation Commission of Canada, Honouring the Truth, Reconciling for the Future Summary of the Final Report of the Truth and Reconciliation Commission of Canada (2015): http://nctr.ca/assets/reports/Final%20Reports/Executive_Summary_English_Web.pdf (last accessed 2 October 2023).

[62] See, for example: Ruth Slade, *The Belgian Congo* (Oxford University Press 1960); David Renton and David Seddon, *The Congo: Plunder and Resistance* (Leo Zeilig 2007).

[63] For example: Philip Stern, *The Company-State: Corporate Sovereignty and the Early Modern Foundations of the British Empire in India* (Oxford University Press 2011), in particular Chapter 3.

[64] See the analysis in: Rowan Nicholson, 'Was the Colonisation of Australia an Invasion of Sovereign Territory?' (2019) 20(2) *Melbourne Journal of International Law* 1.

[65] Ian Brownlie, *Principles of International Law*, 6th edition (Oxford University Press 2003) 76.

The harm in these circumstances, at least insofar as political community is concerned, is not one perpetuated against the dominated government (assuming that one still exists). This is only the form that such domination takes. Instead, the issue is how colonised populations are affected by unilateral foreign control of their governance institutions. Such control characteristically limits the artefactual value of dominated institutions, as well as making it harder for them to function as focuses and forums, because the subject population is more causally removed from those who actually wield political power over them, all other things being equal, than a non-colonised population would be. This fact limits the degree to which colonised peoples can benefit from these three dimensions of institutional value.

Where plenary rule is exercised exclusively or substantially from abroad, this causal alienation is particularly evident. It was present, for instance, within pre-1948 Kelantan, where an Agreement of 1910 required the Sultan to eschew all international relations not conducted through the British government and, with the exception of issues relating to Islam and Malay custom, to comply wholly with the advice of their British adviser.[66] So extreme were these restrictions that, as Crawford observes, 'it is difficult to see that the Government of Kelantan had any real power at all'.[67] Under such conditions, it is highly implausible that Kelantanese governance was conducted purely, or even primarily, in response to the political activity of the Kelantanese people. Indeed, the very fact that the 1910 Agreement explicitly stipulated that domestic policy was to fall largely under foreign (that is, British) control indicates otherwise. Further support can be found for this proposition, both in Kelantan and elsewhere, by observing the 'weak legal pluralism' instituted by such colonial arrangements.[68] The legal orders imposed upon colonised peoples often created jurisdictional space for Indigenous customs or religious practices while simultaneously restricting them to particular ethnic groups, areas of social life, or geographical areas.[69] This weakly pluralistic approach, although it enabled Indigenous law to survive through colonial 'recognition', also insulated colonial rule from local influence. Tolerated customs characteristically governed what were then considered to be private matters – marriage, the family, and so on – rather than public concerns, such as criminal regulation and international relations.[70] By conceding control over the

[66] Agreement respecting the Administration of Kelantan (Great Britain-Kelantan) (adopted 22 October 1910) 103 BFSP 518, Articles 1 and 2.

[67] Crawford (n 3) 77.

[68] John Griffiths, 'What Is Legal Pluralism' (1986) 24 *Journal of Legal Pluralism* 1, 5.

[69] Ibid 7.

[70] Ibid.

former, the supremacy of colonial powers and their foreign policy interests could be maintained.[71]

Taken together, these two consequentialist concerns – the deleterious conditions imposed by colonialism and the causal alienation it affects between populations and those with political power – help to explain why inter-governmental domination is at odds with the normative foundations of political community. A second kind of reason for this normative opposition, of which colonialism is once again paradigmatic, consists in the relational wrong that inter-governmental domination effects. Namely, even if none of the above consequences were to pertain, political action within the dominated community would still be objectively disrespected, simply by the fact that its population would be denied an institutional structure that is primarily concerned with governing *them*, as opposed to any other population. Consider the British government's relationship with colonial India. During colonial rule, the former directly governed England, Wales, Scotland, and (at least to some extent) Ireland. Whilst almost certainly not legitimate in respect of those populations (see Chapters 6 and 7), the British government at least purported to exist for their benefit and/or primarily for the purpose of preventing endemic conflict amongst them.[72] Individuals living within Britain thereby lived under institutions whose governance was nominally an end, rather than a means. Conversely, the British government did not even purport to govern India solely for the benefit of those who lived there: British nationals were considered to have a stake in colonial government as well.[73] This problem was most intense during the rule of the British East India Company,[74] which

[71] This continues to be a tool through which Indigenous peoples are suppressed, albeit one via which, in more recent times, their sovereignty can be reasserted, see: Alex Green and Jennifer Hendry, 'Non-Positivist Legal Pluralism and Crises of Legitimacy in Settler-States' (2020) 14(2) *Journal of Comparative Law* 267.

[72] Demonstrating this throughout British legal history is well beyond the scope of this book. Indicative phrasing can nonetheless be found in: the Bill of Rights 1689 (UK); *Entick v Carrington & Others* [1765] EWHC KB J98 (UK).

[73] This primarily turned upon the supposed benefits of trade. See the various sources cited by: Pramod Nayar, *Colonial Voices: The Discourses of Empire* (Wiley-Blackwell 2012), 57–59. This asymmetry and concomitant disrespect existed in even the most enlightened of contemporary sources: in his *Speech on Fox's East India Bill* (1 December 1783), Edmund Burke argued that the conduct of the East India Company could either be a 'great disgrace or great glory to the whole British nation' (E. H. Payne (ed.), *Selected Works of Edmund Burke* (Liberty Fund 1990), Volume 4). As David Armitage's analysis illustrates, this notion of unequal benefit pervaded British imperial discourse since its inception (*The Ideological Origins of the British Empire* (Cambridge University Press 2000) 146–169).

[74] See, the initially sparse but increasing oversight granted by: Regulating Act 1773 (UK); East India Company Act 1784 (UK); Amending Act of 1786 (UK), which ended with government being formally vested in the Crown by the Government of India Act 1858 (UK).

governed primarily in line with private economic interests, supposedly for the benefit of the Empire at large.[75] British colonial subjects in India, unlike their metropolitan counterparts, were governed by institutions that officially served an additional political community (Britain itself), to which the former lacked membership. This formal-come-rhetorical asymmetry expressed a distinct form of disrespect for the capacity of these colonial subjects to meet the normative challenges that self-government represents. It constituted, as it were, a sort of political infantalisation because it implied that the metropolitan polity was 'mature' enough to merit direct governance, whereas their colonial counterparts were not.[76]

These arguments explain what is problematic about inter-governmental domination from the point of view of political community. However, they also provide the independence antecedent with more determinate and ascertainable legal content.[77] First, any entity that *emerges* as a colony, whether or not it is labelled as one, will struggle to demonstrate that it is sufficiently conducive to valuable politics, when compared to non-dominated communities. Second, this point can, by virtue of the same set of arguments, also be extended to the case of puppet-states, which, like colonies, are governed wholly or substantially from abroad, notwithstanding their nominal independence. Historical examples include Manchukuo, which existed between 1932 and 1945,[78] and Croatia under German control between 1941 and 1945.[79] Contemporary examples include the so-called Donetsk People's Republic and Luhansk People's Republic, which

[75] For analysis of 'mercantile colonialism', see: Matthew Craven, 'Colonialism and Domination' in Bardo Fassbender and Anne Peters (eds.), *The Oxford Handbook of the History of International Law* (Oxford University Press 2012) 863–889, 870–874.

[76] This was, in fact, the explicit policy position of more than one colonial power, see: Winthrop Jordan, *The White Man's Burden: Historical Origins of Racism in the United States* (Oxford University Press 1973), in particular Chapters 1 and 2; Ntina Tzouvala, *Capitalism As Civilisation: A History of International Law* (Cambridge University Press 2020), in particular Chapters 1 and 2.

[77] Undermining the independence of an existing state differs from *maintaining* an entity's colonial or puppet status in at least two relevant ways: (a) unlike the latter, the former always involves subjecting an existing, independent community to the wrongs discussed in this subsection, and (b) reasons of international stability, linked to the presumption of continuing statehood, are also violated by attempts of this kind.

[78] Both the Lytton Commission's Report of October 1932, and the Assembly of the League of Nations, found Manchukuo to be governed wholly by the Empire of Japan, following a fabricated independence movement, see: Quincy Wright, *Legal Problems in the Far Eastern Conflict: Part I, The Legal Background in the Far East* (Arns Pr Inc 1969) 57–58; Sino-Japanese Dispute – Advisory Committee of the Special Assembly, Resolution of 24 February 1933 (1933) League of Nations Official Journal Spec Supp 101/I, 87.

[79] *Socony Vacuum Oil Co. Claim* (1954) 21 ILR 55, 58–62.

are generally accepted, at the time of writing, to be puppet-states of the Russian Federation by virtue of the extent of Russian military, financial, and logistical support, and the control exercised over them by Russia in respect of their international relations.[80] Further analysis of these two cases is provided in Chapter 4. For now, the salient point is that within all such entities, no matter what the material conditions within them are for individual political actors, governance from abroad carries with it both causal alienation and relational disrespect.

Third, the normatively pressing nature of the above considerations also explains why a clear lack of actual independence must be taken to rebut any formal indicators that this antecedent has been satisfied. Indicators of the latter sort establish a presumption in favour of independence because they are more straightforwardly ascertainable, at least in complex and contested cases, than the often-messy social reality of governmental (non-)domination. However, the importance of not attributing statehood to entities that arise due to inter-governmental domination clearly outweighs this merely epistemic utility.

The final set of explanatory points is that neither small size, scarce resources, international alliances, nor shared policy orientations evince an absence of independence, because none of them implicate inter-governmental domination. In the case of unusually small states or those with uncharacteristically limited resources, their material disadvantages may place them at risk from the domineering behaviour of foreign governments. However, this does not equate to an absence of governmental autonomy on their part: it is always the fact of foreign control and not its particular causes, which has salience *vis-à-vis* statehood as political community. Turning to alliances and shared policy orientations, the absence of inter-governmental domination in such circumstances is conclusive against them derogating from actual independence. Indeed, absent such domination, the fact that a given community has legally formalised ties to other polities speaks to the richness of their respective political traditions, rather than to their lack of independence.[81]

80 Marc Weller, 'Russia's Recognition of the "Separatist Republics" in Ukraine was Manifestly Unlawful' *EJIL: Talk!*, 9 March 2022: www.ejiltalk.org/russias-recognition-of-the-separatist-republics-in-ukraine-was-manifestly-unlawful/ (last accessed 2 October 2023); Thomas de Waal, *Uncertain Ground: Engaging with Europe's De Facto States and Breakaway Territories* (Carnegie 2018) 62–66.

81 In Chapter 4, I develop this argument more extensively in relation to the political value of foreign recognition. Although recognition characteristically operates as a precursor to alliances or shared policy programmes, many of my arguments there hold equally in this context, for largely the same reasons.

3.4.2 *Formal Indicators of Independence*

Where independence is formally indicated, and no clear contrary evidence of inter-governmental domination is present, satisfaction of this antecedent can be presumed. The clearest examples of such formal indicators are explicit commitments by 'parent' states to transfer governmental competence, whether in the form of the devolution of power over some portion of that state's own territory, or via the 'metropolitan' grant of independence to an overseas colony. In the latter set of cases, statehood as political community supports a very strong epistemic presumption of postcolonial independence, for the reasons established below. It is particularly important, *vis-à-vis* respect for political capacity, that the extant populations of non-self-governing territories should be afforded the legal space to develop as independent political communities, even (or perhaps especially) where they have limited actual independence at the moment of formal granting.[82] Methods for effecting formal grants of this kind have included domestic legislation, the termination of treaties of protection, and constitutive treaties of the sort discussed above, in Section 3.2.[83]

Nonetheless, whatever form such transferences take, the mere fact of their occurrence may not be sufficient for formal independence to be indicated. Consider, once again, pre-1948 Kelantan: although allegedly a protectorate – an independent state enjoying the legally guaranteed protection of another entity – its formal subjugation through various international legal instruments rendered it more akin to a colony.[84] Judge Huber, in the *Island of Palmas* case, distinguished protectorates of this colonial sort from 'true' international protectorates, the independence of which he held to be on a surer footing.[85]

Fine questions also arise where such formal grants of independence, whether exercises in decolonisation or otherwise, are incremental rather than total. According to Crawford, 'a devolving unit is to be considered independent when it possesses virtually complete internal autonomy and some

[82] This presumption, whilst firmer even than the more general presumption noted immediately above, is not irrebuttable in circumstances where actual independence is severely lacking. Consider French control of the formally independent Syria and Lebanon between 1942 and 1946. Despite the purported transfer of 'all rights and prerogatives of an independence and sovereign State, limited only by the exigencies of the war and the security of its territory' (*Papers Relating to the Foreign Relations of the United States*, 1941/III, 786) the French government exacted such control over the Syrian and Lebanese institutions – particularly in civilian matters – that the United States refused recognition (see further: Crawford (n 3) 83–85). This refusal, given social reality at the time, took place without offending the precepts of political community.

[83] Crawford (n 3) 331.

[84] Ibid 77.

[85] 2 *RIAA* 829 (1928), p. 858.

substantial competence in international relations, which the metropolitan State is bound by law, convention, or treaty to respect'.[86] One consequence of this is that any formal indication of discretionary rights to intervene in the internal affairs of a putative state, or any special claims of right over the relevant government, call independence into question, even if they are not always conclusive proof of dependence.[87] Statehood as political community assesses such cases, as it does with all matters arising under the independence antecedent, by examining whether they demonstrate actual or formal inter-governmental domination.

On the question of special claims of right, consider Great Britain's claimed entitlement to bind its Dominions to the 1924 Treaty of Lausanne without the consent of their respective governments. This suggested a relationship of dominance between Briton and the Dominions on a formal level, which must be held inconsistent with at least the appearance of their independence. Canada, for instance, was only formally recognised as equal and independent in 1931, when the Statute of Westminster was passed by the British Parliament, and even then did not gain full formal authority until 1982, with the passage of the Canada Act by the United Kingdom Parliament. Contrast this, for example, with the relationship between the European Union and its Member States. There can be no serious suggestion that EU Membership results in domination, notwithstanding the fact that some obligations under EU law are non-voluntary and that non-compliance can result in liability.[88] Article 50 of the Treaty of Lisbon permits any Member State to withdraw unilaterally from the EU, assuming that it has complied with the appropriate procedure.[89] Even if some EU law can bind without consent, the applicability of that law rests on continued association, voluntary at the governmental level, which assumes the equality and independence of EU Member States.

Formally indicated discretionary authority to intervene in domestic affairs is more controversial than special claims of right, since it is generally considered to be inconsistent with independence, even when subject to consent.[90] Statehood as political community suggests that the scope of such purported authority is more important than its consensual nature when determining whether or not it indicates inter-governmental domination. Truly endemic

86 Crawford (n 3) 358.
87 Ibid 71–72.
88 Case C-6/90 *Andrea Francovich and Danila Bonifaci and Others v Italian Republic* [1991] ECR I-05357.
89 Treaty of Lisbon amending the Treaty on European Union and the Treaty establishing the European Community [2007] OJ C306/1, Article 50.
90 Crawford (n 3) 71.

assertions of foreign authority, absent significant countervailing evidence, must be taken to suggest a relationship of dominance at the formal level. In extreme cases, any formal indications of independence will be lacking altogether, such that nascent statehood ought not to be presumed. One example of this was the British protectorate of Bahrain in the late nineteenth century. By an agreement of 22 December 1880,[91] Bahrain was purportedly obligated to abstain from all international relations without British consent and was subsequently forbidden from doing so entirely following an Exclusive Agreement of 13 March 1892.[92] Its position was, in formal terms, similar to that of pre-1948 Kelantan, as analysed above. Although the British government described Bahrain as an independent state during this period, the extent of their control over Bahraini foreign policy renders this assertion highly doubtful.[93]

A more marginal case is the Principality of Monaco, which, despite high levels of international recognition,[94] possessed quite limited formal indicators of its independence until relatively recently. Under its 1918 Treaty with France, Monaco was 'to exercise its rights of sovereignty entirely in accord with the political, military, naval and economic interests of France',[95] while its territory was only alienable to France.[96] Succession to the throne required French governmental approval and, if the royal line was broken, Monaco's territory was to form a new state protected by France.[97] This position, which afforded significant French discretion over Monegasque internal and constitutional affairs, was ameliorated by the 2002 Treaty between France and Monaco. That agreement formally broadened Monaco's governmental autonomy, requiring that it only observe 'the *fundamental* interests of the French Republic in the political, economic, security and defense areas'[98] [emphasis added]. The 2002 Treaty also

91 Agreement signed by the Chief of Bahrain (Great Britain-Bahrain) (adopted 22 December 1880), Charles Aitchison, *Treaties, Agreements and Sanads Relating to India and Neighbouring Countries* (1933), Vol. XI, 237.

92 Treaty between Great Britain and the Chief of Bahrain, 22 March 1892, 176 CTS 467.

93 Husain Al-Baharna, *The Legal Status of the Arabian Gulf States: A Study of Their Treaty Relations and Their International Problems* (Manchester University Press 1968), 79–80; Alfred Kamanda, *A Study of the Legal Status of Protectorates in Public International Law* (Les Presses de Savoie 1961) 85–88, 158.

94 For an interesting visual representation, see: Map of Bilateral Relations, *Gouvernement Princier, Principauté de Monaco*: http://en.gouv.mc/Policy-Practice/Monaco-Worldwide/Diplomacy-and-International-Presence/Map-of-Bilateral-Relations (last accessed 2 October 2023).

95 Treaty establishing the relations of France with the Principality of Monaco (with exchange of letters) (adopted 17 July 1918, entered into force 23 June 1919) 981 UNTS 363, Article 1.

96 Ibid., Article 2.

97 Ibid.

98 Treaty intended to adapt and strengthen friendship and cooperation relations between the Principality of Monaco and the French Republic (adopted 24 October 2002, entered into force 1 December 2005) 48 AFDI 792, Article 1.

makes Monaco's territory unalienable, whilst ensuring that breaks in the line of succession must be handled in accordance with its domestic constitution.[99] Furthermore, the new instrument recognises the 'independence and sovereignty' of Monaco as something that France has an obligation to defend.[100] These changes were implemented to better suit 'present realities' and to place Monaco on a more formally equal footing with France.[101] In particular, the absence of French discretion in Monegasque royal succession and the narrowing of the French interests that Monaco is obligated to protect reduces the degree of inter-governmental domination formally available to France.

There are several formal restrictions upon governmental freedom that do not imply relationships of domination and so do not indicate dependence. For example, domestic constitutional limitations are generally consistent with the independent instantiation of political community because, unless such limitations were imposed by unilateral foreign decree, they cannot even be provisionally linked to inter-governmental domination. Where foreign governments *were* involved in the promulgation of the relevant constitutional provisions, however, attention must be given to the substance of the formal limitations in question. Consider the purportedly unalterable first forty-eight provisions of the 1960 Constitution of the Republic of Cyprus,[102] which was formed under the influence of foreign powers.[103] They do not formally subject Cyprus to the authority of any foreign government, suggesting that any inter-governmental domination that may have existed during the formation of the 1960 Constitution was short lived. In such circumstances, statehood as political community asks whether the relevant constitutional provisions help to ground governance institutions that serve as political focuses and forums, and whether they might either have or enable some artefactual value. Nothing within the limitations set by the 1960 Constitution formally prevents the creation of governments and institutions that focus political activity. Furthermore, several provisions provide guarantees that enable the functioning of political forums.[104]

99 Ibid Article 3.

100 Ibid Article 1.

101 Ibid Preamble.

102 Constitution of the Republic of Cyprus, 16 April 1960 (Republic of Cyprus), Article 182(1), Annex III.

103 As Crawford notes, the constitution was framed through negotiations between representatives of Greek and Turkish communities subject to amendment and approval of the British government (Crawford (n 3) 242). It was enacted as a United Kingdom Order-in-Council under a United Kingdom statute (The Republic of Cyprus Order-in-Council, SI 1960, No. 1363, p. 1174 (UK); Cyprus Act 1960 (UK)).

104 For instance, Article 31 guarantees voting rights, whilst Article 11 protects free movement, and Article 10 prohibits involuntary servitude.

Whilst more complex and contingent, some artefactual value can also be instantiated by constitutional provisions that forbid legal change.[105] If those provisions were developed substantially in response to either direct or diffuse political activity within the community they purport to govern, then they count to that extent as achievements of the population to which their drafters were responding. Thereafter, what matters is whether the constitutional restrictions in question either prevent, permit, or enable political action that might generate further artefactual value. There is little evidence to suggest that the 1960 Constitution functions so as to limit such activity. Indeed, its protection of fundamental rights must be seen as possessing an enabling effect.

To take yet more examples of non-dominating limitations upon governmental authority, there is no formal indication of dependence where certain competences are exercised on the basis of agency or where authority concerning issues such as defence are shared between two or more states, even if one of the states concerned is the parent state of another within such an association.[106] Relationships of genuine cooperation and delegation are the antithesis of inter-state domination, such that statehood as political community raises no objection to independence in such circumstances. For example, the Principality of Liechtenstein makes use of Austrian prisons under the 1982 Treaty on Accommodation of Prisoners, without any indication of formal dependence arising.[107] Such circumstances exhibit no external, unilateral exercises of control or claims of unequal right, and so none of the problematic normative eventualities analysed above are at issue. The same reasoning holds *vis-à-vis* entities bound by international legal obligations and those belonging to various international organisations.[108] Indeed, an evident capacity to hold international obligations, especially where such obligations were voluntarily undertaken by the entity concerned, is better understood as a formal indication that the independence antecedent is satisfied, rather than as a derogation from it.[109]

[105] See generally: Michael Wilkinson, 'Between Freedom and Law: Hannah Arendt on the Promise of Modern Revolution and the Burden of "The Tradition"' in Marco Goldoni and Christopher McCorkindale (eds.), *Hannah Arendt and the Law* (Hart Publishing 2011).

[106] Crawford (n 3) 70–71.

[107] For more on the use of foreign institutions by 'microstates', see: Jorri Duursma, *Fragmentation and the International Relations of Micro-States: Self-Determination and Statehood* (Cambridge University Press 1996), 161–170, 274–288.

[108] Crawford (n 3) 69–71.

[109] Article 1(d), Montevideo Convention; Endicott (n 52) 245–251.

3.4.3 *Decolonisation and the Right to Gain Independence*

In addition to explicating the independence antecedent as such, statehood as political community also clarifies the adjacent but prior issue of why colonies constitute 'self-determination units' with presumptive claims to become independent states.[110] Most straightforwardly, given the deleterious and disrespectful conditions to which non-self-governing peoples tend to be subjected, reversing this unjust state of affairs is of evident importance *vis-à-vis* political community. More complexly, the fact that it is ex-colonies themselves that should emerge as states, rather than some different set of non-continuous entities within or upon their erstwhile territory, follows from the scalar natures of both actual independence and political community. As argued above, neither colonies nor puppet-states sufficiently instantiate the potential for valuable politics to emerge as independent states themselves. However, because this potential itself is scalar, colonies ordinarily instantiate political community sufficiently to warrant the right to develop statehood. What counts as negligible instantiation for the purposes of state creation, in other words, is not necessarily negligible for all legal purposes, including for the purposes of establishing existing colonies as self-determination units.

This holds because, although conditions there might be woefully inadequate in many respects, colonies usually possess some features of valuable politics. Colonial institutions allow for *some* focusing of political activity, even where this is hampered by causal alienation and oppressive governance practices, whilst the relative territorial stability their extant boundaries provide, at least in the absence of endemic violence, can enable at least *some* valuable political forums to develop. This admittedly limited potential for more robust political activity is nonetheless sufficient for us to speak of 'the people' of non-self-governing territories, notwithstanding their demographic and historical diversity and the fact of their subjugation to foreign powers.

For example, although Kenya has historically encompassed culturally and ethnically diverse peoples, its history as a colony entailed that, at the point of its independence, one could speak of 'Kenyans' in a non-reductive manner. The population of Kenya then satisfied at least the residence condition of *Non-Voluntary Membership* and had, prior to independence from British domination, at least some opportunity to act meaningfully in relation to the

110 Antonio Cassese, *Self-Determination of Peoples: A Legal Reappraisal* (Cambridge University Press 1998) 71–76, 130–131.

moral duty implied by that membership condition.[111] Captured by the *uti possidetis iuris* principle as it applies within the context of the decolonisation movement, considerations of this sort are sufficient to establish a presumption of existential continuity between non-self-governing territories and the postcolonial states that succeed them. Under such circumstances, a shared political history of resisting colonial oppression is sufficient to establish discrete peoples within those territories, who then gain the right to pursue independent statehood within those existing territorial boundaries.[112]

3.5 CONCLUSION

The antecedents of statehood are legal principles that specify the factual prerequisites that nascent entities must satisfy before they can mount plausible statehood claims. Taken collectively, they set minimum conditions for state creation, which statehood as political community explicates in terms of the ethical value that territorially delimited polities enable for their members. The antecedents of population, territory, effective government, and independence each partake of this shared ethical foundation in slightly different ways and yet are also mutually reinforcing by virtue of their underlying normative coherence.

Moreover, although they do not require that emerging states possess governmental legitimacy, nor that they are perfectly just, the antecedents of statehood, when understood through the lens of political community, constitute a normatively attractive set of minimum conditions. They emphasise a threshold for nascent statehood based upon the potential for ethically valuable politics within the community in question, which both humanises and concretises otherwise austere and nebulous legal concepts such as governmental 'effectiveness'. This normative appeal helps to explicate their legal salience

111 This does not imply that pre-independence Kenyans had a moral obligation to support or uphold British colonial institutions simply because those institutions provided relative domestic peace. The collective duty that corresponds to the residence condition of *Non-Voluntary Membership* is 'only' an obligation to ensure that *some* set of institutions exists that can effectively forestall endemic conflict. It does not entail loyalty, come what may, to whatever set of institutions happens to fulfil that role at any given moment in time. As noted in Chapter 2, the ethical value of politics is entirely consistent with wholesale constitutional reform and, in some circumstances, even with complete revolution.

112 Within international practice, this is supported by: Article 22, Covenant of the League of Nations (adopted 28 June 1919, entered into force 10 January 1920); Articles 1(2) and 73–91, Charter of the United Nations (adopted 26 June 1945, entered into force 24 October 1945) 1 UNTS XVI; UNGA Resolution 1514 (VX) (14 December 1960) UN Doc A/RES/1514(XV); UNGA Resolution 1541 (XV) (15 December 1960) UN Doc A/RES/1541(XV); UNGA Resolution 2625 (XXV) (24 October 1970) UN Doc A/RES/25/2625(XXV).

via rational reconstruction: we can take the antecedents of statehood seriously as requirements for state creation because it makes normative sense for existing members of the international community to interrogate novel statehood claims in relation to them.

When it comes to applying the principles articulated in this chapter, I emphasised that none are immutable or inflexible criteria, which must be met in the same manner or to the same degree in every case. Instead, I presented them as factors that must be considered within a holistic exercise of judgement, which must be undertaken with an eye to historical peculiarity and contemporary social context. The contribution that each antecedent makes, when understood in this manner, is to render more concrete and ascertainable the question of whether or not a particular entity has made a plausible claim to have emerged *as a political community of the relevant kind*. When combined with our capacity to reason analogically, not only to past instances of state creation but also to contemporary paradigms of established statehood, this rational reconstruction of international law offers considerable guidance for both the discernment of plausible statehood claims and, consequently, the exercise of international recognition. The following chapter continues this work by articulating five procedural principles, which further condition state creation in relation to entities that have, to some non-negligible extent, satisfied the antecedents detailed here.

4

Five Procedural Principles

Chapter 3 discussed the 'antecedents of statehood': the legal perquisites characteristically necessary for plausible statehood claims. These elements – a permanent population, a more or less defined territory, an 'effective' government, and relative political independence – are accepted by many international lawyers to be necessary for state creation in at least one form or another. The originality of my own account was threefold. First, I argued that the antecedents of statehood do not form an immutable list of necessary criteria for the emergence of new states but rather different modes through which the moral and ethical values of 'political community' can be demonstrably instantiated in social reality. Second, I claimed that an exercise of holistic judgement is required to identify when, as a set, those antecedents have been sufficiently satisfied for a plausible statehood claim to be made, and that this claim should be understood as a claim to *be* a political community of the relevant kind. Third, I contended that each antecedent can be independently explained and justified in terms of political community, such that their threshold requirements must be interpreted in light of what that set of values requires.

Despite the importance of these antecedents within state creation, presenting a plausible statehood claim is insufficient to guarantee that statehood will arise. In this chapter, I establish five procedural principles that condition the process through which statehood accrues. Unlike the antecedents mentioned above, which concern the intrinsic properties that a nascent community must display, these principles each relate to the manner in which such communities emerge. They can be split into two sets. There are two principles that condition state creation by establishing processes through which political action can be either instantiated or enhanced. These are the 'recognition principle' and 'referendum principle', which concern respectively the effects of foreign recognition and the salience of independence referendums. Second, there are three principles that condition state creation by prohibiting, or rendering far more onerous, the emergence of new states through means that undermine political ethics. These are the 'negative self-determination principle', the 'peace principle', and the 'territorial integrity principle'.

All five principles can be primarily explained and justified in terms of political community, such that their existence, legal implications, and presumptive justifiability turns upon the extent to which they reflect those moral and ethical values. Taken together with the antecedents of statehood, they establish a legal framework through which alleged instances of state creation can be holistically assessed. Insofar as these principles are procedural, they are concerned with various means through which various international legal actors, including the nascent community itself, can manage the process of state creation. Their concern is to ensure that both the capacity for political action, and respect for the intrinsic value of politics, is enhanced and safeguarded to the greatest extent possible.

4.1 THE RECOGNITION PRINCIPLE

As discussed briefly in the Introduction, doctrinal scholars continue to disagree about whether foreign recognition is 'constitutive' or merely 'declaratory' of statehood. The persistence of this disagreement, as I alluded to there, is largely because the role of recognition is underdetermined by the available social facts. Without undertaking rational reconstruction, we have no means to determine which view of recognition *should* be adopted, be it constitutive, declaratory, or something else entirely. In this section, I argue that statehood as political community not only provides a way forward but also eliminates the constitutive-declaratory dichotomy itself. Unlike scholars such as Nicholson or Vidmar, who hold widespread recognition to provide an independent basis for state creation,[1] or Crawford, who argues that it fulfils only an epistemic role,[2] I adopt a position similar to that of Charles de Visscher, who contended that foreign recognition during state creation is just one factor to be considered amongst many, and that it has both constitutive and declaratory elements.[3]

1 Rowan Nicholson, *Statehood and the State-Like in International Law* (Oxford University Press 2019) 127–140; Jure Vidmar, *Democratic Statehood in International Law: The Emergence of New States in Post-cold War Practice* (Bloomsbury Publishing 2013) 43–46.

2 James Crawford, *The Creation of States in International Law* (Oxford University Press 2007) 27–28.

3 Charles de Visscher. *Problems d'interpretation judiciaire en droit international public* (A Pedone 1963) 191; Charles de Visscher, *Théories et Réalités*, 4th edition (A Pedone 1970) 258.

At bottom, statehood as political community holds that entities fully satisfying the antecedents of statehood, which emerge in compliance with the other principles listed in this chapter, simply *are* states, whether or not they receive foreign recognition. Entities like the Republic of Somaliland, which I reference in Section 4.5, are best viewed for this reason as actual but non-recognised states,[4] rather than as non-state entities for want of international recognition. This position also fits statehood-adjacent' legal practice, such as the commonplace expectation that non-recognised states are routinely expected to comply with international law, as illustrated by the treatment of Israel and North Korea throughout the Arab-Israeli Conflict and the Korean War.[5] Formal recognition, as such examples suggest, is not the only descriptive fact that can be reconstructed as indicating 'state-like' treatment. Statehood as political community helps to make normative sense of such material.

Nonetheless, political ethics suggests that it would be wrong to think that recognition had no impact upon state creation, even though it is not strictly necessary. The granting of recognition is not normatively inert, either in its expressive force or its material effects. As Vaughan Lowe observes, it is widely accepted that the 'practical effects' of recognition are causally advantageous to the development of independent statehood.[6] However, the normative profile of such effects has particular significance *vis-à-vis* political community, as I have argued at some length elsewhere.[7] In addition to being facilitated and instantiated by governance institutions that regulate purely domestic affairs, ethically valuable politics can thrive in relation to international relations. The actions our governments take towards foreign communities, and the attitudes these actions express towards them, create a unique international profile that characterises our communities no less than the governmental profiles created by actions that are more self-regarding. This is all the more evident when international relations extend beyond mere respect for the political independence of foreign states into relationships of cooperation or coordination. Just as an individual is partly defined by the company they keep, so too is the political ethos of a community influenced by its external affairs. Membership within international organisations, collaboration through international trade, and transnational solidarity on matters such as collective security, all represent

4 Nicholson comes close to endorsing this position; however, he remains hesitant: (n 1) 190–192.

5 Ian Brownlie, *International Use of Force by States* (Oxford University Press 1963) 380.

6 Hersch Lauterpacht, *Recognition in International Law* (Cambridge University Press 2012) 6, 32–33; Vaughan Lowe, *International Law* (Oxford University Press 2007) 163.

7 Alex Green, 'Successful Secession and the Value of International Recognition' in Jure Vidmar, Sarah McGibbon, and Lea Raible (eds.), *Research Handbook on Secession* (Edward Elgar 2023).

ways in which political communities can develop ethically valuable traditions of international relations. Indeed, even the creation of international law, whether through the signing and ratification of treaties or the generation of state practice and the promulgation of *opinio juris*, constitutes an external expression of politics within a particular community. Such histories of governmental action form political focuses of the sort contemplated in Chapter 2. Moreover, to the extent that international relations within a given state are causally responsive to its domestic political activity, the external actions of its government can have artefactual value as well.

However, communities can only develop international relations with value of these kinds if other communities are willing to enter into such relations with them. Mutual recognition of statehood is the most explicit and often the most straightforward means of initiating such relationships. Where recognition is granted or exchanged, the political value of international relations has begun to accrue, even if only in nascent form.[8] Ethically valuable politics is, to that extent, both facilitated and instantiated. Admittedly, international relations are possible without formal recognition. Consider Taiwan, which maintains informal relations (and a number of bilateral treaty arrangements) with several established states. It is also a non-state member of some international organisations, such as the World Trade Organisation (as an independent customs territory) and the Commission for the Conservation of Southern Bluefin Tuna (CCSBT) (as a 'Fishing Entity' member of its Extended Commission and Extended Scientific Committee).[9] However, notwithstanding this potential for less formal relationships or *ad hoc* legal statuses, non-recognised entities characteristically find it much more difficult to develop ethically valuable international relations of the relevant kind. Taiwan's membership in the CCSBT is a case in point: between the 1993 Convention for the Conservation of Southern Bluefin Tuna, and the CCSBT's adoption of the Resolution to Establish an Extended Commission and an Extended Scientific Committee in 2001, Taiwanese representatives were limited to observer status within the CCSBT and had to push for the voting rights they currently possess within the Extended Commission.[10]

[8] Recognition tends to be almost immediately followed by other diplomatic activity, which will itself strengthen the degree to which this conclusion holds in a particular case (Lowe (n 6) 163).

[9] Although notably not the United Nations, from which it was displaced by the Peoples' Republic of China in 1971, see: United Nations General Assembly (UNGA) Resolution 2758 (XXVI) (25 October 1971) UN Doc A/RES/2758(XXVI).

[10] Andrew Serdy, 'Bringing Taiwan into the International Fisheries Fold: The Legal Personality of a Fishing Entity' (2005) 75(1) *British Yearbook of International Law* 183, 186–191.

Such uphill struggles demonstrate that formal recognition is at least instrumental for full engagement with the international community.

This line of argument establishes the normative salience of recognition from the perspective of recognised communities. However, acts of recognition also have important implications for recognising states. Due to the formal commitment it represents, recognition is normatively unique amongst the causal precursors to diplomatic relations. Although non-recognised entities can possess statehood notwithstanding their treatment by foreign powers, a recognised community has formal assurances that it will be afforded the presumptive benefits typically attached to legal statehood. This is not to suggest that recognition itself grounds those benefits: they arguably pertain wherever statehood exists as an independent legal fact. However, recognition nonetheless induces receiving states to rely upon an international commitment to their legal status. An analogy can be drawn with inter-personal promises. If I falsely promise to you, or break an existing promise without proper justification, I wrongfully undermine the knowledge base upon which you rely when conducting your personal affairs.[11] This may cause you various forms of material harm, but it also expresses a discrete form of disrespect for your individual agency. Recognition places *granting* states in a similar position. They indicate through the commencement of formal diplomatic relations that they respect the recognised community as a state, thereby making themselves doubly liable should they subsequently fail to do so. Violations of territorial integrity or political independence, for example, take on an additional normative dimension: they become bilateral betrayals as well as international wrongs.[12]

These two reasons clarify why statehood as political community entails that recognition can have a partial constitutive effect. First, it develops nascent states as political communities by enmeshing them within international relations. Second, it strengthens the reasons established states have to treat nascent entities as though they possessed statehood. The explanatory advantage of embracing some constitutive potency is well rehearsed: it allows us to explain cases where the antecedents of statehood were not otherwise sufficiently fulfilled.[13] Consider Monaco, which has long enjoyed considerable recognition notwithstanding its history of limited political independence, or Bosnia-Herzegovina, which received widespread recognition even though

[11] Ronald Dworkin, *Justice for Hedgehogs* (Harvard University Press 2011) 300–315.

[12] Jean Charpentier characterises this (in more formal legal terms) as the 'opposability' of international obligations to recognising states, see: *Le Reconnaissance Internationale et L'Évolution du Drois de Gens* (A Pedon 1956) 217–225.

[13] Nicholson (n 1) 129–130.

the control its government initially exercised over its claimed territory was minimal.[14] Some might dismiss these examples as legal mistakes, whereby recognition was genuine but premature, or as cases where diplomatic formality was used to hide *realpolitik*.[15] Admittedly, *realpolitik* will often influence recognition decisions. However, statehood as political community gives us important reasons not to overstate the normative impact of that influence. In the above cases, as in others, recognition constitutively contributes to statehood because it normatively underwrites the value of political community itself. This alone is sufficient to yield what we might call the 'recognition principle' of state creation: that all other things being equal, formal acts of foreign recognition bolster the strength of extant statehood claims, with near-universal recognition significantly lowering the threshold for evidencing statehood's antecedents.

4.1.1 *The Epistemic Value of Recognition*

As stated above, I support a hybrid approach to recognition, whereby it not only has constitutive effect but also serves the important function of 'resolv[ing] uncertainties as to status and allow[ing] new situations to be regularised'.[16] This matters for statehood as political community because, as argued in Chapter 3, the antecedents of statehood do not function as a list of fixed and immutable requirements but rather as connected variables within an overall scheme of normative evaluation. This flexible framework, although normatively appealing in other respects, makes it likely that hotly contested or difficult cases of state creation will arise, where it is unclear whether a plausible statehood claim exists or not. International law requires a mechanism for providing clarity and formal recognition is at least one way in which this might be achieved. According to Lauterpacht, something of this sort forms the primary function and value of recognition within the law of state creation.[17]

On a purely constitutive account of recognition, such as Lauterpacht's own, the exclusive emphasis upon recognition by established states makes complete

[14] Roland Rich, 'Recognition of States: The Collapse of Yugoslavia and the Soviet Union' (1993) 4 *European Journal of International Law* 56.

[15] Victor Kattan, 'Book Review: Jure Vidmar, Democratic Statehood in International Law: The Emergence of New States in Post-cold War Practice' (2015) 78(2) *Modern Law Review* 394, 395–397.

[16] Crawford (n 2) 27.

[17] Lauterpacht (n 6) 55. In Chapter 5, I ask whether positions of this kind are better explained by what I call the 'stability thesis': my positive arguments in this subsection should be read alongside my negative claims there.

sense. If foreign recognition alone determines statehood, it follows that its presence or absence will be uniquely probative *vis-à-vis* international legal status. By contrast, if state creation is not exhausted by recognition, what stands in favour of relying upon *this* means for settling contested or difficult cases, rather than any other? We might argue that no alternative body exists with an established practice of adjudicating upon such matters. The UN General Assembly could, in principle at least, ask the ICJ for advisory opinions on 'hard cases'. However, such a request has never been made, at least not explicitly.[18] Practically speaking, therefore, the responsibility falls to established states. But practical necessity cannot show that state representatives are best able to judge such matters or even that they are better placed to do so than other kinds of observers. Why then treat formal recognition as peculiarly probative rather than academic analysis or civil society opinion? It can scarcely be because the former is less politically charged.

Even if states themselves are solely responsible for generating the law of state creation, it need not follow that they are best placed to apply the legal principles they produce. There is no obvious reason why state representatives would be more likely to successfully apply the law than, say, an international judge. Unless this point can be addressed, the epistemic reliance I have so far placed upon foreign recognition would seem to be *ad hoc*. Fortunately, the constitutive contribution of recognition according to statehood as political community allows us to co-opt the determinative-epistemic entailment described above. The epistemic value of recognition supervenes upon its normative capacity to strengthen existing statehood claims as a matter of independent legal fact. That value is more modest than under a purely constitutive view, such as Lauterpacht's, where recognition forms the sole basis for state creation, or under a hybrid-alternative model, such as Nicholson's, where widespread recognition forms a sufficient but non-necessary condition for emergence. Nonetheless, it permits us to rely upon recognition when analysing contested or difficult cases without begging the question *vis-à-vis* its epistemic power. Moreover, whilst scholars such as de Visscher have already advanced kind of hybrid model I advocate here, statehood as political community provides it with an underlying normative basis, which refutes Crawford's contention that, when deciding between the constitutive and declaratory views, 'at a fundamental level a choice must be made'.[19]

[18] It is arguable that this request was made in *Accordance with International Law of the Unilateral Declaration of Independence in Respect of Kosovo* (Advisory Opinion) [2010] ICJ Rep 403 (see the *Separate Declaration of Judge Simma*, 478–481).

[19] Crawford (n 2) 27.

4.1.2 *Recognition as a Liberty*

Statehood as political community also clarifies why international legal practice is often cited as not supporting a duty to recognise.[20] Although the value of politics can be both facilitated and instantiated via international recognition itself, no obligation to recognise follows from this because that same value also entails the importance of a presumptive liberty to grant recognition, which is logically inconsistent with the existence of a duty to do so. International relations provide an important means for developing a discrete political tradition. A duty to interact on particular terms, beyond the 'arms-length' requirements secured by mutually beneficial rights to political independence, territorial integrity, and so on, would unduly limit this means. Consider once again the analogous case of friendship, which exists only where our mutual and uncoerced associations routinely motivate us to go above and beyond what we typically owe each other simply by virtue of our shared humanity.[21] Friendship would be greatly impoverished if it was motivated purely by an impersonal sense of duty. The position is similar *vis-à-vis* diplomatic relations, although the normative relationship between mutually recognising states is far thinner than the ones that exist between friends. Although mutual recognition does not necessitate entering into any further relations, such as alliance or confederation, it does signify the beginnings of formal discourse through the exchange of embassies or other diplomatic representatives. Such exchanges imply a judgement about the worthiness of closer association, thereby expressing something about what the communities involved value in 'outsiders': an important element of the political 'ethos' that each community must develop. In this way, recognition creates a unique focus for domestic political activity, as evidenced, for example, by debates within the United Kingdom over the legal status of the State of Palestine and the position that should be taken in relation to the recognition of that state.[22]

4.1.3 *Collective Non-recognition*

Nonetheless, the liberty to recognise has limits. Wholly tyrannical states, which either oppress or destroy the political capacities of their populations, cannot

[20] *Conference on Yugoslavia, Arbitration Commission, Opinion 10* (1992) 92 ILR 206, para 4; Nicholson (n 1) 190; Vidmar (n 1) 43–44; Cf. Lauterpacht (n 6) 12–22, 26–37; and (possibly) *Reference re Secession of Quebec* [1998] 2 SCR 217 (Canada), para 111.

[21] John Finnis, *Natural Law and Natural Rights*, 2nd edition (Oxford University Press 2011) 141–143.

[22] 'Palestine and Israel', HC Deb 13 October 2014, vol 586, cols 61–131.

receive recognition without fundamentally contradicting statehood as political community. Recognition in such circumstances would be both wrongful and ineffectual: the emergence of truly tyrannical entities instead creates a collective duty of non-recognition on the part of the international community.[23] For example, any recognition of the Islamic State entity, or 'Daesh' as it was sometimes called, would have breached international law and in any event had no legal effect. Offering international support for such entities via the extension of recognition is wrongful for two reasons. First, and most importantly, it further undermines the political capacities of individuals within the relevant territory by expressively bolstering an oppressive regime. Second, it subverts international law itself by publicly endorsing manifestly insupportable views about both statehood and state creation. These considerations do not obligate states to completely shun entities like Islamic State; international peace might justify *ad hoc* interactions with them; however, they heavily weigh against the sort of formalised, ongoing relations implied by recognition.

This common duty to not recognise tyrannical entities is supported by international practices surrounding collective non-recognition in general, which are perhaps most obvious in relation to the cases of Manchukuo,[24] Namibia,[25] and Kuwait,[26] as well as Southern Rhodesia, the Bantustans, Northern Cyprus,[27] and both the Donetsk and Luhansk People's Republics.[28] As Crawford argues, the practice of coordinating a denial of recognition is 'enjoined by the status – or lack of it – of the entity in question…[but] goes beyond this in that it reinforces the legal position, and helps to prevent the consolidation of unlawful situations'.[29] This has characteristically been carried out under the auspices of the UN Security Council, for instance through Resolutions 217 (1965), 253 (1968), 277 (1970) in the case of Southern Rhodesia,[30] and 541 (1983) and 550 (1984) in

[23] Although I present this conclusion primarily in normative terms, other scholars have grounded it exclusively within international legal practice, see: Karl Zemanek, 'New Trends in the Enforcement of *Erga Omnes* Obligations' (2000) 4 *Max Planck Yearbook of United Nations Law* 1; Crawford (n 2) 158.

[24] Robert Langer, *Seizure of Territory: Stimson Doctrine and Related Principles in Legal Theory and Diplomatic Practice* (Greenwood Press 1947) 50–60, 95–99.

[25] *Legal Consequences for States of the Continued Presence of South Africa in Namibia (South West Africa) notwithstanding Security Council Resolution 276 (1970)* (Advisory Opinion) [1971] ICJ Rep 6, paras 122–127.

[26] Crawford (n 2) 159.

[27] See Section 4.3 for discussion of these cases.

[28] See Sections 4.4 and 4.5 for discussion of both.

[29] Crawford (n 2) 159.

[30] United Nations Security Council (UNSC) Resolution 217 (20 November 1965) UN Doc S/RES/217; UNSC Resolution 253 (29 May 1968) UN Doc S/RES/253; UNSC Resolution 277 (18 March 1970) UN Doc S/RES/277.

the case of Northern Cyprus.[31] In both cases, the entities claiming statehood violated political community by breaching the 'negative self-determination principle' considered below. Indeed, collective non-recognition typically occurs only when mandated by one or more of the three principles identified at the outset of this chapter as disrupting or forestalling state creation through means that undermine political ethics. These are negative self-determination, territorial integrity, and the prohibition on the threat or use of force.

In light of these points, I must augment my earlier characterisation of the recognition principle. This principle holds that, all other things being equal, any formal recognition offered by foreign governments, although not necessary for state creation, will bolster extant claims to independent statehood *unless* recognition would, in all the relevant circumstances, undermine the moral and ethical values of political community. In the latter eventuality, a collective duty of non-recognition arises, which supplants the default liberty that each state enjoys to grant recognition on its own terms.

4.2 THE REFERENDUM PRINCIPLE

In the *Western Sahara* Advisory Opinion,[32] the ICJ held that paragraph 2 of General Assembly Resolution 1514 (XV),[33] which holds all people to have a right to 'freely determine their political status', implies that 'a free and genuine expression of the will of the peoples concerned' is necessary for the emergence of new states.[34] Moreover, in that same opinion, the Court stressed the importance of General Assembly resolution 2625 (XXV),[35] which provides that:

> The establishment of a sovereign and independent State, the free association or integration with an independent State or the emergence into any other political status *freely determined by a people* constitute modes of implementing the right of self-determination by that people.[36] [ICJ's emphasis]

31 UNSC Resolution 541 (18 November 1983) UN Doc S/RES/541; UNSC Resolution 550 (11 May 1984) UN Doc S/RES/550.

32 *Western Sahara* (Advisory Opinion) [1975] ICJ Rep 12, paras 55–59.

33 United Nations General Assembly (UNGA) Resolution 1514 (VX) (14 December 1960) UN Doc A/RES/1514(XV).

34 *Western Sahara*, para 55. Drawing upon the Declaration, the Court in fact considered three circumstances where 'a free and genuine expression of will' would be required on the part of a non-self-governing territories: (1) where state creation takes place; (2) where a formal association is created with an existing state; and (3) where an existing state integrates the non-self-governing entity into their own territory.

35 UNGA Resolution 2625 (XXV) (24 October 1970) UN Doc A/RES/25/2625(XXV).

36 *Western Sahara*, para 58.

On the basis of this treatment, Vidmar contends that state creation will require an appropriately administered independence referendum, unless majority support for independent statehood within the relevant territorial unit is unusually clear.[37] This suggestion certainly fits international practice to at least some degree. For example, the Republic of Croatia held an independence referendum on 19 May 1991, which was noted with at least some approval by the Badinter Commission.[38] Bosnia-Herzegovina concluded a similar process on 1 March 1992,[39] as did Macedonia on 8 September 1991.[40] Within the Union of Socialist Soviet Republics (USSR), an all-Union referendum on the future of the USSR was held on 17 March 1991,[41] which was boycotted by six out of the fifteen republics.[42] These included the Republic of Lithuania, which held its own referendum on 9 February 1991,[43] the Republic of Armenia, which did likewise on 21 September 1991,[44] and the Republics of Estonia and Latvia, which both held their own votes on 3 March 1991.[45] Prior to the dissolution of the USSR, two participating republics (Turkmenistan and Ukraine) held special referendums on 8 December 1991.[46] On 29 December 1991, after the USSR had already dissolved, further referendums were held in the Republics of Azerbaijan and Uzbekistan.[47] Outwith the post-USSR context, the State of Eritrea emerged following a UN-observed referendum held between 23 and 25 April 1993.[48] In a similar vein, the Democratic Republic of Timor-Leste held an independence referendum under UN auspices.[49] In addition, Montenegro

37 Vidmar (n 1) 169, 198.

38 *Conference on Yugoslavia, Arbitration Commission, Opinion* 5 (1992) 92 ILR 188, point 4.

39 Interestingly, the ICJ held that Bosnia-Herzegovina actually became a state on the date that the referendum results were announced: *Application of the Convention on the Prevention and Punishment of the Crime of Genocide (Bosnia and Herzegovina v Serbia and Montenegro)* (Preliminary Objections: Judgement) [1996] ICJ Rep 595, para 23.

40 *Conference on Yugoslavia, Arbitration Commission, Opinion* 6 (1992) 92 ILR 182, para 4.

41 H. Brady and C. Kaplan, 'Eastern Europe and the Former Soviet Union' in D Butler and A Ranney (eds.), *Referendums Around the World: The Growing Use of Direct Democracy* (AEI Press 1994) 186.

42 Ibid 188.

43 Vidmar (n 1) 185.

44 Ibid 193.

45 Ibid 185.

46 Brady and Kaplan (n 41) 201.

47 Ibid 193.

48 'Elections in Eritrea', available at: https://africanelections.tripod.com/er.html (last checked 1 September 2023).

49 United Nations General Assembly (UNGA) 'Question of East Timor: Report of the Secretary General' (5 May 1999) UN Doc A/53/951 'Annex I: The Agreement between the Republic of Indonesia and the Portuguese Republic on the Question of East Timor'; 'Annex II: The Agreement Regarding the Modalities for the Popular Consultation of the East Timorese through a Direct Ballot'; UNSC Resolution 1246 (11 June 1999) UN Doc S/RES/1246.

held a European Union monitored referendum on 21 May 2006, through the Independence Referendum Act of that year.[50] Finally, the Republic of South Sudan arose from a six-year process of emergence instigated by the 2005 Comprehensive Peace Agreement,[51] which culminated in a referendum under the Southern Sudan Referendum Act (2009).

However, notwithstanding the extent of the practice cited above, it appears clear that genuine political communities can emerge without any real expression of popular will.[52] The Czech and Slovak Republics, for example, emerged without referendums. So too did Serbia and Montenegro, which initially arose as the Federal Republic of Yugoslavia (FRY). Admittedly, the FRY originally claimed to be a continuation of the SFRY, which complicates this case somewhat.[53] Nonetheless, the seeming absence of referendums remains an issue in all three examples. In the case of the FRY, Vidmar argues that 'the absence of significant independence movements at the time…[left] little doubt that the Serbs and Montenegrins favoured the association'.[54] This seems too quick. Although the absence of dissent may track shared preferences for independence, it may also or instead correspond to other motivations, such as fear of personal repercussions for opposition, apathy, or ambivalence. Contemporary political communities are too pluralistic for us to assume shared preferences in the absence of significant positive evidence. This is particularly true in circumstances of state dissolution, secession, and devolution, beset as they usually are by political controversy.

Such evidential difficulties undermine the very notion of 'popular will' itself, as I argue more fully in Chapter 7. As such, and notwithstanding the literal meaning of the relevant paragraphs of the *Western Sahara* opinion, and that of the resolutions cited therein, it is more fruitful to understand international law on this point as requiring something slightly different. According to statehood as political community, entities created via popular political engagement, enabled in good faith by the relevant authorities, have stronger claims

50 The Act on the Referendum on State-Legal Status of the Republic of Montenegro, Official Gazette of the Republic of Montenegro, No. 12/06 (2 March 2006) (Republic of Montenegro), Article 6.

51 The Comprehensive Peace Agreement between The Government of The Republic of The Sudan and The Sudan People's Liberation Movement/Sudan People's Liberation Army (adopted 9 January 2005), Article 222(2).

52 Cf. Daniel Moeckli and Nils Reimann, 'Independence Referendums in International Law' in Jure Vidmar, Sarah McGibbon, and Lea Raible(eds.), *Research Handbook on Secession* (Edward Elgar 2022).

53 Constitution of the Federal Republic of Yugoslavia 1992 (Federal Republic of Yugoslavia), Preamble.

54 Vidmar (n 1) 184–185.

to statehood than they would otherwise. This holds because politics itself is a confluence of individual participatory actions, and if the creation of states can be observed to result from a collective effort of this kind, respect for political capacity itself will be evidenced within that process. Referendums matter, not because they capture the 'will of the people' – at best, they express the overlapping preferences of a majority – but because they function as both focuses and forums for political action, which speak to the character of the nascent community that may emerge from them.[55] Moreover, any state that emerges partly in response to an independence referendum necessarily possesses at least some artefactual value as a political product by virtue of existing causally downstream from that referendum itself. This is sufficient, from the perspective of statehood as political community, to hold that entities created via appropriate referendums will have a stronger claim to statehood than they would otherwise.

However, this cannot entail that referendums are necessary for state creation. For that stronger position to hold, the importance of holding referendums would have to normatively outweigh the countervailing value of genuine political communities accruing statehood in their absence. Only then would international law be justified in denying statehood to a community that might otherwise qualify for that status. It is not obvious that such reasons exist. On the one hand, an unambiguously phrased independence referendum signals that a nascent community both respects, and has begun to facilitate, the political action of its population. Outwith circumstances of civil war or other endemic violence, in which sufficiently widespread and uncoerced political participation will often be impossible, the provision of referendums seems like a relatively minimal commitment on the part of the relevant authorities, given the gravity of what is typically at stake. Commitments of this kind, where present, aid judgements about the advisability of recognition from the point of view of statehood as political community, as well as making questions related to the date of commencement easier to address. Although rarely negligible, the cost of organising appropriate referendums will rarely justify foregoing these advantages altogether, particularly given the availability of United Nations assistance (as in the cases of Eritrea and East Timor). This suggests that referendums should usually be required.

[55] On the potential dangers and misuses of referendums, see: Sze Hong Lam, 'To Perfect the Imperfect Title: How Referenda were Historically Manipulated to Justify Territorial Conquests by Nations' *EJIL: Talk!*, 1 October 2022: www.ejiltalk.org/to-perfect-the-imperfect-title-how-referenda-were-historically-manipulated-to-justify-territorial-conquest-by-nations/ (last accessed 2 October 2023).

On the other hand, it would seem perverse from the perspective of political community for international law to deny ethical, moral, and social reality by refusing to impart statehood upon communities such as Serbia and Montenegro, the Czech Republic, or the Slovak Republic, simply because no popular vote occasioned their emergence. There is a qualitative difference between failing to facilitate popular participation during state creation and attempting to forge a state through the aggressive use of force, mass disenfranchisement, or the displacement of persons. In the former case, political action is only undermined insofar as it is not actively facilitated. In the latter, the capacity for political action is not just implicitly denied or disrespected but actively attacked and undermined. This distinction matters within international law, as my subsequent discussion demonstrates. Political communities can last for an extremely long time – sometimes hundreds of years – during which the international community can either recognise and respect them as sites of political action or refuse to do so, despite all evidence to the contrary. Refusing to impart statehood in perpetuity simply because no referendum has taken place is tantamount to the latter. In light of this, the precise position in relation to independence referendums must be reconstructed carefully.

Accepting that such referendums should ordinarily be available, while nonetheless acknowledging that their absence should not constitute an absolute bar to state creation, statehood as political community recommends an intermediary position, which I call the 'referendum principle'. A weak rebuttable presumption in favour of independence referendums should be taken to exist, which places the burden upon nascent communities either to provide them, to request UN or other authoritative external facilitation, or to somehow publicly justify their absence. Such justifications might point to tumultuous domestic circumstances following protracted civil war or perhaps to obstruction by the relevant 'parent' state, from which the nascent community wishes to secede. In the event that no such action is undertaken and no justification is forthcoming, the presumption will operate so as to raise significantly the standard to which a nascent entity must satisfy the antecedents of statehood before full independence can be gained. Failure to provide a referendum, in other words, should be seen to warrant considerably heightened scrutiny in relation to the instantiation and facilitation of ethically valuable politics.[56]

[56] Although it somewhat tortures the language of that text, this strikes me as the most attractive reading of the Badinter Commission's implication that popular participation during the process of state creation is just one way amongst many in which collective self-determination might be demonstrably respected: *Conference on Yugoslavia, Arbitration Commission, Opinion 1* (1991) 92 ILR 162.

4.3 THE NEGATIVE SELF-DETERMINATION PRINCIPLE

According to Crawford, 'self-determination is, at the most basic level, a principle concerned with the right to be a State'.[57] Statehood as political community explains one sense in which this claim might be true: states are the primary (or, more accurately, the default) means through which individuals enjoy collective self-determination under international law. Insofar as they form the populations of states, they can self-determine as members of *those* political communities. In the case of established states, the enjoyment of collective self-determination chiefly entails juridical equality with other communities, the capacity to create international law, and presumptive entitlements to both territorial integrity and relative political independence.[58] However, within the context of state creation, self-determination has also been argued to block statehood where emergence would licence the formal disenfranchisement or political subordination of large sections of the relevant population. As Crawford puts the point, where certain of its precepts would be violated, self-determination 'suspend[s] statehood until the constitutional and governmental structure of the territory is brought into line with this principle'.[59] This view has received significant criticism in recent scholarship.[60] In this section, I defend it as correct in principle *vis-à-vis* statehood as political community.

In terms of international practice, two cases are of paradigmatic importance. The first is the Turkish Republic of Northern Cyprus, which emerged in 1974 under a Turkish Cypriot administration with military support from

[57] Crawford (n 2) 107. International legal practise concerning 'internal' self-determination arguably addresses governmental legitimacy, in the sense addressed within Chapters 6 and 7, and so is wholly distinct from the law of state creation, see: Antonio Cassese, *Self-Determination of Peoples: A Legal Reappraisal* (Cambridge University Press 1995) 101–140. Similarly, the right to development and some cultural rights might be considered components of self-determination, also falling outside the immediate scope of political ethics, see: Roland Rich, 'The Right to Development: A Right of Peoples?' in James Crawford (ed.), *The Rights of Peoples* (Oxford University Press 1988) 39–54; Lyndel Prott, 'Cultural Rights as Peoples' Rights in International Law' in ibid 93–106. For the non-state self-determination claims of Indigenous peoples, which are somewhat inconsistently supported by international practice, see: Richard Falk, 'The Rights of Peoples (In Particular Indigenous Peoples)' in ibid 17–37; Garth Nettheim, 'Peoples' and 'Populations' – Indigenous Peoples and the Rights of Peoples' in ibid 107–126; Jennifer Hendry, 'A Legally Pluralist Approach to the *Bakassi Peninsula* Case' in Damian Gonzalez-Salzberg and Loveday Hodson (eds.), *Research Methods for International Human Rights Law: Beyond the Traditional Paradigm* (Routledge 2020).

[58] UNGA Resolution 2625 (XXV) (24 October 1970) UN Doc A/RES/25/2625(XXV), Annex; Charter of the United Nations (adopted 26 June 1945, entered into force 24 October 1945) 1 UNTS XVI, Articles 1 and 2; *Jurisdictional Immunities of the State (Germany v Italy: Greece intervening)* (Merits) [2012] ICJ Rep 99, para 57.

[59] Crawford (n 2) 129–131.

[60] Nicholson (n 1) 175–180; Vidmar (n 1) 61–62.

the Republic of Turkey.[61] Its creation resulted in some 211,000 Greek Cypriots being displaced from the North, whilst those who remained faced severe restrictions upon their liberty, most notably in terms of freedom of movement.[62] The history of Cypriot intercommunal conflict is too complex to do justice here.[63] It suffices to note that the mass expulsion of Greek Cypriots from Northern Cyprus excluded a considerable proportion of the North's extant population from its erstwhile political life. No entity created via these means, particularly not one secured by a foreign state's illegal use of force,[64] can plausibly be held to have arisen consistently with the ethical value of politics.

The second paradigmatic case is Southern Rhodesia, which declared independence from the United Kingdom on 11 November 1965 under the moniker 'Rhodesia'.[65] Controlled by a white minority and unopposed militarily by the United Kingdom, it nonetheless attracted condemnation from both the Security Council and the General Assembly for its policies of racial segregation and discrimination, including but not limited to the delineation of suffrage along racial lines.[66] In both cases, governmental violence either disrupted, wholly removed, or doubled down upon the deprivation of the capacity for political action amongst large sections of the relevant populations. The collective non-recognition that followed in both cases can, or so I contend, be reconstructed in light of this as complying with a 'negative self-determination' principle, which blocks the accrual of statehood until such situations are resolved in favour of enfranchisement and non-domination.

A similar approach can be taken in circumstances where established states attempt to grant independence to parts of their territory in order to disenfranchise habitual residents. When the government of South Africa tried to establish the 'Bantustans' of Transkei,[67] Bophuthatswana,[68] Venda[69] and Ciskei,[70]

[61] *Loizidou and Cyprus (intervening) v Turkey* (1997) 23 EHRR 513, paras 16–23.

[62] *Cyprus v Turkey* (2002) 35 EHRR 30, paras 28–48 (this was held by the Court to violate Article 8 of the European Convention on Human Rights, see: paras 165–176).

[63] For an interesting collection of essays on the topic, see: Yiannis Papadakis, Nicos Peristianis, and Gisela Welz (eds.), *Divided Cyprus: Modernity, History, and an Island in Conflict* (Indiana University Press 2006).

[64] Press statement of Robin Cook, Secretary of State for Foreign and Commonwealth Affairs, 16 December 1997, reprinted in Geoffrey Marston (ed.) 'United Kingdom Materials on International Law 1997' (1997) 68(1) *British Yearbook of International Law* 520.

[65] John Dugard, *Recognition and the United Nations* (Grotius 1987) 90–98.

[66] UNGA Resolution 2022 (XX) (5 November 1965) UN Doc A/RES/2022(XX); UNGA Resolution 2024 (XX) (11 November 1965) UN Doc A/RES/2024(XX); see also note 31 above.

[67] Status of Transkei Act, 1976 (No. 100 of 1976) (South Africa).

[68] Status of Bophuthatswana Act, 1977 (No. 89 of 1977) (South Africa).

[69] Status of Venda Act, 1979 (No. 107 of 1979) (South Africa).

[70] Status of Ciskei Act, 1981 (No. 110 of 1981) (South Africa).

none of the resulting entities received recognition from any third state.[71] This collective non-recognition was again supported by both the General Assembly and the Security Council.[72] As put by the Security Council President, the Bantustans policy was not a genuine attempt to create independent states on an ethno-cultural basis but was 'designed to divide and dispossess the African people and establish client states under [South Africa's] dominion in order to perpetuate *apartheid*'.[73] This effectively divested large sections of the South African population of their nationality and drew up boundaries so as to distribute land along racial lines, which is arguably a freestanding violation of international law.[74] It also excluded many 'non-white' South Africans from political participation, utilising a nominal grant of independence to further subordinate them to the violent rule of a minority class.

At the normative level, the case for the negative self-determination principle operating as a block to the accrual of statehood in circumstances such as this departs from five distinct but connected wrongs. All of these wrongs, as demonstrated by the above examples, are occasioned by mass disenfranchisement and political subordination, conducted upon cultural, ethnic, geographical, linguistic, or similar lines. First, all deliberate disenfranchisement and other forms of political subordination disrupt existing political activity. By excluding those previously able to participate, disenfranchising regimes knowingly or carelessly undermine the capacity of such individuals to act reasonably through political action. As argued in Chapter 5, this infantilises or otherwise disrespects those individuals as political agents, which constitutes a unique form of expressive wrong.

Second, and somewhat similarly, individuals subordinated via expulsion from an aspiring state's territory are forced to abandon their political projects, leaving them both symbolically and physically alienated from any institutional successes to which they previously contributed. This not only expressively

71 Crawford (n 2) 342–343.

72 UNGA Resolution 2775E (XXVI) (29 November 1971) UN Doc A/RES/2775(XXVI)E; UNGA 2923E (XXVII) (15 November 1972) UN Doc A/RES/2923(XXVII)E; UNGA Resolution 3151G (XXVIII) (14 December 1973) UN Doc A/RES/3151(XXVIII)G; UNGA Resolution 3324E (XXIX) (16 December 1974) UN Doc A/RES/3324(XXIX)E; UNGA Resolution 3411D (XXX) (28 November 1975) UN Doc A/RES/3411(XXX)D; UNGA Resolution 31/6A (26 October 1976) UN Doc A/RES/31/6A; UNSC Resolution 264 (20 March 1969) UN Doc S/RES/264; UNSC Resolution 402 (22 December 1976) UN Doc S/RES/402; UNSC Resolution 407 (25 May 1977) UN Doc S/RES/407; UNSC Resolution 417 (31 October 1977) UN Doc S/RES/417; UNSC Resolution 556 (23 October 1984) UN Doc S/RES/556; UNSC Resolution 581 (13 February 1986) UN Doc S/RES/581.

73 UNSC 'Note by the President of the Security Council' (21 September 1979) UN Doc S/13549.

74 Crawford (n 2) 338–341, 344–345.

devalues their personal narratives as contributors to a particular community but also implies a callousness as to their ongoing political lives. One problematic consequence of statelessness (although by no means the most important consequence) is the characteristic difficulties displaced and unprotected persons face when participating politically anywhere.[75]

Third, wholly disenfranchised and subordinated groups are necessarily excluded from accessing the governance institutions of the aspiring state as forums for political activity. They are left, characteristically, with only the physical space demarcated by the territory of nascent entity within which to act politically. Since their disenfranchisement may well emanate from the constitution of the aspiring state – and, to that extent, be entrenched within its governance practices – any claim that the nascent community permits ongoing opportunities for their political participation will be extremely weak. Fourth, and connectedly, disenfranchised and subordinated groups usually find it difficult to benefit from any other domestic political forums that enjoy the acceptance of the nascent regime, such as national trade unions or formally registered political parties. Although such individuals may be able to establish unsanctioned political forums of their own and can certainly use the forums of their oppressors as political focuses,[76] their vestigial capacity for political action *vis-à-vis* dominant groups will be problematically asymmetric. Fifth and finally, as argued in Chapter 2, where the *violent* oppression of disenfranchised or subordinated groups is particularly severe, their general capacity to engage in political projects will suffer as a result of this endemic violence.[77]

All five wrongs are characteristic of the cases such as Northern Cyprus and Southern Rhodesia. What is more, all five proceed from a discrete form of governmental wrongdoing. However, this point does not imply that the negative self-determination principle requires governmental perfection: as I discuss in Chapters 6 and 7, it is entirely possible for states to emerge without governments that are even characteristically legitimate. Naturally, any unjustified disenfranchisement, and certainly all widespread political subordination, will harm the legitimacy of offending governments; however, that is not the point at issue here. As Crawford puts it:

[75] William Conklin, *Statelessness: The Enigma of the International Community* (Hart Publishing 2014) 113–117.

[76] As I argue in Chapter 2, very few regimes that secure civil peace are *completely* devoid of political value.

[77] As regards the negative self-determination principle, this point was mirrored within: *Application of the Convention on the Prevention and Punishment of the Crime of Genocide (Bosnia and Herzegovina v Serbia and Montenegro)* (Pleadings: Memorial, Bosnia and Herzegovina) [2007] ICJ Rep 43, p. 43, para 233.

> while such actions may delegitimize the government, they do not affect the State as such…[the] point [is] a more limited one: that where a particular people has a right of self-determination in respect of a territory, no government will be recognized which comes into existence and seeks to control that territory as a State in violation of self-determination[78]

What matters for negative self-determination is not the extent to which governments are legitimate but whether ethically valuable politics is sufficiently disrupted via the process of state creation for us to doubt whether it remains possible for the disenfranchised group while those circumstances persist. In this respect, the negative self-determination principle forms a procedural corollary to the notion that 'effectiveness' requires a government that is characteristically facilitative of political action.[79] Its function is to ensure that subordinated groups are not 'left behind' during the creation process, such that politics is shut off from them by the territorial gerrymandering of their oppressors.

Notwithstanding the attractiveness of the negative self-determination principle, what it takes for nascent communities to overcome it should not be overstated. The facilitation of valuable politics does not require full-fledged non-discrimination on the part of emerging states. The initial constitutions of the Republics of Cyprus, Fiji, Malawi, and Zimbabwe, as well as that of New Zealand, all provided for governmental appointment mechanisms that treated particular ethnic groups preferentially.[80] Moreover, the State of Israel remains formally committed to promoting and protecting a particular ethno-cultural group.[81] Although such constitutional arrangements raise questions of legitimacy, equality, justice, and fairness,[82] they do not contravene negative self-determination. If governance within a putative state allows for a sufficient level of authentic and reasonable political activity to take place *outside* the group(s) it privileges, that entity is not only capable of mounting a plausible statehood claim but will also be able to demonstrate sufficient procedural compliance with political ethics to either not trigger the negative self-determination principle or to overcome its prohibitive effect.

Israel itself is quite an interesting case, which merits brief reflection, even though doing its complex history full justice here would be impossible. It is

78 Crawford (n 2) 131.

79 See Chapter 3.

80 Crawford (n 2) 333–334.

81 Sammy Smooha, 'The Model of Ethnic Democracy: Israel as a Jewish and Democratic State' (2002) 8(4) *Nations and Nationalism* 475.

82 Ronald Dworkin, 'Democracy and Religion: America and Israel', *Ian Thompson Forum on World Issues, 20th Anniversary Season*, University of Nabraska-Lincoln, October 2008: https://mediahub.unl.edu/media/546 (last accessed 2 October 2023).

at least arguable that what is now the State of Israel emerged in violation of the negative self-determination principle, given the violent displacement that characterised the seizure of its territory.[83] If this was so, then it follows that its initial claim to statehood would have been blocked, at least until a sufficient degree of enfranchisement and non-domination was established. Whatever the case, this period of legal suspension would have been reasonably brief: subsequent to its emergence, non-Jews within Israel were afforded a reasonably significant capacity for political action, notwithstanding the aforementioned ethno-cultural inequality within Israeli politics. Although an initial violation of the negative self-determination principle can block statehood, changes in circumstances may reverse this position. Even if Israel was not a state in 1948, when its independence was declared,[84] or even in 1949, when it was admitted as a Member State of the UN,[85] it certainly possesses that status now.

It is also possible that Israeli statehood was never blocked in this manner. The above comments assume that the negative self-determination principle existed within international law at the time of Israel's creation. However, although I would be prepared to contend that it did, this is by no means clear. International legal practice in support of negative self-determination was at that point quite thin on the ground: the situations in the Bantustans, Northern Cyprus, and Southern Rhodesia had not yet taken place.[86] This intimates a key difference between the law of state creation, even when understood to be a branch of political morality, and the normative implications of political ethics when conceived wholly in the abstract. To be sure that a particular principle existed at any given time, sufficient international practice must support that conclusion, even on the 'Grotian' view adopted here. Although it is arguable that the negative self-determination principle might be derived purely *a priori* from other principles of international law, such as the proper construction of the effectiveness antecedent or the prohibition on the threat or use of force, such claims must be made with some degree of caution.

Whatever the precise status of Israel was in the middle of the last century, the foregoing discussion allows us to provide a final formation of the negative self-determination principle as it exists today. Whenever state creation is attempted through means that cause the mass disenfranchisement or political subordination of a significant group within the relevant territorial unit, or whenever independence is nominally granted to a particular entity to the same

83 John Quigley, *The Statehood of Palestine: International Law in the Middle East Conflict* (Cambridge University Press 2010) 120–121.

84 Declaration of the Establishment of the State of Israel, 14 May 1948 (State of Israel).

85 UNGA Resolution 273 (11 May 1949) UN Doc A/RES/273(III).

86 Crawford (n 2) 434.

effect, statehood will not accrue until this situation is resolved. Alongside and to ensure the implementation of this normative 'block', which arises automatically when the negative self-determination principle is triggered, international law will also impose a duty of collective non-recognition on the part of the international community (see Section 4.1.3). This parallel duty persists until the normative block triggered by negative self-determination lapses. Triggers for the negative self-determination principle may present themselves either as ongoing features of an emerging entity's governance (the text and application of its basic legal instruments, for example) or as something undertaken to permit the entity in question to take a particular form (such as the mass expulsion of persons). In either case, statehood as political community requires that statehood be denied until sufficient facilitation of political action is restored.

4.4 THE INTERNATIONAL PEACE PRINCIPLE

As argued in Chapter 2, war is not just the continuation of politics with other means. Endemic violence is both antithetical to political community and destructive of political action. We cannot pursue justice and legitimacy as we ought when our daily lives are preoccupied with immediate self-preservation. This precarity is particularly evident within international armed conflicts, where private individuals caught between warring governments often suffer extreme deprivation. Article 2(4) of the UN Charter prohibits 'the threat or use of force against the territorial and political independence of any State' and this prohibition generates perhaps the most important procedural element of state creation: the 'international peace principle'. This principle holds that states cannot be created solely through the unlawful use or threat of force, such that no attempt at state creation grounded purely upon the international use of such force can succeed.[87] As with negative self-determination, the international peace principle operates autonomously; however, it is both supported and occasioned by a parallel duty of collective non-recognition, which binds the international community *erga omnes*.

Practice in support of this principle is often complicated by the fact that entities created through the unlawful use of force characteristically operate as puppet states, such as Manchukuo in the 1930s, which was ruled by the Empire of Japan,[88] North Cyprus immediately after its creation by Turkey,[89]

[87] See Subsection 4.5.1 for the importance of 'solely' and 'purely' within this formulation.
[88] Crawford (n 2) 132–133.
[89] *Cyprus v Turkey*, para 77.

or Transdniestra, which is supported almost entirely by the Russian Federation.[90] Indeed, Crawford goes so far as to present the relationship between statehood and the unlawful use of force as one of presumption, arguing that 'entities created by the use of force or during a period of belligerent occupation' are assumed to fail what I have called the independence antecedent.[91] Nonetheless, this 'contingent judgement',[92] to use Crawford's own phrase, is best separated out from the international peace principle itself. As Nicholson argues, it would undermine the proposition that the annexation of territory was unlawful if there was no concomitant prohibition upon the creation of states through unlawful force.[93] Both the ICJ's reading of General Assembly resolution 2625 (XXV) in *Wall in the Occupied Palestinian Territory* and various Security Council resolutions support the former position, such that normative coherence seems to require the latter.[94] The necessity for such coherence is evident, as Nicholson demonstrates, from how the 'Republic of Crimea' was used by Russia in 2014 as a thinly veiled means to appropriate territory from Ukraine. The General Assembly's condemnation of the Russian annexation in 2014 should be read as covering 'both attempts to annex Ukrainian territory directly…*and* attempts to create friendly new states on the territory (suggesting that…[state creation] could not be used to avoid the norm about annexation)'.[95]

This being understood, it becomes easier to discern the very strong trend in support of the international peace principle within practice over the last century or so. Two recent examples provide perhaps the starkest illustration: the Donetsk People's Republic and the Luhansk People's Republic, which declared independence from Ukraine on 7 and 27 April 2014.[96] Referendums were held in both entities on 11 May 2014, subject to several allegations of

[90] *Ilaşcu and Others and Romania (intervening) v Moldova and Russian Federation* (2005) 40 EHRR 1030, para 392.

[91] Crawford (n 2) 132–133.

[92] Ibid 344.

[93] Nicholson (n 1) 166–167.

[94] *Legal Consequences of the Construction on a Wall in Occupied Palestinian Territory* (Advisory Opinion) [2004] ICJ Rep 136, para 87; UNSC Resolution 242 (22 November 1967) UN Doc S/RES/242; UNSC Resolution 478 (20 August 1980) UN Doc S/RES/478; UNSC Resolution 662 (9 August 1990) UN Doc S/RES/662; see also note 32 above and: Claus Kreß, 'The International Court of Justice and the "Principle of Non-Use of Force"' in Marc Weller (ed.), *The Oxford Handbook of the Use of Force in International Law* (Oxford University Press 2015).

[95] Nicholson (n 1) 167; UNGA Resolution 68/262 (27 March 2014) UN Doc A/RES/68/262.

[96] 'Ukraine Crisis: Protesters Declare Donetsk "republic"', *BBC News*, 7 April 2014: www.bbc.co.uk/news/world-europe-26919928 (last accessed 2 October 2023); 'Separatists Declare "People's Republic" in Ukraine's Luhansk', *RadioFreeEurope*, 28 April 2014: www.rferl.org/a/separatists-declare-luhansk-peoples-republic/25364894.html (last accessed 2 October 2023).

voting fraud, intimidation, and other procedural irregularities.[97] After initial military conflicts, in which Russia allegedly played an important role,[98] a so-called 'static war' persisted between the two Donbas entities and Ukraine until, on 25 February 2022, Russia invaded. Importantly for present purposes, this was preceded, on 21 February, by Russia formally recognising the independence of both entities.[99] The reaction of the international community was almost unanimous: to date, no governments save those of Syria and North Korea have joined Russia in recognising either entity, and several states made unilateral declarations decrying both Russia's unlawful use of force and its wrongful recognition of Donetsk and Luhansk.[100] On 25 February 2002, Russia used its veto to prevent passage of a Security Council resolution that would have, amongst other things, demanded the reversal of Russian recognition,[101] whereas the General Assembly, on 2 March, adopted a resolution with precisely the same terms.[102] Despite Russian attempts to ground the legality of its military action and recognition upon both Article 51 of the UN Charter

[97] 'Ukraine Rebels Hold Referendums in Donetsk and Luhansk', *BBC News*, 11 May 2014: www.bbc.co.uk/news/world-europe-27360146 (last accessed 2 October 2023); David Blair, 'The "Disappeared" Whose Voices Will Be Silent in Vote on Self-Rule in Ukraine's East', *The Telegraph*, 10 May 2014: www.telegraph.co.uk/news/worldnews/europe/ukraine/10822420/The-disappeared-whose-voices-will-be-silent-in-vote-on-self-rule-in-Ukraines-east.html (last accessed 2 October 2023); Atika Shubert and Ben Brumfeld, 'Polls Close in Eastern Ukraine Amid Allegations of Fraud and Double-Voting', *CNN*, 11 May 2014: http://edition.cnn.com/2014/05/11/world/europe/ukraine-crisis/ (last accessed 2 October 2023); 'Reports: 100,000 "Yes" Ballots for Referendum Intercepted in Sloviansk', *Kyiv Post*, 10 May 2014: www.kyivpost.com/post/9088 (last accessed 2 October 2023).

[98] Donald Jensen, 'Moscow in the Donbas: Command, Control, Crime and the Minsk Peace Process' (2017) *NATO Defence College* 1, 3–6.

[99] Executive Order No. 71. On the Recognition of the Donetsk People's Republic, 21 February 2023 (in Russian): http://publication.pravo.gov.ru/Document/View/0001202202220002 (last accessed 2 October 2023) (Russian Federation); Executive Order No. 72. On the Recognition of the Lugansk People's Republic, 21 February 2023 (in Russian): http://publication.pravo.gov.ru/Document/View/0001202202220001 (last accessed 2 October 2023) (Russian Federation).

[100] For example: UNSC Verbatim Record (21 February 2022) UN Doc S/PV.8970; Joint Expeditionary Force, JEF Defence Ministers – Joint Statement, 22 February 2022: www.stjornarradid.is/library/04-Raduneytin/Utanrikisraduneytid/PDF-skjol/20220222_JEF%20DEFMINS_JOINT%20STATEMENT_FINAL.pdf (last accessed 2 October 2023); Boris Johnson, Statement to Parliament, HC Deb 22 February 2022, vol 709, cols 173–175 (UK); Executive Order 14065 – Blocking Property of Certain Persons and Prohibiting Certain Transactions with Respect to Continued Russian Efforts to Undermine the Sovereignty and Territorial Integrity of Ukraine, 21 February 2022 (United States).

[101] United Nations, 'Security Council Fails to Adopt Draft Resolution on Ending Ukraine Crisis, as Russian Federation Wields Veto', *Press Release*, 25 February 2022, UN Doc SC/14808: https://press.un.org/en/2022/sc14808.doc.htm (last accessed 2 October 2023).

[102] UNGA Resolution ES-11/1 (2 March 2022) UN Doc A/RES/ES-11/1, paras 2–6; see also: UNGA Resolution 377A (V) (3 November 1950) UN Doc A/RES/377(V)A.

and the 1948 Genocide Convention,[103] international opinion remains firmly against the legality of either, as well as against the statehood of either Donbas entity. As such, the 'creation' of Donetsk and Luhansk is best viewed as an attempt to manipulate international law to facilitate conquest and therefore as void by operation of the international peace principle.[104]

Normatively speaking, the case for the international peace principle is clear from the perspective of statehood as political community. Although, historically speaking, many states were created through violent conquest, the contemporary conception of statehood as a territorial forum for political action is antithetical to the use of force in international relations. The law of state creation, as the branch of international law concerned with the initial delimitation of our political communities, cannot consistently licence such an extreme form of domination. Although all truly endemic violence is inimical to political action, the distinction between international armed conflict and domestic armed conflict is key. When a political community descends into civil war, due to a genuinely internal collapse of power and authority, politics in the sense that concerns us has already ceased. At that point, there is no reason, *vis-à-vis* political community, to insist that no new states arise. Indeed, the institution of civil peace, even within part of an otherwise anarchic territory, is something to celebrate from this point of view, and a new state may well be conducive to that end.[105] However, the same cannot hold in relation to conflicts with their origin in an unlawful use or threat of force within the meaning of Article 2(4). This distinction might seem odd from the perspective of private individuals, who will suffer the deprivations of endemic violence irrespective of whether its proximate causes are foreign or domestic.

[103] Allegations of genocide as a trigger for intervention were made by President Vladimir Putin on 24 February 2022, in an address available here: http://en.kremlin.ru/events/president/news/67843 (last accessed 2 October 2023). This line of argument appears to be less frequently adopted, likely due to ICJ proceedings currently being brought by Ukraine, see: *Allegations of Genocide under the Convention on the Prevention and Punishment of the Crime of Genocide (Ukraine v Russian Federation)*, (Application Instituting Proceedings) General List No. 182 [2022] ICJ 1. For the official position of Russia on Article 51, see: UNSC Verbatim Record (21 February 2022) UN Doc S/PV.8970, p.11.

[104] Since both entities are puppet states, lacking political independence, they have in any event no plausible statehood claim, see: Marc Weller, 'Russia's Recognition of the "Separatist Republics" in Ukraine was Manifestly Unlawful' *EJIL: Talk!*, 9 March 2022: www.ejiltalk.org/russias-recognition-of-the-separatist-republics-in-ukraine-was-manifestly-unlawful/ (last accessed 2 October 2023).

[105] Complications can arise under contemporary international law to the extent that any criminal funding of secession movements leads to those movements beings considered 'terrorists', see: Elizabeth Chadwick, 'National Liberation in the Context of Post- and Non-Colonial Struggles for Self-Determination' in Marc Weller (ed.), *The Oxford Handbook of the Use of Force in International Law* (Oxford University Press 2015) 853–856.

Nonetheless, from a communal perspective, whereas genuine civil war represents the tragic breakdown of politics, foreign attempts to annex, destabilise, or destroy an existing state constitute an orchestrated disruption. The latter is a species of inter-governmental domination, within the same wrongful family as colonialism, and cannot be tolerated by either statehood as political community or the prohibition on the threat or use of force itself.[106] This explains the international dimension of the peace principle, as well as its nature as an absolute bar upon the creation of states through such unlawful methods. War is the ultimate political violation, and the law of state creation protects established communities from being torn apart by such means.

4.5 THE TERRITORIAL INTEGRITY PRINCIPLE

Since nascent political communities typically arise on the territory of existing states, state creation will almost always create at least an apparent tension with the territorial integrity of such 'parent' states.[107] According to statehood as political community, territorial integrity as an entitlement of established states can be explained as follows. As argued in Chapter 1, our political communities are defined in part by two discrete moral duties that we owe to our compatriots. These duties are fundamentally obligations to promote stability, legitimacy, and justice within and amongst the complete set of all those to whom we are duty-bound. Furthermore, as argued in Chapter 3, the indeterminacy that would otherwise arise over the scope of these duties is with reference to the factual control exercised over the relevant territorial unit and its governance institutions. From this perspective, the primary political units recognised by international law (that is, states) are constituted by a combination of established social facts and normative obligations, giving us discrete ethical challenges in relation to these historically contingent groups. Characteristically, attempting to sever or dissolve such groups by disrupting their extant territorial limits therefore risks undermining the ongoing political projects of the relevant populations. Territorial integrity matters, in other words, because political communities must be given both space and time within which to develop.

As a matter of international practice, this principle is commonly assumed to apply only between established states.[108] This argumentative line stems from

[106] See generally: Kevin Heller, 'The Illegality of "Genuine" Unilateral Humanitarian Intervention' (2021) 32(2) *European Journal of International Law* 613.

[107] Vidmar (n 1) 63.

[108] Marko Milanovic, 'A Footnote on Secession' *EJIL: Talk!*, 26 October 2017: www.ejiltalk.org/a-footnote-on-secession/ (last accessed 2 October 2023).

the *Kosovo* advisory opinion, in which the ICJ rejected the argument that all unilateral declarations of independence are unlawful because they necessarily violate territorial integrity.[109] The Court held, instead, that because territorial integrity applies only to international relations, nothing about that principle itself can prevent such declarations from being lawful.[110] That finding drew upon some state-centric wording within Principle 1 of General Assembly resolution 2625 (XXVI), which was accepted to reflect customary law in the *Nicaragua* case.[111] The text in question, which the ICJ also considered to cohere with Article IV of the Final Act of the Helsinki Conference on Security and Co-operation in Europe (1975),[112] characterises the law as follows:

> The principle that States shall refrain in their international relations from the threat or use of force against the territorial integrity or political independence of any State, or in any other manner inconsistent with the purposes of the United Nations.

Interestingly, however, as Vidmar correctly observes,[113] the Court in *Kosovo* omitted mention of Principle 5 of that same resolution, which not only provides that '[e]very State shall refrain from any action aimed at the partial or total disruption of national unity and territorial integrity of any other State or county' but also includes the following text:

> Nothing in the forgoing paragraphs [referring to the right of self-determination as that attaches to non-state 'peoples'] shall be construed as authorizing or encouraging any action which would dismember or impair, totally or in part, the territorial integrity or political unity of sovereign and independent States conducting themselves in compliance with the principle of equal rights and self-determination of peoples as described above and thus possessed of a government representing the whole people belonging to the territory without distinction to race, creed or colour.

Given that nothing within *Nicaragua* implies that only Principle 1 of Resolution 2625 (XXVI) represents customary international law, such that every other principle therein somehow has lesser status, the foregoing text must imply that territorial integrity also applies outwith international relations.[114] This entails

[109] *Kosovo*, para 80.
[110] Ibid.
[111] *Case Concerning Military and Paramilitary Activities in and against Nicaragua (Nicaraagua v United States of America)* (Merits) [1986] ICJ Rep 14, paras 191–193.
[112] 'The participating States will respect the territorial integrity of each of the participating States'.
[113] Jure Vidmar, 'The *Kosovo* Advisory Opinion Scrutinized' (2011) 24 *Leiden Journal of International Law* 335, 368–369.
[114] Principle 2, for example, is cited by the Court at paragraph 192.

at least the possibility that non-state entities, including potential secession movements, are implicated by the territorial integrity of their parent states.[115]

In light of this somewhat conflicting practice, statehood as political community suggests three connected points within the procedural law of state creation, which together comprise what I call the 'territorial integrity principle'. First, and most straightforwardly, the territorial integrity of a parent state only raises issues where it coincides with a title claim over the territory in question. When state creation results from the total dissolution of a parent state, as in the case of the successor states of the SFRY, there is no parent entity capable of making such a claim, so the territorial integrity principle cannot apply. Conversely, in many cases of nascent statehood, it is the consent of parent states that facilitates the creation of new communities. This was the case, for example, with the grant of colonial independence issued to the Belgian Congo in 1960 and the 1946 withdrawal of the United States from the Republic of the Philippines.[116] In such cases, the territorial integrity principle is not engaged because consent removes any claim to territorial title that parent states might otherwise make. Indeed, assuming that the parent state sufficiently instantiates the normative elements of political community, granting independence to some portion of its extant territory can be a valuable defining event in its political history.

The same holds in relation to consensual merger, either to form new entities, or simply to become subsumed within an existing state. If the merger itself exhibits respect for the political capacities of the relevant populations, such unions are one mode through which valuable institutional traditions can develop. This was the case, for example, with the unification of Berlin under quadripartite administration, the German Democratic Republic (GDR), and the Federal Republic of Germany (FRG).[117] The process leading to the GDR's merger with the FRG was marked by the relative absence of violence and a proliferation of peaceful political protest, inter-state negotiations, and representative elections.[118] Not only was territorial integrity not

[115] This is supported, for example, by the preamble to UNSC Resolution 2249 (20 November 2015) UN Doc S/RES/2249, which describes Daesh as a 'threat to the security of the Iraqi people *and territory*' [my emphasis].

[116] On the latter, see: (1946) 15 Department of State Bulletin 66.

[117] I assume here that at least the GDR and FRG were separate states at some stage prior to 1990, see: *International Registration of Trade Mark (Germany) Case* (1959) 28 ILR 82; Francis Mann, *Studies in International Law* (Clarendon Press 1973) 549–550, 675–679; Quincy Wright, 'Some Legal Aspects of the Berlin Crisis' (1961) 55(4) *American Journal of International Law* 959, 960. The legal status of Berlin was less clear at the relevant time, see: I.D. Henry and M.C. Wood, *The Legal Status of Berlin* (Grotius Publishing 1987); Crawford (n 2) 459–466.

[118] This 'Peaceful Revolution', which led to the fall of the Berlin Wall, crippled the Socialist Unity Party. On 1 December 1989, the GDR parliament struck their right to rule from the

at issue within this process but also ethically valuable political action itself blossomed throughout.

Second, in circumstances where state creation is attempted solely via an unlawful use or threat of force within the meaning of Article 2(4) of the UN Charter, the effect of the territorial integrity principle is coextensive with that of the international peace principle. This was so, for example, in relation to the Republic of Crimea, as well as in that of the Donetsk and Luhansk People's Republics, as discussed in Section 4.4. The effect of territorial integrity in these circumstances is to ground a strong presumption of state continuity on the part of the established community, safeguarding its existence and dimensions against unlawful and void attempts at state creation.[119] That is the effect, amongst other things, of the international practice reflected by Principle 1 of General Assembly Resolution 2625 (XXVI).

4.5.1 *The Baseline Presumption*

Third, and perhaps more controversially, statehood as political community suggests that in the absence of the consent or dissolution of the parent state, a presumption against emerging statehood will *sometimes* exist even when no unlawful foreign intervention has taken place. The default normative position here is as follows. The two moral duties we owe to our compatriots, which help to define our communities and contour the political dimension of our ethical lives, can be wrongfully frustrated not just by imperialist foreign powers but also by those of our compatriots who seek without appropriate justification to abandon the collective project represented by our established state. This is the normative corollary of the international practice encapsulated within Principle 5 of Resolution 2625 (XXVI). As articulated in *Reference re Secession of Quebec*:

> …a right to secession only arises under the principle of self-determination of peoples at international law where 'a people' is governed as part of a colonial

constitution, leading to their resignation on 3 December and disbandment on 18 December. The political manoeuvres and protests both preceding and following this were intentionally non-violent. See generally: Karsten Timmer, *Vom Aufbruch zum Umbruch: Die Bürgerbewegung in der DDR 1989* (Vandenhoeck & Ruprecht 2000) 276–279; Von Nadja Klinger, 'Bühne der Freiheit', *Der Tagesspiegel*, 4 November 2009: https://web.archive.org/web/20091108171522/http://www.tagesspiegel.de/zeitung/Die-Dritte-Seite-Mauerfall-4-November-Deutsches-Theater%3Bart705%2C2940530 (last accessed 2 October 2023); Russell Dalton (ed.), *The New Germany Votes: Unification and the Creation of the New Party System* (Berg Publishing 1993).

119 See also the Conclusion of this text.

> empire; where 'a people' is subject to alien subjugation, domination and exploitation; and possibly where 'a people' is denied any meaningful exercise of its right to self-determination within the state of which it forms a part. In other circumstances, *peoples are expected to achieve self-determination within the framework of their existing state.*[120] [emphasis added]

This formulation by the Supreme Court of Canada has recently been endorsed, effectively verbatim, by the Supreme Court of the United Kingdom.[121] My discussion in Chapter 3, when establishing the independence antecedent, implicitly endorsed the first two grounds for secession listed there, which are now largely of historical interest, at least as regards state creation.[122] Statehood as political community also endorses the third ground, which I address in some detail below. However, the presently relevant point is not whether (or when) international law grants a right to secession but how it responds to attempted secession, even in the absence of such a right. Consistent with the ICJ in *Kosovo*, statehood as political community holds unilateral secession as such to be lawful.[123] Unlike the conception of territorial integrity developed by the ICJ, however, the one adopted here does not leave the 'sphere of legal neutrality' created by international law's permissive position completely without procedural contours.[124] Instead, it works alongside the referendum principle as a means for contextually determining the level of scrutiny that must be applied when assessing both compliance with the antecedents of statehood and the sufficiency of foreign recognition. The strength of this presumption must not be overstated. Unlike the international peace principle, it is not an absolute bar upon state creation, nor is it a situation-contingent 'block', like the negative self-determination principle. Instead, it amounts to this: all other things being equal, in the absence of parent state consent or dissolution, a nascent entity must typically demonstrate the instantiation of political community more clearly and for a longer period of time than they would otherwise.

The approach outlined above helps to explain how, for example, Somaliland might be considered a state, notwithstanding its total lack of foreign recognition. Formally a British protectorate, and fleetingly independent from 26 to 30 June 1960, what is now the Republic of Somaliland was until 17 May 1991 undisputedly part of what is now the Federal Republic of Somalia.[125] At the

[120] *Re Secession of Quebec*, para 154.

[121] *Reference by the Lord Advocate of devolution issues under paragraph 34 of schedule 6 of the Scotland Act 1998* [2022] UKSC 31 (UK), paras 88–89.

[122] In particular, Subsections 3.4.1 and 3.4.3.

[123] *Kosovo*, paras 79–81, 84.

[124] This phrase is Vidmar's, see: (n 1) 52–53.

[125] Crawford (n 2) 412–413.

time Somaliland declared independence, civil war had plunged Somalia itself into what was to be prolonged anarchy.[126] The evidence largely suggests that, by contrast, Somaliland swiftly became relatively stable, continuously satisfying the antecedents of statehood to a far greater extent.[127] Indeed, Nicholson notes that '[i]ts parent state "virtually and substantially abandoned the struggle for supremacy" (which generally indicates that a unilateral secession entity has become effective)'.[128] From the perspective of statehood as political community, notwithstanding the breakdown of civil peace, on 17 May 1991 Somalia was almost certainly protected against the nascent Somaliland by the territorial integrity principle. As the observable effectiveness of Somaliland endured, however, particularly in juxtaposition to the enduring anarchy within Somalia itself, the presumption that principle establishes moved closer towards the point of rebuttal.[129] Therefore, notwithstanding its aforementioned lack of foreign recognition, insofar as we might claim statehood for Somaliland today, statehood as political community provides a rationale for that shift in its status. The territorial integrity principle may ground a presumption against state creation in the absence of consent or dissolution, however, that presumption is not unshakeable.

The normative justification for this presumption is twofold. First, the necessity for a strong presumption against emerging statehood grounded upon territorial integrity alone is limited by the independent operation of both the negative self-determination principle and the international peace principle. Through their operation, territorial integrity receives significant protection, particularly from attempts at state creation grounded solely within internationally wrongful acts. Second, as argued in Chapter 2, there are some circumstances in which the radical reform or abolition of our governance institutions will evince greater respect for their artefactual value than would be demonstrated by our continued toleration. This holds no less for the possibility of secession than it does for other things: sometimes the best course of action

[126] Scott Pegg, *International Society and the De Facto State* (Ashgate 1998) 85–97.

[127] For instance: UNSC 'Report of the Secretary-General on the situation in Somalia' (19 December 2000) UN Doc S/2000/1211, para 34; UNSC 'Report of the Secretary-General on the Situation in Somalia' (11 October 2001) UN Doc S/2001/963, paras 18–19; UNSC 'Report of the Secretary-General on the Situation in Somalia' (21 February 2002) UN Doc S/2002/198, para 28; *Hagi-Salad v Ashcroft*, 359 F 3d 1044, 1046 (8th Cir 2004, Loken CJ) (United States); Judgment of 30 October 2003, 4 UE 4952/96.A (Hesse Administrative Court, Kassel) (Federal Republic of Germany).

[128] Nicholson (n 1) 190, citing William Harcourt, *Letters by Historicus on Some Questions of International Law* (Macmillan 1863) 9.

[129] It is significant, for example, that Somaliland from 1993 onwards made considerable inroads into restoring and maintaining public infrastructure, while its parent state did not, see: UNSC 'Report of the Secretary-General on the Situation in Somalia' (25 October 2002) UN Doc S/2001/1202, para 55.

within a deeply divided community, where politics has effectively become impossible, will be to make that division formal. Since extant national government(s) may well fail to acknowledge this, statehood as political community makes room for the possibility of state creation notwithstanding their consent, as long as the antecedents of statehood are sufficiently instantiated or where their relative absence is supplemented to a sufficient degree by acts of foreign recognition. There is one situation, however, in which this presumption will be absent altogether: the case of remedial secession, to which I now turn.

4.5.2 *Remedial Secession*

Unlike circumstances of consent and dissolution, unilateral secession always creates tension with territorial integrity. As just explained, statehood as political community establishes a presumption against state creation within the territory of established communities. Notwithstanding difficult cases, like that of Somaliland, this is borne out by the preponderance of international practice: as Crawford notes, no unilaterally seceding entity has been admitted to the UN since its inception in 1945, contrary to the wishes of its parent state.[130] This being so, the presumption that territorial integrity ordinarily creates must either be outweighed or removed. Outweighing takes place whenever a nascent entity has either or both a significant degree of foreign recognition and a clear instantiation of political community through the antecedents of statehood. In such cases, assuming that no other procedural principles were violated, and especially if the nascent entity achieved a suitably administered independence referendum, the presumption established by territorial integrity is forcibly overcome by reference to recalcitrant political reality. Conversely, the presumption is removed entirely whenever the relevant parent state itself dissolves or else consents to the independence of the nascent community. In those circumstances, there is either no parent entity remaining to ground the territorial integrity principle or its application has been waived in relation to the newly defined territory of the emerging state.

There is, however, one more manner in which the presumption can be removed entirely. Political philosophers, and even some doctrinal lawyers, have argued that where governments perpetrate particularly severe and widespread human rights abuses within a discrete area of their territory, that territorial unit will have a right to 'remedial' secession.[131] As we have seen,

[130] Crawford (n 2) 390.

[131] Allen Buchanan, 'Theories of Secession' (1997) 26(1) *Philosophy & Public Affairs* 31; Lea Brilmayer, 'Secession and Self-Determination: A Territorial Interpretation' (1991) 16(1)

this position was supported as a matter of law by the Supreme Court of Canada in *Quebec* and by the UK Supreme Court in *Reference by the Lord Advocate*.[132] In *Kosovo*, the ICJ held that it was not necessary to address the issue of remedial secession; however, it noted that 'radically different views were expressed by those taking part in the proceedings and expressing a position on the question'.[133] As a result, and in particular given Russia's reliance upon the doctrine in support of its unlawful aggression against Ukraine,[134] the existence of a right to remedial secession remains highly controversial. Nonetheless, and despite its default position on territorial integrity, statehood as political community supports the existence of such a right under international law.[135]

Consider the secession of the People's Republic of Bangladesh from the Islamic Republic of Pakistan. Following elections in December 1970, the Bengali Awami League, seeking provincial autonomy for East Pakistan, won a clear majority in the National Assembly of Pakistan.[136] The central government in Islamabad suspended the Assembly's inaugural session in 1 March 1971 and imposed martial law in East Pakistan on 25 March of that year.[137] This involved extreme violence against the local population, seemingly amounting to genocide,[138] and caused some ten million Bengalis to seek refuge in India.[139] While still engaged in armed struggle against government forces, the Awami League declared independence on 10 April 1971.

Yale Journal of International Law 177, 197; Simone F. van den Driest, 'Crimea's Separation from Ukraine: An Analysis of the Right to Self-Determination and (Remedial) Secession in International Law' (2015) 62 *Netherlands International Law Review* 329, 340–341.

132 Supra notes 20, 120, and 121, with adjoining text.

133 *Kosovo* Advisory Opinion, supra (n 19), paras 49–51, 82–83.

134 Sergii Masol, 'Orwellian Rulings of the Russian Constitutional Court on the Donetsk, Kherson, Luhansk and Zaporizhzhia Provinces of Ukraine' *EJIL: Talk!*, 25 October 2022: www.ejiltalk.org/orwellian-rulings-of-the-russian-constitutional-court-on-the-donetsk-kherson-luhansk-and-zaporizhzhia-provinces-of-ukraine/ (last accessed 2 October 2023); see also, in relation to Abkhazia and South Ossetia: Statement by the Ministry of Foreign Affairs of Russia, Doc.1246, 26 August 2008, analysed in Marc Weller, *Negotiating the Final Status of Kosovo* (EU Institute for Security Studies 2008) 86–87.

135 To that extent political community mirrors Steven Ratner's view that General Assembly resolution 2625 (XXV) creates only limited space for a unilateral right to secede: Steven Ratner, *The Thin Justice of International Law: A Moral Reckoning of the Law of Nations* (Oxford University Press 2015) 149.

136 Crawford (n 2) 141.

137 International Commission of Jurists, 'East Pakistan Staff Study' (1972) 8 *ICJ Review* 23, 26.

138 Ibid 30–34; Ved Nanda, 'Self-determination in International Law: The Tragic Tale of Two Cities – Islamabad (West Pakistan) and Dacca (East Pakistan)' (1972) 66 *American Journal of International Law* 321, 336.

139 Crawford (n 2) 141.

India invaded East Pakistan in early December 1971 and was instrumental in the swift surrender of Western Pakistani forces.[140] Notwithstanding the fact that Indian troops remained until the end of March 1972, by that point more than fifty states had recognised the emergence of Bangladesh, with no state beyond Pakistan raising any objection.[141] Although Bangladesh was not admitted to the United Nations until after it received recognition from Pakistan in 1974, this was arguably due only to an earlier Chinese veto of the first draft Security Council resolution proposing its admission.[142] The General Assembly had in fact called for the admission of Bangladesh in November 1972.[143]

The interests protected by fundamental human rights generate weighty normative reasons that may outweigh many countervailing concerns.[144] Some scholars may wish to characterise India's otherwise unlawful intervention as justified to the extent that the territorial integrity of Pakistan was outweighed by such reasons.[145] However, insofar as statehood as political community supports remedial secession, the relevant *en masse* human rights violations stand in a different relation to territorial integrity. As in East Pakistan, some violations committed by parent states undermine the very possibility of valuable politics within particular areas of their territory. This weakens, rather than outweighs, the normative force of territorial integrity *vis-à-vis* those victimised areas. In sufficiently extreme cases, such abuses will be so deeply at odds with political community itself that any claim to territorial integrity in relation to those areas will be entirely removed. This was seemingly the case in East Pakistan. The people within that territory, just like any other group, possessed an interest in undertaking valuable politics. Moreover, in March 1971, it became implausible to claim that this interest could still be satisfied by retaining membership of Pakistan. As such, it must be concluded that East Pakistan gained the right to develop their own political community via secession: a right which

140 Ibid.

141 Christopher Dugard and David Raič, 'The Role of Recognition in the Law and Practice of Secession' in Marcelo G. Kohen (ed.), *Secession: International Law Perspectives* (Cambridge University Press 2006) 94, 123

142 Ibid 122.

143 UNGA Resolution 2937 (XXVII) (29 November 1972) UN Doc A/RES/2937(XXVII).

144 Allen Buchanan, *Justice, Legitimacy, and Self-Determination: Moral Foundations for International Law* (Oxford University Press 2003) 118–142.

145 As Thomas Franck argues, this implies that if India's intervention was unlawful, it was almost certainly because they acted unilaterally, rather than because East Pakistan had no entitlement to establish itself as a state (*Fairness in International Law and Institutions* (Oxford University Press 1998) 161); see also: Jean Salmon, 'Naissance et reconnaissance du Blanga-Desh' in Josef Tittle (ed.), *Multitudo legum ius unum: Festschrift für Wilhelm Wengler* (Interrecht 1973) vol 1, 490.

dissolved in its entirely any countervailing claim to territorial integrity on the part of their violent and oppressive parent state.[146]

Such remedial rights to secede are entitlements to *develop* statehood, rather than automatic conferrals of that status. Statehood must still be achieved by sufficiently instantiating political community via the antecedents of statehood, supported as appropriate by sufficient international recognition. Nonetheless, the existence of this right is indispensable for explaining why Bangladesh was able to emerge at all, notwithstanding India's seemingly unlawful use of force within East Pakistan.[147] Given Islamabad's military superiority, some manner of international intervention would always have been necessary before Bangladesh could demonstrate either effectiveness or independence. However, East Pakistan declared independence before any intervention took place: before, in other words, it had the logistical capacity to develop as an independent state, free from the military oppression of West Pakistan. Given the international peace principle, only East Pakistan's prior and remedial right to secede could explain how Bangladesh could emerge and be recognised so swiftly.[148] Unlike the emergence of states such as the Republics of Angola, Mozambique, or Guinea-Bissau, Bangladesh was not an ex-colony struggling against a recalcitrant imperial power to assert its acknowledged right to external self-determination.[149] Moreover, although East Pakistan was ethnically, culturally, and linguistically distinct from the West,[150] the same holds for many sub-state entities in relation to which no freestanding right to secession is implicated by international practice.

Conversely, the total oppression of East Pakistan explains its entitlement to remedial emergence, notwithstanding any procedural illegality perpetrated by India. Unlike violations of Article 2(4) designed to exert inter-governmental

146 Nicholson warns against arguments of this kind, calling them 'largely after-the-fact explanation[s] of an event that might be explicable in some other way': (n 1) 184. However, within an area of practice as factually complex as that of state creation, it would seem as though such reconstructions – for that is what such arguments clearly are – are not only justifiable but also the only sort of conclusive analyses we can hope to achieve. A superior characterisation is provided by Crawford (n 2) 142, with whom I agree: '…it is hard to conceive of any non-colonial situation more apt for the description "*carence de souveraineté*" than East Bengal after 25 March 1971. Genocide is the clearest case of abuse of sovereignty, and this factor, together with the territorial and political coherence of East Bengal in 1971, qualified East Bengal as a self-determination unit'.

147 van den Driest (n 131) 346; Christian Okeke, *Controversial Subjects of Contemporary International Law* (Rotterdam University Press 1974) 142–157.

148 Franck (n 145); Salmon (n 145).

149 UNGA Resolution 3181 (XXVIII) (17 December 1973) UN Doc A/RES/3181(XXVIII), para 1.

150 Willem van Schendel, *A History of Bangladesh* (Cambridge University Press 2015), particularly Chapters 11 to 15.

domination, whether through the annexation, conquest, or otherwise unjustified subversion of extant communities, India's use of force in 1971 is better understood as an unlawful means of securing a legally mandated end.[151] On this interpretation, the international peace principle was not engaged, even though the prohibition on the threat or use of force may have been, because the force in question was not the sole basis for state creation but merely the method through which an independent right to secession was secured.[152] None of this goes so far as to render lawful any otherwise unlawful uses of force. It does, however, entail that where countervailing claims to territorial integrity are removed by the right to secede, any unlawful uses of force that may occur do not prevent statehood from accruing. This conclusion, I suggest, is far more appealing than understanding Bangladesh to have emerged because India forced the international community to accept a *fait accompli*. Indeed, assuming my foregoing argument to be correct, the absence of collective action, exemplified by Resolution 2793's silence on the issue of external self-determination,[153] constituted a failure on the part of the international community to support the emergence of Bangladesh through legally authorised intervention.[154]

4.6 CONCLUSION

The procedural principles of state creation can be summarised as follows: First, the 'recognition principle' holds that formal recognition by foreign governments, while not necessary for statehood, strengthens extant claims unless such recognition would, in all the relevant circumstances, operate so as to undermine the moral and ethical values of political community. In that event, a collective duty of non-recognition supplants the default liberty to recognise that each state possesses. Second, the 'referendum principle' holds that, at least in the ordinary course of events, a weak rebuttable presumption against statehood

[151] Naturally, this is not the position that India adopted, see: Nigel Rodley, 'Humanitarian Intervention' in Marc Weller (ed.), *The Oxford Handbook of the Use of Force in International Law* (Oxford University Press 2015) 781.

[152] This is what distinguishes the emergence of Bangladesh from the attempted creation of entities such as Donetsk, Luhansk, and the Republic of Crimea. Russia's cynical invocation of remedial secession, complete with apparently unevidenced allegations of genocide, lacks the clear factual basis present in the former case, see: *Allegations of Genocide under the Convention on the Prevention and Punishment of the Crime of Genocide (Ukraine v Russian Federation)* (Provisional Measures, Order of 16 March 2022) [2022] ICJ Rep 211, para 59.

[153] UNGA Resolution 2793 (XXVI) (7 December 1971) UN Doc A/RES/2793(XXVI).

[154] That inaction might be explained by a desire to avoid protracted conflict between two states then committed to the development of nuclear weapons. (Although I do not discuss them here, similar international failures might be said to have occurred in relation to the attempted secession of Biafra from Nigeria (1967–1970) and some of the attempts of Kurdistan to secede from Iraq.)

will arise unless an appropriate independence referendum is provided, at least in the absence of an appropriate public justification for why facilitating public participation is not possible. If such a presumption arises, a greater degree of either or both foreign recognition and the demonstrable satisfaction of the antecedents of statehood will be required. Third, the 'negative self-determination principle' holds that the accrual of statehood will be temporarily blocked wherever an entity arises so as to cause mass disenfranchisement or political subordination. Only when that situation is resolved in favour of sufficient political inclusion can state creation proceed. Fourth, the international peace principle holds that statehood will be impossible where the sole basis for the emergence of a new entity is an unlawful use or threat of force within the meaning of Article 2(4). This does not cover genuinely internal military or paramilitary struggles, nor does it apply in cases where an entitlement to remedial secession pertains; however, where it does exist, that prohibition is absolute. Fifth, the territorial integrity principle holds that a rebuttable presumption against statehood arises in all circumstances where state creation is attempted without either the consent or the dissolution of the parent state. This presumption can be overcome where nascent entities have either or both widespread foreign recognition and a clear instantiation of political community through the antecedents of statehood, assuming that no other procedural principles have been breached. Moreover, the presumption can be removed altogether in circumstances where the nascent entity gains a right to remedial secession. In the latter case, such a right arises where the normative basis for territorial integrity itself is undermined *vis-à-vis* the seceding entity, by virtue of extreme violent oppression exacted upon the population of the territory in question.

These conclusions, taken together with the antecedents of statehood, raise a crucial point about state creation in general. The emergence of new states will rarely result from single acts. Sometimes specific events, such as the promulgation of a 'constitutive' treaty text or an internationally monitored independence referendum, can have singular importance. In particular, they can help determine the date of commencement, upon which a new state is formally deemed to exist. Nonetheless, statehood as political community suggests that the status of nascent entities turns upon the outcome of a holistic judgement, taking into account not only the internal properties of a given community in light of their unique historical circumstances and contemporary social context but also an assessment of the process through which they emerge. What matters is always the degree to which the moral and ethical values of a political community are instantiated by a nascent entity *and* whether that entity arises in a manner consistent with respect for political ethics itself.

PART II

STABILITY, LEGITIMACY, AND DEMOCRACY

5

The Stability Thesis

In Part I of this book, I argued that statehood accrues only when genuine political communities emerge in a manner coherent with the ethical value of politics. This characterisation of international law challenges more traditional understandings of its normative content. In Part II, I defend this rational reconstruction from two potential criticisms. In short, these criticisms are that statehood as political community is either too morally ambitious as a reconstruction of international law or else not ambitious enough. The first holds that international law – and in particular those elements governing state creation – should eschew considerations of political ethics and instead focus upon maintaining international stability. That is the concern of this chapter, which investigates whether an exclusive focus upon the importance of maintaining stability in international relations can provide a convincing reconstruction of the law that governs state creation. The suggestion that stability might possess this explanatory power, which I call the 'stability thesis', can be found in Steven Ratner's claim that the 'thin justice of international law' is first and foremost concerned with the promotion of peace,[1] and in Patrick Capps' emphasis upon the stability-value of 'effectiveness' when it comes to creating new states.[2] Finally, it can be found in the arguments of those such as Lassa Oppenheim and Prosper Weil, who suggest that the value of international law in general turns upon its ability to forestall (and swiftly resolve) international disputes.[3]

[1] Steven Ratner, *The Thin Justice of International Law: A Moral Reckoning of the Law of Nations* (Oxford University Press 2015) 184–190. See also Ratner's assertion that the promotion of international peace is one of the 'basic values' of international law (at 65).

[2] Patrick Capps, *Human Dignity and the Foundations of International Law* (Hart Publishing 2009) 258–264.

[3] Lassa Oppenheim, 'The Science of International Law: Its Task and Method' (1908) 2 *American Journal of International Law* 313, 314; Prosper Weil, 'Towards Relative Normativity in International Law?' (1983) 77(3) *American Journal of International Law* 413; Ingrid Wuerth, 'International Law in the Post-Human Rights Era' (2017) 96 *Texas Law Review* 279.

The stability thesis also provides one plausible reconstruction of Crawford's claim that 'effectiveness is the dominant principle' governing state creation.[4] As I shall argue, the emphasis Crawford's formulation places upon social facticity – to the effective exclusion of moral judgements – coheres quite strongly with at least one version of the stability thesis and so provides an important and *prima facie* plausible alternative to statehood as political community, particularly as regards my own arguments about how 'effectiveness' should be understood.

One brief word of clarification. Like statehood as political community itself, the stability thesis need not hold the values it emphasises to be the *only* ones relevant to the law of state creation. For instance, the importance of treating like cases alike is arguably always relevant to questions of when and why new states arise, and that principle at least seemingly implicates both fairness and the international rule of law. Indeed, since the value of the rule of law might be cashed out in a number of ways, this implies that considerations beyond those of international stability might be implicated wherever new states arise, even if the stability thesis is true. Nonetheless, like statehood as political community, the stability thesis *is* committed to the idea that the values it emphasises have explanatory primacy *vis-à-vis* state creation. It claims that it is impossible to understand the existence, legal implications, or normative salience of the principles that govern the emergence of statehood without understanding that the promotion of international stability is their primary function.

Although this chapter is largely critical of that claim, it has some constructive implications. Relative stability in international relations *does* matter – that much seems impossible to deny – so the real question is to what extent the importance of its promotion governs the emergence of states. The following critique will establish just how much justificatory and explanatory work stability can do in this area of law: an exercise that enhances our understanding of statehood as political community itself. In particular, I argue that whilst it is normatively imperative for the law of state creation to remain consistent with the maintenance of global peace, statehood as political community in fact fares no worse than the stability thesis in that respect, notwithstanding the premium the latter places upon the avoidance of all conflict.

5.1 CHARACTERISING THE STABILITY THESIS

The stability thesis holds that legal statehood can and should accrue only under particular conditions because those conditions are conducive to peace

[4] James Crawford, *The Creation of States in International Law*, 2nd edition (Oxford University Press 2007) 96.

and friendly relations at the international level. Two versions of this argument will be discussed here. The first claims that the only principles actually germane to state creation are those upon which almost the entire international community has already agreed. Restricting the content of the law to such a *modus vivendi* (allegedly) limits misunderstanding and disagreement, which in turn avoids conflict. I draw this austere reconstruction from 'normative positivists', such as Oppenheim and Weil, who famously argued for the importance of clarity and stability in international law.[5]

In what follows, I deny that international legal practice is currently conducive to such a stabilising convergence of views, and, as a result, this rational reconstruction fails to get off the ground. If this version of the stability thesis were true, then we would expect to see relatively few entrenched disagreements or divergences in approach amongst state representatives, international judges and arbitrators, and leading academics. Instead, we would expect to see a relatively stable and clear pattern of consistent beliefs and behaviour, which would *uncontroversially* yield a single set of standards governing emerging statehood. In this chapter, I claim that this is not so.

The second version of the stability thesis suggests that the principles most frequently cited as governing emerging statehood – no matter how potentially controversial their legal status may be – have normative implications that are conducive to peace and friendly relations, such that their existence and normative weight should be primarily understood in those terms. This chapter casts doubt upon that idea as well. Once more, my concern is not whether there are *any* stability-related considerations relevant to state creation: I assume that there are at least some. What concerns me is whether peace and friendly relations have explanatory primacy in relation to this area of law, to the exclusion of political ethics.

Both versions of the stability thesis fit the view that international peace is the ultimate purpose, not just of the law on emerging statehood but of international law in general. As such, they cohere with several claims about the moral foundations of the rights and powers of states that fall beyond the immediate scope of this book. These are worth exemplifying, however, because many international lawyers are likely to find them intuitive, which may be thought to strengthen the *prima facie* plausibility of the stability thesis.

For instance, proponents of either version of that thesis may also hold that state representatives should (and do) have the power to make international laws because their doing so also contributes to an international *modus vivendi*:

[5] Oppenheim (n 3); Weil (n 3).

states are more likely to comply with laws that their representatives played a role in generating.[6] Furthermore, as Ratner argues, equal status as lawmakers: (i) goes some way to combating the exploitation of the weak by the strong and (ii) increases the likelihood that weaker states will attempt to resolve disputes through legally regulated means.[7] This promotes peace and makes friendly relations at least a little more likely. Such claims are partly empirical and, whilst it is not clear how they could be tested, seem plausible enough to lend the stability thesis some credence.

To take another example, stability may well explain the presumption of state continuity. As evident from cases like the dissolution of the Socialist Federal Republic of Yugoslavia, the extinction of statehood is often occasioned by violence.[8] What is more, there are no obvious gains to be made in terms of international stability by an automatic revocation of statehood in response to domestic anarchy. This suggests that continuing statehood should be presumed unless there are strong (stability-related) reasons for holding otherwise. This argument seems adequate to explain the reluctance of international practice to accept the loss of statehood once that status has accrued, at least in very many cases, and it stands in favour of both versions of the stability thesis that they cohere with such views.

Notwithstanding the force of these points, this chapter takes a critical view of the claim that stability has explanatory primacy in relation to the law that governs state creation. First, it denies that an international *modus vivendi* exists in relation to the law in question, given the disagreement and divergent practice that currently surrounds the creation of new states. Second, I argue that even if sufficient consensus did exist for a *modus vivendi* to emerge, such a coincidence of views could do relatively little to ensure international peace and security. Having argued that this version of the stability thesis fails in both respects, I then ask whether the principles most frequently cited as governing the emergence of new states have normative content that is particularly conducive to international peace and friendly relations. I contend that whilst some stability-value can be located in such principles, the degree to which that value pertains is insufficient to defend the second version of the stability thesis. At best, stability plays a secondary role to political community when it comes to understanding the creation of states under international law.

6 Martti Koskenniemi, *From Apology to Utopia: The Structure of International Legal Argument* (Cambridge University Press 2005) 17–23.

7 Ratner (n 1) 198–200.

8 Ibid 149–150, 162–165.

5.2 AMBIGUITY OVER THE RELEVANCE OF RECOGNITION

Whilst the statehood of some entities is paradigmatic, international legal practice contains considerable scope for disagreement over when and why that status arises. As canvassed in Chapter 4, one such ambiguity concerns the legal implications of new states being recognised by foreign governments. According to one view, international recognition constitutes statehood, whereas on the other, it is purely declaratory.[9] The traditional declaratory view is largely based upon Article 1 of the Montevideo Convention on the Rights and Duties of States, which, as referenced throughout Chapter 3, holds statehood to pertain wherever there is an independent and 'effective' government of a more or less defined territory and permanent population.[10] Composite views also exist, whereby the recognition of a 'sufficient' number of other states is necessary in addition to the Montevideo criteria, as do arguments that allow for either recognition or satisfaction of the Montevideo criteria to ground statehood.[11] As Chapters 3 and 4 detailed, statehood as political community provides an alternative view, both of the meaning of 'effectiveness' and of the contribution made to state creation by foreign recognition. In this chapter, I take a step back from these deliberately controversial claims to consider a range of more orthodox views. If the first version of the stability thesis were correct, we should expect to see at least an uncontroversial majority view, which can thereby function as a *modus vivendi* within international practice.

Some scholars argue that the 'pure' declaratory view predominates, at least amongst academic lawyers.[12] This may be true. However, even if it is, such uniform scholarly opinion would be insufficient to defend the notion that international law on this point constitutes a *modus vivendi*. The vast majority of state practice fits all three of the more orthodox views mentioned above, and agreement within the academy does not entail agreement amongst state representatives. Whilst state practice contains few statements to the effect that

9 Crawford (n 4) 12–22.

10 Rosalyn Higgins, *Problems and Processes: International Law and How We Use It* (Oxford University Press 1994) 39–42; Thomas Baty, *The Canons of International Law* (John Murray 1930) 11–13; Franz Von Liszt, *Das Völkerrecht: Systematisch Dargesellt* (Auflage 1904) 65–66, 70–72; Crawford (n 4) 37–89. I have not listed the final Montevideo criterion here because most of those who endorse the declaratory position accept Crawford's argument that 'the capacity to enter into relations with other states' is in a *result* of statehood, rather than an antecedent of it.

11 Higgins (n 10) 42; Gerald Kreijen, 'The Transformation of Sovereignty and African Independence: No Shortcuts to Statehood' in Gerald Kreijen (ed.), *State, Sovereignty and International Governance* (Oxford University Press 2002) 92; Rowan Nicholson, *Statehood and the State-Like in International Law* (Oxford University Press 2019) 127–141.

12 Crawford (n 4) 25.

recognition is constitutive, neither does it contain many outright denials of that proposition. Statements alluding to the importance of recognising communities with independent and effective governments *might* be motivated by a declaratory approach. However, they could just as easily be motivated by beliefs about the appropriate criteria for undertaking constitutive recognition. Consider, for example, the comments of the American Delegate to the United Nations Security Council on the topic of Israel in 1948:

> When [recognition] was exercised by my Government, *it was done as a practical step*, in recognition of realities; the existence of things and the recognition of a change that had actually taken place.[13] [Emphasis added]

There is nothing here that points conclusively in one direction, rather than the other. The delegate *might* have been referencing the effectiveness of Israeli territorial control, but the precise *legal* role this factor played in the United States' reasoning was left wholly undisclosed. Compounding such characteristic sidestepping of the underlying legal issues is the fact that many statements by state representatives deal only with the advisability of recognition in purely instrumental terms, focusing on practical and political advantages and disadvantages.[14]

Moreover, many statements that do invoke the relevant law are simply ambiguous on their face. For example, within Lord Carrington's speech to the House of Lords in 1980, which set out a change in British policy on the recognition of governments, his Lordship averred, 'we have decided that we shall no longer accord recognition to Governments. The British Government recognise States in accordance with common international doctrine'.[15] It *might* be argued that this language suggests the declaratory view, at least insofar as state recognition is implicated. Lord Carrington speaks of 'States' as receiving recognition, not 'putative states' or 'non-state entities'. But such fine textual parsing seems both artificial and unmotivated. The most natural reading is simply equivocal. A rational reconstruction of such material would bring greater determinacy by invoking normative considerations to make a (necessarily controversial) argument for why particular statements *should* be read one way and not the other. This, however, is not

[13] United Nations Security Council (UNSC) Official Records, No. 68, 3rd Year, p. 16.

[14] To take one example: Telegram From the Department of State to the Mission to the North Atlantic Treaty Organization and Regional Organizations National Archives and Records Administration, Document 108, Foreign Relations of the United States, 1964–1968, Volume XXI, Near East Region; Arabian Peninsula: https://history.state.gov/historicaldocuments/frus1964-68v21/d108#fn:1.3.2.1.6.61.6.4 (last accessed 2 October 2023).

[15] HL Deb 28 April 1980 vol 408 cols 1121–1122.

available on the first version of the stability thesis, which mandates an uncontroversial international consensus.

Finally, most established states meet all of the Montevideo criteria *and* have widespread recognition. Furthermore, for every unusual case pulling in one direction, there is a contravening example that fits the other view more easily. On the declaratory side of things, many entities are treated as though they are states by those that nonetheless deny them recognition. Israel, for example, is not recognised by many Arab states that nonetheless respect its territorial integrity by refraining from unauthorised flyovers with military aircraft. Similarly, the non-recognition of North Korea did not prevent that entity from being treated as a state for the purposes of applying international law to it during the Korean War.[16] Conversely, cases like Southern Rhodesia – where compliance with traditional understandings of the Montevideo criteria was met with almost total non-recognition – could easily pull in the opposite direction. Taiwan provides another example: it clearly satisfies Montevideo but is almost universally recognised as part of China, rather than as a separate state.[17] Conversely, the Vatican City is widely recognised as a state, despite fitting Montevideo rather awkwardly, at anything beyond a purely formal level. Statehood as political community, dependent as it is upon a controversial rational reconstruction, *departs* from this kind of ambiguity in international legal practice. The stability-based suggestion that the law of state creation embodies a *modus vivendi* sits far less happily with ambiguity of this sort.

5.3 AMBIGUITY WITHIN DECLARATORY VIEW

Whilst the constitutive theory admits only one variable in matters of state creation (that is, foreign recognition), the declaratory view admits the possibility of additional variables beyond the Montevideo criteria. The proposition that new states must not arise as a direct result of the unlawful use of force is one such possibility, and, notwithstanding cases such as Bangladesh, there is a solid line of international practice supporting that proposition. Some

16 Ian Brownlie, *International Law and the Use of Force by States* (Oxford University Press 1963) 380.

17 Taiwan's government does not claim statehood, which helps to explain Taiwan's lack of recognition. But explaining Taiwan's status requires more than the assertion that 'a government can only be recognised for what it claims to be' (D. P. O'Connell, 'The Status of Formosa and the Chinese Recognition Problem' (1956) 50 *American Journal of International Law* 405, 415). Governments sometimes claim to represent what they do not: the Taiwanese government's claim to represent 'Greater China' exemplifies this. In this respect, it is possible that Taiwan is both less and more than its government claims.

suggestions, however, are far more controversial and create serious difficulties for the first version of the stability thesis, insofar as it applies to the declaratory view of recognition. For instance, as discussed at some length in Chapter 4, it is arguable that Southern Rhodesia was never a state because its emergence violated the principle of self-determination. Under that principle, governments should not disenfranchise sections of their populations on the basis of their supposed racial traits, yet that is exactly what Southern Rhodesia was constituted to achieve.[18] So whilst the government of Southern Rhodesia represented an entity that seemed to satisfy Montevideo, its claim was blocked because it did not accept the *de jure* equal status of the ethnic groups under its claimed jurisdiction.

The point for now – quite independently of my arguments in Part I – is that the declaratory view makes space for disagreement over its 'criteria for statehood'. Are the Montevideo criteria enough, or are there more requirements that must be met? Some version of the negative self-determination principle seems a plausible candidate – and often receives academic support[19] – but examples of its application are not numerous enough to produce the sort of established trend required for an international *modus vivendi*.[20] We might tentatively expect most state representatives to accept some account of that principle, given the international community's reaction to Southern Rhodesia.[21] However, this would be a prediction, not evidence of consensus *per se*.[22] That episode might as easily evidence an *ad hoc* aversion to racism or support for an alternative criterion of representative government with universal suffrage. In Chapter 4, it was substantive considerations of political ethics that allowed us to cement the connection between this episode of collective non-recognition and the importance of collective self-determination. But such rational reconstruction is not available when a substantively uncontroversial *modus vivendi* is at issue: we would need a clear

[18] In particular, see the self-determination 'safeguard clause' in principle 5, paragraph 7 of UNGA Resolution 2625 (XXV) (24 October 1970) UN Doc A/RES/25/2625(XXV), Annex. See also: Antonio Cassese, *Self-Determination of Peoples: A Legal Reappraisal* (Cambridge University Press 1995) 108–118.

[19] For example: Crawford (n 4) 129–131.

[20] Perhaps the most comparable case – the non-recognition of South African Bantustans – cannot assist us because those entities were puppet states of South Africa in all but name, see: UNGA Resolution 2775E (XXVI) (29 November 1971) UN Doc A/RES/2775(XXVI)E; UNGA Resolution 3411D (XXX) (28 November 1975) UN Doc A/RES/3411(XXX)D. See Chapter 4 for more on this example.

[21] UNGA Resolution 2022 (XX) (5 November 1965) UN Doc A/RES/2022(XX); UNGA Resolution 2024 (XX) (11 November 1965) UN Doc A/RES/2024(XX).

[22] By 'consensus' I mean circumstances where the vast majority of beliefs (about the requirements for emergence) converge; this is less exacting than unanimity.

trend within international practice, demonstrating an unambiguous view amongst the majority of state representatives. This simply does not exist, due in part to the relatively limited number of data points available for us to form an empirical view one way or another. This leaves the declaratory view in a state of ambiguity, which enhances the potential for disagreement over precisely what its conditions for state creation might be. Ironically, this indeterminacy leaves the consensus-based version of the stability thesis worse off than statehood as political community, at least as far as clarity over these conditions is concerned.

5.4 AMBIGUITY WITHIN THE CONSTITUTIVE VIEW

Despite attributing statehood only to entities in receipt of foreign recognition, the constitutive view fares little better in terms of potential controversy. Several questions, in particular, persist. First, is constitutive recognition 'relative', such that entities gain statehood that is opposable against those who formally recognise them but not against those that do not? Alternatively, is it collective in that many acts of recognition are required before a new state can emerge 'objectively'?[23] Second, if recognition is collective, what constitutes 'sufficient' recognition for statehood to arise? Third, what role (if any) does collective recognition through the United Nations (UN) play?

On the first issue, both Lauterpacht and Kelsen took a relativistic approach.[24] For them, to take a couple of examples, Palestine would be a state for the purposes of its international relations with Russia and Tunisia but not when dealing with the United States or Israel. Similarly, Kosovo would be a state for the purposes of relations with the United Kingdom and Bulgaria but not when dealing with China or Brazil. I consider the independent 'stability-value' of this position below. For now, we must ask whether international practice supports such 'relativity' to the extent that a consensus exists in its favour. The answer is, once again, underdetermined by the available data. Whilst many governments publish the considerations that at least nominally guide their recognition decisions, they typically do not detail their understanding of the legal consequences of recognition.

23 On the distinction between 'subjectivist' and 'objectivist' understandings of statehood, see: Jean d'Aspremont, 'The International Law of Statehood: Craftsmanship for the Elucidation and Regulation of Births and Deaths in the International Society' (2014) 29 *Connecticut Journal of International Law* 201, 206–210.

24 Hersh Lauterpacht, *Recognition in International Law* (Cambridge University Press 1947) 50, 58; Hans Kelsen, 'Recognition in International Law: Theoretical Observations' (1941) 35(4) *American Journal of International Law* 605, 609.

Consider the example of Bosnia-Herzegovina. Although the Badinter Commission came down squarely on the side of the declaratory view when reporting on that entity's legal status,[25] Roland Rich argues that state practice at that time actually supported the constitutive view.[26] He claims that in many cases, international recognition was quite premature, evidencing an attempt to constitute Bosnia-Herzegovina as a state before the independence of its government could be established. Assume for now that this is true: on the available descriptive facts alone, it is nonetheless impossible to assess whether this supports a relativistic conception of constitutive recognition. One might think that a rush to recognise evidences a belief in the legal importance of widespread recognition. But as Lowe points out, foreign recognition has clear benefits for political stability, whatever its legal effect.[27] State representatives of course know this, meaning that a rush to recognise Bosnia-Herzegovina can also be explained by a desire to hurry things along politically. Relativity is not touched either way. It is perhaps no accident that the most common arguments levelled against relativistic constitutive recognition are conceptual rather than grounded in state practice.[28]

Now consider the alternative: that recognition is not relativistic and that a sufficiently large number of such acts will constitute a state so as to bind third parties. Many doctrinal scholars hold constitutive recognition to be collective in this way.[29] Two questions nonetheless persist. First, how widespread does such recognition need to be? Second, what role (if any) is occupied by the collective recognition mechanisms of the UN? In relation to the first, most established states enjoy near universal recognition. This reality, whilst limiting practical problems when it comes to the identification of existing states, makes it harder to answer whether any consensus exists on the legal implications of widespread recognition because we have fewer marginal cases through which to identify a reliable trend (without, of course, undertaking a

[25] *Conference on Yugoslavia, Arbitration Commission, Opinion 1* (1991) 92 ILR 162.

[26] Roland Rich, 'Recognition of States: The Collapse of Yugoslavia and the Soviet Union' (1993) 4 *European Journal of International Law* 33, 56.

[27] Vaughan Lowe, *International Law* (Oxford University Press 2007) 163.

[28] Crawford (n 4) 19–22; Krystyna Marek, *Identity and Continuity of States in Public International Law* (Librairie E. Droz 1954) 132–139, 145–150.

[29] Higgins (n 10) 42 n.11; Ti-Chiang Chen, *The International Law of Recognition with Special Reference to Great Britain and United States* (Frederick A. Praeger Inc. 1951) 18 n.41; Ralph Wilde, 'Recognition in International Law' in *Recognition of States: the Consequences of Recognition or Non-recognition in UK and International Law*, Summary of the International Law Discussion Group meeting held at Chatham House (4 February 2010) 7; Robert Jennings and Arthur Watts (eds.), *Oppenheim's International Law: Volume 1 Peace*, 9th edition (Oxford University Press 2008) 133; Cf. Crawford (n 4) 438.

controversial rational reconstruction). Take the example of Palestine, which on 29 November 2012 was given 'Non-Member Observer State' status by the UN General Assembly.[30] Assume for now that all votes in favour of this resolution were acts of recognition in Palestine's favour and the fact that they were taken within the context of the UN framework was immaterial. Assume also that Palestine was not a state before these votes were made. The question becomes whether 138 acts of recognition were sufficient to constitute Palestine as a state.[31] That is well over half the states currently existing, including three out of five permanent members of the UN Security Council (the United States voted against and the United Kingdom abstained). The most we can say solely on the basis of such descriptive facts is that a claim to statehood would be plausible.[32] As Marek points out, absent a substantive principle governing the requisite degree of recognition, the mere fact of a majority tells us nothing.[33] We would need to engage in rational reconstruction to move past this point; however, the version of the stability thesis now under discussion forbids us from doing so.

As this example also shows, UN mechanisms for collective recognition raise as many questions as they answer. This leads us to a final set of ambiguities. What is the legal effect (if any) of the General Assembly asserting the statehood of an entity? Is UN membership a means of collective recognition (or maybe an additional declaratory 'criterion')? There are generally recognised states that are not UN members, and some UN members remain unrecognised by others. Nonetheless, some authors consider an entity's membership status to be particularly probative in relation to its statehood. Martin Dixon argues that UN membership itself constitutes 'an almost irrebutable presumption of statehood', whilst non-membership does 'not necessarily constitute a denial'.[34] Similarly, John Dugard has argued that, through admission and directed non-recognition, the UN has 'for practical purposes become the collective arbiter of statehood'.[35] On the other hand, as Crawford points out, in most cases, the UN has admitted new members only

[30] UNGA Resolution 67/19 (29 November 2012) UN Doc A/RES/67/19.

[31] The vote was 138 in favour, 9 against and 41 abstaining, see: Press Release, 'UN General Assembly GA/11317. General Assembly Votes Overwhelmingly to Accord Palestine "Non-Member Observer State" Status in United Nations', 29 November 2012: www.un.org/press/en/2012/ga11317.doc.htm (last accessed 2 October 2023).

[32] John Quigley, *The Statehood of Palestine* (Cambridge University Press 2010) 234–235.

[33] Marek (n 28) 133.

[34] Martin Dixon, *Textbook on International Law* (Oxford University Press 2013) 118; Jure Vidmar, *Democratic Statehood in International Law: The Emergence of New States in Post-cold War Practice* (Bloomsbury Publishing 2013) 239.

[35] John Dugard, *Recognition and the United Nations* (Grotius Publications 1987) 126.

after regional disputes over their status have been resolved bilaterally.[36] Even Bangladesh, whose admission was called for by the UN General Assembly in November 1972, was not actually admitted until December 1974, by which time its statehood had already been recognised by Pakistan.[37] The 1972 resolution may have had a political impact, in the broader sense of *realpolitik*, but this alone cannot establish its legal effect. The legal ambiguity of such measures – and of admissions decisions themselves – must be accepted if our search is for a *modus vivendi*: there is not enough evidence of consensus on the legal effect of such resolutions amongst state representatives. The substantive ethical considerations that statehood as political community uses to impose coherence and to increase determinacy are not available under this version of the stability thesis, and therefore, once again, the latter is left worse off in terms of legal clarity, despite the emphasis it nominally places upon that interpretive ideal.

5.5 A FURTHER POSSIBILITY AND SOME CONCLUSIONS

In addition to these more traditional versions of the declaratory and constitutive views, it is worth noting Vidmar's argument that (post-Cold War) practice requires states to emerge from a 'democratic political process'.[38] He argues that *neither* recognition nor the Montevideo criteria have a monopoly on the emergence of new states. At best, they are factors to be considered during state creation.[39] On his account, the easiest way a new state can emerge is through the consensual dissolution of the 'parent' state, or through that community's consent.[40] In the absence of this, Vidmar argues that new claims to statehood must be ratified through a political process – involving international administration and/or constitutive acts of recognition – that places emphasis on popular referendums and commitments to maintain representative institutions.[41] What is more, he accepts that sometimes these modes of state creation blur into each other, so that, for example, an internationalised administration can procure the consent of the parent state.[42] Whatever its substantive merits (Vidmar does not attempt rational reconstruction), this close reading of

36 Crawford (n 4) 182.

37 UNGA Resolution 2937 (XXVII) (29 November 1972) UN Doc A/RES/2937(XXVII); UNGA Resolution 3203 (XXIX) (17 September 1974) UN Doc A/RES/3202(XXIX); UNSC Resolution 351 (10 June 1974) UN Doc S/RES/351.

38 Vidmar (n 34) 235, 242. For substantive discussion of his views, see Chapter 4.

39 Ibid 10.

40 Ibid 63, 66–77.

41 Ibid 63, 78–138, 169–199, 242, 247–248, 253.

42 Ibid 63.

international practice is directly at odds both with the constitutive and declaratory views of recognition, serving as further evidence for the ambiguity that practice creates.

Assessing whether the consensus-based version of the stability thesis fits international practice does not require us to resolve the recognition debate or to ease the tensions within the declaratory and constitutive views. It suffices to note that, because legal practice remains ambiguous, the existence of a *modus vivendi* is doubtful. True, international politics is not mired in endless disagreement over the status of putative states. But this does not entail a causal link between current practice surrounding state creation and the maintenance of international stability. Entrenched disagreement can be avoided in international relations through *ad hoc* compromise without the need for generally accepted legal standards. Returning to a previous example, Taiwan enjoys legally binding agreements with many states, including bilateral investment treaties with India and Thailand (amongst others), despite its atypical status.[43] It is a member of a number of international organisations, such as the WTO, and party to a number of multilateral treaties, such as the Convention for the Conservation of the Southern Blue-fin Tuna (1993).

This suggests that case-by-case compromise may achieve stability even without an established consensus on the applicable international principles. This is not to say that widely accepted standards, where they exist, do not enhance stability to at least some degree. Neither is it to claim that consensus-based international law might not have some other value. The point is that, given the possibility of *ad hoc* compromise, there is no reason to believe that relative stability in international relations is evidence of *generally accepted* criteria for the emergence of new states. The stability thesis cannot look to the absence of endemic unworkability in inter-state politics to confirm its explanatory power. Indeed, this state of affairs supports the stability thesis no more than any other interpretation of the relevant law, including statehood as political community, which, as we have seen, has additional normative resources through which to promote the coherence and determinacy of the relevant legal standards. At bottom, considering the extent of disagreement and ambiguity in the relevant practice we can conclude that, whatever its substantive merits, the notion that a valuable *modus vivendi* governs state creation simply does not fit.

43 Agreement between the India Taipei Association in Taipei and The Taipei Economic and Cultural Center in New Delhi on The Promotion and Protection of Investments (adopted 17 October 2002, entered into force 28 November 2002); Agreement between the Taipei Economic and Trade Office in Thailand and the Thailand Trade and Economic Office in Taipei for the Promotion and Protection of Investments (adopted and entered into force 30 April 1996).

5.6 THE STABILITY-VALUE OF CONSENSUS ON THE EMERGENCE OF STATES

International relations can operate quite stably by way of *ad hoc* compromise. So just how instrumental is it for peace and friendly relations that a legal consensus exists on state creation? Other areas of international law seem more directly implicated in the avoidance of war, given that new states arise relatively infrequently.[44] Take the prohibition on the use or threat of force in international relations.[45] The pain and suffering, breaches of individual rights, disruption of politics, environmental damage, and loss of cultural artefacts risked by international and domestic armed conflicts are clearly worth avoiding.[46] A stability-based explanation of that principle seems sensible. What is more, following Franck, we might accept that part of this stability-value lies in that principle's more-or-less uncontested content: the fact that the prohibition is categorical and generally accepted reinforces its role in the promotion of peace.[47] However, this would still hold in circumstances where the law governing state creation is not subject to the same level of clarity or agreement.

Of course, rational reconstructions of emerging statehood sensitive to the value of peace may well be better justified, in the sense of being more normatively attractive, than those that are not. Moreover, reconstructions that cohere with principles like those expressed in Article 2(4) of the UN Charter will be stronger in terms of their 'global' coherence with international law in general. But consistency and coherence are not the same as identity. As argued in Part I, statehood as political community sets great store by the maintenance of peace, yet nonetheless does not make the avoidance of conflict as an end in itself. By contrast, the version of the stability thesis currently under discussion is not just *sensitive* to the importance of peace but takes the avoidance of conflict to be such a pressing and important goal that no criteria for statehood can or should arise in the absence of international consensus.

What would be gained, normatively speaking, by accepting this view? It is hard to see how peace would be better served if it were adopted. Not only do peace and friendly relations have independent political and economic appeal,

44 Crawford (n 4) 727–740.

45 There is some empirical evidence to show that this principle (and others) in fact contributes to greater peace: James Crawford, *Chance, Order, Change: The Course of International Law, General Course on Public International Law* (Brill 2014) 44–47.

46 Ratner (n 1) 67–70, 103–126.

47 Thomas Franck, 'Humanitarian Intervention' in Samantha Besson and John Tasioulas (eds.), *The Philosophy of International Law* (Oxford University Press 2010) 539–542.

but other legal principles already promote them.[48] Conversely, any reconstruction of state creation that values *more* than peace and friendly relations will have a justificatory advantage if it maintains a sufficient level of respect for those values. Statehood as political community is one such theory: the antecedents of statehood outlined in Chapter 3 and the procedural principles detailed in Chapter 4 all reflect the aversion to endemic conflict, both domestic and international, expressed throughout Chapters 1 and 2.

But what if an international *modus vivendi* would also facilitate a reduction of contentious disputes, rather than 'only' promoting their resolution through peaceful means? International disputes cost resources, whether conducted before adjudicative bodies or otherwise, and the price is ultimately paid by the populations of the states involved. Perhaps purely consensus-based standards on the creation of new states would minimise divisiveness by presumptively settling or avoiding highly contested questions? That *might* reduce the number and length of disputes surrounding the legal status of particular entities. However, as the following example suggests, we can afford to be sceptical about this possibility.

Kosovo has been recognised by 117 UN member states since its declaration of independence on 17 February 2008, raising a plausible but not uncontroversial claim to statehood.[49] If the principles of state creation were less contentious, Kosovo's long-disputed status would likely have been less controversial. This counterfactual may seem attractive. However, the benefits that consensus would afford should not be overstated. First, the disputed status of a territorial unit does not preclude it from legally regulated international relations: non-state entities are often treated as if they were states for certain purposes. (That is not to say that no moral harm is done by failures to recognise statehood, only that recognition is not necessary for *stable* relations.) Second, recognition does not imply that friendly relations will always follow, whilst internationally abjured states may suffer from *internal* instability even though they are generally recognised. Under our imagined conditions of a clear consensus on international law, Kosovo would probably still have friendly relations with those states well disposed towards it and either indifference or acrimony from others. Once again, this is not to dismiss the value of clear international law *tout court*, only to put its relative importance into perspective within the context of state creation.

[48] Michael Walzer (*Just and Unjust War* (Basic Books 2015) 57) suggests that the principle of territorial integrity might be justified in similar terms.

[49] www.kosovothanksyou.com/ (last accessed 2 October 2023); see also the recent finding of the Court of Justice of the European Union in: Case C-632/20 *Spain v Commission* (CJEU, 17 January 2023).

5.7 THE STABILITY-VALUE OF CONSTITUTIVE RECOGNITION

I now turn to the second version of the stability thesis, which holds that the law governing state creation is best characterised in terms of its *substantive* contributions to peace and friendly relations, whether or not it is capable of functioning as a *modus vivendi*. I draw this position from Ratner's claim that international law is first and foremost concerned with the promotion of peace[50] and from Capps' emphasis upon the stability-value of 'effectiveness' when it comes to identifying new states.[51] To critique it, I consider whether constitutive recognition and/or the most commonly cited declaratory criteria are best understood in terms of their stability-value. Once again, my interest is in the explanatory *primacy* of stability. I do not doubt that peace and friendly relations matter, nor do I deny the importance of coordination and the speedy resolution of disputes. However, I doubt that these considerations have overriding importance when it comes to understanding the law that governs state creation: on the contrary, they make for a somewhat implausible and 'thin' rational reconstruction.

First, consider the proposition that a state can only exist where it has received the recognition of other states, either in aggregate or on a relative basis. For Lauterpacht, the stability-value of the constitutive view lies in its simplicity. He claimed that stable international relations require a simple means for identifying the subjects of international law, and since there is no central authority to perform that function, the burden must fall upon state representatives.[52] According to him, any criteria for statehood beyond recognition would necessarily produce controversy, both over the appropriateness of those criteria as such and also over how they should be applied in practice. My previous discussion of the declaratory view lends some credence to his fears: there is both ambiguity and controversy there, after all. However, international law is replete with controversial principles and their applications to particular facts. What makes it so important to avoid controversy about state creation?[53] As argued above, eliminating controversy on this topic would do relatively little to enhance international stability. Furthermore, as Crawford points out, international law has relatively few state-subjects, and the status of the vast majority is not in question.[54] This being so, serious disagreement will arise only in hard cases, where controversy would most likely exist anyway.

50 Ratner (n 1) 184–190.
51 Capps (n 2) 258–264.
52 Lauterpacht (n 24) 55.
53 Crawford (n 4) 20.
54 Ibid 21.

What else might be said for the stability-value of the constitutive view? It may help states avoid unforeseen liability, thereby reducing the number of contentious international disputes. On the relativistic account of constitutive recognition, it is conceivable that states would only have obligations to the entities that they recognise. Since recognition is usually held to be a legally unregulated choice, this would appear to place the creation of inter-state obligations at least partially under the obligated state's control.[55] Furthermore, official acts of recognition are often easier to discern than the more complex and normatively laden assessments that, in Chapters 3 and 4, I argued to be necessary when identifying the satisfaction of statehood's antecedents and international law's five procedural principles. This might suggest that even on the collective account of constitutive recognition, the holders of inter-state rights would be easier to identify, which may well lessen the chances of states being landed with unforeseen legal obligations. As I shall now argue, whilst there is some truth to this, we can afford to be sceptical about the normative weight of these stability-focused considerations.

5.7.1 *Relativistic Recognition*

There are two points to be made here. First, it is generally agreed that some international obligations exist *erga omnes* (that is, on the part of all states and owed to every member of the international community). Some of these can be derived from the rights of self-determination units and 'the outlawing of acts of aggression, and of genocide…[and] the principles and rules concerning the basic rights of the human person, including protection from slavery and racial discrimination', whilst others include a number of obligations 'relating to preservation of the environment of the high seas' and several obligations under international humanitarian law.[56] Relativistic constitutive recognition sits uneasily with the existence of such obligations. If an entity only counts as a state for those who recognise it, then it can only have rights as a state against entities that engage with it on that basis. The very notion of states having

[55] Lauterpacht controversially regarded it to be a legal duty ((n 24) 61–66, 73–76). It is generally accepted that a state can have a duty not to recognise entities under certain circumstances (Crawford (n 4) 157–173). However, the existence of this duty would, at most, *forestall* inter-state obligations.

[56] *Barcelona Traction, Light and Power Company Ltd (Belgium v Spain)* (Merits) [1970] ICJ Rep 3, 32; *Application of the Convention on the Prevention and Punishment of the Crime of Genocide (Bosnia and Herzegovina v Serbia and Montenegro)* (Preliminary Objections: Judgement) [1996] ICJ Rep 595, p. 616; *Case Concerning East Timor (Portugal v Australia)* (Merits) [1995] ICJ Rep 90, p. 120; *Legal Consequences of the Construction on a Wall in Occupied Palestinian Territory* (Advisory Opinion) [2004] ICJ Rep 136, p. 199.

rights correlative to obligations owed to the entire international community would be nonsense because such a community could only ever 'exist' relatively speaking. The difficulty is not so much that this risks incoherence in the law, although it does.[57] Rather, the established practice surrounding *erga omnes* obligations would most likely create legal controversy if it were forced to exist alongside relativistic constitutive recognition. This suggests that, in one respect at least, the relativistic model is as apt to create disagreement as to promote stability.[58]

Second, whilst entities without statehood can possess rights under international law, it is generally accepted that some rights belong to states alone. For instance, on many accounts, it is only state representatives who can create customary international law.[59] Whether we accept this or not, state representatives have a special place in international lawmaking because their explicit or implicit support for the existence of a principle is generally taken to be necessary.[60] Conversely, the law-making powers of international organisations

[57] Logical consistency, but not normative coherence, could abide *erga omnes* obligations being applicable amongst all mutually recognising entities: whilst such a position is *possible*, in the sense of inviting no self-contradiction, it renders 'international community' entirely empty. Nicholson makes an analogous but stronger claim of logical inconsistency in relation to *ius cogens* (peremptory) principles on the basis that relativistic recognition implies the relativity of international law *tout court*. This follows because, supposedly, under a relativist system of state creation the only international obligations possible are those arising between states that recognise each other, meaning that no principles with peremptory effect could exist, see: (n 11) 122–123). But this is debatable: relativistic recognition does not *logically entail* such extreme voluntarism, even though these positions are clearly consistent (and arguably coherent) with each other. After all, even the most committed voluntarist must assume at least one principle *not* based on consent (i.e., *pacta sunt servanda*), so there is no *logical* constraint upon them accepting more than one.

[58] Admittedly, this is speculation because no firm consensus exists in favour of this model. However, there is some basis for it in the confusion already caused (and resolved) in relation to the interplay between *erga omnes* obligations and the consent-based jurisdiction of the ICJ: *Armed Activities on the Territory of the Congo (New Application: 2002) (Democratic Republic of the Congo v Rwanda)* (Jurisdiction and Admissibility: Judgment) [2006] ICJ Rep 6, 32.

[59] Most often, this claim is nuanced by the argument that other entities enjoy a law-determining role only to the extent that they reflect or collect the practice of state representatives: Lowe (n 27) 90–93; James Crawford, *Brownlie's Principles on Public International Law*, 8th edition (Oxford University Press 2013) 42–43; *Case Concerning Military and Paramilitary Activities in and against Nicaragua (Nicaraagua v United States of America)* (Merits) [1986] ICJ Rep 14, para 188; Lewis Henkin, *International Law: Politics and Values* (Springer 2015) 26–44; Hugh Thirlway, *The Sources of International Law* (Oxford University Press 2014) 63–81.

[60] As Vaughn Lowe ((n 27) 45) notes: 'International lawyers and international tribunals still look primarily, if not exclusively, to the practices of States, and the practice of States is implicitly regarded as being the practice that is recorded in official publications, such as law reports, statutes, records of parliamentary proceedings, and statements issued by the departments of central government'.

and tribunals are contested, whilst non-state self-determination units are arguably incapable of contributing to customary law formation.[61] Such matters are controversial enough on their own. If an entity can possess statehood in some of its relations but not others, then the legal effect of its practice would be more complex and likely more controversial. This would hardly advance international stability: any rational reconstruction that suggested otherwise would be flawed.

It is also generally accepted that states have a greater degree of freedom in respect of their foreign policy and internal affairs than many non-state territorial units.[62] If correct, this implies a number of obligations of non-intervention but only where statehood pertains.[63] The ability to forestall these obligations via a refusal to grant recognition: (i) makes individual recognition decisions far more significant, which may well lead to animosity when disagreement emerges and (ii) seems independently inconsistent with peace and friendly relations. The stability thesis, as a result, cannot rely upon relativistic recognition to supply a method of state creation that is substantively conducive to conflict-avoidance.

5.7.2 *Collective Recognition and Recognition in General*

Collective recognition faces another set of complexities as far as stability is concerned, all of which stem from the 'internal' ambiguity of recognition itself. First, how many acts of recognition are required to constitute a state? If a few acts are sufficient, the obligations of the entire international community could be altered by a handful of states.[64] Under such conditions, the controversy risked by recognition would create its own tensions, potentially risking either a rush to recognise or a hesitance to do so, neither of which would aid stability. This is not the only issue. Assume instead that the requisite number of recognitions could be universally agreed upon and was relatively high: is an

61 I infer this from the state-centric nature of customary law-determination and the common the assertion that non-state territorial entities have a 'limited set of rights' and a 'qualified international status'. For example: Antonio Cassese, *Self-Determination of Peoples: A Legal Reappraisal* (Cambridge University Press 1995) 168–169; Malcolm Shaw, 'The International Status of National Liberation Movements' (1983) 5 *Liverpool Law Review* 19, 33–34; Crawford (n 59) 117–118, 123–124.

62 Charter of the United Nations (adopted 26 June 1945, entered into force 24 October 1945) 1 UNTS XVI, Article 2(7); [1986] ICJ Rep14, para 265.

63 *Corfu Channel (United Kingdom of Great Britain and Northern Ireland v Albania)*, (Merits) [1949] ICJ Rep 4, 35; UN Charter, Article 2(4); [1986] ICJ Rep 14, p. 107. It is arguable that this also gives rise to the law on foreign state immunity, see: Crawford (n 59) 489–506.

64 N. A. Maryan Green, *International Law: Law of Peace*, 3rd edition (Pitman 1987) 34.

official act of recognition always necessary, or is implicit recognition sufficient to constitute statehood?[65] It holds for either view of constitutive recognition that if implicit acts are sufficient, further problems arise.

According to Lauterpacht, whilst accrediting and receiving diplomatic representatives is 'properly regarded as both a mode of and as an irrebuttable presumption of recognition', bilateral treaties will only imply recognition where there is no reasonable doubt as to the intention of the recognising state.[66] It seems clear that the establishment or acceptance of an embassy is sufficient to evidence recognition of statehood, whereas that of a mere delegation is not: there would be little point in distinguishing the two otherwise.[67] But under what circumstances would it be unreasonable to doubt the recognition of statehood via bilateral treaty? Lauterpacht suggests that comprehensive treaties of commerce and navigation are particularly clear examples, but such multipurpose instruments are less common today than when he was writing.[68] This creates problems of scale *vis-à-vis* recognition and inter-state relations. For example, can bilateral investment treaties imply recognition? What about when combined with a double taxation agreement?

Singapore does not formally recognise Taiwan as a state. However, on 7 November 2013 both entities signed the Agreement between Singapore and the Separate Customs Territory of Taiwan, Penghu, Kinmen, and Matsu on Economic Partnership. That agreement addresses many traditional areas of commerce while also regulating electronic commerce, investment, and intellectual property cooperation. Is a multipurpose agreement such as this sufficient to imply recognition? If not, might it count towards such an implication? Brownlie believed that 'informal relations, without the intent to recognise in the political sense, especially if they persist, have probative value on the issue of statehood'.[69] This may suggest that such treaties have at least preliminary relevance. Indeed, even the particular terms of a treaty – for instance, whether entities like Taiwan are described merely as 'separate customs unions' – aid us only to the extent that they should, as a matter of general principle, be accorded priority over other considerations of the sort that Brownlie mentions. My point here is not that treaties of this kind *necessarily* entail recognition but that once we move beyond formal acts of recognition, the justificatory

65 Nii Lante Wallace-Bruce, *Claims to Statehood in International Law* (Carlton Press 1994) 74.
66 Lauterpacht (n 24) 378.
67 For example, in 2010, the United States accepted a Palestinian 'Delegation General' in Washington but continued its policy of refusing to recognise Palestinian statehood.
68 Lauterpacht (n 24) 378; John Coyle, 'The Treaty of Friendship, Commerce and Navigation in the Modern Era' (2013) 51 *Columbia Journal of Transnational Law* 302, 327–343.
69 Ian Brownlie, *Principles of Public International Law*, 5th edition (Clarendon Press 1998) 94.

connection between constitutive recognition and the stability thesis gets weaker because it gets progressively harder to determine how much 'inter-state' interaction is sufficient for recognition to become implied.

The final issue faced by a stability-focused reconstruction of constitutive recognition is perhaps the most important. Both versions of the constitutive view remove controversy from the law of state creation only by relegating it to the realm of unregulated international relations. Disagreement about recognition *policy* threatens the stability of international relations no less than disagreement over the content of the law. Avoiding legal controversy, for example by favouring recognition as the sole means for state creation, *might* prevent the law itself from becoming controversial, but it cannot eliminate whatever controversy nonetheless arises from its use. In fact, stability may well be served by subsuming such controversy within the law. A range of unprincipled motivations may hold sway in purely political decisions, whereas legal arguments must proceed within the procedural constraints of international legal practice. Given these points, it is difficult to see how the legal relevance of recognition can be explained primarily in terms of its stability-value.

5.8 THE STABILITY-VALUE OF THE DECLARATORY CRITERIA

Within the declaratory view, the elements with the most obvious stability-value are the Montevideo criteria, at least when 'effective' government is read restrictively to mean merely 'stable' government, rather than the normatively richer reconstruction entailed by statehood as political community. As Ratner points out, international peace is served by having territorial entities regulated by international law to the fullest degree possible (that is, as states), not least because this affords presumptive territorial integrity and participation in international lawmaking, both of which promote stability.[70] It is certainly plausible that, when 'effective' governments emerge, denying them statehood would most likely invite their animosity.[71] Nonetheless, Ratner admits that such a traditional interpretation of Montevideo does not possess an *unqualified* stability-value. Granting statehood to seemingly stable entities that emerge from secessionist movements will only enhance peace where the 'parent'

[70] Ratner (n 1) 187; Capps (n 2) 264–265; Jeremy Waldron, 'Two Concepts of Self-Determination' in Samantha Besson and John Tasioulas (eds.), *The Philosophy of International Law* (Oxford University Press 2010) 407; Allen Buchanan, *Justice, Legitimacy, and Self-Determination: Moral Foundations for International Law* (Oxford University Press 2004) 265.

[71] Thomas Baty, 'Can an Anarchy Be a State?' (1934) 28(3) *American Journal of International Law* 444.

state already expects and accepts that consequence.[72] Often, this requires the drawn-out involvement of the international community. Where there is controversy between the seceding entity and its parent, violence is apt to follow, as the recent histories of Kosovo, East Timor, and Palestine show. As Ratner points out, promising statehood whenever an effective government is established may exacerbate this problem by providing an incentive for secession.[73]

Adding to Ratner's point, many violently oppressive regimes maintain independent control of 'their' territory. Given this fact, understanding Montevideo *purely* in terms of relative stability risks indifference to tyranny. This would place the law of statehood in *prima facie* tension with those elements of international human rights law that protect our liberty: a difficulty that statehood as political community does not face. More to the current point however, violent oppression often produces revolts, which also endanger peace. Consider Syria, where, in March 2011, protests against the government of President Bashar al-Assad were met with force by security forces, prompting further protests and uprisings that spiralled downwards into a conflict with serious implications for the stability of the surrounding region.[74] As with many contemporary conflicts, the causes, events, and implications of the Syrian civil war are disputed. What can be said is that, prior to the events of 2011, President Assad's government was in factual control of Syria's territory to a substantial degree, albeit with not infrequent resort to authoritarian means.[75] Clearly, the satisfaction of a stability-focused reconstruction of the Montevideo criteria is no guarantee of peace.

True, the Montevideo criteria are often argued to underdetermine what is required for states to emerge. Recall my argument in Chapter 4 that an emerging entity in breach of the 'negative self-determination principle' may not be able to successfully claim statehood and that, where new communities emerge through the unlawful use of external force, their independence is blocked

[72] Ratner relies upon the examples of the internationalised decolonisation movement and the breakup of the Union of Soviet Socialist Republics ((n 1) 188).

[73] Ibid 187.

[74] Raymond Hinnebusch, Omar Imady and Tina Zintl, 'Civil Resistance in the Syrian Uprising: From Peaceful Protest to Sectarian Civil War' in Adam Roberts, Michael Willis, Rory McCarthy and Timothy Ash (eds.), *Civil Resistance in the Arab Spring: Triumphs and Disasters* (Oxford University Press 2016) 231, 239–240. For an interesting first-hand account of life under Assad's government throughout the 2011 protests, see: Khawla Dunia, 'And the Demonstrations Go On', Robin Moger (trans.) in Layla Al-Zubaidi and Mattew Cassel (eds.), *Writing Revolution: The Voices from Tunis to Damascus* (I.B. Tauris 2013) 179–208.

[75] For an analysis of the nature of government under Presidents Hafiz al-Assad and Bashar al-Assad, see: Lisa Wedeen, *Ambiguities of Domination: Politics, Rhetoric, and Symbols in Contemporary Syria*, 2nd edition (University of Chicago Press 1999).

(the international peace principle). Crawford makes broadly similar claims about international legal practice, albeit without invoking the normative resources of political ethics.[76] Such principles, together with the presumption of territorial integrity, seemingly promote stability by placing legal roadblocks in the path of secession and interventionist movements. Any plausible reconstruction of the law governing state creation must address this, and the stability thesis clearly does so.

However, as argued above, more than one explanation of the law governing the creation of new states might cohere with whatever stability-value these procedural principles possess. As I argued in Chapters 3 and 4, statehood as political community does exactly that. Therefore, even though we should accept the relative stability-value of principles such as negative self-determination and territorial integrity, that alone cannot demonstrate the *superior* explanatory power of the stability thesis. The most we can say is that these aspects of international law are consistent with any reconstruction that values peace.

Indeed, elements of these principles seem to pull in the other direction: Crawford suggests that the prohibition upon state creation through the unlawful use of force may be suspended where the emerging entity is a self-determination unit. In such circumstances, whatever right *to* statehood previously existed will survive the illegality in question.[77] There may well be value to such a principle, but it is difficult to reconstruct in terms of stability. Whilst it might be said to protect the legitimate expectations of self-determination units, this exception may also incentivise armed intervention whenever it is argued that an entity constitutes a self-determination unit. This happened, as discussed in Chapter 4, in relation to Bangladesh and more recently (although that argument was not plausible) in the cases of Donetsk and Luhansk. Since the law on self-determination units is subject to some ambiguity and, as recent events demonstrate, is also apt for deliberate misinterpretation and abuse, the stability-value of this principle is qualified at best.[78]

Even if a wholly traditional interpretation of Montevideo was widely accepted as sufficient for state creation, ambiguity might remain when attempting to identify whether the criteria therein have been satisfied. First, how stable must governmental control be for statehood to emerge? Crawford argues that international law 'lays down no specific requirements as to the

[76] Crawford (n 4) 139–147.

[77] Ibid 148.

[78] The Annex to UNGA Resolution 1541 (XV) (15 December 1960) UN Doc A/RES/1541(XV) provides guidance on this for entities that are neither trust nor mandated territories, for which there is no international agreement to the effect that the right exists. However, the application of the principles therein to concrete cases will almost always involve controversy.

nature and extent of…control, except that it include some degree of maintenance of law and order and the establishment of basic institutions'.[79] The evident looseness of this interpretation may well produce controversy, such that we cannot expect too much from it when our goal is to forestall or settle disputes. Admittedly, this is no less the case for the interpretation of 'effectiveness' entailed by political community; however, that reconstruction of state creation does not turn upon the avoidance of legal controversy to the same extent that the stability thesis does. Nonetheless, I would contend that it certainly fairs no worse than the stability thesis in this respect: some controversy seems inevitable.

It *is* generally accepted (whatever the merits of this position might be) that statehood requires unified government, so that the institutions of a territory must in some sense 'work together', rather than operating in a wholly independent or 'competing' manner. For instance, in *Western Sahara*, the ICJ held the Islamic Republic of Mauritania was incorrect to assert that in 1884 the Bilad Shinguitti was anything more than an area with a certain cultural, linguistic, economic, and religious character. At that time, emirates such as the Adrar, Trarza, and Tagant, as well as a number of less structurally complex communities, all enjoyed considerable political independence within the Bilad Shinguitti. That independence was (at least allegedly) too great to justify any legal personality, let alone discrete statehood, on the part of the Bilad Shinguitti itself.[80] This principle *might* further international stability, if only insofar as it would seem to simplify international relations; however, its stability-value must be viewed as marginal, given the already referenced capacity of international relations to produce stability via *ad hoc* arrangements and compromise.

Moreover, the above point does nothing to settle the question (noted in Chapter 3) of just how much factual control governments must have over their claimed territory. Take the example of the DRC, which came into being on 30 June 1960, following a grant of independence by Belgium. Within the next few months, the government broke down into two factions as the nascent state descended into a conflict marked by nationalist secession movements, illegal foreign intervention, widespread international aid, and peacekeeping interventions by UN forces.[81] Notwithstanding the lack of independent governmental control, Crawford argues (citing as evidence its swift international

[79] Crawford (n 4) 59; *Western Sahara* (Advisory Opinion) [1975] ICJ Rep 12, para 94.

[80] (n 79) para 147.

[81] UNGA Resolution 1498 (XV) (22 November 1960) UN Doc A/RES/1498(XV); UNGA Resolution 1599 (XV) (15 April 1961) UN Doc A/RES/1599(XV); UNSC Resolution 143 (13 July 1960) UN Doc S/RES/143; UNSC Resolution 145 (22 July 1960) UN Doc S/RES/145; UNSC Resolution 146 (1 August 1960) UN Doc S/RES/146; see also Crawford (n 4) 56–57.

recognition and unopposed UN membership) that 'there can be little doubt that in 1960 the Congo was a State in the full sense of the term'.[82]

To rationalise this, Crawford notes that the Belgian grant of independence left the DRC's territory otherwise unclaimed, contrasting it with situations in which territorial title is opposed and where the degree of factual control must be greater for statehood to arise.[83] Whilst that may be true – I adopt the same position in Chapter 3 – it nonetheless undermines the explanatory power of the stability thesis. True, *denying* statehood to the DRC in the 1960s would have done little to enhance the stability of the region, particularly in light of the foreign intervention prevalent throughout the conflict. However, the alternatives are similarly stark. On the one hand, if the degree of governmental control required is so low that it would always admit entities like the DRC in 1960, then it is capacious enough to admit near anarchy. That would rob it of the analytical power required to address disputes over state creation, since almost anything would count as 'effective government' for such purposes.[84] On the other hand, if efficacy should have *relative* weight in certain situations, then the possibility arises for debate over what other factors should be determinative and when. None of this is even to mention the vexed question of how high the bar of government effectiveness should be set to *maximise* international stability, even assuming that one could investigate this with any real degree of rigour.

As this exemplifies, there are two stability-related difficulties with the Montevideo efficacy requirement. First, controversy and misunderstanding are risked when settling upon a sufficient standard of control. Second, the complex facts involved in a particular case might make it difficult to identify when that standard (whatever it is) has been met in practice.[85] The second issue may also arise when trying to judge how *independent* a government must be for statehood to emerge.[86] The chief difficulty here is distinguishing the influence of foreign policies, which is a normal feature of international politics, from instances of intergovernmental domination, which derogate from *de facto* independence (see Chapter 3). For instance, in Syria on 27 September

82 Crawford (n 4) 57.

83 Ibid 58–59.

84 On this basis, Crawford's conception of the declaratory view has sometimes been identified with a denial of the efficacy principle as the central criterion for statehood, see: Thomas Grant, 'Defining Statehood: The Montevideo Convention and Its Discontents' (1998) 37 *Columbian Journal of Transnational Law* 403, 435.

85 Colin Warbrick, 'States and Recognition in International Law' in Malcolm Evans (ed.), *International Law*, 2nd edition (Oxford University Press 2006) 233.

86 Although he is relatively optimistic about the ease identifying instances of *de facto* independence, Crawford admits that 'the...degree of real governmental power at the disposal of the authorities of the putative State...may raise serious problems of appreciation' ((n 4) 72).

1941, French Delegate-General Catroux read a proclamation to the effect that the then-mandate territory was to 'exercise at once all rights and prerogatives of an independent and sovereign state, limited only by the exigencies of the war and the security of its territory'.[87] The United Kingdom afforded recognition soon after.[88] However, the United States refused to recognise Syria's statehood on the basis that the degree of independence held by the Syrian government was too limited, given the power exercised by General Catroux in civil matters on France's behalf.[89] The United States only recognised the independence of Syria on 5 September 1944, following a transfer of governmental powers (including 'the right to make law and legislate') from the French Delegate-General, which began on 1 January 1944.[90] On the assumption that Class A mandate territories did not possess statehood by default upon their creation, the United States was probably correct in its approach to independence. However, the British position (mistaken or not) suggests that the scope for disagreement over *de facto* independence can be sufficient to place that antecedent in tension with the stability thesis, at least on complex facts like those in 1940s Syria.

Somewhat ameliorating these problems, Crawford identifies two presumptions related to formal independence that operate upon the requirement to demonstrate *de facto* governmental autonomy. First, formal independence, whether granted by a parent state (as in the example of the DRC) or asserted in a domestic constitution, will result in a presumption of statehood unless the relevant State's creation was attended by serious illegality (see the connected discussion

87 Telegram from The Consul General at Beirut (Engert) to the Secretary of State, Document 381, Foreign Relations of the United States Diplomatic Papers, 1941, The British Commonwealth; The Near East and Africa, Volume III, p. 786: https://history.state.gov/historicaldocuments/frus1941v03/d849 (last accessed 2 October 2023).

88 HC Deb 27 October 1943, vol 393, col 157.

89 Telegram from The Secretary of State to the Diplomatic Agent and Consul General at Beirut (Wadsworth), Document 103, Foreign Relations of the United States Diplomatic Papers, 1943, The Near East and Africa, Volume IV, p. 966: https://history.state.gov/historicaldocuments/frus1943v04/d1024 (last accessed 2 October 2023); Memorandum of Conversation, by the Chief of the Division of Near Eastern Affairs (Alling), Foreign Relations of the United States: Diplomatic Papers, 1943, The Near East and Africa, Volume IV, p. 970: https://history.state.gov/historicaldocuments/frus1943v04/d1028 (last accessed 2 October 2023).

90 Telegram from The Secretary of State to the Diplomatic Agent and Consul General at Beirut (Wadsworth), Document 134, Foreign Relations of the United States: Diplomatic Papers, 1944, The Near East, South Asia, and Africa, The Far East, Volume V, p. 774: https://history.state.gov/historicaldocuments/frus1944v05/d848 (last accessed 2 October 2023); Telegram from The American Representative to the French Committee of National Liberation (Wilson) to the Secretary of State, Document 265, Foreign Relations of the United States: Diplomatic Papers, 1943, The Near East and Africa, Volume IV, p. 1055: https://history.state.gov/historicaldocuments/frus1943v04/d1112 (last accessed 2 October 2023).

of self-determination and the unlawful use of force above).[91] That presumption may be overturned by clear evidence that the nascent state's government is subject to substantial external control (the US refusal to recognise Syria may well be a case in point). Second, where formal independence has been granted by a 'parent' state, it is presumed to extend to the whole of the territory in question.[92]

These presumptions may help to promote stability; however, they need not. As mentioned above, the Belgian Congo was granted independence on 30 June 1960, as a complete unit. It is well established that this process was rushed, with the first genuine multiparty talks on independence and potential government taking place on 20 January 1960, a mere five months previously.[93] Many former colonial officers remained in their posts and by 1960 no Congolese had achieved more than adjunct rank in the armed forces.[94] This swiftly resulted in conflict when General Emile Janssens, having refused to promote Africans to senior positions, went so far as to state 'before independence = after independence' on 5 July 1960. The resulting mutiny and lasting disorder in the armed forces robbed the new government of much of its control.[95] As this episode suggests, inappropriately managed grants of formal independence may create their own instability, even if they are morally mandatory for other reasons. A presumption of statehood under such circumstances will do little to promote stability if actual independence is not present.

These arguments do not entail that questions regarding 'sufficient' levels of governmental control or independence are doomed to complete indeterminacy. As argued in Chapter 3, there are thresholds of municipal stability and institutional autonomy that will normally be required for statehood to emerge. Rather, the difficulty is answering such questions in a way that would satisfy the stability thesis. The existence of a determinate answer to a legal question does not imply that the finding of it will be uncontroversial. There is scope to disagree about the requisite level of control and independence, not to mention about whether, as a matter of descriptive fact, that level has been reached in a particular case. Because the stability thesis prioritises the avoidance of disagreement and conflict in international relations, this scope for controversy limits its capacity to explain the Montevideo criteria. Statehood as political community, which does not look to the avoidance of controversy for the ultimate source of its explanatory power, suffers no such difficulty.

91 Crawford (n 4) 89.

92 Ibid.

93 Emizet François Kisangani, *Civil Wars in the Democratic Republic of Congo, 1960–2010* (Lynne Rienner Publishers 2012) 16.

94 Thomas Kanza, *Conflict in the Congo: The Rise and Fall of Lumumba* (Penguin 1972) 192.

95 Kisangani (n 93) 17.

5.9 CONCLUSION

The law that governs the emergence of statehood cannot be explained primarily in terms of the moral importance of international stability. This chapter argued that the gains to international stability promised by this area of law are not particularly significant. First, I argued that reliance upon consensus-based conditions for statehood is not feasible, given the ambiguity and disagreement present in international practice. Second, I noted that even if an international *modus vivendi* on state creation were available, it would add little to the stability of international relations. Third, I argued that the principles most commonly cited as governing state creation would not make a significant or unequivocal contribution to international stability, even if their existence was legally uncontroversial. This suggests that the stability thesis offers an implausible reconstruction of the law on emerging statehood.

Nonetheless, reflection upon the value of international stability yields an important insight. Although the normative considerations that underpin the law of state creation may not be exhausted by the importance of stability, any reconstruction of this area of law must give stability the relative weight it deserves. Throughout my discussion, I accepted the importance of international peace and friendly relations. The promotion of these values is an important underlying justification for several paradigmatic principles of international law, such as the prohibition on the use or threat of force in international relations. I also observed that it counts strongly in favour of the stability thesis that it apparently coheres with generally accepted legal positions like the presumption of continuing statehood. Nonetheless, when discussing these points, I also noted the distinction between: (i) an area of international law being *consistent* with the value of peace and (ii) that same area of law being *primarily geared towards* avoiding conflict. It is important that the former is true of the law governing state creation: any reconstruction of that law sensitive to the value of peace will cohere with the stability-value of principles such as the prohibition on the use or threat of force and the presumption of continuing statehood. However, it will possess this coherence without the need to adopt peace as an end in itself. What is more, if the same explanation can support values *beyond* peace, its normative appeal can only increase. It will, in short, be a more attractive, and therefore more apt, rational reconstruction. That, I suggest, is precisely the position of statehood as political community.

6

The Legitimacy Thesis

Statehood as political community, or so I have argued, provides a more convincing rational reconstruction of the law that governs state creation than the stability thesis. This is due, at least in part, to it being a normatively 'thicker' theory, which draws upon the resources of political ethics to explicate the law and thereby better elucidates the substantive importance of the legal principles it endorses. However, some may worry that my approach has been insufficiently demanding and believe that an even 'thicker' normative approach is required. Specifically, they may contend that no reconstruction of the law on state creation can be plausible unless it foregrounds the importance of states possessing legitimate governments. For such critics, statehood as political community may well 'fit' international practice, but it cannot begin to justify it – even on a provisional basis – meaning that, ultimately, it must fail as a rational reconstruction.

Chapters 6 and 7 defend my arguments in Part I against this assertion. They do so by critiquing arguments that foreground legitimacy, first in general and then with specific reference to democratic values. The view I refer to from now on as the 'legitimacy thesis' is that no rational reconstruction of the law that governs state creation can be normatively plausible unless it treats considerations of governmental legitimacy as possessing explanatory primacy in relation to that area of law. This strikes at the heart of statehood as political community because that theory explicitly denies that states require legitimate governments in order to emerge. Indeed, it explains several aspects of the relevant law in reference to ethical considerations that themselves turn on a *lack* of legitimacy.

The legitimacy thesis is also worth examining, simply on its own merits. Governments characteristically claim to be legitimate, both on their own behalf and in relation to the state institutions they occupy, and subjecting this rhetoric to close scrutiny can only inform our understanding of international law.

More specifically, if states can emerge without legitimate governments (or legitimate governance institutions) and, what is more, if this fact can make normative sense, then we will have learned something interesting about the *nature* of statehood in existential terms. Such a discovery would be all the more important given that, as I shall argue, several political philosophers, and even some international lawyers, link the idea of statehood to that of legitimacy, such that, or so they claim, we cannot properly understand one without the other.

With this in mind, Sections 6.1 and 6.2 address what it means to investigate governmental legitimacy, after which I examine and reject the claim that, due to their overriding importance, considerations of governmental legitimacy *must* condition the emergence of new states. Sections 6.4, 6.5, and 6.6 of this chapter each consider a discrete legitimacy-focused rational reconstruction of the law governing state creation, each of which emphasises different legitimacy-related factors: civil peace, 'civil incorporation', and popular consent. All three reconstructions converge on a single point: they take their discrete conceptions of legitimacy to set necessary conditions for state creation, such that 'illegitimate entities' cannot gain that status. Because of this, I argue that all three reconstructions face the same difficulty: they either appreciate the demanding nature of legitimacy and, in so doing, fail to 'fit' the existence of the vast majority of contemporary states, or they explain sufficient instances of contemporary statehood but fail to justify the emergence of those states with reference to a normatively plausible conception of legitimacy.

6.1 THE LEGITIMACY QUESTION

Legitimacy concerns 'justified governance' in the sense that, where governmental legitimacy pertains, there must be a sufficient normative justification for the governance practices in question.[1] This is sometimes conflated with the descriptive fact of (some or most) people *believing* governance to be justified.[2] For example, Thomas Franck writes:

> In the international context, legitimacy is achieved if – or to the extent that – those addressed by a rule, or by a rule-making institution, perceive the rule or institution to have come into being and to be operating in accordance with generally accepted principles of right process.[3]

[1] Christopher Morris, *An Essay on the Modern State* (Cambridge University Press 1998) 102–103.

[2] Christopher Thomas, 'The Uses and Abuses of Legitimacy in International Law' (2014) 34(4) *Oxford Journal of Legal Studies* 729, 738–745

[3] Thomas Franck, 'The Emerging Right to Democratic Governance' (1992) 86(1) *American Journal of International Law* 46, 51.

Franck relies upon the writings of Locke, Madison, and Jefferson, all of whom advanced theories of that kind.[4] His apparent conflation of normative questions about legitimacy with descriptive questions about perceptions or beliefs is most likely due to an implicit reliance upon the consent-based theories of such authors. At the core of such theories is the premise that popular acquiescence to governance is both necessary and sufficient for its justification. However, consent-based accounts of legitimacy are not the only such theories to be had. Furthermore, under the most convincing consent-based accounts, widespread belief in the legitimacy of a particular entity is not equivalent to effective consent. I return to these points below. For now, I want to emphasise the distinction between the descriptive fact of a moral belief and the normative fact of its truth or falsehood. I am concerned with normative facts here, just as I have been throughout my analysis up to this point.

Turning to the substance of the legitimacy question, I take governance to require justification because it: (a) involves elevating *some* people (rather than others) to positions of power;[5] and (b) enables those elevated to utilise the threat of collective force as a means for coercion. For these purposes, I understand coercion to be the exploitation of another person's capacity to reason by changing the options available to them.[6] For instance, threats of incarceration coerce us by making disobedience dramatically less advantageous. In its strongest form, governmental legitimacy consists in the right to engage in activity of the above sort, such that it would be wrong for (most) other people to undermine it. More modestly, it equates to the permissibility of such behaviour. I rely upon both senses in what follows.

This characterisation employs three substantive premises. First, I take differences in political power to be problematic because the equal status of individuals is at least seemingly inconsistent with it: if we are all equals, then why should only some of us govern?[7] Second, coercion also creates an 'equality problem' insofar as the victim's decisions become at least partly a function of

4 Ibid 49.

5 Many such positions at least implicitly involve those elevated acting as *representatives* of their community. This sense of representation is particularly relevant at the international level, although it has domestic implications as well. It involves 'speaking for' the community, in the sense of 'acting in their place' (Hanna Pitkin, *The Concept of Representation* (University of California Press 1967) 82). The point is not that such individuals actually *are* representative of those they govern (which might justify this aspect of governance) but that they *act as though they were* (ibid). Representative institutions as a justification for governance are considered in Chapter 7.

6 Robert Nozick, *Socratic Puzzles* (Harvard University Press 1997) 15–44.

7 Allen Buchanan, *Justice, Legitimacy, and Self-Determination: Moral Foundations for International Law* (Oxford University Press 2003) 242–243.

the coercer's will. This process subordinates one individual to another, instantiating inequality. Third, coercion poses an 'autonomy problem' because it manipulates people into pursuing ends that they would not have otherwise chosen to prioritise. Assuming that we accept the independent and equal value of autonomous agents, these properties establish the presumptive wrongfulness of governance. For now, at least, they also help define it as a distinct kind of human activity.

Several of these premises and distinctions will, I hope, be familiar from Part I. However, it warrants mention that, despite overlap in the conceptual frameworks employed both here and there, the instantiation of political community and the instantiation of legitimacy are both normatively and conceptually distinct. Legitimacy pertains, as I shall argue, only where the presumptive wrong of governance has been either outweighed or dissolved. Whilst governments can be more or less legitimate, this means only that some of their actions are legitimate whilst others are not. Incomplete legitimacy always gives us something to regret, since it implies the continuation of wrongful behaviour. Imperfect instantiations of political community, on the other hand, show only that the relevant community is imperfectly constituted for maximal political participation, which in itself does not entail the presence of wrongdoing. The fact that communities can be both valuable and subject to illegitimate governance evidences the moral complexity of politics.

6.2 INVESTIGATING LEGITIMACY

Now that legitimacy has been characterised, the appropriate objects of a legitimacy analysis must be identified. There are at least four: (1) particular acts of governance, (2) governments, (3) governance institutions, and (4) 'the state' taken as a whole. Equivocation between these four things ought to be avoided, since it obfuscates our enquiry into the role that legitimacy may play within the law governing state creation.

The first is the most conceptually fundamental. Governance, because it is a kind of activity, can be broken down into its constitutive behaviours. Individual acts of governmental coercion, whether by judges, police, ministers, or civil servants, can all be individually judged in terms of their legitimacy. This indicates that *some* governance acts within a particular community might be legitimate, whilst others might not. For instance, the hierarchical social structures and coercion necessary to maintain a minimal degree of public order might always be legitimate. It does not follow that *all* the activity of those who institute these things will be. As noted in Chapter 1, contemporary governance characteristically attempts far more than the maintenance of civil peace.

At a more general level, we might ask whether a government *as a whole* is legitimate. Throughout Part I, the definition of 'government' I adopted was deliberately quite loose. Now, it is important to be more precise. For present purposes, by 'government', I mean the group of people within a community that: (a) successfully maintain some degree of public order and (b) do so via the monopolisation of (more or less) centralised coercion. Characteristically, governments are coextensive with the complete set of people engaged in acts of governance. For instance, the government of France will include its ministers, civil servants, judges, police, armed forces, and so on. This clarifies the nature of the contention 'government X is legitimate'. Since governmental actions can (and should) be assessed individually, legitimacy claims about governments must concern the legitimacy of their activity in aggregate. This makes claims about the overall legitimacy of governments rather robust. They amount to saying that the complete set of a government's activity is at least characteristically justified, notwithstanding the equality and autonomy problems mentioned above.

6.2.1 *Institutional Legitimacy*

Claims about institutions are more complex, such that further nuance is required, notwithstanding the separate attention they received in Chapter 2. Such institutions come in at least two forms, although they are comparable in terms of their relationship to the activity of governance and their possession of an organisational structure, containing 'roles, functions, procedures and processes'.[8] Some very simple governance institutions exist as social conventions. These pertain where: (a) considerable convergence in practice exists relating to a particular kind of governance activity and (b) the individuals involved in that activity share a disposition towards their convergent behaviour, perhaps amounting to a shared belief in its obligatory nature.[9] An example might be a convention of hereditary succession, whereby those 'practicing' monarchy organise themselves around a shared belief that the first-born sons of dead rulers should inherit power. Institutions constituted by conventions like these need not be legal in nature: it is enough that they have some kind of role in the organisation of governance.

[8] Ibid 2. Following Rom Hare, we might say that institutions characteristically possess an 'interlocking double-structure of persons-as-role-holders or office-bearers and the like, and of social practices involving both expressive and practical aims and outcomes' (*Social Being* (Blackwell 1979) 97).

[9] H. L. A. Hart, *The Concept of Law*, 3rd edition (Oxford University Press 2012) 88–91.

Legally constituted governance institutions are different. As argued in the introduction, international law exists to the extent that a combination of practices and normative reasons determine and explain the salience of its constitutive principles. This, or so I argue there, is what motivates the rational reconstruction of legal practice as an exercise in discovering *de lege lata*. This is no less true in the domestic context, insofar as we must analyse the legal institutions with which I am now concerned.[10] Specifically, legally constituted governance institutions exist as a combination of their constitutive principles and the governance practices that partly determine those principles. Returning to the idea of 'organisations', we can say that the legal principles constituting governance institutions both entail and explain the coordination of activity around the performance of particular tasks (such as the promulgation of legal texts) that are characteristic of modern governance.

Consider the Westminster Parliament in the United Kingdom. Parliament is not the building in which its meetings are held, nor is it reducible to the individual members of which it is comprised.[11] Neither is it just what such people habitually or conventionally do in that building. Instead, there are a number of related normative considerations, which collectively determine and explain the relevance of those descriptive facts to the legal principles that constitute Parliament.[12] They establish everything from the relevance of its conventional rules for the creation of legislative texts to the legal effect that those documents have. These principles are not reducible to the practices that ground their existence. Nonetheless, the former only exist in the way that they do because of the latter.[13]

Whether they are legally constituted or not, we can assess the legitimacy of governance institutions in two ways. First, the practices that constitute them (at least those involving presumptively problematic hierarchies and reliance upon centralised coercion) can be assessed for legitimacy on an individual basis. Second, and at a more general level, we can ask whether the normative foundations of the conventions or principles that constitute the relevant institutions are sufficient to justify: (a) any hierarchical structures or acts of centralised coercion that form part of their constitutive practices; or (b) any structures or acts of this kind *outside* their constitutive practices that nonetheless contribute towards governance within the relevant community. For instance,

10 Ronald Dworkin, *Law's Empire* (Hart Publishing 1986) 87–113.

11 Ibid 63–66.

12 Whilst I take no position on what these considerations are, they plausibly include the value of: (a) holding the executive to account, (b) being accountable to an electorate, and (c) producing more or less clear pieces of legislation for the purpose of social coordination.

13 Mark Greenberg, 'How Facts Make Law' (2004) 10 *Legal Theory* 157, 164–171.

we might ask whether there is anything about judicial institutions that helps to justify their reliance on centralised coercion when handing down rulings. To take another example, we can ask whether anything about the nature of legislatures helps to justify coercion on the basis of laws that are partly determined by statutory texts.

6.2.2 *Legitimate Principles vs. Legitimate Conventions*

Although both conventional standards and legal principles can be assessed in this manner, the object of assessment is arguably different for each. In the case of legal principles, it is their normative implications. On the understanding of law canvassed in the Introduction, principles necessarily give effect to at least some normative reasons. The crucial point is that this holds even in relation to legal principles that are insufficient to justify (or even to excuse) *any* hierarchical structures or coercive acts. For instance, the importance of social coordination, which can be promoted by clear regulations, may give us *pro tanto* reasons to comply with legal principles that are partly determined by statutory texts (coordination is, at least characteristically, socially beneficial). The institution that promulgated those texts may nonetheless be illegitimate insofar as it possesses an inegalitarian structure or sanctions a range of unjustified coercive acts. I return to this point below.

The correspondence between conventions and normative considerations is more incidental. Conventions themselves are descriptive (social) facts and may well track nothing of any real value. Conversely, the widespread dispositions that partly constitute conventions may reflect normative reasons of some kind. Ultimately, whether or not a particular convention happens to possess normative value is, for this reason, contingent. As such, the normative implications of compliance with conventions can also be assessed in terms of legitimacy. For instance, even in circumstances where they would not count as law, we can still meaningfully ask whether complying with hereditary succession conventions would adequately address the equality and autonomy problems.

6.2.3 *States and 'the State'*

International law attributes statehood to territorial entities inclusive of their populations (see Chapter 3). This matters because legitimacy concerns the relationship between those exercising power and those subject to it. States inclusive of their populations can be neither legitimate nor illegitimate, since populations are those *in respect of whom* legitimacy pertains. This is epitomised by the fact that whilst 'the state' may change following revolution, international practice suggests that neither changes of government nor even the most fundamental institutional shifts will necessarily result in the loss of statehood.[14]

When philosophers talk about 'the state', they have something else in mind.[15] This is the complete set of a community's governance institutions, or at least the most 'basic' or 'fundamental' institutions within that set.[16] As such, the phrase 'state X is legitimate' is at least partly concerned with the claim that something about a particular set of institutions is capable of justifying governance within the relevant community.[17] Most of the rational reconstructions discussed over the next two chapters rely on claims of this kind. Specifically, they argue that state creation can only occur when the nascent community either possesses, or can be demonstrably evidenced to be developing, an institutional framework that legitimises most governance acts undertaken within its territory. Just like claiming that a government is legitimate, this sets the bar quite high. It is not enough that *some* governance institutions justify *some* hierarchies and *some* centralised coercion: in each case, the institutions in question must justify *the preponderance* of governance within the relevant community.

Two final comments are in order. First, as noted above, whether or not a government is legitimate is contingent upon the overall behaviour of that group. To a large extent, institutional legitimacy over time is also contingent upon this because the conventions and principles that constitute governance institutions are almost always grounded upon the activities of governments. Should governments routinely act inconsistently with what their governance institutions nominally require, the latter's existence 'on the books' does little

[14] Consider Iraq after 2003, which underwent several changes in constitutional structure but nonetheless maintained identity (See: UNSC Resolution 1483 (22 May 2003) UN Doc S/RES/1483; UNSC Resolution 1546 (8 June 2004) UN Doc S/RES/1546; UNSC Resolution 1619 (11 August 2005) UN Doc S/RES/1619; UNSC Resolution 1637 (8 November 2005) UN Doc S/RES/1637; UNSC Resolution 1700 (10 August 2006) UN Doc S/RES/1700; UNSC Resolution 1723 (28 November 2006) UN Doc S/RES/1723). See also: Krystina Marek, *Identity and Continuity of States in Public International Law* (Librairie E. Droz 1954) 24–26.

[15] Buchanan (n 7) 281–282.

[16] John Rawls considered the 'basic structure of society' to include 'the political constitution and the principal economic and social arrangements. Thus, the legal protection of freedom of thought and liberty of conscience, competitive markets, private property in the means of production, and the monogamous family are examples of major social institutions' (*A Theory of Justice* (Belknap Press 1999) 6). Whilst this admits a number of non-coercive institutions, it is nonetheless suggestive of my intended scope. Governance need not be restricted to the legislature, executive, and judiciary.

[17] Buchanan (n 7) 283.

to establish legitimate governance. Indeed, where the subversion of institutional standards becomes endemic, it is doubtful whether the relevant institutions will continue to exist at all.[18] As such, the truth of the claim that 'state X is legitimate' will be partly contingent upon the government(s) of that state being characteristically legitimate on an ongoing basis. As I argue below, we have good reasons to doubt that this union of governmental and institutional legitimacy ever existed within the vast majority of states. This conclusion casts considerable doubt upon the plausibility of the legitimacy thesis as a rational reconstruction of the law on state creation. However, before examining particular versions of this thesis, I shall address a general argument in favour of legitimacy-based accounts of the relevant law.

Second, legitimacy, as I have characterised it so far, is 'internal' in relation to any given community, in that it concerns the relationship between the governing and the governed. Nonetheless, it is also possible to speak of 'external' legitimacy, in the sense of a moral right for a state or government not to be subverted or eliminated by a foreign power.[19] This separation matters because, although some scholars treat the two positions as normatively linked, such that all losses of internal legitimacy occasion at least some liability to foreign intervention,[20] it does not necessarily follow that 'intervention is justified whenever revolution is'.[21] The distinctive contribution of the legitimacy thesis turns on its assertion that *internal* legitimacy of some sort provides a necessary condition for state creation. Focusing upon internal matters in this way is justified, at least for present purposes, because it is

[18] Many state representatives *claim* to govern through legitimate institutions, but such claims cannot establish legitimate institutions *as such*. Where they fall within a set of governance practices that make a plausible attempt at legitimate governance, claims of this sort help to establish standards against which those practices can be assessed. For instance, a great deal of 'institutional practise' in Iceland employs the language of equality. Insofar as Icelandic governance fails in egalitarian terms, it can be criticised not only for inegalitarian behaviour but also for failing to meet the standards its own governance institutions require. Not all governments that make claims of this kind can be assessed in this way. Whatever the normative status of governance within the Democratic People's Republic of Korea may be, it cannot be plausibly considered republican or democratic. Everything we know about governance in that state belies the republican and democratic value of its nominal status. There is no sense in which anti-democratic behaviour on the part of Supreme Leader Kim Jong-un would be a betrayal of tradition, even if it is deplorable for other reasons.

[19] Michael Walzer, 'The Moral Standing of States: A Response to Four Critics' (1980) 9(3) *Philosophy & Public Affairs* 209, 214.

[20] Andrew Altman and Christopher Heath Wellman, *A Liberal Theory of International Justice* (Oxford University Press 2009) 100.

[21] Michael Walzer, *Just and Unjust Wars: A Moral Argument with Historical Illustrations* (Basic Books 2006) 89.

entirely possible that different normative considerations could govern the law and morality of foreign intervention from those that govern the emergence of states.[22]

6.3 BUCHANAN'S CHALLENGE

Governments that act wrongfully provide us with reasons to oppose (or mitigate) their wrongful behaviour, but this is typically not enough to warrant either dismantling them or refusing to impart statehood upon their respective communities. This point also cuts the other way: just because it would be wrong to remove a government (or to deny their community statehood), it does not imply that governance within their community characteristically overcomes either the equality or autonomy problems. The reconstructions I examine below deny this distinction. They claim that it would be wrong for statehood to emerge other than within the context of characteristically legitimate governance. To make this case, they might rely upon an argument I call 'Buchanan's challenge' (after the philosopher who developed it). This proceeds as follows:

> If international law recognized as legitimate states entities that were *not* internally politically legitimate...then it would thereby confer legitimacy on entities that are not morally justified in wielding political power...[and because] recognition *supports* and *enhances* the ability...to wield political power, which includes coercion...[this] amounts to being an accomplice to injustice, since the morally unjustifiable exercise of political power is itself an injustice.[23]

On this basis, the reconstructions I examine below might be backstopped by the argument that state creation must turn on the presence of governmental legitimacy. It is incoherent – or so that argument might go – for a rational reconstruction to endorse an injustice. This is an intuitively appealing position. Nonetheless, I believe it should be rejected. In fact, foreign governments may sometimes act unjustly by refusing to recognise states with characteristically illegitimate governance. This is so because hierarchical practices can be worthy of support notwithstanding their wrongful reliance upon widespread coercion. Statehood as political community provides several reasons to believe this; however, there are at least three others.

[22] One explanatory strength of statehood as political community is that it relies on the same set of normative reasons to explain both things (see Chapter 4); however, we need not assume anything of that sort in order to interrogate the legitimacy thesis.

[23] Buchanan (n 7) 270.

The first expands upon a point mentioned above. Governance can have a limited kind of practical authority insofar as its constitutive practices may partly determine legal principles with which its subjects have (*pro tanto*) reasons to comply. Crucially, this can hold even when it is unjustifiable for governments to enforce the principles in question coercively. That may seem counter-intuitive, particularly to those who assume that legitimacy is less demanding than authority.[24] But there are many instances where we can have duties to do something that no one has the right to coerce us into doing. Most of the promises we make and many of the inter-personal associations we enter into give us duties of this kind. It seems plausible that domestic governance can produce obligations of a similar sort. If we grant: (a) the possibility of authoritative law without legitimate governance and (b) that living under authoritative law is to some extent beneficial,[25] then we have a reason to support institutions that provide such law, even though many governance activities they support may lack legitimacy. Admittedly, this does not establish that such institutions should be offered our support in general and all-things-considered. Nonetheless, it suggests one reason that at least partially offsets the unattractiveness of 'illegitimate statehood'.

Second, in its original context at least, Buchanan's challenge is a proposal for universal reform.[26] It asks *all* state representatives to discriminate between legitimate and illegitimate regimes on the assumption that their own domestic arrangements are already legitimate.[27] As I argue in what follows, this assumption does not reflect social reality. As such, we must ask whether it would be just for contemporary state representatives to deny recognition to emerging communities with illegitimate governments when their own governance practices also lack it. The incongruence of holding other communities to standards that one's own government violates is not only a matter of brute inconsistency but also one of (un)equal respect. Imagine a government that fails to recognise another state because the latter possesses illegitimate institutions under some plausible conception of justified governance. Unless that government meets

24 Ibid 239.

25 Liam Murphy, *What Makes Law: An Introduction to the Philosophy of Law* (Cambridge University Press 2014) 125–126.

26 Buchanan (n 7) 269–270.

27 Buchanan's criteria for legitimacy are quite modest, being intentionally 'aspirational towards legitimacy' rather than reflecting its true content. In a nutshell these conditions are: (a) that states protect the 'basic human rights' of those they deploy govern, both within their lawful jurisdiction and beyond; (b) that they do so by means that are human rights compliant; and (c) that they do not come into being via the violent or otherwise unlawful overthrow of an existing legitimate state (ibid 266–267, 275). In the case of emerging states, Buchanan requires that there be a credible commitment to the first two of these requirements (ibid 271).

the requirements of the very same conception, they implicitly devalue their own subjects when they refuse recognition. Although they may not intend to dismiss their subjects' equal status as human beings, the latter are entitled to infer disrespect from the fact that those in power *act* as if another community is entitled to a level of legitimacy that they are not.

Hypocritically refusing recognition risks publicly disrespecting equality via an expressive act. However, there is also a risk that refusing to recognise illegitimate states will lead to harm of a more tangible sort. This is the third reason to reject rational reconstructions of state creation premised upon Buchanan's challenge. As argued in Chapter 5, although the law governing state creation is not primarily explicable in relation to international stability, it must at least be consistent with the value of peace and friendly relations. In particular, it should not significantly detract from the possibility of securing these ends. There are at least two reasons to suspect that refusing recognition to illegitimate entities might violate this desideratum.

First, granting statehood to nascent communities can help stabilise regional politics. In Chapter 5, I considered the possibility that Bosnia-Herzegovina was subject to 'premature recognition' motivated by a desire for clear political boundaries within a troubled region. On this interpretation, Bosnia-Herzegovina emerged notwithstanding its government's relatively low degree of effective and independent control. Since political instability sometimes leads to violent conflict, particularly in regions where such conflict preceded the emergence of new regimes, a refusal to grant statehood to any community that does not enjoy legitimate governance could lead to further violence. Where this is likely to occur, any law that made legitimacy a condition for statehood would be complicit in risking the furtherance of conflict, placing it in direct tension with peace and friendly relations.

Second, as noted in Chapter 5, when comparatively small or economically weak communities are granted equal lawmaking powers through the conferral of statehood, their governments may become more likely to resolve international disputes through legal means. This will arguably also pertain between powerful states as long as their levels of potential influence are to some extent comparable. Ratner points out that, under these conditions, bringing governments within the ambit of the international legal system by granting their communities statehood enhances the prospects for dialogue by setting a starting point for negotiation.[28] All other things being equal, this suggests that the more inclusive the law of state creation is, the more likely it is to be consistent

[28] Steven Ratner, *The Thin Justice of International Law: A Moral Reckoning of the Law of Nations* (Oxford University Press 2015) 199.

with peace and friendly relations. Adopting a position that frustrates these important goals demonstrates ambivalence towards the possibility of conflict, which is itself a form of injustice.

To summarise, it may be unjust to refuse to recognise an illegitimate state if: (a) its governance institutions help to generate at least some authoritative law, (b) refusing to recognise it would constitute a hypocritical act of disrespect, and/or (c) doing so would be inconsistent with the value of peace and friendly relations. Admittedly, non-recognition of an 'illegitimate state' will not always result in instability, nor do governance institutions necessarily produce practice that grounds binding obligations. Furthermore, if the government withholding recognition is itself legitimate, their withholding will not constitute the kind of disrespect contemplated above. Nonetheless, it seems plausible that these concerns will arise frequently enough to justify a more inclusive set of principles than those contemplated by Buchanan's challenge (or the legitimacy thesis). This possibility is sufficient to rebut the claim that legitimacy is so important that no rational reconstruction could be plausible without making it a condition for state creation. With this objection out of the way, I shall now consider three legitimacy-focused reconstructions of the relevant law. I argue that they all either fail to 'fit' the current state of international practice or else adopt an implausible conception of legitimacy.

6.4 HOBBES' THESIS

In this section, I ask whether all governments who successfully secure civil peace are thereby legitimate, such that domestic stability should be considered necessary for state creation *for reasons of legitimacy*. This possibility should not be confused with the account of state creation considered in Chapter 5, which concerned the instrumental value of international peace and friendly relations. The contention now being examined (which I call 'Hobbes' thesis', after its creator) is that governments that successfully secure civil peace necessarily overcome the equality and autonomy problems. Hobbes thesis, like each of the substantive views considered in this chapter, supplies a discrete conception of legitimacy with which one might seek to articulate the legitimacy thesis.

Thomas Hobbes was primarily concerned with whether private individuals have a duty to obey their governments.[29] These aspects of his argument are complex, containing some (questionable) claims about the normative relevance of, and conditions for, individual consent.[30] I shall not address them

[29] Thomas Hobbes, *Leviathan* (Penguin Classics 1997) 114–115.
[30] Ibid 87–97, 107–110, 115–118.

here: there are more compelling consent-based arguments that deal directly with legitimacy, some of which I consider below. What interests me is a seeming afterthought in his *Leviathan*:

> …the state of man can never be without some incommodity or other; and the greatest, that in any form of government can possibly happen to people in general, is scarce sensible, in respect of the miseries, and horrible calamities, that accompany a civil war; or that dissolute condition of masterless men, without subjection to laws, and a coercive power to tie their hands from rapine and revenge…[31]

Hobbes may have intended this passage to backstop his arguments about the rationality of individual consent. Nonetheless, it suggests the possibility of governance being justified on the basis of the 'horrible calamities' of anarchy. This claim is intuitively plausible, especially given events within the previous decade. We may justly criticise the regimes of Bashar al-Assad, Muammar Gaddafi, and Saddam Hussain, but the events during and after their removals from power resulted in a considerable loss of life.[32] Building such intuitions into a more structured philosophical argument, Massimo Renzo argues that governmental coercion is justified out of collective self-defence.[33] Like Hobbes, Renzo sees anarchy as intrinsically dangerous and considers those who oppose the creation of stable states to be responsible for posing a serious threat to others, even if they lack any malicious intent or negligence in so doing.[34] Applying this to the law of state creation, we might argue anarchy to be so dangerous that: (a) governments capable of maintaining civil peace govern as a matter of right and (b) international law must support those governments by offering their communities statehood.

Note the form of this claim. Unlike most versions of the legitimacy thesis, Hobbes' thesis does not purport to 'dissolve' the equality and autonomy problems. Instead, it claims that the need for civil peace 'outweighs' the wrongfulness of political hierarchies and centralised coercion. When presumptive wrongfulness is dissolved, the reasons that make something wrongful no longer apply in that particular context. For instance, at least part of what makes

[31] Ibid 122.

[32] On 23 April 2016, Staffan de Mistura estimated the Syrian death-toll to be around 400,000: Aljazeera, 'Syria Death Toll: UN Envoy Estimates 400,000 Killed', 23 April 2016: www.aljazeera.com/news/2016/04/staffan-de-mistura-400000-killed-syria-civil-war-160423055735629.html (last accessed 2 October 2023). The Iraq Body Count Project estimates between 186,968 and 210,380 civilian deaths from violence since 2003: www.iraqbodycount.org/database/ (last accessed 2 October 2023).

[33] Massimo Renzo, 'State Legitimacy and Self-Defence' (2011) 30(5) *Law and Philosophy* 575, 580.

[34] Ibid 582–586.

physical violence wrong is that it involves using someone else's body for ends that they have not chosen: when you punch me, you violate my autonomy. However, when we agree to a boxing match, the presumptive wrongfulness of your punch is 'dissolved' by the nature of our cooperative enterprise: it is an exercise of my autonomy to engage in combat sports. Contrast this with justified promise-breaking. Generally speaking, breaking promises is wrong because it knowingly or recklessly undermines the knowledge base upon which other people judge how best to act.[35] Say that I break my promise to join you for dinner because I have to take my father to the hospital at the last minute. I have not dissolved the presumptive wrongfulness of failing to keep my word: doing so remains something to regret because promissory reasons still apply to me in that context. Nonetheless, the pressing nature of helping my father justifies letting you down: the relevant promissory reasons have been outweighed. The same distinction holds for legitimacy. Dissolving the wrongfulness of governance means that there is nothing to regret about activity of that kind because the reasons that make it wrong no longer apply within that particular context. Outweighing it means that governance is only justifiable 'all-things-considered' and that the necessity of governing is something that we can justifiably regret. Hobbes' thesis claims the latter.

6.4.1 *Can Hobbes' Thesis Explain International Practice?*

Most established states have governments that exercise sufficient control over their territory to maintain a relatively constant degree of public order, meaning that Hobbes' thesis has no obvious difficulty explaining why those entities gained statehood. Admittedly, the problem of how much public order is 'enough' still applies, although this creates fewer problems in the present context than it did in Chapter 5. For Hobbes, what mattered was avoiding complete lawlessness – a 'state of nature' within which a war of 'everyman, against everyman' pertains.[36] If we take this to be the appropriate threshold, fine questions about when states fall above or below the requisite level may remain, but they will be few and far between. For instance, whilst we should regret that 2019 saw 39,682 people in the United States die from firearm-related injuries alone, 12 people dead in every 100,000 scarcely amounts to anarchy.[37] Cases

35 Ronald Dworkin, *Justice for Hedgehogs* (Harvard University Press 2011) 305; Thomas Scanlon, 'Promises and Practices' (1990) 19(3) *Philosophy & Public Affairs* 199.

36 Hobbes (n 29) 84, para 8.

37 Philip Alpers, Amélie Rossetti, and Daniel Salinas, 'United States – Gun Facts, Figures and the Law', *Sydney School of Public Health, The University of Sydney: GunPolicy.org*, 2022: www.gunpolicy.org/firearms/region/united-states (last accessed 2 October 2023).

like Somalia are more difficult, where civil war has been a constant feature of life for many years.

Nonetheless, unlike the stability thesis, Hobbes' thesis does not turn upon its ability to minimise international disagreement, meaning that potential controversy over the existence of a sufficiently stable state is not fatal. True, accurately and uncontroversially identifying states would ensure that effective governmental arrangements received the recognition and support that Hobbes' thesis says they merit. However, whilst eliminating/minimising controversy is imperative for the stability thesis, those arguing for Hobbes' thesis can simply accept hard cases as inevitable. They may also make the more austere claim that, where controversy over state creation exists because the requisite degree of civil peace cannot be clearly ascertained, the entity in question does not adequately instantiate the value of stable governance.[38] At best, such an entity would be a nascent community and can be treated with respect out of political expedience rather than obligation.

Notwithstanding the explanatory power mentioned above, the latter possibility also exposes some difficulties faced by Hobbes' thesis. Because it emphasises stable government to such a degree, it will struggle to explain some of the international practice mentioned in the previous chapter. First, there are cases of actual and attempted state creation where the existence of civil peace did not seem determinative. Consider Southern Rhodesia, where an effective entity was refused recognition, or Bosnia-Herzegovina, where recognition was granted before that entity's government had control over large areas of its claimed territory.[39] Second, an exclusive focus on public order risks ignoring the independence (or otherwise) of governmental control. Protectorates, puppet states, and colonies are all capable of enjoying civil peace. True, the international status of the former two is controversial.[40] However, colonies are clearly not states, even though in recent history they were characteristically treated as self-determination units with a presumptive claim to statehood. Nonetheless, as Chapter 5 noted when discussing the effects of rapid decolonisation in the

[38] Carl Schmitt, *Der Leviatha in der Staatslehre des Thomas Hobbes: Sinn und Fehlschlag eines politischen Symbols* (Klett-Cotta 1995) 72. See also: Thomas Baty, 'Can an Anarchy Be a State' (1934) 28(3) *American Journal of International Law* 444, 446, who writes, 'International legitimacy is simply the legitimate right to rule, conferred by the fact of having ruled, and it is an all-important thing; because whenever there is a contest for power in a given country, so long as one of the parties is the legitimate ruler in this sense, he sustains the continued existence of the country as a state until his efforts to maintain himself are hopeless'.

[39] Jure Vidmar, *Democratic Statehood in International Law: The Emergence of New States in Post-cold War Practice* (Bloomsbury Publishing 2013) 98.

[40] James Crawford, *The Creation of States in International Law*, 2nd edition (Oxford University Press 2007) 76–83.

DRC, sometimes the maintenance of colonial rule might *protect* civil peace, at least in the short term. This suggests an unsettling possibility: because Hobbes' thesis claims that *stable* governance is both necessary and sufficient for legitimacy, it implies that empires can maintain justified dominance over their colonies, as long as they maintain peace there. What is more, it may even *licence* the creation of colonies where stability would be enhanced by doing so. If Hobbes' thesis really does imply as much, it is clearly in tension with all international legal practice that supports the importance of decolonisation.

6.4.2 *Is Hobbes' Thesis Normatively Plausible?*

As the above point exemplifies, civil peace alone is almost certainly insufficient for legitimacy. However, this is worth examining in some detail because, if this is correct, Hobbes' thesis will be inadequate to provide the legitimacy thesis with normative foundations. To use Hobbes' own words, the argument for the sufficiency of civil peace departs from the plausible premise that anarchy leads to our lives becoming 'solitary, poor, nasty, brutish, and short'.[41] In *Leviathan*, he supports this by making three empirical generalisations about human psychology.[42] I shall not interrogate these here: total anarchy is clearly undesirable, whether due to the likelihood of endemic violence, the increased probability of resources being wasted in the absence of a legally structured market, or the resulting impracticality of pursuing more complex goods, such as art or literature. The question is where to go from there. Hobbes advocates complete and multilateral surrender to an absolute ruler on the basis that only such an entity can secure civil peace.[43] I shall not dwell on this: convincing refutations exist, not to mention numerous examples of functional 'checks and balances'.[44] The enduring appeal of Hobbes' argument, particularly in the form set out above, is its more cautious assertion that no matter how bad one's government may be, the prospect of anarchy (whether through civil war or *inter regnum*) is terrible enough to make rebellion wrong; hence the right to govern that attaches to all stable governments.[45] It is this claim that interests me.

41 Hobbes (n 29) 84, para 9.

42 According to Hobbes, humankind is naturally motivated by competition, diffidence, and glory, which collectively and inevitably lead us into conflict out of desire for material gain, fear of others, and a lust for greater reputation (ibid 83–84; David Gauthier, *The Logic of Leviathan: The Moral and Political Theory of Thomas Hobbes* (Clarendon Press 1969) 91).

43 Hobbes (n 29) 86–88, 111–122, 215.

44 Paul DeHart, 'Leviathan Leashed: The Incoherence of Absolute Sovereign Power' (2013) 25(1) *Critical Review* 1; Morris Silver, 'Economic Theory of the Constitutional Separation of Powers' (1977) 29(1) *Public Choice* 95.

45 Hobbes (n 29) 222–223.

It seems likely that governance is only permissible where the would-be government is capable of maintaining a minimal degree of public order. Absent this condition, the strength of an *aspiring* government is often just one threat amongst many: an additional menace within anarchy and not yet a solution to anything.[46] However, the most this shows is that the ability to secure civil peace is a necessary condition for the liberty to govern, not a sufficient condition for the right to do so. The permissibility of doing something (in this case, governing) is not equivalent to an entitlement to do that thing. An organisation capable of stable governance may do no wrong, under certain conditions, by taking it, but more is needed for it to be wrong to oppose or unseat them. What Hobbes' thesis *can* explain is why the provision of civil peace should be 'bumped up' to a necessary (but insufficient) condition for an entitlement to govern, rather than remaining a condition for a 'mere' liberty to do so. To unseat a government that maintains civil peace is to risk exposing others to the dangers of endemic violence. Even so, it is insufficient to entail that we are 'obliged, in order to maintain the state, to act against faith, against charity, against humanity'.[47]

There are two primary reasons for thinking that, notwithstanding the point just conceded, the maintenance of civil peace is insufficient to legitimise most contemporary governance. First, the dangers of anarchy can only justify actions that maintain order. Governance involves far more than the preservation of peace, and when we move beyond this very basic goal, Hobbes' thesis has very little to say.[48] There might be many reasons to support governmental attempts to achieve, for example, a more egalitarian distribution of wealth or improved industrial capacity, but the avoidance of a 'state of nature' cannot rank high amongst them. Hobbes implied that peace justifies a *general* right to employ centralised coercion because unless governments are *generally* obeyed, they cannot maintain order.[49] However, whilst the dangers of anarchy might – in purely prudential terms – justify tolerating the existence of governments that engage in coercive activity that is unnecessary for the provision of civil peace, it does not follow that it is permissible for such governments to behave as they do.

Even if we interpret Hobbes as making a purely prudential point, we can afford to be sceptical about the notion that public order will break down if

46 There is anecdotal support for this in contemporary civil conflicts, where government forces pose a threat to civilians simply through their continued attempts to (re)establish control. Whether those attempts are justified or not is unimportant: what matters for these purposes is that continued violence *from anyone* creates danger.

47 Niccolò Machiavelli, *The Prince* (1552), XVIII, 65.

48 Renzo accepts this in his articulation of what I call 'Hobbes' thesis': (n 33) 579.

49 Hobbes (n 29) 112–113.

we do not support each and every use of centralised coercion. For one thing, it is plausible to suppose that people have various motivations for complying with domestic law, many of which have little to do with their fears about enforcement.[50] The content of some laws may be viewed as just, traditional, or supported by rule of law considerations.[51] Furthermore, as Liam Murphy points out, any stability-based obligations we have to support the *status quo* necessarily turn upon the likely impact of our actions.[52] An act of defiance will usually have such a minimal impact on civil peace that invoking the dangers of anarchy to justify restraint seems wrongheaded. Conversely, widespread dissent within an army or civil service can result in such chaos that the value of supporting governance in that context has more bite.[53] What is more, we can quite easily imagine large numbers of people ignoring certain edicts whilst obeying others, with the result that whilst some aspects of governance flounder, civil peace survives.[54] For instance, whilst widespread violations of copyright law might undermine attempts to regulate the music industry, this scarcely endangers civil peace.

The second reason why the maintenance of civil peace is insufficient for legitimacy is that stable governments can be extremely dangerous without considerable checks upon their power. We might appeal to the many international crimes perpetrated against people by their own governments.[55] We might also point out that the greatest risks posed in situations of civil and international conflict come from entities with more or less stable control over a core territory.[56] The capacity governments have to harness the power of their populations makes them dangerous, especially where individuals or minorities are concerned. The fear and persecution arising from Nazi rule provide one example of this. The racial disenfranchisement in apartheid South Africa provides another. In defence of Hobbes himself, it is not entirely clear whether he would have considered either regime to have instantiated civil peace or not. Circumstances of extreme tyranny may constitute a 'state of nature', especially when large groups of people are in imminent danger from their government.[57]

[50] Hart (n 9) 90.
[51] Max Weber, 'Politics as a Vocation' in H. H. Gerth and C. Wright Mills (eds.), *From Max Weber: Essays in Sociology* (Routledge 1991) 78–79.
[52] Murphy (n 25) 130–142.
[53] Ibid 138–139.
[54] Ibid 130–131.
[55] This history is too extensive to summarise here. The most famous instances remain those tried at Nuremburg: http://nuremberg.law.harvard.edu/php/docs_swi.php?DI=1&text=overview (last accessed 2 October 2023).
[56] The danger posed by Daesh came in large part from its territorial nature and organised structure.
[57] Hobbes (n 29) 144–148.

Exegesis aside, it remains that Hobbes' thesis, at least as articulated above, presumptively licences both tyranny and oppression. In light of this, it is implausible that the conditions it sets are sufficient for legitimacy. Civil peace *is* valuable. Indeed, it may be one of the more important things that governance can provide. It is hard to imagine effective protections for human rights and popular involvement in politics without the maintenance of public order. Nonetheless, this is insufficient to justify the full range of modern governance activities. Since Hobbes' thesis rests upon such an impoverished conception of justifiable governance, it cannot support the notion that legitimacy is necessary for the emergence of statehood. At best, it shows that relatively stable governance might be necessary as an independent matter, a point on which statehood as political community agrees.

6.5 CIVIL INCORPORATION

As argued in Chapter 1, where individuals enjoy unrestricted freedom, mutual incompatibility in their plans creates the risk of conflict. You and I cannot both make exclusive use of the same weights at the gym or eat the same meal for our disparate lunches. If we try, at least one of our conflicting attempts will be frustrated. This injects uncertainty into our plans because, absent some form of coordination, there is a persistent risk of somebody acting incompatibly with us. Similarly, if we cannot rely on each other's word, or trust each other to refrain from physical assault, our ability to engage in day-to-day activity will be severely restricted. Neither of us can properly enjoy our liberty under such conditions. According to one philosophical tradition, law sets rules of conduct, neutral as between each individual, which settle what we can expect in terms of each other's activity. In this section, I ask whether governments and institutions that provide this function (which I call 'civil incorporation') thereby address the equality and autonomy problems. My goal, as with Hobbes' thesis, is to assess whether civil incorporation provides sufficient normative resources to ground the legitimacy thesis as a rational reconstruction of international law.

Immanuel Kant argued that enforceable laws characteristically accomplish civil incorporation, leaving us both better able to exercise our autonomy and properly assured that the same standards of behaviour will be applied equally to all.[58] For instance, enforceable contracts increase individual autonomy by enhancing the reliability of cooperative action amongst strangers.[59]

[58] Immanuel Kant, *The Metaphysics of Morals*, Lara Denis (ed.), Mary Gregor (trans.) (Cambridge University Press 1996) 27–29, 92–94, 97–98.

[59] Ibid 62, 65.

Without domestic contract law, individuals have no guarantee that commercial promises will be kept. Being able to rely upon the enforcement of contractual obligations enables them to undertake projects that would otherwise involve too much risk. Taking another example, enforceable property law allows us to make complex plans in relation to our existing resources.[60] Living in constant apprehension of losing whatever we have accrued severely limits our ability to act autonomously. Enforceable property rights alleviate this difficulty by enhancing the security of our resource base. In a community where everyone enjoys the equal protection of such laws, autonomy is enhanced and equality instantiated; according to Kant, governance in such communities completely dissolves the equality and autonomy problems.[61] According to a legitimacy thesis that places Kantian civil incorporation at its centre, this would make the existence of an appropriate legal system a necessary condition for the accrual of statehood. This mirrors, at least to some extent, Kelsen's argument that states are synonymous with their legal systems.[62] For this reason, albeit with some caution, a 'Kantian legitimacy thesis' might be considered a rational reconstruction of that theory of statehood, which utilises governmental legitimacy as the normative explanans of Kelsen's legal views.

Although Kant makes a persuasive case for why the equal application of particular kinds of law constitutes a necessary condition for legitimacy, it is doubtful whether the legitimacy thesis can rely upon his claims. There are two reasons for this. First, whilst Kant may provide a necessary condition for legitimate governance, his arguments cannot establish what is *sufficient* for that end. Second, whilst an augmented version of Kant's claims may be more attractive, increasing their justificatory power has an adverse effect upon the extent to which they 'fit' international practice. To take the first point, beyond the abstract proposition that coordinative law must be created, identified, applied, and enforced, civil incorporation has few implications for the kinds of institutional practices that should characterise a legal system. For instance, the need for law to coordinate activity amongst equals does not automatically entail the need for representative legislatures or checks and balances between the various branches of government.[63] The most it can imply is that executives should not be able to act without legal authority, since that would subvert equality under the law.[64] Civil incorporation also leaves the correct

60 Ibid 54–55, 89–90.
61 Ibid 50, 99–100.
62 Hans Kelsen, *The Pure Theory of Law* (University of California Press 1967) 286–287.
63 Kant mounted separate arguments to establish the need for, and proper functioning of, the three traditional branches of government: (n 58) 99–103.
64 Ibid 102.

distribution of property undetermined and stops short of endorsing a complete list of fundamental rights.[65] It is concerned only with the equality and autonomy instantiated by the universal application of coordinative laws, not with those values in a broader sense. This results in it having no implications for many of the institutional features that seem intuitively necessary for a complete dissolution of the equality and autonomy problems.

Perhaps in appreciation of this, Patrick Capps' contemporary Kantian account of international law argues that the value of civil incorporation is entailed by a normatively thicker notion of 'human dignity'. According to Capps, 'the state' is legitimate whenever its constitutive institutions both provide civil incorporation *and* guarantee a particular set of human rights.[66] According to him, only when these two conditions are met are the equality and autonomy problems dissolved. Whilst not providing an exhaustive list, Capps describes the relevant human rights as those that safeguard 'freedom' and 'well-being'.[67] Freedom is a person's ability to 'control their behaviour by their unforced choice while having knowledge of relevant circumstances', whilst well-being 'consists in having the various substantive conditions and abilities that are proximately required either for acting at all or for having general chances of success in achieving one's purposes through one's action'.[68] Capps argues that, when understood in these terms, legitimacy explains some paradigmatic elements of international legal practice: the Universal Declaration of Human Rights, the Covenant on Civil and Political Rights, and the United Nations Charter. Whether this is an accurate interpretation of those texts is not immediately relevant:[69] what matters is that Capps uses this rather abstract reconstruction to inform his views on state creation. Ultimately, whilst it employs a plausible understanding of legitimacy, this move seems both unmotivated and artificial.

Capps claims that international law distinguishes between states as they should be and states as they are.[70] For him, states should possess 'those institutions which are necessary to enable a community to restructure its natural social relations in a way that reduces dependency [on the mercy and tolerance

65 For Kant, coercive resource redistribution is permissible but not obligatory (ibid 109–110).

66 Patrick Capps, *Human Dignity and the Foundations of International Law* (Hart Publishing 2009) 194–195, 265.

67 Ibid 112.

68 He takes these definitions from: Alan Gewirth, *The Community of Rights* (Chicago University Press 1996) 13, 15.

69 By way of evidence, he points to a few passages in each document that link the phrase 'human dignity' to the protection of human rights. Capps (n 66) 106–107.

70 Ibid 258.

of others] and enhances human dignity and individual autonomy'.[71] This is attractive: governance institutions *should* promote the greatest possible potential for equal individual flourishing. However, it is unclear to what extent even the most nominally liberal and egalitarian states actually do this. If the relevant metric is compliance with the rule of law and some appropriate level of human rights protection, then we can expect some contemporary states to fall short of the required standard at least some of the time and others to routinely fail to pass muster. This means that Capps' 'enhanced account' of Kantian civil incorporation will struggle in terms of fit.

Capps accepts this.[72] Indeed, he suggests that *revoking* statehood from entities that do not properly instantiate legitimate governance would lead to serious instability in international relations.[73] His argument on this point is convincing. Apart from anything else, considerable transaction costs would be incurred by states 'blipping in and out of existence' in accordance with their levels of domestic legitimacy. This leads him to endorse a 'juridical concept of the state' that is effectively identical to the traditional understanding of the Montevideo criteria examined in Chapter 5.[74] He explains the consequences of this move as follows:

> …statehood is determined by effectiveness alone, and illegal acts under international law can allow sovereign rights to be withdrawn from states via various acts of enforcement…At the far end of this spectrum is the withdrawal of the right to territorial integrity of the state which, in turn, would allow external interference in the internal affairs of the state. Thus, statehood is determined by de facto effectiveness, and legitimacy conditions form the basis of legal norms against which state conduct is judged and coercion by international legal institutions justified.[75]

Whilst it is plausible that some areas of international law promote legitimacy, explaining the entitlements of states in this way risks considerable artificiality. Specifically, it implies that states gain their characteristic entitlements (via the accrual of statehood) due to a characteristically counterfactual *assumption* that their governance institutions are legitimate. For instance, Capps argues that states merit 'non-interference' because independent governance facilitates civil incorporation and human rights protection.[76] Nonetheless, he

[71] Ibid 192.
[72] Ibid 191.
[73] Ibid 265.
[74] Ibid 260–261, 264–265.
[75] Ibid 264–265.
[76] Ibid 194, 260.

maintains that stability – not legitimacy – justifies statehood emerging purely in response to the effective governmental control of territory.[77] This seems unmotivated. By Capps' own admission, 'effectiveness' does not guarantee legitimacy, yet he remains committed to it on the basis of something very like the stability thesis.

6.6 POPULAR CONSENT

Consent-based theories of legitimacy have a pedigree stretching back to Plato but are perhaps best known, in the English-speaking world, from the writings of John Locke.[78] To use Locke's words, such accounts claim that the 'only way whereby any one divests himself of his natural liberty, and puts on the bonds of civil society, is by agreeing with other men to join and unite'.[79] This implies that each of us must consent on an individual basis, before governance can be legitimate.[80] As mentioned above, governance requires justification because it establishes hierarchies through coercive means. This poses the equality and autonomy problems: governance allows some people to subordinate others through means which manipulate them into pursuing ends that they would not otherwise have chosen. Popular consent allegedly dissolves both problems because it makes governance a function of each person's equally valuable and autonomous choice to accept centralised coercion and political hierarchy. Upon first glance, this position seems attractive. Nonetheless, popular consent provides perhaps the most implausible set of normative foundations considered so far. As such, any version of the legitimacy thesis that relies on it must be dismissed.

Consent needs to be genuine and uncoerced to confer legitimacy. It also needs to be clear exactly what one is consenting to and on what terms. That condition is particularly problematic when consenting to contemporary governance because its scope is so broad. Consent-based theories of legitimacy

[77] Ibid 265.

[78] Plato, 'Crito' in *The Last Days of Socrates*, Hugh Tredennick and Harold Tarrant (trans.) (Penguin Books 2003) 78–96: 90–94; John Locke, *Second Treaties of Civil Government* (1690), VII.91 to VIII.112. Like Hobbes, both Plato and Locke were at least as concerned with political authority as legitimacy. However, as above, exegesis is not my primary concern. Since Locke did not separate out the duty to obey from the duty to support governance institutions, I take what he says to relate to both.

[79] Locke (n 78), VIII.95.

[80] We can consent collectively, insofar as that means expressing our consent as a group. However, if consent is to address the autonomy problem, such 'collective' action must be reducible to a number of coinciding, individual acts. You cannot consent *for* me without my authorisation; a majority cannot consent *for* a minority to which it is opposed.

characteristically claim that it is sufficient for us to consent to the rule of particular governments or governance institutions. But the open-ended nature of such consent undermines its autonomy-value: suggesting that I can instantiate autonomy by promising to do whatever somebody else wants in perpetuity stretches that value to breaking-point. What is more, the asymmetric nature of this kind of relationship places it in tension with equality. For instance, it is one thing to say that someone I permit to borrow my books is my equal. It is quite another to believe that I preserve that relationship of equality when I tell them that they can take whatever belongs to me whenever they like.

Consent can only dissolve the autonomy and equality problems when the purported act of consent relates to something that is itself consistent with those values. For example, I cannot instantiate autonomy or equality by consenting to be your slave, meaning that if our governments treat us like slaves, popular consent offers them no legitimacy.[81] Indeed, consent only serves our autonomy and equality when it is given to governments or institutions that are characteristically compatible with those values in almost every other respect.[82] Imagine that you and I consent to a policy that so severely restricts our freedom of movement that we become effectively tied to a very small area of the world – one village, let's say – on an indefinite basis. Moving around freely is an important way in which we can be autonomous. It follows that, since our autonomy is fundamentally undermined by this policy, our government cannot use our consent to justify enforcing it coercively. True, we may *temporarily* give away freedoms like these without abrogating our autonomy or equality. If I freely enter a drug rehabilitation clinic, my prior consent to the programme of treatment is relevant to the justifiability of forcing me to remain on the premises. But in that case, the goal is the furtherance of my autonomy (by freeing me from addiction). This is quite different from a policy that restricts freedom of movement for some other reason and for an indefinite period of time. Arguments of this kind suggest that even if consent is necessary for legitimacy, it is clearly insufficient.

The real difficulty with claiming that statehood emerges only where popular consent has been given is that few (if any) governance practices are consented to in this way. As Leslie Green points out, consent 'is not mere consensus or approval; it is a performative commitment that undertakes an obligation through the very act of consenting'.[83] Typically, we are born into

81 Kant (n 58) 113.
82 Locke (n 78), VII.90–91.
83 Leslie Green, 'Legal Obligation and Authority' in Edward Zalta (ed.), *The Stanford Encyclopedia of Philosophy* (Winter 2012 Edition): http://plato.stanford.edu/archives/win2012/entries/legal-obligation/

the state in which we live and are expected from that day forward to at least *tolerate* governance there.[84] Our consent is never elicited, nor would a refusal to provide it result in our immunity from coercive rule. Even in the highly unlikely eventuality that our ancestors once entered into a civil compact, it is hard to see how their actions could entail contemporary legitimacy.[85] If popular consent *does* justify governance, it must be the consent of the actual, current population that does this work.[86] This implies that if popular consent is necessary for legitimacy, then Locke's criterion of 'every man…consenting with others to make one body politic' is met nowhere.[87] Even if consent was provided at the inception of a new state through the use of an independence referendum – and it is doubtful, despite their *political* value, that such referendums ever provide for this – then the legitimacy conferred by this act would last only so long as the relevant population remained unchanged. Whatever its truth, such an austere account of legitimacy cannot explain the law of state creation.

But what if *some* people – let's say a bare majority – really do consent to governance within a particular community? Would that be enough to say that popular consent had been granted? This relates to the point just mentioned: that popular consent might be given for the emergence of a new state via an independence referendum. Perhaps the legitimacy thesis might trade on the idea of popular consent by arguing that such referendums are legally required. There are two points to make here. First, consent to secession does not entail consent to whatever governance practices follow. At most, it expresses the desire *not* to be governed within the 'parent' community. Second, even if we place this issue to one side, true popular consent cannot be realised by such referendums unless they yield a unanimous result. Locke argued that once a group enters the civil condition, majority decisions can rightly be treated as representing the whole. Nevertheless, he stopped short of suggesting that a majority could enact the social contract on behalf of everyone else.[88] The autonomy-value of consent explains why. Under certain conditions, agreeing to something that would violate my autonomy if undertaken without consent dissolves the autonomy problem. However, this only pertains because offering consent

[84] David Hume, *Essays, Moral, Political, and Literary*, Eugene Miller (ed.) (Liberty Fund 1987) II.XII.7.
[85] Ibid II.XII.8
[86] Ronald Dworkin, *Taking Rights Seriously* (Gerald Duckworth & Co Ltd 1996) 150–158.
[87] Locke (n 78) VIII.97; Leslie Green, 'Associative Obligations and the State' in Justine Burley (ed.), *Dworkin and His Critics* (Blackwell Publishing 2005) 267–268.
[88] Locke (n 78) VIII.95–99.

exercises my autonomy. If someone else purports to consent for me without my authorisation, such an exercise has not occurred, and my autonomy can do no justificatory work in that context.

6.6.1 *Tacit Consent*

Locke argued that consent to governance can be inferred when mature individuals refuse to leave their communities.[89] This might lead us to believe that by remaining within the territory of an emerging state, the relevant population thereby consents to governance there (making it, at least to that extent, legitimate). But can a failure to emigrate really show consent? Hume notes that this cannot generally be so because most people have no real choice in the matter.[90] Moving states is costly, both in terms of material resources and the personal relationships often left behind. What is more, since almost all of the inhabitable globe is under the jurisdiction of one state or another, emigrants must not only bear the cost of leaving but must also find somewhere to take them in. The perils of statelessness are well known: consider the contemporary example of Afghan, Iraqi, and Syrian refugees and their precarious position within Europe. Under such conditions, any decisions to remain can plausibly be explained in terms of practical necessity rather than uncoerced choice. At the very most, remaining within a state indicates a belief that the benefits of leaving are fewer or less pressing than the burdens of doing so. But that is not the same as consenting to governance.

Some, less austere, circumstances really do enable consent through inaction. When a priest asks a wedding congregation to 'speak now or forever hold their peace', failing to speak implies an endorsement of the union, since the format of the ceremony transforms silence into expression. There are also situations where someone can *seem* to have given consent and incur obligations as a result, even though their intentions were different. Consider the social conventions surrounding strangers playing chess in public parks. Say I set up a chess board in one such park and wait for an opponent. Someone approaches, and we agree to play 'a game', although chess itself is never mentioned. I suggest that she goes first. She moves her queenside knight to the square two spaces in front of her queenside castle. In response, I move one of my pawns to that space and knock her knight off the board. She immediately reprimands me for cheating. I reply that this game is not chess but 'smess' and that my move was permissible. My opponent can justifiably feel affronted. Although I never mentioned

[89] Ibid VIII.119–122.
[90] David Hume, *Essays, Moral, Political, and Literary*, II.XII.23–27.

chess, both my conduct and the social context justified her inference that I had agreed to play that game. She could also justifiably complain that I must have known the impression I was giving. Under such conditions, whether I actually intended to play chess is beside the point: I gave the impression of consenting to play and can plausibly be expected to behave *as if* I had done so.[91]

Alleged tacit consent to governance differs from both of these cases. Unlike weddings, there is no ceremony that imparts special meaning upon the decision to remain within a particular territory. Furthermore, unlike in my 'smess' hypothetical, there are no social conventions in relation to which it would be reasonable to infer that everyone who remains within a particular territory thereby agrees to endure governance there. Some societies might have very abstract social conventions in favour of obeying the law, but even then, it would be wrong to infer consent from the mere fact of continued presence. Not only is a convention of this kind too abstract to justify that inference, but as Hume's critique illustrates, there are many non-consensual reasons for enduring illegitimate governance. Given all of the above, popular consent, whether tacit or otherwise, cannot be expected to precondition statehood. Any version of the legitimacy thesis that asserts otherwise will generate a wholly implausible reconstruction of the law.

Similar problems arise for Fernando Tesón's view that individuals guaranteed 'basic' human rights can be 'presumed to consent' to governance, such that the presumptive entitlements that states possess under international law are the 'outward face of [this] legitimacy'.[92] It is wholly implausible that compliance with international human rights law counts as any sort of evidence for popular consent. We can be granted any number of benefits and still not consent to whatever is demanded in exchange. Our lack of consent may be unreasonable, because consent *should* be offered, or ineffectual, because we are obligated in various ways without it, but that consent would be withheld nonetheless. Conversely, it would make consent a redundant synonym for legitimacy to say that governments meeting their human rights obligations should be treated as if they have it. Even if we interpret Téson to mean that popular consent is 'hypothetical', in the sense that it would be rational for individuals to accept the burdens of governance, this demonstrates only that governance is a valuable enterprise, not that it is voluntarily accepted.[93]

[91] The issue is my dishonesty or carelessness when beginning such an interaction: it does not entail that I must *finish* the game. My consent to play with someone gives them no right to force me to continue once I express a desire to stop, or even to complain when I do.

[92] Fernando Tesón, *A Philosophy of International Law* (Westview Press 1998) 2–7, 45–47, 57–58.

[93] Ronald Dworkin, 'Why Efficiency?' (1998) 8(3) *Hofstra Law Review* 563, 574–579.

6.7 CONCLUSION

This chapter began by providing an understanding of legitimacy as either the right to engage in governance or the permissibility of governing. I characterised governance, for these purposes, as the presumptively wrongful elevation of *some* people to positions of power whereby they can utilise the threat of collective force as a means for coercion. This emphasised the same 'equality and autonomy problems' that featured in Chapter 1: governance presumptively affronts both the equality and autonomy of private individuals, such that it stands in need of justification. With this being done, I then specified the appropriate objects of a legitimacy enquiry: particular acts of governance, governments, governance institutions, and 'the state'. I argued that whilst assessing the former two involves examining behaviour, either on an individual basis or in aggregate, the latter two require attention to the legitimacy-value of the conventions or principles that constitute governance institutions.

Turning from these definitional questions, I next considered 'Buchanan's challenge': the argument that imparting statehood upon communities with illegitimate governance is impermissible by virtue of being unjust. Arguing against this, I suggested that foreign governments can often commit injustice by failing to recognise the statehood of such entities. Next, I considered 'Hobbes' thesis': the claim that securing civil peace is sufficient to render governments legitimate, with the implication that establishing civil peace within a particular territory would be sufficient for the accrual of statehood, all other things being equal. I argued that whilst civil peace is undeniably important, theories of state creation based wholly upon Hobbes' thesis cannot account for sufficient international practice, nor can the avoidance of anarchy justify the full range of contemporary governance activities. Following this, I examined two versions of 'civil incorporation' (the view that particular kinds of legal systems serve a legitimising function). Whilst Kant's view contained a plausible condition for legitimacy, I argued it to be insufficient to address the equality and autonomy problems. As such, it could not supply the legitimacy thesis with a sufficiently plausible normative foundation. Conversely, whilst it was more normatively robust, Capps' view took an artificial position on the normative status of most contemporary states. Finally, I assessed rational reconstructions of emerging statehood premised upon the legitimacy-value of popular consent. I concluded that these neither matched social reality nor addressed the equality and autonomy problems. In Chapter 7, I continue this substantive critique by assessing accounts of the legitimacy thesis premised upon the importance of human rights and the value of representative government, both of which appeal to broadly democratic intuitions.

7

Democratic Legitimacy

Chapter 6 introduced the legitimacy thesis and critiqued three substantive versions of that reconstruction. In addition, it established some general philosophical foundations for a legitimacy-based analysis and contended, *contra* Allen Buchanan, that the law governing state creation can justifiably endorse the statehood of communities without legitimate governance. This chapter critiques several further versions of the legitimacy thesis, each of which is centred around some conception of democratic values. The first focuses upon the protection of fundamental human rights as a criterion for governmental legitimacy, whilst the remaining accounts rely instead upon the provision of representative government. I argue that each version of the legitimacy thesis either fails to explain the existence of a sufficient number of established states, such that they cannot be considered a good 'fit', or that they adopt an implausible conception of legitimacy, such that they lack sufficient normative appeal to function as adequate rational reconstructions.

As argued in Chapter 6, legitimacy concerns the justifiability of 'governance': the presumptively wrongful imposition of social hierarchies and use of collective force as a means for coercion. Governance presents 'equality and autonomy problems' insofar as it presumptively violates these values. Theories of legitimacy can either attempt to 'dissolve' these problems by detailing conditions under which they no longer pertain or allege them to be 'outweighed' by contending that the benefits of governance justify violating the values in question. Legitimacy can be assessed in relation to a range of elements: individual acts of governance; 'governments' (understood as groups of people in power); 'governance institutions' (understood as entities comprised of social conventions or legal principles); and 'the state' (understood as the total set of a community's governance institutions). When examining the legitimacy of either governments or 'the state', we are always asking whether various acts of governance undertaken by or through them are *characteristically* justified. The legitimacy thesis, as a rational reconstruction of the law that governs state creation, claims that some appropriate criteria of legitimacy must be satisfied before statehood can arise.

With this in mind, my critique begins with rational reconstructions that emphasise the legitimacy-value of human rights. I draw such views from James Faucett's claim that such rights have conditioned state creation in the past, together with the contention of those such as Patrick Capps and Fernando Tesón that the existence of 'legitimate statehood' turns upon their protection.[1] I argue that, whilst some human rights set necessary conditions for governmental legitimacy, their protection is not sufficient to justify the full range of contemporary governance practices. International legal practice reflects this: to the extent that it supports plausible guarantees of human rights protection as a factor in favour of the accrual of statehood, it remains ambiguous about *why* such guarantees matter. Given the weakness of the normative connection between human rights and governmental legitimacy, I conclude that statehood as a political community provides a more convincing explanation for the existential relevance of human rights than the legitimacy thesis.

Turning to representative government, I claim, contrary to the optimistic predictions of some international lawyers, that international practice does little to support it as necessary for state creation. As to whether such a standard has independent normative appeal, and so might provide a plausible constraint upon the accrual of statehood notwithstanding contemporary legal practice, I examine two arguments for the legitimacy-value of representative institutions. The first proceeds from the egalitarian credentials of majority rule. I contend that it successfully establishes representative government as necessary for legitimacy in some circumstances but, in so doing, sets a threshold for legitimacy that a substantial number of established states fail to meet, further weakening its explanatory power. The second argument turns on the instrumental value of accountability, which is more promising in terms of contemporary 'fit' but nonetheless incapable of addressing the equality and autonomy problems.

7.1 RIGHTS-BASED LEGITIMACY

It seems unlikely that all internationally protected human rights provide necessary conditions for legitimate governance.[2] For instance, Article 7(d) of the

[1] James Fawcett, 'Security Council Resolutions on Rhodesia' (1965) 41 *British Yearbook of International Law* 103, 112; Patrick Capps, *Human Dignity and the Foundations of International Law* (Hart Publishing 2009) 194–195; Fernando Tesón, *A Philosophy of International Law* (Westview Press 1998) 57–66.

[2] George Letsas, *A Theory of Interpretation of the European Convention on Human Rights* (Oxford University Press 2007) 21–26. Some philosophers claim that human rights are

International Covenant on Economic, Social and Cultural Rights (1966) guarantees the right to paid holiday. Whilst clearly conducive to human flourishing within particular social and economic contexts, this entitlement does not obviously address either the equality or autonomy problems. What *does* seem likely is that legitimacy requires at least a 'minimum level' of human rights protection.[3] Governments that fail to provide 'minimally decent conditions' for most of their subjects, most of the time, are unlikely to have adequately addressed either the equality or autonomy problems. The question becomes which entitlements form part of this 'minimum'. Philosophical elaborations tend to be somewhat unspecific.[4] Allen Buchanan lists:

> ...the right to life (the right not to be unjustly killed, that is, without due process of law or in violation of the moral constraints on armed conflict), the right to security of the person, which includes the right to bodily integrity, the right against torture, and the right not to be subject to arbitrary arrest, detention, or imprisonment; the right against enslavement and involuntary servitude; the right to resources for subsistence; the most fundamental rights of due process and equality before the law; the right to freedom from religious persecution and against at least the more damaging and systemic forms of religious discrimination; the right to freedom of expression; the right to association (including the right to marry and have children, but also to associate for political purposes, etc.); and the right against persecution and against at least the more damaging and systematic forms of discrimination on grounds of ethnicity, race, gender, or sexual preference.[5]

Similarly, Fernando Tesón considers 'the core meaning of international human rights law' to include at least the right to life, freedom from torture and probably 'the right to physical integrity...the right to a fair trial, freedom

necessarily connected to the limits of rightful governance, in that breaches of those rights justify international intervention, see: John Rawls, *The Law of Peoples with 'The Idea of Public Reason Revisited'* (Harvard University Press 1999) 79; Joseph Raz, 'Human Rights without Foundations' in Samantha Besson and John Tasioulas (eds.), *The Philosophy of International Law* (Oxford University Press 2010) 332.

3 Letsas (n 2) 22.

4 John Rawls considers Articles 3 to 18 of the Universal Declaration of Human Rights 1948 to be 'human rights proper' and himself lists the rights to life, liberty, property, and formal equality (Rawls (n 2) 65, 80). Dworkin suggests that there is just one basic right: the 'right to be treated *as* a human being whose dignity fundamentally matters' (Ronald Dworkin, *Justice for Hedgehogs* (Harvard University Press 2011) 335–338). Reasonable disagreement clearly pertains even *before* we consider requisite degrees of compliance. Like Buchanan, neither Rawls nor Dworkin are particularly clear about what constitutes sufficient compliance in concrete cases.

5 Allen Buchanan, *Justice, Legitimacy and Self-Determination: Moral Foundations for International Law* (Oxford University Press 2003) 129.

of expression, freedom of association, freedom of movement…[and] the prohibition of discrimination', as well as 'subsistence rights or basic socio-economic rights'.[6]

Whilst indicative, such lists are quite abstract. First, the meaning of the individual entitlements they include is not altogether clear: what counts as 'subsistence', 'torture', 'fundamental rights of due process', or 'free expression' for the purposes of establishing legitimate governance? It seems plausible that the rights necessary to dissolve the equality and autonomy problems are less extensive than those required to secure perfect justice, although it is by no means obvious where that line should be drawn. For instance, does 'torture' for these purposes include any treatment that might be considered degrading or only that which causes some 'inappropriate' level of suffering?[7] Such lists also leave questions of distribution unanswered. How many people must enjoy these protections within a particular community before governance there becomes characteristically legitimate? Finally, they are vague as to the relevance of context. Given global disparities in wealth and other resources, how should we judge whether particular governments are offering enough protection to legitimise their activities?[8] My point is not that there are *no* answers to such questions, but that talk of 'basicness' and 'fundamentality' offers very little help when identifying the threshold for legitimacy.

These questions must be answered if rights-based legitimacy is to meaningfully condition state creation without risking prohibitive obscurity. Buchanan recognises this problem and suggests that the content of human rights can be specified through democratically legitimate institutions at the domestic level.[9] This is an attractive proposal for reform but is of limited assistance when rationally reconstructing contemporary law. As I argue below, there is little reason to believe that sufficiently legitimate institutions currently exist in most states. Given this point, international legal practice is the obvious place to turn. Minimalist conceptions of rights-based legitimacy will be less obscure if international law can be shown to yield normatively plausible implications for the nature, distribution, and contextual application of human rights, insofar as those entitlements demonstrably bolster governmental legitimacy within the context of state creation.

6 Fernando Tesón, 'International Human Rights and Cultural Relativism' (1984–1985) 25(4) *Virginia Journal of International Law* 869, 873; Tesón (n 1) 5.

7 Buchanan offers no guidance on questions like this beyond alluding to the protections necessary 'for a good human life or at least a minimally decent life': (n 5) 129.

8 Ibid 181–185.

9 Ibid 186–190.

7.1.1 *Can Minimal Rights-Based Legitimacy Explain International Practice?*

It is doubtful whether sufficient practice of this kind exists. This is not to say that credible governmental commitments to honour some human rights are irrelevant to state creation. In fact, their relevance is entailed by statehood as political community (see Chapter 3). Nonetheless, it is by no means clear that such commitments are always necessary for state creation or that their legal relevance is best explained in terms of their legitimacy-value. In fact, contemporary legal practice is largely equivocal on both points: almost all global and regional human rights instruments establish obligations only for existing states, leaving state creation completely untouched.

The most obviously relevant text is the European Community Guidelines on the Recognition of New States in Eastern Europe and the Soviet Union, mentioned in Chapter 3, which made recognition conditional upon evidence of 'respect for the provisions … in the Charter of Paris, especially with regard to…human rights'.[10] In turn, the most relevant provisions of the Charter of Paris for a New Europe (1990) provide three lists of commitments, to be maintained without discrimination. The first includes the freedoms of expression, association, peaceful assembly, and movement. The second lists the freedoms from arbitrary arrest and detention, and torture or other cruel, inhuman or degrading treatment or punishment. The final list references the right to know and act upon one's rights, as well as the right to free and fair elections, fair and public trials, the ownership of property, and the right to engage in 'individual enterprise'. Perhaps most strikingly, this list ends with a general commitment to the protection economic, social, and cultural rights.[11]

Whilst the EC Guidelines plausibly help to establish human rights as relevant to state creation, their invocation of the Charter of Paris leaves open the question of *why* such principles are relevant. In this respect, the Charter of Paris is just one more list of abstract entitlements, albeit one now endorsed by particular states for the purposes of issuing recognition. There is nothing intrinsic to that list which necessitates reading it in terms of governmental legitimacy. What is more, even assuming that we *should* read it in those terms, questions of meaning, distribution, and contextual application still remain in relation to the human rights it references. Practice of this kind is too unspecific to yield anything beyond nominal requirements for state creation: the

10 European Community: Declaration on Yugoslavia and on the Guidelines on the Recognition of New States (1992) 31 ILM 1485: 1487.

11 Charter of Paris for a New Europe (1991) 30 ILM 193: 194.

threshold remains too obscure to establish a plausible and clear threshold for governmental legitimacy.[12] Such relative ambiguity creates less of an issue for statehood as political community, since the latter is not only more normatively capacious than the legitimacy thesis but can also draw upon a broader range of contextual information – such as the antecedents of statehood and the procedural principles of state creation – to determine whether the ethical value of politics has been sufficiently instantiated and respected. But a rights-based conception of the legitimacy thesis cannot claim likewise: governmental legitimacy is both more categorical and more normatively demanding than the instantiation of political ethics.

Similar ambiguity *vis-à-vis* governmental legitimacy and human rights can be found in past instances of non-recognition. Take James Fawcett's claim that non-recognition was legally required in the case of Southern Rhodesia because its emergence was characterised by the breach of 'certain civil and political rights'.[13] If true in that case, a similar argument might explain the more recent example of Northern Cyprus. This seems plausible: I endorsed an analogous claim in Chapter 4, although I characterised both cases in terms of negative self-determination. But nothing about the possibility of human rights principles preventing some entities from gaining statehood entails that they do so *for reasons of governmental legitimacy*. Statehood as political community provides its own reconstruction of this practice, using the very same normative foundations it employs to explicate, for example, the antecedents of statehood and the salience of foreign recognition. Rational reconstructions based upon the legitimacy-value of human rights protection lack the means to secure such coherence, making them comparatively inferior in terms of their explanatory power.

12 When applying these standards to the entities that emerged following the dissolution of the Socialist Federal Republic of Yugoslavia, the Badinter Commission focused mainly upon the text of various constitutional provisions (for example: *Conference on Yugoslavia, Arbitration Commission, Opinion 5* (1992) 92 ILR 188; *Conference on Yugoslavia, Arbitration Commission, Opinion 6* (1992) 92 ILR 182; *Conference on Yugoslavia, Arbitration Commission, Opinion 7* (1992) 31(6) ILM 1512). Such provisions, by their very nature, were characteristically no less abstract than the Charter of Paris itself. True, this form of review is probably the most that can be expected in relation to nascent states, which usually lack a distinct tradition of governance in light of which to make more informed judgements about legitimacy. However, this does little to aid the legitimacy thesis. If anything, the provisional form that human rights commitments must take during the emergence of new states fits better with statehood as political community, which is necessarily forward-looking, focused as it is upon the potential for politics to take place within a given community.

13 J. E. S. Fawcett, 'Security Council Resolutions on Rhodesia' (1965) 41 *British Yearbook of International Law* 103, 112.

7.1.2 *Is Minimal Rights Protection Sufficient for Legitimacy?*

Compounding this explanatory ambiguity are difficulties related to normative plausibility. The more minimalist an account of rights-based legitimacy becomes, the less able it is to justify the full range of governance activities characteristic of contemporary states. Whilst the importance of 'basic' rights might justify taking steps towards securing those rights within a given community, it cannot justify acts of coercion and political hierarchies that are *not* necessary for this purpose. This mirrors the problem faced by Hobbes' thesis in Chapter 6: whilst we might accept that civil peace is one of the most important things that governance can achieve, this cannot entail a plenary entitlement to govern on the part of governments that forestall anarchy.

Since governance can be assessed at the level of individual acts, it is implausible that *all* contemporary political hierarchies and coercive practices are justifiable in terms of a restricted set of human rights. To take a simplified example, elevating some individuals to positions of power so that they can utilise centralised coercion might be justified insofar as they secure free expression for all. Being able to communicate and receive information is an important means through which our autonomy can be exercised, and insofar as the same protections are offered to all of us, our equality is respected. However, it would be strange to claim that this protection of free speech also justifies, for example, the coercively enforced public funding of cultural heritage sites. The equality and autonomy problems raised by that additional governmental activity require separate resolution. Abstracting up, we can say that whilst the coercion and hierarchies necessary to secure minimally decent lives for all might be justified, the value of everyone having a minimally decent life cannot justify governance practices that are not necessary for securing that end. At the very most, the fact that governance is necessary for the protection of our most fundamental rights might justify an obligation not to unseat governments that provide benefits of this kind. However, as argued in the previous chapter, saying that governments should not be removed is not equivalent to proclaiming them legitimate. This casts doubt upon any rational reconstruction of state creation that hopes to characterise the role of human rights within this area of law in terms of governmental legitimacy. As such, this version of the legitimacy thesis must be rejected, notwithstanding its likely appeal to those with commitments to liberal democracy.

7.2 REPRESENTATIVE GOVERNMENT IN INTERNATIONAL PRACTICE

Are representative institutions reliable indicators of legitimate governance, such that their presence should be considered necessary for state creation?

Assume for now that 'representative government' requires the kind of national-level institutions present in communities such as the United States or France. Generally – there is no need to be more exacting just yet – this implies a legislature and executive, the members of which are subject to relatively frequent and regular popular election in which near universal suffrage is enjoyed by the population of the relevant territory.[14] As argued in Chapter 3, credible commitments to provide such institutions will typically indicate greater 'effectiveness' on the part of the relevant government. However, the suggestion that such institutional arrangements are *necessary* preconditions for statehood fits uneasily with legal practice. The classic rebuttal of that suggestion can be found in the *Nicaragua* case, where the ICJ held that 'adherence by a State to any particular [political] doctrine does not constitute a violation of customary international law; to hold otherwise would make nonsense of the fundamental principle of State sovereignty on which the whole of international law rests, and the freedom of choice of the political, social, economic, and cultural system of a State'.[15]

Subsequent practice is, perhaps, more equivocal. On the one hand, the United Nations has a well-established practice of monitoring national elections, which began with aiding newly postcolonial states in the appointment of governments. After the monitoring of the Nicaraguan elections in 1990, it became relatively unremarkable for such aid to be extended to established states as well.[16] There is also a relatively well developed body of international human rights law that supports an individual right to participate in the regular election of governmental representatives.[17] The EC Guidelines mentioned in

14 Such legislatures and executives may be formally separate (for example, the United States of America) but need not be (for example, the United Kingdom). I use 'near universal suffrage' to capture the disenfranchisement of children, resident non-citizens, and incarcerated individuals, which remains widespread in many Western states.

15 *Case Concerning Military and Paramilitary Activities in and against Nicaragua (Nicaraagua v United States of America)* (Merits) [1986] ICJ Rep 14, para 263.

16 Gregory Fox, 'The Right to Political Participation in International Law' (1–4 April 1991) 86 *Proceedings of the General Meeting (American Society of International Law)* 249, 251; Gregory Fox and Bradley Roth, 'Democracy and International Law' (2001) 27(3) *Review of International Studies* 327, 328–330.

17 International Covenant on Civil and Political Rights (adopted 16 December 1966, entered into force 23 March 1976) 999 UNTS 171, Article 25; Protocol to the European Convention for the Protection of Human Rights and Fundamental Freedoms (adopted 20 March 1952, entered into force 18 May 1954) 213 UNTS 262, Article 3; American Convention on Human Rights (adopted 22 November 1969, entered into force 18 July 1978) 1144 UNTS 143, Article 23; United Nations Human Rights Committee 'General comment adopted by the Human Rights Committee under article 40, paragraph 4, of the International Covenant on Civil and Political Rights' (27 August 1996) UN Doc CCPR/C/21/Rev.l/Add.7; *Chiiko Bwalya v Zambia* (27 July 1993) Communication No. 314/1988 CCPR/C/48/D/314/1988; *Greek Case* (1969) 2 Yearbook of the European Convention on Human Rights 186 (Report of 5 November 1969), 180; *Socialist*

the previous sections, in conjunction with the Charter of Paris, also committed a number of states to recognising only 'democratic regimes', at least within the post-Cold War context.[18] Nonetheless, UN monitoring of elections often takes place with the consent of the host state's government, so the aforementioned trends may as easily reflect domestic political choice as a requirement of international law.[19] What is more, UN membership is not contingent upon the presence of representative institutions in the applicant state. This means that, to the extent that UN membership is at least indicative of statehood, representative government is not required.[20]

Most importantly, whilst some states appear to make the perceived democratic quality of a foreign regime a condition for recognition, many established states enjoy near universal recognition even though they manifestly lack representative government.[21] For this reason, most scholars in favour of an international principle requiring representative government argue that it is 'emerging', not that it currently exists.[22] For such a principle to arise as a plausible precondition for statehood, many more existing states would need representative institutions. As argued in Chapter 6, the incongruity of requiring a particular form of governance from emerging states without demanding the same from established states risks both legal incoherence and expressive disrespect. This is not to say that a pro-representation 'sea change' is impossible

Party and Others v Turkey (1999) 27 EHRR 51; *Matthews v United Kingdom* (1999) 28 EHRR 361; Inter-American Commission on Human Rights Resolution 01/09 (17 May 1990) OEA/Ser.L/V/11.77, doc. 7, rev.1; Organisation of American States, 'Texts Approved by the General Assembly at Its Sixteenth Special Session in Connection with the Amendments to the Charter of the Organization' OEA/Ser.P/ AG/doc. 11 (XVI-E/92) (14 December 1992).

18 European Community (n 10) 1487; Charter of Paris (n 11) 194.

19 Fox and Roth (n 16) 338, 344.

20 Whilst it is true that the UN Charter sometimes uses the word 'State' in an idiosyncratic manner, membership decisions pursuant to Article 4(1) broadly reflect the notion that members must be states for the purposes of international law. For a detailed analysis, see: James Crawford, *The Creation of States in International Law*, 2nd edition (Oxford University Press 2007) 179–190; Rosalyn Higgins, *The Development of International Law through the Political Organs of the United Nations* (Oxford University Press 1963) 11–57.

21 Sean Murphy, 'Democratic Legitimacy and the Recognition of States and Governments' (1999) 48(3) *International and Comparative Law Quarterly* 545, 556; Fox and Roth (n 16) 337.

22 Thomas Franck, 'The Emerging Right to Democratic Governance' (1992) 86(1) *American Journal of International Law* 46, 50; Fox and Roth (n 16) 337; This position is further undermined by the apparent halt of global democratisation: Thomas Carothers, 'Empirical Perspectives on the Emerging Norm of Democracy in International Law' (1–4 April 1992) 86 *Proceedings of the Annual Meeting (American Society of International Law)* 261, 263–264; Jean d'Aspremont, 'The Rise and Fall of Democracy Governance in International Law: A Reply to Susan Marks' (2011) 22(2) *European Journal of International Law* 549, 552–563; Susan Marks, 'What Has Become of the Emerging Right to Democratic Governance?' (2011) 22(2) *European Journal of International Law* 507.

or undesirable; simply that a much higher degree of 'fit' is required before we can announce its advent, unless a *seriously* persuasive normative case can be mounted for why that principle should be held to exist notwithstanding the current condition of international practice.[23] It is to the latter possibility that I now turn.

7.3 EQUALITY, MAJORITY RULE, AND THE JUSTIFICATION GAP

The notion that state creation requires the provision of representative institutions may appeal to the value of instantiating political equality.[24] In this section, I argue that although arguments of this sort provide plausible partial dissolutions of the equality problem, they ultimately fail to show that representative institutions are sufficient for legitimacy. As such, the legitimacy thesis cannot plausibly rely upon arguments of this kind to make up for the lack of support international legal practice provides for a criterion of representative government.

Whilst there are many versions of these egalitarian arguments, they all turn upon the supposed legitimacy-value of majoritarian governance institutions. Unlike other decision-making mechanisms, 'majority rule provides all participants with an equal chance of giving salience to their own views over what ought to be done over matters of common concern'.[25] It is not equality of influence that is alleged here but an equal degree of 'minimal decisiveness'.[26] As Bruce Ackerman explains that concept:

> If, say, there are 99 people in an Assembly, then majority-rule gives me a decisive voice when the rest of you are split 49–49; and the same is true of your decision as well. When confronted with the prospect of a tied vote,

[23] Franck (n 22) 50.

[24] Samantha Besson, 'The Authority of International Law – Lifting the State Veil' (2009) 31 *Sydney Law Review* 343, 354–355; Buchanan (n 5) 249–260; Jeremy Waldron, *Law and Disagreement* (Oxford University Press 1999) 101–118; Ronald Dworkin, *Sovereign Virtue: The Theory and Practice of Equality* (Havard University Press 2020) 200–203; Henry Richardson, *Democratic Autonomy* (Oxford University Press 2002) 28; Thomas Christiano, 'The Authority of Democracy' (2004) 12(3) *The Journal of Political Philosophy* 266, 269; Thomas Christiano, *The Constitution of Equality: Democratic Authority and Its Limits* (Oxford University Press 2008) 75–130; Charles Beitz, *Political Equality* (Princeton University Press 1989) 45, 113.

[25] Besson (n 24) 354.

[26] It would be unrealistic and undesirable to require equality of influence, given that the *sine qua non* of politics is diversity, both in viewpoint and personality. Any attempt to do so would abrogate political self-expression. Absent discursively inappropriate attempts to increase influence, such as coercion or dishonesty, the only way in which influence may justifiably be restricted is indirectly, through a limitation upon the resources available to political actors (Dworkin (n 24) 194–198).

> the majoritarian does not appeal to some unresponsive decision procedure, but instead recognizes each citizen's right to have his considered judgement determine the social outcome.[27]

On this account, governance institutions that offer minimal decisiveness respect equality because: (a) each participant has the opportunity to determine the outcome of collective decisions that effect the course of their own lives,[28] and (b) no one person has more of an opportunity to do so than anyone else.[29] This goes some way towards dissolving the equality problem, or so the argument goes, because it makes governance a function of egalitarian procedures. The principle alleged to emerge from such reasoning is that 'the inequality that political power inevitably involves is justifiable if every citizen can participate as an equal in determining who will wield the power and how it will be wielded'.[30]

Arguments of this sort constitute a plausible first step towards demonstrating the legitimacy of majoritarian institutions. Nonetheless, there are at least three unresolved issues. Two of these complicate the position on majority rule, whilst the third poses a serious objection to it as a justification for representative government. First, although the above argument shows that majority rule can be consistent with equality, the most that this establishes is that governance via majoritarian institutions is not always wrong. But this cannot be sufficient to demonstrate legitimacy, particularly not in the strong sense of a *right* to impose hierarchies and engage in centralised coercion. Most likely, some version of Hobbes' thesis must also be satisfied, not to mention the necessity of somehow addressing the autonomy problem, which the above argument from equality does not touch. However, given that majoritarian processes are clearly more egalitarian than decision-making by one or more individuals shy of the whole effected group, majority rule seems like a plausible condition for governmental legitimacy. However, as I argue below, this conclusion actually undermines, rather than strengthens, the egalitarian case for representative government, both as an independent matter and as a condition of emerging statehood.

27 Bruce Ackerman, *Social Justice and the Liberal State* (Yale University Press 1980) 283.

28 Thomas Christiano develops a complex version of this argument, whereby those engaged in national-level politics inhabit a 'common world' within which their interests are almost always equally implicated to some degree, due to the complex relations of competition and mutual reliance that pertain within municipal society: (n 24) 78–95. This is designed to capture the possibility that, outside such 'common worlds', individuals might be effected by decisions without being effected to a roughly equal degree.

29 Waldron (n 24) 108–109.

30 Buchanan (n 5) 250.

7.3.1 'Democracy-Plus'

The second complicating factor is that even if majoritarian institutions help to dissolve the equality problem, at best they amount to a necessary but insufficient condition for doing so. The basic problem is simple: an egalitarian decision-making procedure can produce substantively inegalitarian decisions. Leaving aside the possibility that the legislation or policies produced by majority rule might also be problematic for a host of other reasons, the possibility of inegalitarian outcomes raises a problem of coherence. Equality can be disrespected by advancing inegalitarian standards of behaviour through egalitarian means, in much the same way that it can be disrespected by advancing egalitarian standards through non-egalitarian means. In one situation, the means disrespect equality; in the other, the ends do so.[31] If legitimacy requires respect for equality, *both* the means for adopting decisions, *and* those decisions themselves, should be consistent with the equal status of persons. It is not obvious that individual minimal decisiveness over the creation of legislation or policy is of greater egalitarian import than, for example, the equal distribution of resources or the equal protection of certain freedoms.

Nonetheless, some scholars maintain that egalitarian decision-making must be afforded priority, even at the expense of egalitarian outcomes. By far the most common argument of this sort appeals to the fact that there is disagreement about what equality requires.[32] For instance, Jeremy Waldron argues that respect 'has to do with how we treat each other's *beliefs* about justice in circumstances where none of them is self-certifying, not how we treat the truth about justice itself (which, after all, never appears in politics *in propria persona*, but only – if at all – in the form of somebody's controversial belief)'.[33] To quote at greater length from Thomas Christiano:

> If I were to change things regardless of what others think, I am in effect saying that my judgment on these matters is better than theirs in a way that is contradicted by all that I know about the limitations of people's capacities for judgments. I am in effect treating myself like a god or the others like children. Since that is not the relationship between us and since they have the same interests in having their judgments respected as I do, I must respect their judgments.[34]

31 Beitz (n 24) 64.

32 I restrict myself to equality here because that is the value currently at issue. However, everything discussed in this paragraph could easily relate to other values, such as justice or autonomy.

33 Waldron (n 24) 111.

34 Christiano (n 24) 98.

But why is respecting others' political beliefs (via majority rule) *more* pressing than, for example, promoting their individual capacities to further personal goals through the egalitarian reallocation of resources or demonstrating substantive respect for their autonomy by guaranteeing an equal set of individual rights? Majority rule may be the most respectful means of settling upon and pursuing these ends. Indeed, assuming that it furthers them at least as well as alternative modes of decision-making, it would be inegalitarian not to offer it our support.[35] However, that only establishes majoritarian institutions as *necessary* to dissolve the equality problem, not sufficient. This problem is effectively conceded by Christiano, who accepts that the legitimacy of such institutions is restricted by the application of substantive rights with egalitarian foundations as well as the need to provide an equal 'economic minimum'.[36] This approach is attractive. However, it reveals a difficulty that not only affects Christiano's 'democracy-plus' position but also Waldron's more austere insistence on the illimitability of majoritarian institutions.

Christiano's argument is that substantive egalitarian constraints upon majoritarian institutions are justified by the same considerations that establish the value of majority rule, such that where majoritarian institutions violate these bounds, they operate *ultra vires*.[37] Nonetheless, this is exactly the sort of controversial political thesis that people can (and do) disagree about. By appealing to it, Christiano undercuts his argument that rebellious action against majoritarian institutions necessarily disrespects equality. What if a majority held, on whatever spurious basis, that ethnic discrimination against some vulnerable minority group was *not* a violation of equality? Would that minority be bound to submit to such a decision, or else be in peril of evincing disrespect? That seems implausible. However, what makes the inegalitarian nature of such discrimination an ascertainable enough normative fact, such that their resistance would not be disrespectful? The intuitive or widespread nature of our belief in the wrongfulness of ethnic discrimination cannot be the reason, for such things are geographically and temporally contingent. Neither can it be that this belief is one that everyone *should* accept, for there are many such beliefs that are nonetheless highly controversial. On this basis, it may be thought that Waldron's more austere position is to be preferred.

Waldron believes, for much the same reasons as Christiano, that majoritarian institutions can establish legitimacy, notwithstanding the possibility of inegalitarian outcomes, assuming that they are appropriately constituted.

35 Buchanan (n 5) 252.
36 Christiano (n 24) 97–98, 260–300.
37 Ibid 133–189, 264–266.

However, unlike Christiano, he argues that *any* attempt to curtail such institutions demonstrates 'a combination of self-assurance and mistrust: self-assurance in the proponent's conviction that what he is putting forward really *is* a matter of fundamental right and that he has captured it adequately...and mistrust, implicit in his view that any alternative conception...is so likely to be wrong-headed or ill-motivated that *his own* formulation is to be elevated immediately'.[38] This, he says, is incompatible with the equal respect that we owe our political equals. Let us assume that Waldron is correct: that it is always wrong, by virtue of equality, to limit or resist the decisions of appropriately constituted majoritarian institutions. It may be tempting to suppose that this goes well beyond addressing the equality problem and actually establishes legitimacy itself: even if majority rule produces substantively inegalitarian outcomes as a matter of objective fact *and* cannot answer the autonomy problem, as long as everyone has a duty not to subvert such institutions (because doing so would be inegalitarian) any governance conducted through them must at least be tolerated.

Nonetheless, there are two reasons to believe that Waldron fails to establish the sufficiency of majority rule. First, like Christiano's claims about the appropriate limitations on majority rule, Waldron's justification for the impermissibility of limitation or resistance is a contestable political argument. Indeed, the notion that egalitarian respect concerns 'how we treat each other's *beliefs* about justice' has exactly the same status, *qua* political belief, as any controversial theory about distributive justice or human rights. To establish this, we need only ask how one might respond if someone were to challenge Waldron's claim. In answering revolutionary authoritarians, for example, majoritarians can only respond that such people misunderstand either the importance of equality or what it requires in terms of institutional design. However, this response is no more nor less than a contestable philosophical *claim* that authoritarian views on institutional design cannot be accommodated within legitimate political structures as a matter of normative fact.

This is not to suggest that equality does not require respect for the beliefs of others. Nor does it necessarily imply that majority rule is not sometimes optimally respectful in the face of disagreement. But it does show that all governance necessarily involves instituting potentially controversial opinions at some level. The public justification of majority rule must ultimately depend

[38] Waldron (n 24) 221–222. This quotation is taken from a passage discussing attempts to curtail majoritarian legislatures through the entrenchment of constitutional rights. The point is nonetheless applicable to all instances of opposition, resistance, or rebellion to the rule of majoritarian institutions.

upon a direct appeal to normative reasons rather than to some underlying consensus or majoritarian procedure (that is, unless we are to tempt infinite regress).[39] Now, if this is the case for questions of institutional design, why not also for matters of legal and political substance, such as the provision of an equal basic income or rights to marriage equality? The rejoinder cannot be that these substantive commitments are ones with which others may disagree, for that is no less true for matters of institutional design.[40] This apparent equivalence between substantive and procedural egalitarian commitments brings us full circle. Even if challenging or limiting majoritarian institutions necessarily demonstrates some inegalitarian disrespect, the legitimacy of such institutions nonetheless seems contingent upon them acting within certain egalitarian bounds. To hold otherwise, and so to ignore the equivalence of our substantive and procedural commitments, would be to arbitrarily prioritise the latter at the expense of the former. To avoid this, we should accept that, *vis-à-vis* equality, majoritarian institutions are insufficient for governmental legitimacy.

The second reason why Waldron fails to demonstrate the sufficiency of majority rule for governmental legitimacy is that, whilst he might have established the presumptive wrongfulness of subverting majority decision-making, it does not follow that majoritarian institutions are sufficient to justify *governance by coercive means*. To say that governance institutions are legitimate in the strong sense described in Chapter 6 is to say that at least some people have obligations not to subvert the existence of those institutions and obligations not to oppose governmental coercion when it is exercised in accordance with their institutional procedures. Waldron's argument may help to establish the former but, unaided, it cannot support the latter. Coercion is presumptively wrong because it subordinates the victim to the will of their coercer. This violates the equal status of those parties as autonomous agents. In line with the above justification for majority rule, these concerns can be partly dissolved by affording everyone minimal decisiveness over the adoption of coercively enforceable policies or legislative texts. However, the presence of majoritarian

[39] This is not to say that fine questions of institutional design (for example, whether to require a bare or super-majority) should not be open to discussion on majoritarian terms. My point is rather that this kind of concrete dispute necessarily assumes the mandatory nature of majority rule.

[40] Wojciech Sadurski argues that the egalitarian nature of majority rule is 'undisputed', such that 'our' consensus extends that far but no further ('Law's Legitimacy and "Democracy-Plus"' (2006) 26(2) *Oxford Journal of Legal Studies* 377, 395–396, 406–408). If 'we' are defined to exclude the many non-democrats out there, then this might be true; otherwise, it is clearly false.

institutions says nothing about other important ways in which coercion must be squared with equality, such as through compliance with the rule of law.[41]

Furthermore, unless coercion by majority rule produces sufficiently egalitarian conditions, such as an appropriate degree of economic equality and the enjoyment of sufficient individual liberty, it will still violate equality because it will maintain (or create) unequal capacities to act autonomously. To take an extreme example, a super-majoritarian decision to enforce slavery will violate equality even if the enslaved minority had the opportunity to vote on the decision in question. Resistance by that minority may well disrespect the beliefs of the majority insofar as the justice of slavery was genuinely in contention. However, it is wholly implausible that such resistance would be *wrong*. Given this, majoritarian institutions must be (at best) a necessary but insufficient condition for governmental legitimacy.

7.3.2 *The Justification Gap*

The final issue with majoritarian legitimacy arguments concerns their capacity to explain the alleged legitimacy-value of contemporary representative government. The egalitarian conception of majority rule requires the public to have minimal decisiveness over the creation of both legislation and policy. By contrast, the fact of minimal decisiveness over the election of legislative or executive representatives entails almost nothing for minimal decisiveness over the legislation those representatives vote for or the policies they endorse. Only with regular popular voting on all legislation and major policy decisions can majority rule meaningfully determine governance. But if this is what legitimacy requires, then the last fully legitimate governance institutions – and by extension the last legitimate states – were found in entities like pre-Macedonian Athens (assuming, *contra* 'democracy-plus', that we can overlook their gendered political participation and slave economies). If true, this would be a very serious objection to the legitimacy thesis *qua* rational reconstruction.

The typical answer to this line of argument is that 'direct democracy' is unworkable, given the size of modern states.[42] That is plausible, although perhaps somewhat limited in terms of institutional imagination.[43] Whatever

[41] Jennifer Hendry and I argue this in detail elsewhere, see: Alex Green and Jennifer Hendry, '*Ad Hominem* Criminalisation and the Rule of Law: The Egalitarian Case Against Knife Crime Prevention Orders' (2022) 42(2) *Oxford Journal of Legal Studies* 634.

[42] Christiano (n 24) 105; Waldron (n 24) 109–110 (footnote 60).

[43] For critiques along these lines, see Roberto Unger: *False Necessity: Anti-necessitarian Social Theory in the Service of Radical Democracy*, 2nd edition (Verso Books 2004); *Plasticity into*

the case, it cannot follow that, because true majority rule is impracticable, 'the next best thing' will be sufficiently egalitarian to dissolve the equality problem. It must be shown that contemporary representative government instantiates equality to an appropriate degree. As Buchanan observes, the election of representative regimes, even under ideal majoritarian conditions, 'does not actually achieve equality of political power…[instead it] contribute[s] to equalising power over the *allocation* of inequalities in political power'.[44] In contemporary representative systems, this not only pertains to minor administrative positions but sometimes to institutions that purport to possess plenary legislative power, such as the United Kingdom's Westminster Parliament.

Is minimal decisiveness over the election of the powerful necessary to render governance legitimate? The most we can say is that it can be, but only where there is no option but to delegate substantial power, which is to say where majority rule in the strict sense is impossible. In such circumstances, the same egalitarian justification applies to the election of representatives as to the majoritarian creation of legislation and policy. It would disrespect the equal status of an individual to exclude them from this electoral process and, wherever the election of representatives is the most we can do, it is superior in terms of equality to any other mode of political appointment. However, it does not follow that legislation and policy adopted by elected representatives merits the same degree of respect as that adopted by a majority of the populous. The difference in degree can be intuitively grasped by comparing motions passed by representative institutions and those passed by popular referendums. When a referendum is ignored, the views of the majority are disrespected. When the motions of representative assemblies are ignored, the views of those chosen by the majority are disrespected (and even this assumes that the assembly in question proportionately represents its electorate).

There is equivalence between the wrongfulness of these two things only if elected representatives act as accurate proxies or delegates for those they represent.[45] But how can they? The circumstances of politics are those of plurality and difference, where no two individuals are identical in origin, outlook, or interests. Imagine a fictional state with roughly the population

Power (Verso Books 2004). For an interesting case study of possible alternatives, see: Maura Duffy, '(Re)conceptualising Democracy: The Limitations of Benchmarks Based on Neoliberal Democracy and the Need for Alternatives' (2015) 36(8) *Third World Quarterly* 1472.

44 Buchanan (n 5) 251.

45 Hanna Pitkin, *The Concept of Representation* (University of California Press 1967) 146; Dimitrios Kyritsis, 'Representation and Waldron's Objection to Judicial Review' (2006) 26(4) *Oxford Journal of Legal Studies* 733, 742.

of, for example, the Republic of Kenya. Assume proportional representation, whereby its legislative assembly is appointed in direct relation to the votes cast for particular parties. Assume furthermore that every one of its (to pick a number) six political parties develops an extensive manifesto on virtually every matter of public concern that is made available sufficiently far in advance of the relevant election. Now assume that each member of the electorate has read and understood every manifesto, individually forming a view on the desirability of each after personal reflection and public debate. Assume also that everyone votes. Even if the identity of individual representatives remains immaterial,[46] the following are not only possible but likely, given plurality and diversity: (a) many individuals will agree with some, but not all, of the manifesto they vote for; (b) many individuals voting for the same manifesto will differ as to the relative importance of its contents; (c) some individuals may have no strong preference for any manifesto; and (d) some will have a negative preference (that a particular option not be adopted) and vote for another manifesto on that basis.[47] It is practically impossible for any representative to act as an accurate proxy for the wishes of so diverse a multitude.[48] They will almost always be acting contrary to the preferences of someone they represent.[49]

Why would it be disrespectful for those whose preferences were not actually represented on a particular matter to resist the coercive enforcement of

[46] Many representatives do not view their role as one of delegation, or else their perception of their role varies, depending upon the issue they are voting on: Warren Miller and Donald Stokes, 'Constituency Influence in Congress' (1963) 57 *American Political Science Review* 45; Robert Erikson, Norman Luttbeg, and William Holloway, 'Knowing One's District: How Legislators Predict Referendum Voting' (1975) 19 *American Journal of Political Science* 231; Ronald Hedlund and H. Paul Friesema, 'Representatives' Perceptions of Constituency Opinion' (1972) 34 *Journal of Politics* 730.

[47] These problems (and others) ground the concerns of Jean-Jacques Rousseau ('On the Social Contract' in Jean-Jacques Rousseau, *The Basic Political Writings*, Donald Cress (trans.) (Hackett Publishing Company 1987) 198): 'Sovereignty cannot be represented for the same reason that it cannot be alienated. It consists in the general will, and the will does not allow of being represented. It is either itself or something else; there is nothing in between'.

[48] For analyses of such complexities, see: Donald McCrone and James Kuklinski, 'The Delegate Theory of Representation' (1979) 23(2) *American Journal of Political Science* 278; Andrew Rehfeld, 'Representation Rethought: On Trustees, Delegates, and Gyroscopes in the Study of Political Representation and Democracy' (2009) 103(2) *The American Political Science Review* 214.

[49] Christiano (n 24) 105–106 overlooks this possibility, claiming that: '…citizens are charged with the task of defining the aims the society is to pursue while legislators are charged with the tasks of implementing and devising the means to those aims through the making of legislation. As long as the legislative assembly proportionally represents the aims that citizens have chosen and the legislators are faithful to those aims while pursuing the appropriate compromises and means, the requirement of political equality can be met'.

legislation or policy adopted by their elected assembly?[50] It cannot be because they had minimal decisiveness over the decision in question. Given the likelihood that even those in an electoral majority will disagree on important matters, our support for a particular representative will not necessarily entail popular support for what that representative does. This means that private individuals will lack minimal decisiveness whenever their views diverge from the decisions of their representatives. Under contemporary representative systems, all private individuals have is intermittent minimal decisiveness over who gets to make legislation and policy for them.[51]

This might be the best we can hope for under some conditions. However, it is not clear that all contemporary states are such that such representative distance is a universally necessary second best to genuine majority rule.[52] For instance, the Federal Constitution of the Swiss Confederation makes provision in Articles 138 to 142 (under Title IV) for compulsory and optional referendums on a range of matters. Of particular note is Article 141(a), under which a mere 50,000 signatures are required to call a referendum on any federal act. Although these rules exist within the context of a constitutional framework within which individual Cantons have considerable autonomy, they show that direct resort to majority rule is possible at the national level, at least more often than the alleged 'necessity' of representative government seems to suggest. Given these factual complexities, it is by no means clear that representative government can replace majority rule as an egalitarian condition for legitimacy.

Assuming that the equality problem could be dissolved by private individuals having minimal decisiveness over the election of their governments, do those

[50] When discussing representation directly, Waldron ('Representative Lawmaking' (2009) 89 *Boston Law Review* 335, 345–354) tackles the problem of opposing preferences and opinions by speaking instead of objective interests. 'A representative stands for something (348): in a democratic system, she stands *for* a whole array of constituents who have voted for (or against) her or participated in the voting process by which she was chosen. But she also stands for her constituents under *certain auspices*: she stands for them geographically, in constituency-based systems; she stands for them jurisdictionally, in federal systems; and she stands for them ideologically, in systems of party representation, particularly party-proportional representation. And because she stands for them under those auspices, her standing for them involves abstraction from their personal decision-making. She stands for the interest of the northeast district, or she stands as the junior senator from New York, or she stands as a representative of the Liberal Democratic Party'. (Drawing upon Nadia Urbinati's *Representative Democracy: Principles and Genealogy* (Chicago University Press 2009) and 'Representation as Advocacy: A Study of Democratic Deliberation' (2000) 28(6) *Political Theory* 758.) However, it is not clear how this helps. The metaphor of geographical or jurisdictional areas having 'interests' obscures the reality that such units are comprised of people with diverse interests, which may sometimes overlap but may as easily conflict.

[51] Kyritsis (n 45) 744–745.

[52] Pitkin (n 45) 84–85.

subject to modern representative institutions actually possess minimal decisiveness of this kind? The answer to this question is both empirical and dependent upon the state in question, making it too complex to settle here. However, a few indicative observations can be made. First, in many modern representative systems, most potential representatives are put forward by large political parties with non-universal membership. Such organisations have procedures for determining who runs for election over which the public lacks minimal decisiveness.[53] For instance, under the proportionate representation system in Israel, appointees are placed on party lists in ranking order, with only those at the top of the list having much chance of being elected. As Gordon Tullock points out, this has enabled particular candidates to be 'blackballed' by their respective parties, simply by being moved down the lists.[54] Second, although individuals subject to representative assemblies are able to vote for individual candidates (in a constituency system) or parties (under proportional representation), they are not afforded the opportunity to vote for *assemblies* as such. However, as Jean-Pierre Benoit and Lewis Kornhauser note, the result of the electoral process is always a particular combination of representatives, which results in a unique discursive dynamic and decisional matrix.[55] Third, where election is by geographical constituency, it is almost never the case that two constituencies within the same jurisdiction are the same size. For example, in the United Kingdom's 2015 general election, the voting population of its largest constituency was around 105,400, whilst that of its smallest was 20,900.[56] Given that the egalitarian credentials of minimal decisiveness rest on each voter possessing equal 'buying power', incongruence such as this casts serious doubt upon the egalitarian credentials of many contemporary representative systems.

This analysis leaves the legitimacy thesis in an effectively unworkable position insofar as it turns upon the provision of majoritarian representative institutions. Not only is there scant support for a criterion of representative government in international legal practice but also, as I have argued, there are

[53] This may result in some elements of society having enhanced access to potential representatives with whom they can identify, which implies that others will be unable to exercise minimal decisiveness over the choice they *would* like to have had, were things differently constituted, see: Hannah Dawson, 'Do They Look Like Me? Rethinking Representation and Its Relationship with Freedom' (2014) 21(2) *Juncture* 136.

[54] Gordon Tullock, 'Thoughts about Representative Government' (1994) 10 *European Journal of Political Economy* 27, 34.

[55] Jean-Pierre Benoit and Lewis Kornhauser, 'Social Choice in a Representative Democracy' (1994) 88(1) *The American Political Science Review* 185, 185–188.

[56] Office for National Statistics (UK), Statistical bulletin, 'Electoral Statistics for UK: 2015': www.ons.gov.uk/peoplepopulationandcommunity/elections/electoralregistration/bulletins/electoralstatisticsforuk/2015#parliamentary-electors (last accessed 2 October 2023).

good reasons to doubt that majoritarian institutions are sufficient to establish governmental legitimacy, even if they might be necessary under some conditions. Moreover, notwithstanding the egalitarian credentials of majority rule, there are good reasons to reject the suggestion that contemporary representative government shares these credentials. This version of the legitimacy thesis, it seems, is a total non-starter.

7.4 ACCOUNTABILITY

Given its apparent lack of egalitarian credentials, one might be tempted to look elsewhere in order to support representative government as a criteria for statehood under the legitimacy thesis. One advantage of representative government is the enhanced accountability that comes with relatively frequent and regular popular elections when compared to the conditions of unelected leadership.[57] The periodic removal or confirmation of officials lessens the possibility of persistently unpopular rule, which provides a potential means for preventing tyranny. The framers of the United States Constitution recognised this, understanding the people 'not as rulers but as *judges* able to check the legislature'.[58] Beyond increasing the likelihood that the legislation and policies adopted over extended periods of time will be tolerable to a majority of those governed, popular checks on power may also promote other goods.[59] For instance, John Stuart Mill believed that keeping a check on government promotes intelligence, practical knowledge, and moral sensibility amongst the governed.[60] There is also evidence that domestic accountability tends to produce international restraint in matters of war (at least *between* states with representative institutions).[61] But are such benefits enough to render accountability either necessary or sufficient for legitimacy?

57 Waldron (n 50) 335; Jeremy Waldron, 'The Core of the Case against Judicial Review' (2006) 115 *Yale Law Journal* 1346, 1348.

58 Jonathan Macey, 'Representative Democracy' (1993) 16 *Harvard Journal of Law and Public Policy* 49, 51–52, citing: James Madison, *The Federalist No. 10*, Clinton Rossiter (ed.) (New American Library 1961) 82–83; James Madison, *The Federalist No. 51*, Clinton Rossiter (ed.) (New American Library 1961) 323–324.

59 Pitkin (n 45) 57.

60 John Stuart Mill, 'Considerations on Representative Government' in *On Liberty and Other Essays*, John Gray (ed.) (Oxford University Press 1991) 239–242, 249–256.

61 Michael Doyle, 'Kant, Liberal Legacies, and Foreign Affairs: Part I' (1980) 12(3) *Philosophy & Public Affairs* 205; Michael Doyle, 'Kant, Liberal Legacies, and Foreign Affairs: Part II' (1980) 12(4) *Philosophy & Public Affairs* 323; Michael Doyle, 'Liberalism and World Politics' (1986) 80(4) *The American Political Science Review* 1151; Rodolph Rummel, 'Libertarianism and International Violence' (1983) 27(1) *Journal of Conflict Resolution* 27; David Garnham, 'War-Proneness, War-Weariness, and Regime Type: 1916–1980' (1986) 23(3) *Journal of Peace Research* 279.

It seems plausible that accountability may advance civil peace, at least in some circumstances, and insofar as it does, it may be necessary for legitimacy. However, this cannot advance our understanding of the law governing state creation very far. Unless we accept the questionable empirical premise that Western-style representative government will *always* advance civil peace, the notion that it sometimes may amounts to little more than a qualified sociological addendum to Hobbes' thesis, as examined and dismissed in Chapter 6. More interesting is whether accountability dissolves the equality or autonomy problems.

Understood in isolation, the value of accountability relations themselves is insufficient. When individuals and institutions are held accountable, this necessarily involves an appeal to particular standards. We are accountable as parents, partners, or politicians, but never in the abstract.[62] Sometimes people are accountable in a purely personal capacity, for instance, for breaking promises or negligently causing harm. However, even then, we implicitly invoke standards that prescribe how that individual should have behaved, whether those standards are partly conventional, purely moral, or legal in nature. This means that whether a particular instance of accountability also instantiates the values of autonomy or equality will depend upon the content of the standards in relation to which accountability is established. For instance, accountability *per se* is perfectly consistent with many inegalitarian features of contemporary representative arrangements, such as the absence of popular voting on the final composition of legislative assemblies and the unequal sizes of electoral constituencies. Since accountability's relationship to equality and autonomy is contingent in this way, it cannot dissolve either the equality or autonomy problems. We must examine the institutional framework and substantive principles of the community in question to determine whether a given system of representative government measures up.

However, functioning accountability relations sometimes instantiate a value that cannot be reduced to the importance of the standards to which the individuals in question are held accountable. If the standards in relation to which an individual is judged are normatively appropriate to their particular social or political context, then the fact that one party *offers* accountability to another expresses an acknowledgement that the second party's interests are at stake in the activity of the first.[63] This expression instantiates a kind of

62 Cf. Pitkin (n 45) 58.

63 There is no intrinsic value to accountability relations that do not correspond to some set of objective interests that the supervising party has in the accountable party's activity. For instance, no one has an objective interest in preventing consenting adults from engaging

respect, albeit one more limited than that required to dissolve the equality or autonomy problems. Making yourself accountable to someone with objective interests in your own activity enables their agency in pursuing those interests and so avoids treating them as mere objects or bearers of externalities. This is not always the motivation for establishing accountability relations, but it is characteristic of those relations, at least if the standards of behaviour invoked are apt. Moreover, this sort of respect for agency is normatively important. It is difficult to imagine a legitimate government that fails to enable the agency of its subjects through accountability of some kind. This may render accountability necessary for legitimacy. Nonetheless, it cannot make it sufficient.

In terms of establishing necessity, the relationship between agency and coercion creates a problem. People cannot be coerced unless they have agency, since successful coercion requires targets who can respond to changes in their overall interests.[64] Although both people and rocks can be forcibly moved, rocks lack agency and cannot be coerced. Since it trades upon the fact of its existence, every attempt to coerce us involves an implicit recognition of our agency, meaning that there is no 'agency problem' with coercion, governmental or otherwise. Whilst it seems possible that institutional accountability is necessary to fully recognise the agency of the governed, it is arguable that the very fact of coercive rule publicly recognises it as well. That this particular form of recognition stands in need of further justification speaks to equality and autonomy, not to agency. This suggests that, if and when accountability is necessary for governmental legitimacy, this has more to do with its contingent and extrinsic importance to securing substantive justice rather than the intrinsic value of accountability relations themselves.

In terms of establishing sufficiency, nothing about enabling agency necessarily implies equal status, since relative overall status can be asymmetric in either direction, even when accountability pertains. A soldier's accountability to her commander proceeds on the basis of the latter's superior status. Conversely, in the *Case of Proclamations*, King James I of England was held accountable to his judiciary notwithstanding his allegedly superior social, political, and legal status.[65] Neither does enabling someone's agency

in homosexual activity, so it enables no one's agency to have such relationships subject to 'accountability' via criminal law. Furthermore, no accountability relation that implicitly denies the value of agency can truly instantiate that value. The historical relationship of some slaves to their masters was one of complete subservience, such that the agency of the slaves was effectively denied. This deep contradiction prevents any coherent understanding of agency from justifying the 'accountability' of slaves.

[64] Robert Nozick, *Socratic Puzzles* (Harvard University Press 1997) 15–44.

[65] *Case of Proclamations* [1607] EWHC J23 (KB) (UK).

necessarily instantiate full respect for their autonomy. Someone holding you to account could be otherwise relatively restricted in their autonomous decision-making: in a governmental context, the fact that a particular regime permits me to participate in free and fair elections says nothing about the other freedoms it may fail to afford me.

Moreover, the degree of intrinsic value present in accountability relations depends upon the mode of its instantiation. In some contemporary representative systems, the respect articulated for agency will be minimal because the accountability afforded is relatively thin. For instance, the power to deny reappointment to a political representative provides minimal accountability, especially where it is infrequently and irregularly available. Prior to the 2011 Fixed-term Parliaments Act, the United Kingdom held general elections when the government deemed it appropriate, subject to some constitutional conventions, such as the rule that elections must be held before the new parliamentary term (roughly every five years). Following the 2011 Act, at least until it was repealed in 2022,[66] elections were ordinarily held every five years but could be called early at the behest of two-thirds of MPs in the House of Commons.[67] On the recently reinstated model, the executive branch, which is only indirectly accountable to voters via election of the legislature, determines when its subjects can hold them to account.[68] On the 2011 model, those directly accountable to their constituents were able to collectively begun the procedure themselves. Any system of accountability in which the accountable exercise either level of control over the means of their accountability can only instantiate minimal respect for the agency of the governed.

Despite its limited normative weight, and unlike the egalitarian arguments considered previously, this understanding of accountability can accommodate trustee models of representation, as most famously articulated by Edmund Burke.[69] For Burke, a representative owes his constituents 'his unbiased opinion, his mature judgement, his enlightened conscience' such that 'he betrays [them], instead of serving [them], if he sacrifices it to [their] opinion'.[70] These views are echoed by Mill, who argued that 'it must be counted upon that the representative will sometimes differ in opinion from the majority of his constituents…the electors will not do wisely, if they insist on absolute conformity

66 Dissolution and Calling of Parliament Act 2022 (UK), Section 1.

67 Fixed-term Parliaments Act 2011 (UK), Sections 1–2.

68 Ibid, Section 2.

69 Edmund Burke, 'Speech to the Electors of Bristol' in E. H. Payne (ed.), *Selected Works of Edmund Burke* (Liberty Fund 1990) Volume 4, 4.1.0–4.1.27.

70 Ibid 4.1.22.

to their opinions, as the condition of his retaining his seat'.[71] However, whatever the merit of such views, their inability to dissolve either the autonomy or equality problems should be clear. Trusteeship might present a more accurate view of political representation, however there is nothing therein that ameliorates the violations of autonomy or equality characteristic of contemporary governance. In this respect, it matters far more what our trustees do than it matters whether they are acting self-consciously in our interests, insofar as they happen to understand them. An elected representative may act reasonably, in the sense articulated in Chapter 1, and nonetheless fail to enhance governmental legitimacy, simply because their conscientious behaviour is wrongheaded. In sum, given the tenuous link between accountability and legitimacy, the former cannot establish the legitimacy-value of representative government. As such, any version of the legitimacy thesis that relies upon the value of popular accountability must be dismissed as implausible.

7.5 CONCLUSION

This chapter argued against several versions of the legitimacy thesis, each of which was in some respect grounded upon democratic values. First, it denied that the relevance of human rights to the creation of states can be explained in terms of legitimacy. The protection of fundamental normative entitlements may set a necessary condition for legitimate governance but such protection cannot be considered either sufficient, or tied sufficiently to governmental legitimacy by international legal practice, for such a rational reconstruction to be plausible. Governmental assurances that particular human rights will be protected are relevant to state creation, as I argued in Chapter 3; however, this can be more elegantly explained in terms of political community.

Second, this chapter argued against state creation turning on the presence of representative government. In the first place, support for such a condition is very thin within international legal practice. Moreover, in normative terms, the presence of representative institutions must be viewed as insufficient to dissolve either the equality or autonomy problems. These conclusions, taken together with those from Chapter 6, suggest that the legitimacy thesis should be rejected altogether. States can indeed emerge without legitimate governments and statehood as political community provides a far more convincing rational reconstruction of the relevant law.

[71] Mill (n 60) 376.

Conclusion

The Nature and Resilience of Statehood

Statehood as political community establishes two sets of legal principles. The first are the antecedents of statehood, which determine the factual prerequisites nascent entities must demonstrate to make plausible statehood claims. I characterised these prerequisites, via rational reconstruction of the relevant legal practice, as the set of conditions which, once satisfied, indicate that a discrete political community of the relevant kind has emerged. The second set of governing principles is procedural, conditioning the emergence of statehood by prescribing the means through which that status can accrue. This set includes not only prohibitions on creating states through the unlawful use or threat of force, or in violation of collective self-determination, but also principles that determine the relevance of independence referendums, foreign recognition, and the territorial integrity of existing states.

Taken together, the antecedents of statehood and these procedural principles establish criteria of judgement that must be referenced whenever novel statehood claims arise. They function as factors within an overall interpretive exercise, the outcome of which must also be informed by contemporary social context and historical particularity, as well as by analogical reference, not only to past instances of attempted state creation but also to the conditions of territorial governance within established states. When identifying whether or not an attempt to create a new state has been successful, statehood as political community therefore requires a complex evaluative process, which is nonetheless streamlined by a number of legal presumptions that operate under the auspices of the principles just summarised.

A detailed summary of this legal framework is provided in the Introduction. In addition to establishing the propositions listed there, I have argued that this area of law possesses a single set of normative foundations, central to which are particular elements of political ethics. Part I pursued this argument by presenting statehood as political community itself, whilst Part II considered several alternative reconstructions, centred around the stability and legitimacy theses, which I argued to be untenable. The law of state creation is not particularly well placed to guarantee international stability and, insofar as peace and friendly relations matters *vis-à-vis* state creation, proceeding under the auspices of statehood as political community would leave the international community no worse off than it would be by acting as though some version of the stability thesis were true. Concurrently, although legitimacy is something that all governance *should* exhibit, any plausible normative threshold for legitimacy would be too demanding to function as a condition for state creation.

On this basis, and by virtue of the independent normative appeal I believe it to hold, I have argued that statehood as political community provides the best available reconstruction of the relevant international practice. However, even readers who agree with me on this point may well ask two further questions. First, what does statehood as political community have to say, if anything, about the continuity and extinction of already established states? Second, what might be said about the *nature* of legal statehood, as opposed to the principles governing the accrual, continuity, or demise of that status? In this concluding chapter, I present some thoughts on both topics, although I reach no definitive conclusions on either. Issues of continuity and 'essence' are sufficiently complex to warrant lengthy analyses on their own. However, they appear alongside discussions of state creation within legal scholarship so often that it merits giving them some consideration here. The reasons for this overlap in treatment turn largely upon the emphasis scholars typically place upon their preferred criteria for state creation within their overall characterisations of legal statehood in general.

For instance, when canvassing issues of continuity, Crawford contends that 'we should treat the determination of identity and continuity as dependent on the basic criteria for statehood',[1] even though he accepts that the threshold necessary to satisfy these criteria is far lower in cases of continuity than it is in circumstances of creation.[2] Similarly, when engaged in an analysis nominally focused upon the essence of statehood and in particular upon the relationship between statehood and international legal personality, Nicholson focuses predominantly upon the various ways in which entities might *gain* statehood, as though questions of essence and creation were largely coextensive.[3] Indeed, Nicholson even goes so far as to claim that principles of effectiveness and

1 James Crawford, *The Creation of States in International Law*, 2nd edition (Oxford University Press 2007) 671.
2 Ibid 59, 89.
3 Rowan Nicholson, *Statehood and the State-Like in International Law* (Oxford University Press 2019) 213–214.

recognition in state creation 'define' statehood, which indicates the totality of the slippage he perceives between these two issues.[4]

Nonetheless, it need not follow that the principles governing the creation of states are closely connected to those that determine their continuity or extinction. Even less can it be said that accounts of what it takes for new states to arise collapse into accounts of the nature of statehood, or vice versa. Indeed, as I shall argue here, although the arguments considered in this book disclose some intriguing possibilities for issues of state continuity and essence, they cannot be considered dispositive of either. Legal scholars should be cautious of assuming that their preferred account of state creation, whatever that account might be, can determine when established states should be considered extinct or even what 'statehood' itself should be taken to mean.

1 RESILIENT STATEHOOD: MATTERS OF CONTINUITY AND EXTINCTION

The law of state continuity has never been more topical. The last decade has seen numerous unlawful attempts at regime change, some successful and others not, whilst territorial destabilisation from insurgent groups has threatened the existence of more than one state. Moreover, the threat of human-caused climate change, and in particular the issue of rising sea-levels, endangers small island, low-lying, and archipelagic states in an altogether unprecedented manner.[5] In light of this, state continuity is poised to become one of the most pressing and controversial issues facing the international legal system over the next few years. However, considerable uncertainty exists over the fitness of existing law to grapple with these challenges.

Despite being questioned recently in the proceedings of the International Law Commission,[6] the existence of the presumption of state continuity is firmly rooted within international legal practice.[7] As alluded to in Chapter 4,

4 Ibid.

5 International Law Commission (ILC) 'Sea-Level Rise in Relation to International Law: Second Issues Paper' (19 April 2022) UN Doc A/CN.4/752, paras 21–56. See also: Derek Wong, 'Sovereignty Sunk? The Position of "Sinking States" at International Law' (2013) 14 *Melbourne Journal of International Law* 346, 359; Jane McAdam, '"Disappearing States", Statelessness and the Boundaries of International Law' in Jane McAdam (ed.), *Climate Change and Displacement: Multidisciplinary Perspectives* (Bloomsbury 2010) 105; Alex Green, '*The Creation of States* as a Cardinal Point: James Crawford's Contribution to International Legal Scholarship' (2023) 40(1) *Australian Year Book of International Law* 67, 81–88.

6 ILC 'Report of the Study Group on Sea-Level Rise in Relation to International Law' (15 July 2022) UN Doc A/CN.4/L.972, paras 50–52.

7 Krystyna Marek, *Identity and Continuity of States in Public International Law* (Librairie E. Droz 1954), see generally Chapter 2; Crawford (n 1) 672–690.

this presumption has links to the procedural function of both territorial integrity and the prohibition upon the use or threat of force within the process of state creation. Correlative to the international peace and territorial integrity principles is the presumption that established states shall maintain their existence and territorial boundaries, notwithstanding such eventualities. Moreover, in the case of established states where governmental control of the relevant territory has been subject to prolonged interruption, such as the DRC or Somalia, nothing but a strong presumption of continuing statehood can explain the legal resilience exhibited.

Consequently, the challenge from the perspective of rational reconstruction is not so much demonstrating the existence of this presumption as elucidating its basis and scope. As noted in Chapter 5, one strength of the stability thesis is the intuitive appeal of a stability-based explanation for this. The continuing existence of states such as the DRC, notwithstanding lengthy periods of civil unrest and almost total lapses in governmental control, seems readily explicable via the internationally stabilising effect of more-or-less fixed territorial boundaries, which a strong presumption of state continuity helps to enforce. The same holds, for example, in relation to the continued existence of the Syrian Arab Republic, notwithstanding similar conditions, albeit aided and abetted in that case by considerable foreign intervention.[8] By establishing a firm presumption of continuing statehood, international law disincentivises imperial warfare by making it less easy to install puppet states or governments.

Nonetheless, the explanatory power that the stability thesis apparently holds begins to waver when we consider the wholly unprecedented likelihood that some low-lying, small island, and archipelagic states will become either unfit for human habitation or even wholly submerged should sea-levels continue to rise. Hitherto, the presumption of continuing statehood has operated solely within circumstances where either effective government or governmental independence have been lost via foreign intervention or domestic unrest. For example, the alleged establishment of Slovakia under German occupation in 1939 did not disrupt the continuity of the Kingdom of Yugoslavia, which maintained a government in exile until the advent of the Socialist Federal Republic of Yugoslavia in 1945.[9] Even in cases of extreme territorial change, such as Poland between 1939 and 1945, no substantial changes in territory,

8 Jehan Bseiso, Michiel Hofman, and Jonathan Whittal (eds.), *Everybody's War: The Politics of Aid in the Syria Crisis* (Oxford University Press 2022); Ohannes Geukjian, *The Russian Military Intervention in Syria* (Queen's University Press 2022).

9 Walter Roberts, *Tito, Mihailović, and The Allies, 1941–1945* (Duke University Press 1987) 312–313.

population, or government have ever involved anything like the total uninhabitability of the relevant land.[10] During that period of instability, Alfred Jarry's famous reference to that same state (in 1896) as '…Poland – that is to say, nowhere' may have seemed apt.[11] However, there was very much a sense in which Poland, for all its territorial and governmental ephemerality, was 'still there' throughout the twentieth century.

The same cannot be said in relation to small island states like the Republic of Mauritius, should sea-levels continue to rise. Rather than inter-state violence, it is the diffuse global effects of excessive carbon emissions that threaten to rob such communities of their land. Despite the obvious injustice of this situation, it is difficult to see how international stability would be served by presuming the continuity of submerged states, since the operation of that presumption can hardly prevent either the factual displacement of the populations in question or the wanton pollution responsible. When it happens, such climate-based mass migration or physical submergence will occur no matter what the law of state continuity has to say, and it is displacement as such, not the formal status of those displaced persons, which poses a threat to both human rights and international peace and security. Rational reconstructions that seek to explain why existential continuity should pertain in such circumstances must therefore reject the stability thesis and look elsewhere.

So how might statehood as political community explain the presumption of state continuity? Most obviously, since endemic violence is inimical to politics, whatever explanatory advantages the stability thesis possesses as regards disincentivising war will also be available with reference to political community.[12] However, since this cannot readily explain why the presumption of state continuity might also function in circumstances of sea-level rise, one further set of arguments merits consideration. These turn on the suggestion that, were it the case that international law permitted states to dissolve following the loss or uninhabitability of their land-based territory, then it would seem to be implicated in a particular sort of injustice *vis-à-vis* political community.

As noted in Chapter 2, one element of 'quasi-independent' value possessed by contemporary governance institutions turns on their capacity to exist as artefacts of political action. Such institutions matter, at least in part, because they represent the collective political endeavours of the populations whose behaviour contributed towards their existence and structure. Importantly, this value can become intergenerational, constituting part of the relevant community's

[10] Crawford (n 1) 692–695.
[11] Alfred Jarry, *Ubu Roi*, Gershon Legman (trans.) (Dover Publications 2003) vi.
[12] See Chapters 4 and 5.

political tradition, and so provide them with existential continuity, as well as identity through time. Once created, continuity and identity of this kind might feasibly survive even a total loss of inhabitable land because the basis of political membership within the relevant community might be said to have altered. Specifically, in addition to the residence and beneficiary conditions, we might formulate a third condition of political membership as follows:

> Any person (P) is a member of a given community (C), where P has contributed, to a non-negligible degree, towards the incremental development of the institutions constituted to govern C.

Call this the 'contribution' condition, which we might include within *Non-Voluntary Membership* insofar as the latter can be repurposed to deal with questions of state continuity. Unlike residence, contribution is not dependent upon territorial delimitation to determine its scope, and unlike the beneficiary condition, it does not depend upon the more-or-less uninterrupted exercise of governmental coercion to be maintained.[13] Discrete acts of political contribution are in one sense eternal, existing within the personal narratives of the individuals concerned. As such, communities defined by their political contributions might survive notwithstanding prolonged interruption, whether from belligerent occupation or sea-level rise. In the former case, continuity is guaranteed by the principle of territorial integrity in combination with the widespread recognition of governments in exile.[14] In the latter, it would be incumbent upon the international community to both recognise and accommodate not only the governments of affected states but their populations as well.

This argument is deliberately provisional, and I do not have the scope to develop it further here. Nonetheless, even the possibility of a contribution condition suggests that political communities *might* endure, notwithstanding an ongoing failure to satisfy the territory antecedent, as long as the institutions that govern them continue to function in some meaningful way. Given this possibility, should international law not extend the presumption of state continuity to communities affected by human-caused climate change, it would thereby tacitly endorse the removal of equal status from those communities, notwithstanding the fact that they otherwise continue to exist.[15] This would be

[13] Fine questions may arise about what constitutes a 'non-negligible degree' of political contribution; however, these might be ameliorated via reference to, for example, voter registration or similar bureaucratic records.

[14] See generally: Katrin Tiroch, 'Governments in Exile' in Rüdiger Wolfrum (ed.), *Max Planck Encyclopedia of Public International Law* (Oxford University Press 2011).

[15] The International Law Commission recently contemplated precisely this: (n 6) paras 52–55.

presumptively unjust, which supports the notion that continuity should be so extended, as a matter of *de lege lata*.[16]

2 THE IDEA OF STATEHOOD: QUESTIONS OF 'NATURE' OR 'ESSENCE'

Given the title of this book, readers may anticipate one particular answer to the question of what states are. Surely, if 'statehood as political community' is committed to anything at all, it must be committed to the view that states *are* political communities. Although this supposition is correct, it is also potentially misleading. Statehood as political community provides a framework for judgement through which legal disputes over emerging statehood should be interrogated and, hopefully, resolved. That is one function of the law that governs state creation. Its other function is to guide the representatives of established states on questions of entitlement and recognition. To that extent, my arguments provide a set of necessary and sufficient conditions for becoming a state. Nascent entities must satisfy, in a holistic and contextually sensitive manner, the antecedents of statehood detailed within Chapter 3 and emerge in a manner consistent with the procedural principles described within Chapter 4. These conditions might permit significant variation from case to case, constituting an overall rubric rather than an inflexible list; however, they are conditions, nonetheless. States must emerge as political communities and do so in a manner consistent with the ethical importance of individual political action. That is the core of my overall claim.

It would make my argument absurd if states routinely emerged without the qualities I attributed to them in Part I. To that extent, statehood as political community addresses one question of 'essence': it is part of the nature of states that, at their inception at least, they are political communities. However, it need not follow, logically speaking, that states must maintain every property of a political community in order to survive. Indeed, as suggested above, established states may well lose their capacity to satisfy the territory, effectiveness, or independence antecedents and still not lose their statehood. This suggests that what it takes to become a state and what it means to be a state might not necessarily be the same thing.

True, there are elements of my argument that pull in the opposite direction. Through my reply to Buchanan's challenge in Chapter 6 and via my reliance upon analogical reasoning in Chapter 3, I am committed to international law imposing upon nascent entities only those statehood criteria

[16] This is not to mention the human costs of what would, in effect, be the creation of mass statelessness by operation of law, see: Green (n 5) 86.

that the preponderance of established states can satisfy as well. There are sound reasons of both fairness and feasibility to support this move as a matter of state creation, but it also entails that statehood as political community is not neutral *vis-à-vis* the properties that established states possess. Indeed, it requires that even if not all established states exist as political communities all of the time, at least the majority must meet that standard most of the time. Were that not the case, then a significant proportion of the evidence I have used to support my rational reconstruction would be unavailable to me. However, even this general observation about the status of established states seems inadequate to account fully for the nature of statehood.

Part of the difficulty turns on the opaqueness of terms like 'nature' or 'essence'. What does it mean, precisely, to ask what states are? According to one account, the nature of something is determined by the necessary and sufficient conditions for being (rather than becoming) that thing.[17] In the same manner that there might be essential and exhaustive requirements for being a cat, the Earth's moon, or the red sportscar you saw last Wednesday, we might also investigate the nature of statehood by asking what the necessary and sufficient conditions are for being a state. Alternatively, some hold that what is most objectively important about an entity, in aesthetic, ethical, or moral terms, is indispensable to its nature.[18] For instance, like those who argue that the fundamental nature of humanity is located within our individual vulnerability, so too we might argue that states are best characterised by their capacity to make war or to govern coercively. Alternatively still, we might say that the nature or essence of a thing consists only in those properties that are *unique* to things of that sort.[19] Just as we distinguish triangles from other two-dimensional shapes on the basis that only triangles have three sides, so too might we distinguish states from other entities on the basis that only states (or at least the state-like) have the right to confer nationality.

Return to the proposition that most established states constitute political communities. Add to that the additional qualification that all states must emerge by satisfying the antecedents of statehood whilst complying with the relevant procedural principles. Notwithstanding everything these conclusions tell us about statehood, it is clear that they underdetermine at least two of the three conceptions of essence just considered. First, the necessary and sufficient conditions for being a state are potentially more numerous than the

[17] John Locke, *An Essay Concerning Human Understanding*, John Yolton (ed.) (Everyman 1993) 238 (III.iii.15).

[18] Aristotle, *Nicomachean Ethics*, Christopher Rowe (trans.) (Oxford University Press 2002) 101–102 (1097b25–1098a20).

[19] Bertrand Russell, *An Inquiry into Meaning and Truth* (George Allen and Unwin 1972) 97–102.

conclusions established by statehood as political community. Statehood comes with characteristic legal capacities, including some more or less abstract rights and duties,[20] which the arguments developed within this monograph cannot establish alone, even if they hint towards them. For instance, no argument within this text entails an immunity from compulsory international jurisdiction,[21] or even powers so paradigmatic as those to create customary international law or to create binding obligations via treaty. But such immunities and powers are surely necessary properties of states as they exist today. Second, although the fact that states constitute political communities is normatively important, it is by no means obvious that this is the most important fact about them. One attractive feature of the legitimacy thesis, for all its other faults *qua* rational reconstruction, is that it seems to grasp something normatively pressing about states as coercive institutions.

Of the three considered, the only conception of essence that statehood as political community might have some claim to satisfy is the last. If no state can emerge without doing so *as* a political community, by satisfying the antecedents of statehood, and if all states must arise through means accordant with the procedural principles mandated by ethically valuable politics, then that is arguably something unique about them. But even if this might *define* statehood in a serviceable manner, it seems insufficient as an account of its nature. We should distinguish questions about the essence of statehood from those concerning whatever workable criteria we might use to identify states for various practical purposes, including but not limited to those of state creation. The enduring appeal of foreign recognition, for example, is that it can be ascertained in a relatively straightforward manner, notwithstanding the ambiguities discussed in Chapter 5. Yet this epistemic benefit hardly offers a unique window into the nature of states as international legal entities.

With these points in mind, I shall briefly review some attempts to elucidate the essence of contemporary statehood, none of which I find particularly convincing. First, we should reject purely nominal characterisations operating at very high levels of abstraction. One example is Jure Vidmar and Lea Raible's account of statehood as a 'customary status under international law', which accrues to territorial units according to the laws of state creation.[22] Such

[20] United Nations General Assembly (UNGA) Resolution 2625 (XXV) (24 October 1970) UN Doc A/RES/25/2625(XXV).

[21] *Jurisdictional Immunities of the State (Germany v Italy: Greece intervening)* (Merits) [2012] ICJ Rep 99, para 57.

[22] Jure Vidmar and Lea Raible, 'State Creation and the Concept of Statehood in International Law' in Jure Vidmar, Sarah McGibbon, and Lea Raible (eds.), *Research Handbook on Secession* (Edward Elgar 2023) 25–27.

propositions are either trite or raise more problems than they solve, depending upon one's view of the relationship between statehood and customary law-making.[23] No less unhelpful is Vidmar and Raible's assumption that statehood necessarily attaches to territorial units, or their connected assertion that 'legal status under international law is [characteristically] territorial in nature'.[24] To begin with, natural persons clearly possess their own status under international law and outnumber territorial entities by many millions to one. Moreover, the assumption that statehood *must* attach to territory may even be problematically backwards-looking, at least from the perspective of state continuity, given the novel threats posed by human-caused climate change.

Potentially more productive accounts focus upon the legal capacities that statehood grounds. Foremost amongst them is Crawford's, who characterises states in line with their 'general legal characteristics' of 'plenary competence to perform acts, make treaties, and so on, in the international sphere…[exclusive competence] with respect to their internal affairs…[freedom from] compulsory jurisdiction…[and] equal status and standing'.[25] In a similar vein, Buchanan characterises statehood as a bundle of rights, including those to territorial integrity and non-interference in internal affairs, the right to make treaties, to engage in '(just) war', and to exercise territorial governance.[26] Comparable characterisations can be found elsewhere.[27] However, these accounts, illuminating as they are about the legal consequences of statehood, leave something to be desired as theories of its nature. Insofar as they provide means to distinguish states from other entities, such as international organisations or non-state armed groups, they serve an important practical function. Nonetheless, since they do not tell us *why* states possess the legal capacities they do, they cannot explicate the internal rationality of statehood as an international legal status. They are doctrinal descriptions, in other words, and not theories.

[23] On the latter point, see Nicholson (n 2) 102–106.

[24] Vidmar and Raible (n 22) 22.

[25] Crawford (n 1) 40–41.

[26] Allen Buchanan, *Justice, Legitimacy, and Self-Determination: Moral Foundations for International Law* (Oxford University Press 2003) 263.

[27] Hersch Lauterpacht, *Recognition in International Law* (Cambridge University Press 2012) 38–66; Ole Spiermann, 'General Legal Characteristics of States: A View from the Past of the Permanent Court of International Justice' in Christine Chinkin and Freya Baetens (eds.), *Sovereignty, Statehood and State Responsibility: Essays in Honour of James Crawford* (Cambridge University Press 2015) 146–152; Jure Vidmar, *Democratic Statehood in International Law: The Emergence of New States in Post-cold War Practice* (Bloomsbury Publishing 2013) 46–50; Steven Ratner, *The Thin Justice of International Law: A Moral Reckoning of the Law of Nations* (Oxford University Press 2015) 103–266; Christopher Morris, *An Essay on the Modern State* (Cambridge University Press 1998) 36–46; John Rawls, *The Law of Peoples with 'The Idea of Public Reason Revisited'* (Harvard University Press 1999) 23–30.

The same problem is faced by Nicholson's account, although he eschews reliance upon the idea of legal capacity.[28] By focusing upon international legal personality, defined as the possession of at least one internationally opposable right or duty,[29] Nicholson characterises statehood 'as the "fullest" degree of personality and related attributes that is presently available in international law',[30] whilst defining 'states in the technical sense' as those entities 'subject to the customary norms giving particular legal relations to entities defined as states and also to the norm that states contribute to [the formation of legally binding international] custom'.[31] This is perfectly serviceable as a 'mere' description;[32] however, it omits almost everything explanatory that we are entitled to expect from an account of statehood's nature. Statehood is an international legal status; that much is clear, whether distinguished by discrete capacities or by particular sets of jural relations. However, the essence of any such status must be the normative position it occupies within the international community,[33] and we cannot fully elucidate that positionality without providing an explanation for why it pertains. We need, in short, a rational reconstruction of *the idea of statehood*, which can render the prescriptive consequences of that status normatively intelligible. No purely descriptive account can accomplish this task.

One attempted reconstruction of this kind is Mortimer Sellers' republican account of statehood, under which states are 'the basic unit[s] within which most power *should* reside, which is to say the largest viable cultural unit or country, within historical borders' (emphasis in original).[34] He takes this characterisation to be wholly dependent upon the provision by states of legitimate governance, which he defines in terms of democratic and rights-respecting institutions that are oriented towards the common good.[35] Whilst it is attractive in some respects, it should be no surprise that I reject this view. As Chapters 6 and 7 demonstrate, although every state should strive for complete legitimacy, very few can plausibly claim to have achieved it. As such,

28 Nicholson (n 3) 28.
29 Ibid 36.
30 Ibid 216.
31 Ibid 144.
32 Nicholson effectively admits this, calling his account 'essentially…a cross-reference' (ibid).
33 Thomas Nagel, 'Personal Rights and Public Space' (1995) 24(2) *Philosophy & Public Affairs* 83, 85.
34 Mortimer Sellers, *Republican Principles in International Law: The Fundamental Requirements of a Just World Order* (Palgrave Macmillan 2006) 102.
35 Ibid 61–62, 99–101 (but see a potentially conflicting definition of statehood at 109); Mortimer Sellers, 'Republican Principles in International Law' (1996) 11(3) *Connecticut Journal of International Law* 419–429 (but, again, see 420 for the potentially conflicting intimation 'not all states are republics').

any theory that characterised contemporary statehood along these lines must either be interpreted as reformist or else as deeply mistaken.

Liberal corollaries to Sellers' republicanism are becoming increasingly popular. Foremost amongst them are Evan Criddle and Evan Fox-Decent's fiduciary theory of statehood, which characterises states as 'purposeful institutions deployed in the service of humanity',[36] mandated to offer 'protection and care' through the provision of Kantian civil incorporation along the lines of that discussed in Chapter 6.[37] Theirs is a formidable and impressive attempt to rationally reconstruct the entirety of international law, to which I cannot do full justice here. However, two general observations are in order.

First, fiduciary theories of this sort, whilst accounting convincingly for international legal regimes such as those protecting human rights, suffer from significant difficulties of fit in relation to the law of statehood. In particular, they necessarily conflate states with governments,[38] the latter of which are more naturally viewed as fiduciary agents, while the states they represent more naturally constitute their respective principals.[39] Obfuscation of this distinction can be found in claims such as 'people and territory are not properly understood as "qualifications" for statehood, as the Montevideo Convention suggests, but rather as structural features that are common to all state-subject relationships', to which Criddle and Fox-Decent cleave. But the distinction matters because international practice differentiates between the recognition of governments and that of states, with non-recognition of the former explicitly leaving the latter untouched.[40] Moreover, the very concept of governments-in-exile, noted above, assumes a schism between the two. Statehood as political community accommodates such points by treating populations as constitutive of the states that help to define them. It raises no objection, by contrast, to treating governments as the fiduciaries of their states, at least for certain purposes.

Second, if international law genuinely attempts to 'distribute sovereignty' by creating states that care for their populations as Kantian fiduciaries,[41] then

[36] Evan Criddle and Evan Fox-Decent, *Fiduciaries of Humanity: How International Law Constitutes Authority* (Oxford University Press 2016) 51.

[37] Ibid 25–31, 50–51.

[38] This mistake is also runs throughout, for example: Jeremy Waldron, 'Are Sovereigns Entitled to the Benefit of the International Rule of Law?' (2011) 22(2) *European Journal of International Law* 315.

[39] Bin Cheng, *General Principles of Law as Applied by International Courts and Tribunals* (Cambridge University Press 1953) 184.

[40] Stefan Talmon, *Recognition of Governments in International Law: With Particular Reference to Governments in Exile* (Oxford University Press 2001) 3–14.

[41] Criddle and Fox-Decent (n 36) 50–51, 63–70.

it must be viewed as a truly spectacular failure. As argued in Chapter 6, the full benefits of Kantian civil incorporation, at least insofar as it might establish governmental legitimacy, are only sporadically provided within established states. Moreover, if international law really was geared towards creating functional fiduciaries on the basis that all individuals merit the same degree of care and protection, then it would pay far closer attention to, for example, the distribution of natural resources amongst states, as well as the relative size of their populations. This is not so, as demonstrated in Chapter 3, suggesting that state creation at least is not concerned with the sorts of fiduciary relationships that Criddle and Fox-Decent impute to statehood in general.

With these critical observations being made, it seems only fitting to end on a more positive note. I have argued that, for all its virtues *qua* rational reconstruction, statehood as political community is not sufficient to elucidate fully the nature of statehood. However, even the limited contribution it does make tells us a great deal. Contemporary states are characteristically not legitimate, but neither are they merely lines on a map, delineated so as to avoid conflict amongst powerful governments. Instead, they are sites of moral and ethical contestation, where authentic and reasonable individuals can strive amongst imperfect communities to promote autonomy and equality whilst forestalling endemic conflict. States might be many other things, both good and bad, but under contemporary international law, they must all emerge with this potential in view.

Where that potential becomes realised, states constitute the primary units within which we pursue justice and legitimacy, whether we achieve it or not. It is perhaps in recognition of this that international law affords them such considerable benefits: it certainly helps to explain the importance of their rights to governmental independence and territorial integrity, as indicated by my arguments within Chapters 3 and 4. The fact that states are political communities might not exhaust their nature, but it does indicate some part of their value. This value is complex and qualified; however, it nonetheless reflects the sublime chaos of human plurality and our collective capacity to struggle onwards, authentically and with meaning.

Bibliography

Ackerman, Bruce, *Social Justice and the Liberal State* (Yale University Press 1980).

Al-Baharna, Husain, *The Legal Status of the Arabian Gulf States: A Study of Their Treaty Relations and Their International Problems* (Manchester University Press 1968).

Aljazeera, 'Syria Death Toll: UN Envoy Estimates 400,000 Killed', 23 April 2016: www.aljazeera.com/news/2016/04/staffan-de-mistura-400000-killed-syria-civil-war-160423055735629.html (last accessed 2 October 2023).

Alpers, Philip, Amélie Rossetti, and Daniel Salinas, 'United States – Gun Facts, Figures and the Law', *Sydney School of Public Health, The University of Sydney: GunPolicy.org*, 2022: www.gunpolicy.org/firearms/region/united-states (last accessed 2 October 2023).

Arendt, Hannah, *On Violence* (Harcourt 1970).

The Human Condition, 2nd ed. (Chicago University Press 1998).

Aristotle, *Nicomachean Ethics*, Christopher Rowe (trans.) (Oxford University Press 2002).

Armitage, David, *The Ideological Origins of the British Empire* (Cambridge University Press 2000).

Barker, Kit, 'The Nature of Responsibility for Gain: Gain, Harm, and Keeping the Lid on Pandora's Box' in Robert Chambers, Mitchell, Charles and James Penner (eds.), *Philosophical Foundations of the Law of Unjust Enrichment* (Oxford University Press 2009).

Baty, Thomas, 'Can an Anarchy Be a State?' (1934) 28(3) *American Journal of International Law* 444.

The Canons of International Law (John Murray 1930).

BBC News, 'Ukraine Crisis: Protesters Declare Donetsk "republic"', 7 April 2014: www.bbc.co.uk/news/world-europe-26919928 (last accessed 2 October 2023).

'Ukraine Rebels Hold Referendums in Donetsk and Luhansk', 11 May 2014: www.bbc.co.uk/news/world-europe-27360146 (last accessed 2 October 2023).

Beitz, Charles, *Political Equality* (Princeton University Press 1989).

Benoit, Jean-Pierre and Lewis Kornhauser, 'Social Choice in a Representative Democracy' (1994) 88(1) *The American Political Science Review* 185.

Besson, Samantha, 'The Authority of International Law – Lifting the State Veil' (2009) 31 *Sydney Law Review* 343.

Birks, Peter, *Unjust Enrichment*, 2nd ed. (Clarendon Press 2005).
Blair, David, 'The "Disappeared" Whose Voices Will Be Silent in Vote on Self-Rule in Ukraine's East', *The Telegraph*, 10 May 2014: www.telegraph.co.uk/news/worldnews/europe/ukraine/10822420/The-disappeared-whose-voices-will-be-silent-in-vote-on-self-rule-in-Ukraines-east.html (last accessed 2 October 2023).
Brady, H. and C. Kaplan, 'Eastern Europe and the Former Soviet Union' in D. Butler and A. Ranney (eds.), *Referendums Around the World: The Growing Use of Direct Democracy* (AEI Press 1994).
Brierly, J. L., 'The Shortcomings of International Law' (1924) 5 *British Yearbook of International Law* 4.
Brilmayer, Lea, 'Secession and Self-Determination: A Territorial Interpretation' (1991) 16(1) *Yale Journal of International Law* 177.
Brownlie, Ian, 'Relations of Nationality in Public International Law' (1963) 39 *British Yearbook of International Law* 284.
International Law and the Use of Force by States (Oxford University Press 1963).
Principles of International Law, 6th ed. (Oxford University Press 2003).
Principles of Public International Law, 5th ed. (Clarendon Press 1998).
Bseiso, Jehan, Michiel Hofman, and Jonathan Whittal (eds.), *Everybody's War: The Politics of Aid in the Syria Crisis* (Oxford University Press 2022).
Buchanan, Allen, 'Theories of Secession' (1997) 26(1) *Philosophy & Public Affairs* 31.
Justice, Legitimacy, and Self-Determination: Moral Foundations for International Law (Oxford University Press 2004).
Burke, Edmund, 'Speech to the Electors of Bristol' in E. H. Payne (ed.), *Selected Works of Edmund Burke* (Liberty Fund 1990) Volume 4.
Cali, Başak, 'On Interpretivism and International Law' (2009) 20(3) *European Journal of International Law* 805.
Capps, Patrick, *Human Dignity and the Foundations of International Law* (Hart Publishing 2009).
Carothers, Thomas, 'Empirical Perspectives on the Emerging Norm of Democracy in International Law' (1–4 April, 1992) 86 *Proceedings of the Annual Meeting (American Society of International Law)* 261.
Carr, E. H., *What Is History?* (Penguin Books 1987).
Carty, Anthony, *The Decay of International Law? A Reappraisal of the Limits of Legal Imagination in International Affairs* (Manchester University Press 1986).
Cassese, Antonio, *Self-Determination of Peoples: A Legal Reappraisal* (Cambridge University Press 1995).
Chadwick, Elizabeth, 'National Liberation in the Context of Post- and Non-Colonial Struggles for Self-Determination' in Marc Weller (ed.), *The Oxford Handbook of the Use of Force in International Law* (Oxford University Press 2015).
Charpentier, Jean, *Le Reconnaissance Internationale et L'Évolution du Drois de Gens* (A Pedon 1956).
Chen, Ti-Chiang, *The International Law of Recognition with Special Reference to Great Britain and United States* (Frederick A. Praeger Inc. 1951).
Cheng, Bin, *General Principles of Law as Applied by International Courts and Tribunals* (Cambridge University Press 1953).
Christiano, Thomas, 'The Authority of Democracy' (2004) 12(3) *The Journal of Political Philosophy* 266.

The Constitution of Equality: Democratic Authority and Its Limits (Oxford University Press 2008).

Conklin, William, *Statelessness: The Enigma of the International Community* (Hart Publishing 2014).

Coyle, John, 'The Treaty of Friendship, Commerce and Navigation in the Modern Era' (2013) 51 *Columbia Journal of Transnational Law* 302.

Craven, Matthew, 'Colonialism and Domination' in Bardo Fassbender and Anne Peters (eds.), *The Oxford Handbook of the History of International Law* (Oxford University Press 2012).

Crawford, James, *Brownlie's Principles on Public International Law*, 8th ed. (Oxford University Press 2013).

Chance, Order, Change: The Course of International Law, General Course on Public International Law (Brill 2014).

The Creation of States in International Law (Oxford University Press 2006) 52–53.

Criddle, Evan and Evan Fox-Decent, *Fiduciaries of Humanity: How International Law Constitutes Authority* (Oxford University Press 2016).

d'Aspremont, Jean, 'The International Law of Statehood: Craftsmanship for the Elucidation and Regulation of Births and Deaths in the International Society' (2014) 29 *Connecticut Journal of International Law* 201.

'The Rise and Fall of Democracy Governance in International Law: A Reply to Susan Marks' (2011) 22(2) *European Journal of International Law* 549, 552–563.

Formalism and the Sources of International Law (Oxford University Press 2011).

Dalton, Russell (ed.), *The New Germany Votes: Unification and the Creation of the New Party System* (Berg Publishing 1993).

Dawson, Hannah, 'Do They Look Like Me? Rethinking Representation and Its Relationship with Freedom' (2014) 21(2) *Juncture* 136.

de Beauvior, Simone, *The Ethics of Ambiguity*, Bernard Frechtman (trans.) (Citadel Press 1948).

de Visscher, Charles, *Problems d'interpretation judiciaire en droit international public* (A Pedone 1963).

Théories et Réalités, 4th ed. (A Pedone 1970).

de Waal, Thomas, *Uncertain Ground: Engaging with Europe's De Facto States and Breakaway Territories* (Carnegie 2018).

DeHart, Paul, 'Leviathan Leashed: The Incoherence of Absolute Sovereign Power' (2013) 25(1) *Critical Review* 1.

Delmas, Candice, *A Duty to Resist: When Disobedience Should Be Uncivil* (Oxford University Press 2018).

Dixon, Martin, *Textbook on International Law* (Oxford University Press 2013).

Doyle, Michael, 'Kant, Liberal Legacies, and Foreign Affairs: Part I' (1980) 12(3) *Philosophy & Public Affairs* 205.

'Kant, Liberal Legacies, and Foreign Affairs: Part II' (1980) 12(4) *Philosophy & Public Affairs* 323.

'Liberalism and World Politics' (1986) 80(4) *The American Political Science Review* 1151.

Duffy, Maura, '(Re)conceptualising Democracy: The Limitations of Benchmarks Based on Neoliberal Democracy and the Need for Alternatives' (2015) 36(8) *Third World Quarterly* 1472.

Dugard, Christopher and David Raič, 'The Role of Recognition in the Law and Practice of Secession' in Marcelo G. Kohen (ed.), *Secession: International Law Perspectives* (Cambridge University Press 2006).
Dugard, John, *Recognition and the United Nations* (Grotius Publications 1987).
Dunia, Khawla, 'And the Demonstrations Go On', Robin Moger (trans.) in Layla Al-Zubaidi and Mattew Cassel (eds.), *Writing Revolution: The Voices from Tunis to Damascus* (I.B. Tauris 2013).
Duursma, Jorri, *Fragmentation and the International Relations of Micro-States: Self-Determination and Statehood* (Cambridge University Press 1996).
Dworkin, Ronald, 'Democracy and Religion: America and Israel', *Ian Thompson Forum on World Issues, 20th Anniversary Season*, University of Nabraska-Lincoln, October 2008: https://mediahub.unl.edu/media/546 (last accessed 2 October 2023).
'Why Efficiency?' (1998) 8(3) *Hofstra Law Review* 563.
Freedom's Law (Harvard University Press 1996).
Justice for Hedgehogs (Harvard University Press 2011).
Law's Empire (Hart 1986).
Sovereign Virtue: The Theory and Practice of Equality (Harvard University Press 2020).
Endicott, Timothy, 'The Logic of Freedom and Power' in Samantha Besson and John Tasioulas (eds.), *The Philosophy of International Law* (Oxford University Press 2010).
Erikson, Robert, Norman Luttbeg, and William Holloway, 'Knowing One's District: How Legislators Predict Referendum Voting' (1975) 19 *American Journal of Political Science* 231.
Evans, Richard, *In Defence of History* (Granta Books 1997).
Falk, Richard, 'The Rights of Peoples (In Particular Indigenous Peoples)' in James Crawford (ed.), *The Rights of Peoples* (Oxford University Press 1988).
Fawcett, James, 'Security Council Resolutions on Rhodesia' (1965) 41 *British Yearbook of International Law* 103.
Finnis, John, *Natural Law and Natural Rights* (Oxford University Press 1980).
Fox, Gregory, 'The Right to Political Participation in International Law' (1–4 April 1991) 86 *Proceedings of the General Meeting (American Society of International Law)* 249.
Fox, Gregory and Bradley Roth, 'Democracy and International Law' (2001) 27(3) *Review of International Studies* 327.
Franck, Thomas, 'Humanitarian Intervention' in Samantha Besson and John Tasioulas (eds.), *The Philosophy of International Law* (Oxford University Press 2010).
'The Emerging Right to Democratic Governance' (1992) 86(1) *American Journal of International Law* 46.
Fairness in International Law and Institutions (Oxford University Press 1998).
Franck, Thomas and Paul Hoffman, 'The Right of Self-Determination in Very Small Places' (1976) 8(3) *New York University Journal of International Law* 331.
French, Duncan (ed.), *Statehood and Self-Determination: Reconciling Tradition and Modernity in International Law* (Cambridge University Press 2013).
Gardener, John, 'Legal Positivism: 5½ Myths' (2001) 46 *American Journal of Jurisprudence* 199.

'Reasons and Abilities: Some Preliminaries' (2013) 58(1) *American Journal of Jurisprudence* 63.
Garnham, David, 'War-Proneness, War-Weariness, and Regime Type: 1916–1980' (1986) 23(3) *Journal of Peace Research* 279.
Gauthier, David, *The Logic of Leviathan: The Moral and Political Theory of Thomas Hobbes* (Clarendon Press 1969) 91.
Geukjian, Ohannes, *The Russian Military Intervention in Syria* (Queen's University Press 2022).
Gewirth, Alan, *The Community of Rights* (Chicago University Press 1996) 13, 15.
Grant, Thomas, 'Annexation of Crimea' (2015) 109(1) *American Journal of International Law* 68.
'Defining Statehood: The Montevideo Convention and Its Discontents' (1998) 37 *Columbian Journal of Transnational Law* 403.
Green, Alex, 'A Political Theory of State Equality' (2023) 14(2) *Transnational Legal Theory* 178.
'Successful Secession and the Value of International Recognition' in Jure Vidmar, Sarah McGibbon, and Lea Raible (eds.), *Research Handbook on Secession* (Edward Elgar 2023).
'*The Creation of States* as a Cardinal Point: James Crawford's Contribution to International Legal Scholarship' (2023) 40(1) *Australian Year Book of International Law* 67.
'The Precarious Rationality of International Law: Critiquing the International Rule of Recognition' (2021) 22(8) *German Law Journal* 1613.
'Three Models of Political Membership: Delineating "The People in Question"' (2021) 41(2) *Oxford Journal of Legal Studies* 565.
Green, Alex and Jennifer Hendry, '*Ad Hominem* Criminalisation and the Rule of Law: The Egalitarian Case Against Knife Crime Prevention Orders' (2022) 42(2) *Oxford Journal of Legal Studies* 634.
'Non-positivist Legal Pluralism and Crises of Legitimacy in Settler-States' (2020) 14(2) *Journal of Comparative Law* 267.
Green, Leslie, 'Associative Obligations and the State' in Justine Burley (ed.), *Dworkin and His Critics* (Blackwell Publishing 2005).
'Legal Obligation and Authority' in Edward Zalta (ed.), *The Stanford Encyclopedia of Philosophy* (Winter 2012 Edition): http://plato.stanford.edu/archives/win2012/entries/legal-obligation/
Green, N. A. Maryan, *International Law: Law of Peace*, 3rd ed. (Pitman 1987).
Greenberg, Mark, 'How Facts Make Law' (2004) 10 *Legal Theory* 157.
Griffiths, John, 'What Is Legal Pluralism' (1986) 24 *Journal of Legal Pluralism* 1, 5.
Grotius, Hugo, *De Jure Belli ac Pacis, Book I* (1652).
Grzybowski, Janis, 'To Be or Not to Be: The Ontological Predicament of State Creation in International Law' (2017) 28(2) *European Journal of International Law* 409.
Habermas, Jürgen, *Inclusion of the Other: Studies in Political Theory* (Polity Press 1998) 116.
Moral Consciousness and Communicative Action, Christian Lenhardt and Shierry Nicholson (trans.) (Polity Press, 1992).
The Structural Transformation of the Public Sphere: An Inquiry into a Category of Bourgeois Society, Thomas Burger (trans.) (Polity Press, 1989)

Hajer, Maarten, 'Discourse Coalitions and the Institutionalization of Practice: The Case of Acid Rain in Britain' in Frank Fischer and John Forester (eds.), *The Argumentative Turn in Policy Analysis and Planning* (Duke University Press 1993).

Hall, William, A *Treaties on International Law* (Clarendon Press 1924).

Harcourt, William, *Letters by Historicus on Some Questions of International Law* (Macmillan 1863).

Hare, Rom, *Social Being* (Blackwell 1979).

Hart, H. L. A., *The Concept of Law*, 3rd ed. (Oxford University Press 2012).

Hedlund, Ronald and H. Paul Friesema, 'Representatives' Perceptions of Constituency Opinion' (1972) 34 *Journal of Politics* 730.

Heller, Kevin, 'The Illegality of "Genuine" Unilateral Humanitarian Intervention' (2021) 32(2) *European Journal of International Law* 613.

Hendry, Jennifer, 'A Legally Pluralist Approach to the *Bakassi Peninsula* Case' in Damian Gonzalez-Salzberg and Loveday Hodson (eds.), *Research Methods for International Human Rights Law: Beyond the Traditional Paradigm* (Routledge 2020).

Henkin, Louis, *International Law: Politics and Values* (Springer 1995).

Henry, I. D. and M. C. Wood, *The Legal Status of Berlin* (Grotius Publishing 1987).

Higgins, Rosalyn, *Problems and Processes: International Law and How We Use It* (Oxford University Press 1994).

The Development of International Law through the Political Organs of the United Nations (Oxford University Press 1963).

Hinnebusch, Raymond, Omar Imady and Tina Zintl, 'Civil Resistance in the Syrian Uprising: From Peaceful Protest to Sectarian Civil War' in Adam Roberts, Michael Willis, Rory McCarthy and Timothy Ash (eds.), *Civil Resistance in the Arab Spring: Triumphs and Disasters* (Oxford University Press 2016).

Hobbes, Thomas, *Leviathan* (Penguin Classics 1997).

Hohfeld, Wesley Newcomb, 'Fundamental Legal Conceptions as Applied in Judicial Reasoning' (1917) 26(8) *The Yale Law Journal* 710.

Hume, David, *Essays, Moral, Political, and Literary*, Eugene Miller (ed.) (Liberty Fund 1987).

International Commission of Jurists, 'East Pakistan Staff Study' (1972) 8 *ICJ Review* 23.

Jarry, Alfred, *Ubu Roi*, Gershon Legman (trans.) (Dover Publications 2003).

Jellinek, Georg, *Allgemeine Staatslehre*, 3rd ed. (Springer 1922).

Jennings, Robert and Arthur Watts (eds.), *Oppenheim's International Law: Volume 1 Peace*, 9th ed. (Oxford University Press 2008).

Jensen, Donald, 'Moscow in the Donbas: Command, Control, Crime and the Minsk Peace Process' (2017) *NATO Defence College* 1.

Jonathan, Macey, 'Representative Democracy' (1993) 16 *Harvard Journal of Law and Public Policy* 49.

Jordan, Winthrop, *The White Man's Burden: Historical Origins of Racism in the United States* (Oxford University Press 1973).

Kamanda, Alfred, A *Study of the Legal Status of Protectorates in Public International Law* (Les Presses de Savoie 1961).

Kant, Immanuel, *The Metaphysics of Morals*, Lara Denis (ed.), Mary Gregor (trans.) (Cambridge University Press 1996).

Kanza, Thomas, *Conflict in the Congo: The Rise and Fall of Lumumba* (Penguin 1972).

Kattan, Victor, 'Book Review: Jure Vidmar, Democratic Statehood in International Law: The Emergence of New States in Post-cold War Practice' (2015) 78(2) *Modern Law Review* 394.

Kelsen, Hans, 'Recognition in International Law: Theoretical Observations' (1941) 35(4) *American Journal of International Law* 605.

'The Pure Theory of Law and Analytical Jurisprudence' (1941) 55(1) *Harvard Law Review* 44.

General Theory of Law and State (Transaction Publishers 2005).

The Pure Theory of Law (California University Press 1967) 286–287.

Kisangani, Emizet, *Civil Wars in the Democratic Republic of Congo, 1960–2010* (Lynne Rienner Publishers 2012).

Klinger, Nadja, 'Bühne der Freiheit', *Der Tagesspiegel*, 4 November 2009: https://web.archive.org/web/20091108171522/ www.tagesspiegel.de/zeitung/Die-Dritte-Seite-Mauerfall-4-November-Deutsches-Theater%3Bart705%2C2940530 (last accessed 2 October 2023).

Koskenniemi, Martti, *From Apology to Utopia: The Structure of International Legal Argument* (Cambridge University Press 2006).

Koss, Mary, Lisa Goodman, Louise Fitzgerald, Nancy Felipe Russo, Gwendolyn Puryear Keita and Angela Browne, *No Safe Haven: Male Violence Against Women at Home, at Work and in the Community* (American Psychological Association 1994).

Kramer, Matthew, *Objectivity and the Rule of Law* (Cambridge University Press 2007).

Kreijen, Gerald, 'The Transformation of Sovereignty and African Independence: No Shortcuts to Statehood' in Gerald Kreijen (ed.), *State, Sovereignty and International Governance* (Oxford University Press 2002).

State Failure, Sovereignty and Effectiveness: Legal Lessons from the Decolonization of Sub-Saharan Africa (Nijhoff 2004).

Kreß, Claus, 'The International Court of Justice and the "Principle of Non-Use of Force"' in Marc Weller (ed.), *The Oxford Handbook of the Use of Force in International Law* (Oxford University Press 2015).

Kyiv Post, 'Reports: 100,000 "Yes" Ballots for Referendum Intercepted in Sloviansk', 10 May 2014: www.kyivpost.com/post/9088 (last accessed 2 October 2023).

Kyritsis, Dimitrios, 'Representation and Waldron's Objection to Judicial Review' (2006) 26(4) *Oxford Journal of Legal Studies* 733.

Lalonde, Suzanne, 'The Role of the *uti possidetis* Principle in the Resolution of Maritime Boundary Disputes' in Christine Chinkin and Freya Baetens (eds.), *Sovereignty, Statehood and State Responsibility: Essays in Honour of James Crawford* (Cambridge University Press 2015).

Lam, Sze Hong, 'To Perfect the Imperfect Title: How Referenda Were Historically Manipulated to Justify Territorial Conquests by Nations' *EJIL: Talk!*, 1 October 2022: www.ejiltalk.org/to-perfect-the-imperfect-title-how-referenda-were-historically-manipulated-to-justify-territorial-conquest-by-nations/ (last accessed 2 October 2023).

Langer, Robert, *Seizure of Territory: Stimson Doctrine and Related Principles in Legal Theory and Diplomatic Practice* (Greenwood Press 1947).

Lauterpacht, Hersch, 'The Grotian Tradition in International Law' (1946) 23(l) *British Yearbook of International Law* l.

Recognition of States in International Law (Cambridge University Press 1947).

Lenin, Vladimir Ilich, *Lenin, Selected Works: Volume 7* (Progress Publishers 1961).
Letsas, George, *A Theory of Interpretation of the European Convention on Human Rights* (Oxford University Press 2007).
Lincoln, Anthony, 'FYI: TMI: Toward a Holistic Social Theory of Information Overload' (2011) 16(3) *First Monday*: http://firstmonday.org/ojs/index.php/fm/article/view/3051/2835 (last accessed 2 October 2023).
Lindley, M. F., *The Acquisition and Government of Backwards Territory in International Law* (Longmans, Green, & Co 1926).
List, Christian and Philip Pettit, *Group Agency: The Possibility, Design, and Status of Corporate Agents* (Oxford University Press 2013).
Locke, John, *An Essay Concerning Human Understanding*, John Yolton (ed.) (Everyman 1993).
Second Treaties of Civil Government (1690).
Lorimer, James, *The Institutes of the Law of Nations: A Treatise of the Jural Relations of Separate Political Communities* (William Blackwood and Sons 1883).
Loughlin, Martin, *The Foundations of Public Law* (Oxford University Press 2010).
The Idea of Public Law (Oxford University Press 2004).
Lowe, Vaughan, *International Law* (Oxford University Press 2007).
Machiavelli, Niccolò, *The Discourses*, Leslie J. Walker (trans.), Bernard Crick (ed.) (Penguin 1983).
The Prince (1552).
Madison, James, *The Federalist No. 10*, Clinton Rossiter (ed.) (New American Library 1961).
The Federalist No. 51, Clinton Rossiter (ed.) (New American Library 1961).
Mann, Francis, *Studies in International Law* (Clarendon Press 1973).
Marek, Krystyna, *Identity and Continuity of States in Public International Law* (Librairie E. Droz 1954).
Marks, Susan, 'What Has Become of the Emerging Right to Democratic Governance?' (2011) 22(2) *European Journal of International Law* 507.
Marston, Geoffrey (ed.) 'United Kingdom Materials on International Law 1997' (1997) 68(1) *British Yearbook of International Law* 520.
Masol, Sergii, 'Orwellian Rulings of the Russian Constitutional Court on the Donetsk, Kherson, Luhansk and Zaporizhzhia Provinces of Ukraine' *EJIL: Talk!*, 25 October 2022: www.ejiltalk.org/orwellian-rulings-of-the-russian-constitutional-court-on-the-donetsk-kherson-luhansk-and-zaporizhzhia-provinces-of-ukraine/ (last accessed 2 October 2023).
McAdam, Jane, '"Disappearing States", Statelessness and the Boundaries of International Law' in Jane McAdam (ed.), *Climate Change and Displacement: Multidisciplinary Perspectives* (Bloomsbury 2010).
McCrone, Donald and James Kuklinski, 'The Delegate Theory of Representation' (1979) 23(2) *American Journal of Political Science* 278.
McDowell, Eleanor, 'Contemporary Practice of the United States Relating to International Law' (1977) 71 *American Journal of International Law* 337.
Metz, Helen, *Somalia: A Country Study*, 4th ed. (Library of Congress 1993).
Milanovic, Marko, 'A Footnote on Secession' *EJIL: Talk!*, 26 October 2017: www.ejiltalk.org/a-footnote-on-secession/ (last accessed 2 October 2023).

Mill, John Stuart, *On Liberty and Other Essays*, John Gray (ed.) (Oxford University Press 1991).

Miller, David, *National Responsibility and Global Justice* (Oxford University Press 2007).

Miller, Warren and Donald Stokes, 'Constituency Influence in Congress' (1963) 57 *American Political Science Review* 45.

Moeckli, Daniel and Nils Reimann, 'Independence Referendums in International Law' in Jure Vidmar, Sarah McGibbon, and Lea Raible(eds.), *Research Handbook on Secession* (Edward Elgar 2022).

Moore, Margaret, 'Is Patriotism an Associative Duty?' (2009) 13(4) *The Journal of Ethics* 383.

Morris, Christopher, *An Essay on the Modern State* (Cambridge University Press 1998).

Murphy, Liam, *What Makes Law: An Introduction to the Philosophy of Law* (Cambridge University Press 2014).

Murphy, Sean, 'Democratic Legitimacy and the Recognition of States and Governments' (1999) 48(3) *International and Comparative Law Quarterly* 545.

Nagel, Thomas, 'Personal Rights and Public Space' (1995) 24(2) *Philosophy & Public Affairs* 83.

Equality and Partiality (Oxford University Press 1995).

Nanda, Ved, 'Self-Determination in International Law: The Tragic Tale of Two Cities – Islamabad (West Pakistan) and Dacca (East Pakistan)' (1972) 66 *American Journal of International Law* 321.

Nayar, Pramod, *Colonial Voices: The Discourses of Empire* (Wiley-Blackwell, 2012).

Nettheim, Garth, 'Peoples' and 'Populations' – Indigenous Peoples and the Rights of Peoples' in James Crawford (ed.), *The Rights of Peoples* (Oxford University Press 1988).

Nicholson, Rowan, 'Was the Colonisation of Australia an Invasion of Sovereign Territory?' (2019) 20(2) *Melbourne Journal of International Law* 1.

Statehood and the State-Like in International Law (Oxford University Press 2019).

Nietzsche, Friedrich, *Beyond Good and Evil*, R. J. Hollingdale (trans.) (Penguin Books 2003)

Thus Spoke Zarathustra, Graham Parks (trans.) (Oxford University Press 2005).

Nozick, Robert, *Anarchy, State, and Utopia* (Blackwell 1974).

Socratic Puzzles (Harvard University Press 1997).

Nusseibeh, Sari, *What Is a Palestinian State Worth?* (Harvard University Press 2011).

O'Connell, D. P., 'The Status of Formosa and the Chinese Recognition Problem' (1956) 50 *American Journal of International Law* 405.

Okeke, Christian, *Controversial Subjects of Contemporary International Law* (Rotterdam University Press 1974).

Oppenheim, Lassa, 'The Science of International Law: Its Task and Method' (1908) 2 *American Journal of International Law* 313.

International Law: A Treatise, Volume 1 (Longmans, Green, and Company 1905).

Parfit, Derek, *On What Matters: Volume One* (Oxford University Press 2011).

Parkinson, John, *Democracy and Public Space: The Physical Sites of Democratic Performance* (Oxford University Press 2012).

Pasternak, Avia, 'Political Rioting: A Moral Assessment' (2019) 46(4) *Philosophy & Public Affairs* 384.

Payne, E. H. (ed.), *Selected Works of Edmund Burke* (Liberty Fund, 1990), Volume 4.

Pegg, Scott, *International Society and the De Facto State* (Ashgate 1998).

Penner, James, *The Idea of Property in Law* (Oxford University Press 2000).

Peters, Anne, 'Crimea: Does "The West" Now Pay the Price for Kosovo?' *EJIL: Talk!*, 22 April 2018: www.ejiltalk.org/crimea-does-the-west-now-pay-the-price-for-kosovo/ (last accessed 2 October 2023).

Pitkin, Hanna, *The Concept of Representation* (University University Press 1967).

Plato, 'Crito' *The Last Days of Socrates* in Hugh Tredennick and Harold Tarrant (trans.) (Penguin Books 2003).

'Euthyphro' *The Last Days of Socrates* in Hugh Tredennick and Harold Tarrant (trans.) (Penguin Books 2003).

Prott, Lyndel, 'Cultural Rights as Peoples' Rights in International Law' in James Crawford (ed.), *The Rights of Peoples* (Oxford University Press 1988).

Pugh, Martin, *State and Society: A Social and Political History of Britain Since 1870*, 4th ed. (Bloomsbury 2012).

Quigley, John, *The Statehood of Palestine: International Law in the Middle East Conflict* (Cambridge University Press 2010).

RadioFreeEurope, 'Separatists Declare "People's Republic" in Ukraine's Luhansk', 28 April 2014: www.rferl.org/a/separatists-declare-luhansk-peoples-republic/25364894.html (last accessed 2 October 2023).

Ramsey, Frank, 'Facts and Propositions' in *Proceedings of the Aristotelian Society, Supplementary Volumes, Vol. 7, Mind, Objectivity and Fact* (1927) 153.

Ratner, Steven, 'Land Feuds and Their Solutions: Finding International Law beyond the Tribunal Chamber' (2006) 100(4) *American Journal of International Law* 808.

Ratner, Steven, *The Thin Justice of International Law: A Moral Reckoning of the Law of Nations* (Oxford University Press 2015).

Rawls, John, 'Legal Obligation and the Duty of Fair Play' in Sidney Hook (ed.), *Law and Philosophy* (New York University Press 1964).

A Theory of Justice (Belknap Press 1999).

Political Liberalism (Columbia University Press 1993).

The Law of Peoples with "The Idea of Public Reason Revisited" (Harvard University Press 1999).

Raz, Joseph, 'Human Rights without Foundations' in Samantha Besson and John Tasioulas (eds.), *The Philosophy of International Law* (Oxford University Press 2010).

Rehfeld, Andrew, 'Representation Rethought: On Trustees, Delegates, and Gyroscopes in the Study of Political Representation and Democracy' (2009) 103(2) *The American Political Science Review* 214.

Renton, David and David Seddon, *The Congo: Plunder and Resistance* (Leo Zeilig 2007).

Renzo, Massimo, 'State Legitimacy and Self-Defence' (2011) 30(5) *Law and Philosophy* 575.

Rich, Roland, 'Recognition of States: The Collapse of Yugoslavia and the Soviet Union' (1993) 4 *European Journal of International Law* 33.

'The Right to Development: A Right of Peoples?' in James Crawford (ed.), *The Rights of Peoples* (Oxford University Press 1988).
Richardson, Henry, *Democratic Autonomy* (Oxford University Press 2002).
Roberts, Walter, *Tito, Mihailović, and The Allies, 1941–1945* (Duke University Press 1987).
Rodley, Nigel, 'Humanitarian Intervention' in Marc Weller (ed.), *The Oxford Handbook of the Use of Force in International Law* (Oxford University Press 2015).
Rousseau, Jean-Jacques, 'On the Social Contract' in Jean-Jacques Rousseau, *The Basic Political Writings*, Donald Cress (trans.) (Hackett Publishing Company 1987).
Rummel, Rodolph, 'Libertarianism and International Violence' (1983) 27(1) *Journal of Conflict Resolution* 27.
Russell, Bertrand, *An Inquiry into Meaning and Truth* (George Allen and Unwin 1972).
Sadurski, Wojciech, 'Law's Legitimacy and "Democracy-Plus"' (2006) 26(2) *Oxford Journal of Legal Studies* 377.
Salmon, Jean, 'Naissance et reconnaissance du Blanga-Desh' in Josef Tittle (ed.), *Multitudo legum ius unum: Festschrift für Wilhelm Wengler* (Interrecht 1973), vol 1.
Scanlon, Thomas, 'Promises and Practices' (1990) 19(3) *Philosophy & Public Affairs* 199.
What We Owe Each Other (Belknap Press 1998).
Scheffler, Samuel, *Boundaries and Allegiances, Problems of Justice and Responsibility in Liberal Thought* (Oxford University Press 2001).
Schmitt, Carl, *Der Leviatha in der Staatslehre des Thomas Hobbes: Sinn und Fehlschlag eines politischen Symbols* (Klett-Cotta 1995).
The Concept of the Political, George Schwab (trans.) (Chicago University Press 1996).
Schwarzenberger, Georg, *Power Politics: An Introduction to the Study of International Relations and Post-war Planning* (Jonatlian Cape 1941).
Sellers, Mortimer, 'Republican Principles in International Law' (1996) 11(3) *Connecticut Journal of International Law* 419.
Republican Principles in International Law: The Fundamental Requirements of a Just World Order (Palgrave Macmillan 2006).
Serdy, Andrew, 'Bringing Taiwan into the International Fisheries Fold: The Legal Personality of a Fishing Entity' (2005) 75(1) *British Yearbook of International Law* 183.
Shaw, Malcolm, 'The International Status of National Liberation Movements' (1983) 5 *Liverpool Law Review* 19.
Shubert, Atika and Ben Brumfeld, 'Polls Close in Eastern Ukraine Amid Allegations of Fraud and Double-Voting', *CNN*, 11 May 2014: http://edition.cnn.com/2014/05/11/world/europe/ukraine-crisis/ (last accessed 2 October 2023).
Silver, Morris, 'Economic Theory of the Constitutional Separation of Powers' (1977) 29(1) *Public Choice* 95.
Simmons, John, *Moral Principles and Political Obligations* (Princeton University Press 1979).
Singer, Peter, 'Famine, Affluence, and Morality' (1972) 1(1) *Philosophy & Public Affairs* 229.
Slade, Ruth, *The Belgian Congo* (Oxford University Press 1960).

Smooha, Sammy, 'The Model of Ethnic Democracy: Israel as a Jewish and Democratic State' (2002) 8(4) *Nations and Nationalism* 475.

Spath, Andrew, 'Change without Revolution: Jordan's Missed Opportunity?' *New Middle East*, 2011: http://new-middle-east.blogspot.co.uk/2011/04/change-without-revolution-jordans.html (last accessed 2 October 2023).

Spiermann, Ole, 'General Legal Characteristics of States: A View from the Past of the Permanent Court of International Justice' in Chinkin, Christine and Freya Baetens (eds.), *Sovereignty, Statehood and State Responsibility: Essays in Honour of James Crawford* (Cambridge University Press 2015).

Stern, Philip, *The Company-State: Corporate Sovereignty and the Early Modern Foundations of the British Empire in India* (Oxford University Press 2011).

Strawson, Peter, 'Truth' (1949) 9(6) *Analysis* 83.

Sunstein, Cass, 'The Law of Group Polarization' (2002) 10(2) *Journal of Political Philosophy* 175.

Talmon, Stefan, *Recognition of Governments in International Law: With Particular Reference to Governments in Exile* (Oxford University Press 2001).

Tasioulas, John, 'In Defence of Relative Normativity: Communitarian Values and the Nicaragua Case' (1996) 16(1) *Oxford Journal of Legal Studies* 85.

Tesón, Fernando, 'International Human Rights and Cultural Relativism' (1984–1985) 25(4) *Virginia Journal of International Law* 869.

A Philosophy of International Law (Westview Press 1998) 57–66.

The Guardian, 'Greenpeace Protesters Spend Night on Parliament Roof', 12 October 2009: www.theguardian.com/environment/2009/oct/12/greenpeace-westminster-roof-protest (last accessed 2 October 2023).

Thirlway, Hugh, *The Sources of International Law* (Oxford University Press 2014).

Thomas, Christopher, 'The Uses and Abuses of Legitimacy in International Law' (2014) 34(4) *Oxford Journal of Legal Studies* 729.

Timmer, Karsten, *Vom Aufbruch zum Umbruch: Die Bürgerbewegung in der DDR 1989* (Vandenhoeck & Ruprecht 2000).

Tiroch, Katrin, 'Governments in Exile' in Rüdiger Wolfrum (ed.), *Max Planck Encyclopedia of Public International Law* (Oxford University Press 2011).

Tullock, Gordon, 'Thoughts about Representative Government' (1994) 10 *European Journal of Political Economy* 27.

Tzouvala, Ntina, *Capitalism as Civilisation: A History of International Law* (Cambridge University Press 2020).

Unger, Roberto, *False Necessity: Anti-necessitarian Social Theory in the Service of Radical Democracy*, 2nd ed. (Verso Books 2004).

Plasticity into Power (Verso Books 2004).

Urbinati, Nadia, 'Representation as Advocacy: A Study of Democratic Deliberation' (2000) 28(6) *Political Theory* 758.

Representative Democracy: Principles and Genealogy (Chicago University Press 2009).

van den Driest, Simone, 'Crimea's Separation from Ukraine: An Analysis of the Right to Self-Determination and (Remedial) Secession in International Law' (2015) 62 *Netherlands International Law Review* 329.

van Schendel, Willem, *A History of Bangladesh* (Cambridge University Press 2015).

Vidmar, Jure, 'The *Kosovo* Advisory Opinion Scrutinized' (2011) 24 *Leiden Journal of International Law* 335.

Democratic Statehood in International Law: The Emergence of New States in Post-cold War Practice (Bloomsbury Publishing 2013).
Vidmar, Jure and Lea Raible, 'State Creation and the Concept of Statehood in International Law' in Jure Vidmar, Sarah McGibbon, and Lea Raible(eds.), *Research Handbook on Secession* (Edward Elgar 2022).
von Clausewitz, Carl, *On War*, Michael Howard and Peter Paret (eds.) (Princeton University Press 1984) 87.
Von Liszt, Franz, *Das Völkerrecht: Systematisch Dargesellt* (Auflage 1904).
Waldron, Jeremy, 'Are Sovereigns Entitled to the Benefit of the International Rule of Law?' (2011) 22(2) *European Journal of International Law* 315.
'Representative Lawmaking' (2009) 89 *Boston Law Review* 335.
'Special Ties and Natural Duties' (1993) 22(1) *Philosophy & Public Affairs* 3.
'The Core of the Case against Judicial Review' (2006) 115 *The Yale Law Journal* 1346.
'Two Concepts of Self-Determination' in Samantha Besson and John Tasioulas (eds.), *The Philosophy of International Law* (Oxford University Press 2010).
Law and Disagreement (Oxford University Press 1999).
Wallace-Bruce, Nii Lante, *Claims to Statehood in International Law* (Carlton Press 1994).
Walzer, Michael, 'The Moral Standing of States: A Response to Four Critics' (1980) 9(3) *Philosophy & Public Affairs* 209.
Just and Unjust War (Basic Books 2015).
Warbrick, Colin, 'States and Recognition in International Law' in Malcolm Evans (ed.), *International Law*, 2nd ed. (Oxford University Press 2006).
Watson, Irene, 'Buried Alive' (2002) 13 *Law and Critique* 253.
Aboriginal Peoples, Colonialism and International Law: Raw Law (Routledge 2014).
Weber, Max, 'Politics as a Vocation' in H. H. Gerth and C. Wright Mills (eds.), *From Max Weber: Essays in Sociology* (Routledge 1991).
Wedeen, Lisa, *Ambiguities of Domination: Politics, Rhetoric, and Symbols in Contemporary Syria*, 2nd ed. (University of Chicago Press 1999).
Weil, Prosper, 'Towards Relative Normativity in International Law?' (1983) 77(3) *American Journal of International Law* 413.
Weinrib, Ernest, 'Restoring Restitution' (2005) 91(3) *Virginia Law Review* 861.
The Idea of Private Law (Oxford University Press 2012).
Weller, Marc, 'Russia's Recognition of the 'Separatist Republics' in Ukraine Was Manifestly Unlawful' *EJIL: Talk!*, 9 March 2022: www.ejiltalk.org/russias-recognition-of-the-separatist-republics-in-ukraine-was-manifestly-unlawful/ (last accessed 2 October 2023).
Negotiating the Final Status of Kosovo (EU Institute for Security Studies 2008).
Wellman, Christopher, 'Friends, Compatriots, and Special Political Obligations' (2001) 29(2) *Political Theory* 217.
Wenar, Leif, 'Responsibility and Severe Poverty' in Thomas Pogge (ed.), *Freedom from Poverty as a Human Right* (Oxford University Press 2007).
Wheaton, Henry, *Elements of International Law* (Clarendon Press 1936).
Whitfield, Bob, *The Extension of the Franchise, 1832–1931* (Heinemann 2001).
Wilde, Ralph, 'Recognition in International Law' in *Recognition of States: The Consequences of Recognition or Non-recognition in UK and International Law*, Summary of the International Law Discussion Group meeting held at Chatham House (4 February 2010) 7.

Wilkinson, Michael, 'Between Freedom and Law: Hannah Arendt on the Promise of Modern Revolution and the Burden of "The Tradition"' in Marco Goldoni and Christopher McCorkindale (eds.), *Hannah Arendt and the Law* (Hart Publishing 2011).

Witty, Patrick, 'Behind the Scenes: Tank Man of Tiananmen', *The New York Times*, 3 June 2009): http://lens.blogs.nytimes.com/2009/06/03/behind-the-scenes-tank-man-of-tiananmen/ (last accessed 2 October 2023).

Wong, Derek, 'Sovereignty Sunk? The Position of "Sinking States" at International Law' (2013) 14 *Melbourne Journal of International Law* 346.

Wright, Quincy, 'Some Legal Aspects of the Berlin Crisis' (1961) 55(4) *American Journal of International Law* 959.

Legal Problems in the Far Eastern Conflict: Part I, The Legal Background in the Far East (Arns Pr Inc 1969).

Wuerth, Ingrid, 'International Law in the Post-Human Rights Era' (2017) 96 *Texas Law Review* 279.

Zemanek, Karl, 'New Trends in the Enforcement of *Erga Omnes* Obligations' (2000) 4 *Max Planck Year Book of United Nations Law* 1.

Index

agency, 220–221
America, United States of, 39, 42, 64, 128, 146, 149, 151, 166, 183, 205, 218
antecedents of statehood
  applied to particular cases, 71–72
  defined, 12–13, 70, 100–101, 223
  effectiveness antecedent, the, 13, 80–85
  independence antecedent, the, 13–14, 85–100
  population antecedent, the, 13, 72–74
  territory antecedent, the, 13, 75–80
Arendt, Hannah, 30, 52–53, 62–63
authenticity, 51, 54, 55, 67, 84, 120, 235
  defined, 39–40
  limits upon, 40–43
  vs autonomy, 40
  vs reasonableness, 32–33, 46–47, 57–59
autonomy, 25–28, 172, 182–183. *See also* legitimacy, autonomy problem, the
  and consent, 192–193
  vs agency, 220–221
  vs authenticity, 40

Bahrain, Kingdom of, 96
Bangladesh, People's Republic of, 132–136, 147, 152, 163
Bantustans, the, 110, 117–118, 121
Belgian Congo. *See* Congo, Democratic Republic of the
Bilad Shinguitti, 164
Bosnia-Herzegovina, 80, 82, 106, 112, 150, 180, 184
British Empire, 89, 90–92, 96, 99, 130. *See also* United Kingdom of Great Britain and Northern Ireland
Buchanan, Allen, 178 181, 198, 200–201, 214, 232
Buchanan's challenge, 178–181, 197, 229

Canada, 95, 130, 133
Capps, Patrick, 141, 156, 190–192, 199
China, People's Republic of, 64, 73, 147, 149
Christiano, Thomas, 209–213
coercion, 25–26, 212, 220
collective self-determination, 2, 52, 111, 116, 120, 127, 130, 135, 136, 148, 223
  as procedural principle, 116–122
  self-determination units, 99–100, 157–159, 163, 184
colonialism, 62, 88–92, 126
colonisation. *See* states, colonies
Congo, Democratic Republic of the, 80, 82, 89, 128, 167, 185, 226
Crawford, James, 3–5, 7, 74, 81, 87, 95, 103, 108, 116, 119, 123, 142, 156, 163–167, 224, 232
Crimea, Republic of, 123, 129
Cyprus, Republic of, 98, 120

Daesh. *See* Islamic State
decolonisation, 78, 80, 94, 99–100, 128
democracy. *See* representative government
diplomatic protection, 2, 78
Donetsk People's Republic, 92, 110, 123–125, 129, 163
Dworkin, Ronald, 10, 11, 20, 39, 59

empire. *See* colonialism
equality, 25–28, 56–57, 172
  and consent, 192–193
  and *Non-Voluntary Membership*, 59
  and representative government, 207–208
ethics, normative, 33, 45, 48, 68
  and personal narratives, 29–30
  defined, 19–20
European Community Guidelines on the Recognition of New States in Eastern Europe and the Soviet Union, 84, 202–203, 206
European Union, the, 45, 95, 113

French Republic, the, 25, 55, 97, 166, 173, 205

genuine political communities, 1, 12, 19–22, 25, 28, 43, 46, 51, 53, 61, 68–70, 73, 106, 113–115, 126, 141, 229–235. *See also* states
Germany, Federal Republic of, 128
governance
  as an activity, 172, 186–187, 204
  defined, 170–172
  as 'effective', 80–85
  as ethically valuable, 60–69
  factually independent, 88–93
  formally independent, 94–99
  and *Non-Voluntary Membership*, 83–84
  as problematic, 25–26, 170–172

Hobbes, Thomas, 54, 181–188
Hobbes' thesis, 181–188, 197, 204, 208, 219
  distinct from the stability thesis, 181, 184
human rights, 67, 68, 81, 162, 188, 199–204, 227
  and 'effectiveness', 84–85
  and remedial secession, 132–135
  and representative government, 209–213
  and tacit consent, 195–197

imperialism. *See* colonialism
India, 73, 89, 91–92, 132–136, 153
International Court of Justice, 108
  Kosovo Advisory Opinion, 126–128, 130, 133
  Nicaragua case, 126–128, 205
  statute of, 9
  Wall in the Occupied Palestinian Territory Advisory Opinion, 123
  Western Sahara Advisory Opinion, 111–113, 164
international law
  the Grotian tradition of, 10–11, 121
  the nature of, 11–12, 20, 174
  the rule of, 142
Islamic State, 84, 110, 187
Israel, State of, 104, 120–121, 146–147, 149, 217

jural relations, 3

Kant, Immanuel, 24, 54, 188–190, 235
Kelantan, British protectorate of, 90–91
Kenya, Republic of, 76, 99, 215
Kosovo, Republic of, 149, 155, 162

Lauterpacht, Hersch, 4, 10–11, 107, 108, 149, 156, 160
legal positivism, 5, 143
  and legal disagreement, 5–7
legitimacy
  and accountability, 218–222
  autonomy problem, the, 23, 25–28, 172, 181–183, 192–193, 197
  and civil peace, 181–188
  of conventions *vs* that of principles, 175
  defined, 170–172, 198–199
  equality problem, the, 23, 25–28, 172, 181, 192–193, 197, 207–208
  of governance institutions, 173–175
  of governments, 173
  and human rights, 190–191, 199–204
  of individual governance acts, 172
  internal *vs* external, 178
  and the rule of law, 188–192, 235
  popular consent, 195
  tacit consent, 195–197
  vs authority, 175, 179
legitimacy thesis, the. *Discussed within Chapters 6&7*. *See also* legitimacy
  and accountability, 218–222
  autonomy problem, the, 208, 219
  civil incorporation, 188–192, 235
  defined, 169–170
  and 'democracy-plus', 209–213
  equality problem, the, 219
  justification gap, the, 213–218
  popular consent, 195
  rights-based legitimacy, 190–191, 199–204
  tacit consent, 195–197
Liechtenstein, Principality of, 98
Locke, John, 171, 192, 194, 195
Luhansk People's Republic, 92, 110, 123–125, 129, 163

Monaco, Principality of, 97, 106
Montevideo Convention on the Rights and Duties of States (1933), 72, 75, 80, 85, 98, 145–147, 152, 161–163, 191, 234
morality, definition of, 20

Nicholson, Rowan, 4–5, 7, 87, 103, 108, 123, 131, 224–225, 233
Non-Voluntary Membership
  beneficiary condition, the, 22, 25–29, 63, 74, 76–78, 83–84, 132–136, 228
  contribition condition, the, 228
  defined, 21–22, 46
  and equality, 57–59
  and political duty, 22–29
  and the population antecedent, 74
  residence condition, the, 22–25, 72–74, 76–77, 83–84, 99, 228
  and state continuity, 228
  and territory, 76–78
normative reasons
  defined, 9
  and the nature of international law, 11–12
  and rational reconstruction, 9–10
North Korea, Democratic People's Republic of, 104, 124, 147
Northern Cyprus, Turkish Republic of, 110, 117, 119, 121, 122, 203

Oppenheim, Lassa, 5, 141, 143

Pakistan, Islamic Republic of, 132–136, 152
Palestine, State of, 109, 149, 151, 162
Paris, Charter of, 84, 202–203, 206
Parkinson, John, 65–67
personal narratives, 30, 32–34, 39–40, 61. *See also* politics
political action, 12–14, 29, 34, 36–39, 43–44, 46, 48–52, 55–59, 91, 98, 102–103, 113–115, 121, 125
  and governance, 60–68, 80–85, 120, 227
political membership. *See Non-Voluntary Membership*
  vs nationality, 74
political morality
  and the nature of international law, 11–12
  political duties, 22–29
  and remedial duties, 132–136
politics
  artefacts of, 61–63, 82, 83, 90, 97–98, 105, 114, 131–132, 227
  defined, 20–21, 69
  degrees of participation, 59–60
  and equality, 56–60, 119
  as an ethical and moral domain, 32–34
  focuses for, 63–67, 73, 75–76, 82–83, 85, 90, 97, 99, 105, 109, 114, 119
  forums for, 65–68, 73, 75–76, 82–83, 85, 90, 97, 99, 114, 119
  and the hazards of being governed, 25–29
  and the hazards of living together, 23–25
  as instrumentally valuable, 44–45
  and modest political burdens, 37–39
  and moral duty. *See* reasonableness
  and peace, 23–25, 52–54, 128–129
  political duty, 22–23
  political successes, 43–44
  relationship with violence, 52–54
  and violence, 54–56, 117, 119, 122, 125–126, 188
procedural principles, 14
  defined, 102–103, 136–137, 223
  international peace principle, the, 14–15, 122–126, 129–131, 135–136, 163, 226
  negative self-determination principle, the, 14–15, 116–122, 130, 131, 148, 163
  recognition principle, the, 14, 103–111
  referendum principle, the, 14, 111–116, 130
  territorial integrity principle, the, 15, 126–136, 226

Quebec, Reference re Secession of, 129–130

rational reconstruction, 1, 48, 55, 68–69, 72, 74, 159, 169, 174, 177, 178, 198–199, 213, 223, 224, 226, 230, 233, 235
  defined, 8–9
  and the Grotian tradition of international law, 10–11
  of Hans Kelsen's views, 189
  and legal disagreement, 7, 100–101, 103, 146, 147, 149, 151
  limits of, 71–72
  and normative reasons, 9–10, 77
  and the sources of international law, 9
Ratner, Steven, 141, 144, 156, 161–162, 180
reasonableness, 30–35, 38, 41, 51, 54, 55, 67, 84, 120, 235
  and attempts, 30–31
  and moral objectivity, 31
  and political duty, 32–34
  and radical change, 63
  as scalar, 32
  vs authenticity, 46–47, 57–59
recognition, 6, 15, 130–132, 137, 203, 223, 231
  of ambiguous and disputed relevance, 4–7, 145–147, 149–153, 155
  collective non-recognition, 109–111
  constitutive or declaratory, 4–7, 103, 106–108, 145–147
  and governmental legitimacy, 178–181
  and justice, 178–181
  libtery to recognise, the, 109
  as procedural principle, 14, 103–111, 132
  as relativistic, 157–159
representative government, 74, 84
  accountability, 218–222
  and equality, 207–208
  and human rights, 209–213
  in international practice, 204–207
  as a poor compromise, 213–218
Republic of China. *See* Taiwan
Russian Federation, 3, 50, 93, 122–125, 133, 149

secession, 2–3, 6, 113, 128, 131, 161–164, 194
  judicial treatment of, 129–130, 132–133
  remedial secession, 15, 132–137
self-authorship. *See* authenticity
social facts, 1, 5, 6, 81–82, 86, 87
  and legal disagreement, 6–7, 103
Somalia, Federal Republic of, 6, 130–131, 226
Somaliland, Republic of, 6–7, 130–131
South Africa, Republic of, 44, 55, 65, 117–118, 187
Southern Rhodesia, 117, 119, 121, 147–149, 184, 203
stability thesis, the, 169, 192, 224, *Discussed within* Chapter 5
  and constitutive recognition, 156–161
  defined, 16, 142–144
  distinct from Hobbes' thesis, 181, 184
  and the presumption of state continuity, 144, 226–227
  and the prohibition on the threat and use of force, 154
  as a reconstruction of the Montevideo Criteria, 161–168

stability thesis, the (cont.)
true value of, 168
value of stability, 73
state continuity, the presumption of, 225–229
and the stability thesis, 144, 226–227
state creation. *See also* statehood as political community
as contentious and contested, 3–7, 145–154
as necessitating legitimate government, 178–181
summarised, 12–15
statehood as political community. *Discussed within* Chapters 1–4 (inclusive)
defined, 1, 12, 19, 223
as a framework for judgement, 15, 223
legal implications, summarised, 12–15
and the prohibition on the threat or use of force, 154–155
vs the legitimacy thesis, 169
vs the stability thesis, 154, 168
states
colonies, 87, 92–94, 99–100, 135, 184–185
as dangerous entities, 2
dissolution of, 15, 112, 113, 128, 129–132, 137, 144, 152
extinction of, 144, 224–229
fiduciary theories of, 234–235
merger of, 128–129
nature of, 229–235
parent states, 2
protectorates, 94, 184
puppet states, 87, 92–93, 99, 122, 184, 226
small island states, 73, 226–228
vs 'the state', 175–176
Swiss Confederation, the, 216
Syrian Arab Republic, 54, 124, 162, 165–166, 226

Taiwan, 105–106, 147, 153, 160–161
territory
as antecedent, 75–80
defined by governance, 83–84
and *Non-Voluntary Membership*, 76–78
as a political forum, 68, 75–76
as procedural principle, 126–136
territorial grants, 78–80
territorial integrity, right to, 126–128, 131–136, 147, 161, 191
territorial title, 75
Tesón, Fernando, 196, 199, 200
tyranny, 13, 60, 65, 83, 84, 89, 162, 187–188

Ukraine, 3, 50, 112, 123–125, 133
Union of Soviet Socialist Republics, 112
United Kingdom of Great Britain and Northern Ireland, 45, 55, 95, 109, 117, 130, 133, 146, 149, 151, 166, 174, 214, 217, 221
United Nations
Charter of the, 122, 124, 125, 129, 136, 137, 154, 190
election monitoring by the, 205
General Assembly of the, 108, 111–112, 117, 118, 122–129, 134, 151–152
and independence referendums, 112, 114
membership of the, 134, 151–152, 206
Security Council of the, 111, 117, 118, 122–125, 134, 146, 151

Vidmar, Jure, 4–6, 103, 112, 113, 127, 152–153, 231–232
violence, 23, 35
defined, 53
as inimical to politics, 21, 53–54, 68, 117, 119, 122, 125–126, 188
as politics, 54–56
relationship with politics, 52–54

Waldron, Jeremy, 209–213
Weil, Prosper, 141, 143

Yugoslavia, Socialist Federal Republic of, 80, 82, 84, 113, 128, 144, 226

www.ingramcontent.com/pod-product-compliance
Ingram Content Group UK Ltd.
Pitfield, Milton Keynes, MK11 3LW, UK
UKHW021957010225
454381UK00008B/83